Islam:
Global Christian Perspectives

Islam:
Global Christian Perspectives

Voices of Majority World Christian Scholars of Islam

Edited by
WAGEEH MIKHAIL

Foreword by
Michael Nazir-Ali

WIPF & STOCK · Eugene, Oregon

ISLAM: GLOBAL CHRISTIAN PERSPECTIVES
Voices of Majority World Christian Scholars of Islam

Wipf & Stock
An Imprint of Wipf and Stock Publishers
199 W. 8th Ave., Suite 3
Eugene, OR 97401

www.wipfandstock.com

PAPERBACK ISBN: 979-8-3852-0524-0
HARDCOVER ISBN: 979-8-3852-0525-7
EBOOK ISBN: 979-8-3852-0526-4

07/29/24

Contents

Foreword vii
MICHAEL NAZIR-ALI

Introduction ix
WAGEEH MIKHAIL

I. HISTORY

1 The Historical Context of Islam 3
THARWAT WAHBA

2 Islam and Judaism 18
ISSA DIAB

3 Early Christian-Muslim Encounters: Timothy I and al-Mahdī as a Model 40
ARA BADALIAN

4 Christian Social Life under Islamic Rule 64
SAM NWOKORO

5 Christian Contributions to the Arab Islamic Civilization 83
ASHOOR YOUSIF

6 Causes of the Decline of the North African Church 126
MARINA BOTROS

II. THEOLOGY

7 Islamic Christology 153
JOHN AZUMAH

8 The Trinity and The Absolute Oneness of God 177
IMAD N. SHEHADEH

9 Sin and Salvation in Islam and Christianity:
A Catholic Perspective 203
COSMAS SARBAH

10 Islamic Philosophy: An Introduction 222
ALEXANDER E. MASSAD

III. MEETING ONE ANOTHER

11 Contemporary Christian-Muslim Relations 247
ANWAR BERHE

12 Religious Extremism against Christians:
A Pakistani Perspective 270
MAQSOOD KAMIL

13 Working for the Common Good 291
PACKIAM T. SAMUEL

14 The Future of Muslim-Christian Dialogue:
A Reflection on the Past 302
WAGEEH MIKHAIL

Foreword

MICHAEL NAZIR-ALI

This collection of essays mostly, but not entirely, by emerging scholars in the Middle East, South Asia, and Africa is very welcome, indeed. It shows that Christians in these parts are studying, researching, and reflecting on the long history of interaction between Islam and the Judeo-Christian tradition. The collection will make a valuable addition to the literature on Christian-Muslim and Jewish-Muslim relations down the ages.

On the one hand, it is important to note the contribution made by Christians and Jews to the emergence of what has come to be called "Islamic civilization" and, on the other, to note the influence of Muslim thought on Christians not only in the Islamic heartlands but also in Europe, in terms, for example, of Ibn Rushd's commentary on Aristotle, Ibn Sina's argument for the existence of God, and much else. When these stories are told today, they should be harbingers of what can happen now and in the future in terms of creative interaction among these traditions of Semitic origin.

In spite of restrictions, the early use of Arabic by Christians in presenting apologetics for their faith is noteworthy, as is their work of translating, more or less, the whole of the Hellenistic philosophical, medical, scientific, and literary corpus either directly from Greek or from Syriac into Arabic. Nor has such interest in Arabic abated down the ages, as can be observed in the contribution made by Christians to the Arab *Nahda*, not only politically and socially but, as we can see from the work of linguists such as Buṭrus *al*-Bustānī and the Christian schools in Syria and Lebanon, to the development of the language as such.

One feature of the interaction that is worth noting is how spiritual terminology from one tradition has been appropriated by the other to express or explain its beliefs and spiritual experiences. Thus, the use of Syriac terms in Islam has been well noted by scholars like Margaret Smith, while the use of Arabic terms to explain Christian beliefs goes back at least to St. John of Damascus. Where there is a shared linguistic and literary heritage, dialogue becomes more possible and easier.

While emphasizing what is in common, the writers have not shied away from discussing the differences regarding the nature of the divine unity, the person and work of Christ, and the effect of sin on human nature. Nor have they failed to note the effects of the *Shari'a* and the *Dhimma* on Christian and Jewish populations and, in particular, how the *Millet* system of the Ottomans gave rise to communities that were defensive, inward-looking, and increasingly dependent on foreign patronage.

They have had to take note of the rise of extremism in its various forms in the Islamic world and the very damaging effects it has had on freedom of thought, speech, and belief, especially, but not only, for Christians and other minorities. They are also, aware, however, of Muslims, for instance, in Indonesia, who are arguing for a view of the relation of religion to the state that welcomes contributions to policies and legislation for the common good from different religious communities rather than just the dominant one or that, in the name of secularity, excludes such contributions altogether.

The scholars writing here need to be encouraged, in every way, to extend, deepen, and develop their interests. They will thus add to the rich storehouse they have already provided in the cause of greater understanding of our neighbours, of dialogue at every level, of peace, both local and global, and of sensitive but clear witness to our faith.

May 2023

Introduction

WAGEEH MIKHAIL

There have been numerous books on Christianity and Islam in recent years. Many Muslim and Christian scholars have worked rigorously to write about Christian-Muslim relations. Each has provided their own perspective on the issue. So, what's the point of a new book on this topic? This book is unique because all contributors live in countries where Christian-Muslims relations are daily realities. These chapters tell stories and experiences of dialogue, challenges, coexistence, mutual understanding, and joint work between Christians and Muslims in a number of countries in the Middle East, Africa, and Asia, such as Egypt, Ethiopia, Ghana, India, Iraq, Jordan, Lebanon, and Nigeria. The contributors know what they write about and live it every day. They come from countries where Christianity and Islam have lived side by side for thousands of years. They even come from different Christian traditions, namely Orthodox, Catholic, and Protestant. They provide unique perspectives on delicate issues that reflect the diverse experiences of Christians living in Muslim-majority countries. Their perspectives on Christian-Muslim relations are balanced and practical. Even when dealing with sensitive issues or describing dangers that surround Christian communities in some Muslim-majority countries, their message is one of peace and reconciliation. Their call is to be Christlike in the midst of difficult circumstances.

Layers of experience throughout history contributing to Christian-Muslim relations in these countries give the following chapters a distinctive character, in which one finds academic arguments mixed with deep life experiences. This is the uniqueness of this volume. However, since these contexts witness different experiences of Christians and Muslims, the chapters of the current volume vary according to social and political circumstances in which Christians and Muslims live. Contributors speak from their perspective, expressing their own convictions and views on Christian-Muslim relations with reverence and kindness.

In fact, one important theme of this volume is its academic and gracious approach to Christian-Muslim relations. Contributors are intentional in excluding polemics and pluralism. Rather, they present a committed Christian position that seeks to spread the message of peace and reconciliation in societies where tension has caused bloodshed and instability.

It is our hope that these chapters help Christians understand Islam and Christian-Muslim relations from a Christlike perspective.

Wageeh Mikhail
Christianity and Islam Engagement Director
Scholar Leaders

I.

History

1

The Historical Context of Islam

THARWAT WAHBA

Islam began in the seventh century when the prophet Muhammad proclaimed that he was the messenger of God. It was an impactful time in the life of Arabs that has affected the rest of the world to the present. Islam sprang from a rich context that has many unique aspects in history, religion, geography, politics, economy, and social life. This background affected Islam not only in its beginning but also in the way it spread and continued.

This chapter will explore the geographical, political, economic, and religious context in which Islam appeared. Although the facts about this context came from both primary and secondary sources, this chapter will not be able to cover the whole subject in detail due to the breadth of studies on early Islam. However, this chapter will help in giving a more synthesized picture of the topic that will help familiarize the reader with the subject and be able to provide an overview of its aspects.

GEOGRAPHY

The Arabian Peninsula is surrounded by saltwater coasts. The northern part is formed by the Zagros collision zone, which lies between the Arabian Plate and Asia. It merges with the desert in Syria with no clear borders. On the northeast there is the Strait of Hormuz and the Arabian (or Persian) Gulf. In the west, the Peninsula is bounded by the Red Sea and the Gulf of Aqaba. On the southeast there is the Arabian Sea, which is part of the Indian Ocean. The Arabian Peninsula includes parts of Iraq and Jordan.[1]

In prehistoric eras, the Arabian Peninsula was a very fertile land, with lush vegetation and running rivers. Remains of large animals have been discovered in the Arabian Peninsula. In the time when Islam started, the center of the Arabian Peninsula was largely dry dessert. The oases are the exception, having some agriculture, but these are very few within the otherwise huge wasteland. In the north and in the south, the seasonal precipitation allowed civilizations to flourish in both Yemen and the Fertile Crescent.[2]

The geographic location helped the Arabs of the south work in maritime and land trade. Thus, their ships traveled to India, Egypt, and Persia. Agriculture also flourished because of the many rivers and dams, of which Marib Dam was the most famous.

The climate of the Arabian Peninsula is generally dry and very hot. It receives very little rain. Although it has a few rivers, it is in general an extremely dry landscape. The rivers that are there, referred to as wadis, are only full during rainy seasons. The dry climate does not permit large scale agricultural development. The number of oases was limited, but they were the places of community that produced some kinds of subsistence civilizations.[3]

The Arabian Peninsula is divided into three major regions. The first, Al-Hijaz, is situated in the northeast of the Peninsula between the southern Levant and eastern Palestine. The second, Arabia Felix, is situated to the south of the Arabian Peninsula: in Yemen, parts of Oman, and parts of Saudi Arabia. The third region, the Arabian Desert, forms the rest of the Arabian Peninsula, especially Najd. The eastern coast of the Peninsula is neither mountainous nor desert. It is, rather, a flat plain with little topography. It extends to the Persian Gulf.[4]

The majority of the population of Arabia before Islam was nomadic, but there were some cities that were centers of commercial activities and religions. The most important cities were Mecca, Medina (Yathrib), and

1. Hitti, *Near East in History*, 12.

2. Payne, *History of Islam*, 1.

3. Al-Tamīmī, *Jaw al-Jazīra al-ʿArabiyya wa-Ātharuhu ʿalā al-Hijrāt al-Sāmiyya*, 37.

4. Hitti, *Near East in History*, 12–13.

Ṭā'if. Mecca was the most important center of trade, as well as being the location of the Kaaba (or Ka'ba). It was one of the most prestigious, holy places in Arabia. Islam honored the Kaaba and considered it the most sacred place in Islam. Some Arabs associated the Kaaba with Adam, Abraham, and Ishmael. In the fifth century, the Kaaba was a place to worship the deities of Arabia's pagan tribes. Mecca's most important pagan deities were Hubal, Allāt, and Al 'Uzza, and their idols were placed in the Kaaba by the Quraysh tribe, where they remained until the rise of Islam in the seventh century.[5]

Medina is about 340 kilometers north of Mecca and about 190 kilometers from the Red Sea. It is situated in a fertile part of the Hejaz. It has streams of water, which made it a suitable place for early Muslims. During the pre-Islamic time until the coming of Muhammad and early Muslims in 622, Medina was known as Yathrib. It was a prominent place in trade and agriculture because of its location in a fertile area of Hejaz. The city was able to produce a decent amount of food and water, and therefore was an important stop for trade caravans. It had a dominant Jewish population until the fifth century, when several Arab tribes became the main political power.[6]

Al-Ṭā'if was considered the second most important population center after Mecca. The Arabs considered it more distinguished than Mecca because it was surrounded by fertile agricultural lands and enjoyed a moderate atmosphere that made it suitable for agriculture. In addition, it had the distinction of a vibrant craft industry. The Thaqif tribe inhabited Ṭā'if until the coming of Islam.[7] Al-Ṭā'if included the most important and most famous Arab market of all, the Okaz market. In the pre-Islamic period, there was a trade fair and a social forum full of all kinds of activities. Arab tribes met for a month each year. They chanted poetry, and they were proud because of their noble tribal roots. The market had an arena for equestrian races and fencing. Okaz was a commercial market for the convoys of merchants coming from the Levant, Persia, Rome, and Yemen.[8]

5. Hitti, *History of the Arabs*, 100.
6. Hitti, *History of the Arabs*, 99.
7. Payne, *History of Islam*, 10–11.
8. Payne, *History of Islam*, 11–12.

RELIGIONS

Religion in Arabia before Islam was a mix of paganism or polytheism, Christianity, and Judaism. Before the rise of Islam, most Bedouin tribes practiced polytheism, most often in the form of animism. Animists believe that non-human entities (animals, plants, and inanimate objects or phenomena) possess a spiritual essence. Totemism and worship of totems or idols representing natural phenomena were also common religious practices in the pre-Islamic world.[9] Polytheists believed in deities and other spirits. A variety of gods and goddesses were worshipped locally. Some of the most important and widely worshiped gods were Hubal, the Syrian god of the moon, and his three daughters, who became the chief goddesses in Mecca. Their names are Allāt, Al-'Uzzá, and Manāt. Allāt was the goddess of the underworld. There are some opinions that consider Allah to be the masculine god of Allāt, both of which were main gods in Mecca. Al-'Uzzá, which means "The Strong," was the goddess of fertility. She was believed to give protection and victory during war. Manāt was the goddess of fate.[10] It was believed that Kaaba had about 360 gods at the advent of Islam.

Hanif

The Hanif religion retained some values from the religion of Abraham but had a weak presence. History also seems to have lost most of the teachings of Lot and Saleh, who, according to the Qur'an, were prophets who prophesied in Arabia before the lifetime of Muhammad. Practitioners of Hanif rejected polytheism, atheism, and everything that was worshiped besides God. Followers of the Hanif religion were a group of pre-Islamic, monotheistic Arabs who embraced the religion of Abraham. Sometimes they were included with the Jews and Christians as monotheists in Arabia before Islam, although some scholars disagree about their historical existence.[11]

Most Islamic historians agree that Hanifs had a prominent role in the emergence of Islam, to the extent of saying that the Prophet himself was a Hanif. They also claimed that the Qur'an did not praise any belief or

9. Hourani, *History of the Arab People*, 9.

10. Hitti, *History of the Arabs*, 98–99.

11. Alī, *Al-Mufaṣṣal fī adyān al- 'Arab qabla al-Islām*, 388.

group as it praised Hanif.[12] According to the Islamic tradition, Muhammad himself was a follower of the Hanif belief system. Because Hanif is mentioned in the Qur'an, some scholars, such as Colin Chapman, claim that Islam was not a new religion in Mecca at the beginning of the sixth century. Instead, they argue that Islam is to be understood as a development of Hanif belief, and that Hanifs were Muslims. According to this line of thinking, the principles of Islam were present on the Arabian Peninsula before Muhammad.[13]

Judaism

There are limited sources on the history of Jews in Arabia before Islam. Most of the news about them came mainly from Islamic sources that described the context of Islam and the environment that witnessed its beginning. Jews lived in the area between Palestine and the city of Yathrib. They also lived in Yemen and Mecca in lesser numbers. They came from Palestine in various times, according to some historians. They came in consecutive waves during the Babylonian exile, the Roman destruction of their temple in 70 AD, and during the Jewish revolt in 135 in the time of Hadrian. In addition to Jewish immigrants, there were Arabs who converted to Judaism according to the book of the Talmud.[14]

The Jews in Arabia were separate from those of Palestine in their customs, language, and religious practices. They worked in agriculture, trade, jewelry, and carpentry. They lived as Arabs in their traditions, clothes, food, and language. They had Arab names and created poetry in Arabic. They mixed with Arab tribes as they married Arabs and gave their daughters in marriage to Arabs. They lived as a minority among pagans, but in some places, such as Yathrib, they were the nobles of the community. They ruled Yathrib until the coming of the Yemeni tribes al-Aws and al-Khazraj. After a series of clashes, the Jews in Yathrib were forced to submit to the rule of the Arab tribes and pay taxes. This happened to avoid wars and killings amongst different tribes, which was common in the years before the advent of Islam. Islamic sources described Jews as people of unorthodox beliefs and immoral practices.[15]

12. Alī, *Al-Mufaṣṣal fī Adyān al- ʿArab qabla al-Islām*, 392.

13. Chapman, *Cross and Crescent*, 91; Ali, *Al-Mufaṣṣal fī Adyān al-ʿArab*, 393.

14. Amīn, *Fajr al-Islām*, 40–41.

15. Alī, *Al-Mufaṣṣal fī Adyān al- ʿArab qabla al-Islām*, 447.

From the beginning of Islam, most Jews did not accept the prophecy of Mohammed but opposed him. Their enmity took many forms, and the Qur'an speaks negatively about Jews in the surahs composed after the Battle of the Trench. Muslims attacked Jews after the Battle of the Trench and made efforts to expel Jews from Arabia alongside Christians and other religions.[16]

Christianity

In Arabia, Christianity spread in the north of the Arabian Peninsula since the first century CE. The day of Pentecost witnessed the presence of Arab Jews in Jerusalem who heard the message of the gospel, and some of them converted to Christianity. The New Testament also mentions Arabia in reference to southern Palestine and northern Arabia, the area to which Saul went after his conversion. The spread of Christianity continued in the northern regions of the Arabian Peninsula, especially in the regions of Syria and Mesopotamia, as well as in the regions that are today called Bahrain. Christianity also spread in the south in the Yemen region, which was influenced by the Ethiopian Christianity that emerged in the fourth century CE, in close association with the Egyptian church in Alexandria.[17]

Historians point out that Christianity spread in the Arabian Peninsula through the migration of Christians from Roman areas, whether because of the destruction of Jerusalem in 70 CE, of Roman persecution, or their search for safer areas. The slave trade also played a role in the spread of Christianity in the regions of Hejaz and Najd. The Arab tribes worked to obtain slaves, especially from the regions of Abyssinia, as well as from throughout the Byzantine Empire. Many of these slaves were Christians, especially girls, who kept their faith and culture. Most of the enslaved Christians were able to read and write, so their Arab masters used them to teach their children, which had great impact on spreading the Christian faith to these children. Likewise, some Arab slave masters married Christian slave girls, who influenced them, and several of them became Christians.

The trade movement also played a key role in the spread of Christianity in the Arabian Peninsula. The summer trade trips went to the

16. Amīn, *Fajr al-Islām*, 42.

17. Chapmam, *Cross and Crescent*, 81.

north, where the number of Christians was large. While winter trips went to the south in Yemen, where Christianity was also strong. These trips were important to expose Arabs to Christianity, which led some tribes to convert.[18] Likewise, Christian merchants visited Arab countries, especially from the Levant and the north of the Arabian Peninsula. Historians say that the Christian Byzantines tried to Christianize some Arab tribes so that it would be easier to deal with them. In addition to trade, Christian monasteries played a role in spreading the Christian faith. Around the trade route there were many monasteries, which the merchants used during their travels to rest and to attain supplies for travel. During their visit to these monasteries, travelers listened to Christian teachings from the monks, and some of them converted to Christianity. The monks from these monasteries also traveled throughout the Arabian Peninsula to spread the Christian faith.[19]

It is worth mentioning that the Christians in the Arabian Peninsula were, in the majority, of those who embraced Nestorian thought as well as Gnostic theology. This helped spread stories about the birth and childhood of Christ and some of his miracles that were not mentioned in the Bible, but rather were told in some apocryphal Gnostic books that narrated such stories.[20] The relationship developed between the Gnostic groups who were present in Egypt and the Arabian Peninsula under the pressure of persecution by the Romans. This was helped by the existence of trade routes across the Red Sea between Egypt and the Arabian Peninsula.[21]

Some studies allude to the existence of a close relationship between the writings of the Gnostics and the Islamic stories about Jesus in the Qur'an, hadith, and hagiographic books. Some of these stories deny the crucifixion of Christ and say that another person put the likeness of Christ on him and died in his place on the cross. In talking about the birth of Christ and his childhood, some Gnostic narrations addressed the virgin birth of Jesus from Mary. These books also talked about the miracles that accompanied Jesus's childhood, such as speaking in the cradle and making birds out of clay. All these influences came due to the presence of Gnostic Christian groups in the fifth and sixth centuries CE in the Arabian Peninsula.[22]

18. Lewis, *Middle East*, 47.
19. Amīn, *Fajr al-Islām*, 45–46.
20. Alī, *Al-Mufaṣṣal fī Adyān al- 'Arab qabla al-Islām*, 542–43.
21. Amīn, *Fajr al-Islām*, 48.
22. Griffith, *Church in the Shadow of the Mosque*, 12–13.

One of the most prominent Christian centers in the south of the Arabian Peninsula is the city of Najran. Christianity entered Najran in the fifth century CE, where the Christology of one nature (monophysite) emerged. It had close contact with Egypt, Nubia, and Abyssinia. Najran became an episcopal chair, making it one of the most important Christian centers in the entire Arabian Peninsula, not just in the south.

In 520 CE, one of the most important religious incidents involving Arabs before Islam occurred: the persecution of Arab Christians in Najran and the emergence of a wave of persecution and martyrdom. After Najran adhered to the Christian faith, about two hundred men and one hundred women were martyred. This was done by the Jewish king Yūsuf Asar Yathar, also known as Dhū Nawas, who ruled the southern Arabian Peninsula. John of Ephesus records that the martyring of the Christians of Najran was undertaken as a response to the rise of Christian persecution of Jews in both the Byzantine and Persian worlds. These events motivated both Byzantine and Abyssinia to increase violence against Jews to avenge the massacre of Christians. This violence led to Christianity spreading in the south of the Arabian Peninsula. Based on these events, Najran became an Arab martyrs' city to which Arabs and others from neighboring countries who embrace the same faith came to visit. The church built for the martyrs was named after Kaaba Najran. Najran and its martyrs were alluded to in Arabic literature as mentioned in the Qur'an. The Prophet praised one of the bishops of Najran. Later, when Mohammed met a delegation from Najran in Yathrib, he delt with them with respect and gave them some privileges to practice their faith, even after they came to an impasse about Christology.[23]

Despite the spread of Christianity in most of the countries of the ancient Near East, it was faced many challenges from outside and from within. From the outside, in the sixth century AD, the Germanic Lombards invaded the Byzantine Empire and the remaining parts of the Roman Empire. Emperor Justinian (527–565 CE) had succeeded earlier in recovering some parts of these lands. External invasions continued from the north and north-east by the Slavic and Bulgarian tribes. The Persians also invaded Syria. These conquests led to the shrinkage of the Roman Empire along with the loss of Syria, Palestine, and Egypt.[24] Although the

23. Badr, *Masiḥiyya ʿabr tarīkhihā fī al-Mashriq*, 440–41.

24. Badr, *Masiḥiyya ʿabr tarīkhihā fī al-Mashriq*, 430.

Byzantines tried to recover what they had lost in these lands, these conflicts led to the weakening of the Byzantine Empire.[25]

It was not only the external invasion that weakened the Christian countries, but the presence of doctrinal differences within, especially after the Council of Chalcedon. This divided the church and created hostility between churches. The theological debate over the nature of Christ was the main issue that led to the division. The churches were divided between the belief that there is one nature of Christ, in which the human and the divine are mixed, and the belief that Christ is one person with two natures. The isolation of the Armenian, Syriac, Coptic, and Nestorian churches also increased because of theological and geographic factors. This made them easy prey for external invasions, whether the Persian or the Islamic expansion.[26]

Manichaeism

Manichaeism is a faith that was widespread during the rise of Islam, including in the Arabian Peninsula. Mani, the founder of Manichaeism, claimed prophethood at the age of twenty-four. He grew up as an ascetic worshiper who did not eat meat and did not drink alcohol. Mani claimed that he was the Paraclete who would call followers to truth and guidance after Jesus. After his acknowledgment of the prophethood of both Jesus and Zoroaster, he said: "I am the man that Jesus preached."[27] Mani claimed that the revelation *waḥy* came to him at the age of thirteen and again at the age of twenty-five.

Manichaeism is considered a Christian Gnostic sect, and churches both East and West agree that it was a dangerous, long-lived heresy. It lasted from the third century CE until the thirteenth century, and many in Syria, Asia Minor, and India embraced it. St. Augustine himself was a Manichean at one time. The most important teaching of Manicheism was about dualism. They believed that there are two gods, the god of light and the god of darkness. Manichaeism philosophy mixes Christianity, Judaism, Buddhism, and Zoroastrianism. Mani used to say that he was the fourth and last prophet, preceded by Christ, Zoroaster, and Buddha.

25. Badr,*Masiḥiyya ʿabr tarīkhihā fī al-Mashriq*, 452.
26. ʿAlī, *Al-Mufaṣṣal fī adyān al- ʿArab qabla al-Islām*, 540–45.
27. Amīn, *Fajr al-Islām*, 164.

He claimed that he was distinguished from them in what he preached and wrote, while they were limited to preaching only.[28]

Mani's teachings spread quickly in Babylon, and from there they spread across the Levant and Palestine. Manichaeism reached the tribes of Taghlib and Ghassan in the north of the Arabian Peninsula. When it came to Egypt, Chrisitan monks seized its teachings and taught them to the public. From Egypt the teachings of Mani spread to North Africa.

Mani rejected the Christian teaching about the crucifixion of Christ, similarly to Qur'anic claims. Mani considered crucifixion a myth and said that he was a pure spiritual Messiah. Manichaeism taught that appropriate fasting is to fast seven days each month. Among the habits of the Manicheans was that a man washes with water after getting up from sleep. Manichaeans prayed twelve times a day in a prescribed sequence of prostrations. There are many similarities between what Mani taught and what Islam claimed regarding Christianity, worship, and the nature of Christ.[29]

POLITICAL LIFE

On the outskirts of the northern Arabian desert were Arab kingdoms, including: the Ghassanids, Palmyra, the Nabateans in the Levant, and the kingdom of Al-Hira in Iraq. These kingdoms were a dividing line between the Arabs and the Persian and Roman empires. The Ghassanid kingdom in the Levant (220–638 CE) goes back to the Azad tribes that migrated from Yemen after the collapse of the Ma'rib Dam and settled in the Levant desert. It had different capitals, the last of which was the Jabiya in the Golan region in present-day Syria. By the end of the sixth century, its rulers weakened and lost their power. Jibla bin al-Ayham was the last of its kings, who supported the Romans against the Muslims in the battle of Yarmouk 13 AH/634 CE, after which the regions of the Ghassanid state became part of the growing Islamic state.[30]

The kingdom of Al-Hira in Iraq (268–633 CE) arose in the third century CE because of the migration of Yemeni tribes. Its capital was Al-Hira, which is located south of Kufa, west of the Euphrates River. One of its most famous kings was Al-Nu'man bin Al-Mundhir (582–609 CE).

28. Amīn, *Fajr El Islām*, 165.

29. Hourani, *History of the Arab People*, 21.

30. Hitti, *History of the Arabs*, 78–79.

Al-Hira was a vassal of the Persian Sassanid state, and Al-Hira supported Persia in the wars against the Romans and their allies.[31]

The population of the Arabian Peninsula itself was divided into nomads and urban dwellers, and the political system was divided into two parts: the tribal system, which was the dominant system, and the semi-monarchy system in Yemen, the Ghassanid, and Al-Hira.[32]

The tribe was the primary unit of the tribal political system and is subject to a system of custom and traditions. Its members are bound by blood and lineage, and the individual is committed to supporting and working for the tribe's interests. A tribe has a hierarchy that is led by the sheikh, who manages the tribe. Usually he leads battles, receives delegations, makes treaties, and settles disputes. Many tribes have a tribal council. It includes the chiefs of the tribe, who undertake the tasks of the affairs of the tribe.[33]

The relationship between Arab tribes varied over time and was sometimes characterized by war, peace, and alliances. Wars arise between Arab tribes for various reasons, such as conflict over water and pasture and for revenge. Among the most famous tribal wars are the Al-Basous and the Fajr Wars.[34]

The Arab tribes in the Hijaz established alliances with each other, the most famous of which is the "Al-Fudul oath," witnessed by the Prophet, where the tribes of Mecca pledged to be united with the oppressed tribes in opposition to outside oppressors, and not to fail one another.[35]

The political system in general was semi-monarchical through heredity in the north and south of the Arabian Peninsula. Some of these kingdoms were influenced by the political systems of the Persians and the Romans. They had a king who managed the country's affairs, protected its borders, and maintained security. Senior officials assisted the king in ruling and managing the affairs of the country. There were also governors of the various regions who were the deputies of the king in the administration of the regions, and each of them was called a "noble." These kingdoms had general councils that were loyal to the king and were made up of high-ranking, wealthy officials and priests.[36]

31. Hoyland, *Arabia and the Arabs*, 49.
32. Hourani, *History of the Arab People*, 12.
33. Hourani, *History of the Arab People*, 105–6.
34. Hitti, *History of the Arabs*, 89.
35. Hourani, *History of the Arab People*, 107.
36. Amīn, *Fajr al-Islām*, 52–53.

The political life in Arabian Peninsula tells us that there was fragmentation of powers and conflicts between kingdoms and tribes. This political atmosphere paved the way for Islam, which called Arabs to be united under the Prophet leadership as one state.

ECONOMIC LIFE

Economic life in Arabian Peninsula depended on a limited number of activities because of the lack of resources. Shepherding was the primary economic activity in the Arabian Peninsula. It was dominated by the desert ecosystem. The breeding of camels, sheep, and goats was widespread. Shepherding forced Arabs to compete for areas capable of growing grass for flocks and herds. The lack of water and the dry weather caused conflicts and wars among tribes. It also colored the Arabian character, writings, and art.

Agriculture was a very minor activity in most parts of Arabia. It was confined to the northern parts of the Arabian Peninsula in the Levant and the southern parts of Yemen. These areas had wells and springs and were on the outskirts of Arabia. The fertile soil and abundance of water, channeled with irrigation projects, helped grow the important crops of date palms and vegetables.[37]

Industry was limited due to the lack of raw materials. Among the most important industries were weapons, pottery vessels, and pearl extraction. In the Arabian Gulf there was the manufacture of jewelry and adornment tools. Arabs depended on imported goods from other parts of the Middle East to cover their needs through trade.[38]

Trade flourished in the Arabian Peninsula, and this was helped by several factors. There were several well-travelled roads of which Arabs had deep knowledge. The Arabs relied on celestial navigation to be guided on land and sea. Yemen had a merchant fleet transporting goods coming from India, Somalia, and Abyssinia to the ports of the Levant and Egypt, and from there to Europe. The Arabs used slaves in their commercial transactions, which were conducted in gold dinars and silver dirhams, and they used a barter system in the markets.[39]

37. Hitti, *History of the Arabs*, 19.
38. Hitti, *Near East in History*, 4.
39. Amīn, *Fajr al-Islām*, 23–24.

Mecca became famous in the country of the Hijaz at the end of the sixth century CE due to its distinguished location, the presence of the Sacred House (the Kaaba), the organization of commercial caravans (such as the winter and summer trips), and the fame of its commercial markets. This unique location and importance led Mecca to be the center of trade and opened the door for it to lead the rise of Islam.[40]

SOCIETY

Arab society before Islam was divided into several layers, which were affected by the economic situation, social status, and the origin to which each class belonged. The upper class consisted of rich, free merchants and owners of large agricultural lands and extensive pastures. The middle class consisted of small traders, owners of limited agricultural lands, and craftsmen. The lower class, which was the majority of the society, consisted of the poor and the slaves.[41]

Arab societies were characterized by different customs. The customs of Arabs have been associated with some religious beliefs that have been shunned by Christians. Some Arabs believed in magic, astrology, and the ability of the hidden forces of the jinn to bring good and to drive away evil.[42]

More positive characteristics common in Arab societies were generosity, fulfillment of covenants, courage, forgiveness, and the refusal to humiliate another. Unpleasant habits found among some Arab tribes consisted of drinking wine, gambling, raiding caravan routes, fanaticism, revenge, and female infanticide.[43]

Arab women had a significant role in the Arabian Peninsula. A woman's role included responsibility as a mother, in addition to her work by spinning sheep's wool and camel hair. Arab women sometimes participated in battles, dressing the wounded, giving water to the warriors, and beating the drums of war to encourage fighting.[44]

40. ʿAlī, *Al-Mufaṣṣal fī Adyān al- ʿArab qabla al-Islām*, 372.
41. Amīn, *Fajr al-Islām*, 135–36.
42. Zwemer, *Influence of Animism on Islam*, 166.
43. Amīn, *Fajr al-Islām*, 57–59.
44. Amein, *Fajr El Islām*, 21.

SCIENCE AND ART

Arabs had learned from the nations around them various fields such as science, literature, art, and architecture. In literature, the Arabs were famous for their poetry and rhetoric. Their markets were not only fields for trade but were also fields for the competition of poets and orators. They used poetry to explain their heritage, victories, and noble roots, and to praise their tribes and kings.[45]

Some sciences were known especially in Arab countries in the north, which were influenced by the civilizations of the Persians and the Romans. Some Arabs, especially Christians, practiced medicine. They were known to treat diseases with natural herbs.[46] Arabs also were skilled in astronomy. They used this knowledge in travel and to determine the beginnings of months. They also used it to determine the times of wind and rain. Arabs also used engineering to build dams and roads in the mountains to connect villages and cities to each other. These sciences were limited to a relatively small number of Arabs who found ways to learn from outside countries, such as the Romans, Egyptians, or Persians.

Arabs were influenced in the art of sculpture and carving by neighboring civilizations, the most famous of which was the city of Al-Hajar in the Nabataean state. It is the home of the people of the Prophet Saleh, and they carved houses in the mountains. They also built castles and fortress around their cities to protect them. One of the most important castles was the Qastal fortress in the Ghassanid state. They also built temples and monasteries, such as the temple of the Sun in Yemen, the monastery of Hind Bint al-Numan in Al-Hira, and the Rusafa Church in the Ghassanid state. Palaces were built for kings and princes, such as Ghamdan Palace in Sana'a, Al-Khornaq in Al-Hira and Al-Mashta in the Ghassanid state.[47]

CONCLUSION

This chapter has sought to cover the big picture of Arabian geography, history, and political, religious, and social life before Islam. All these elements are important to shed light on and give a background to the world in which Islam appeared and then spread. Arab history and civilization

45. Amein, *Fajr El Islām*, 89–92.

46. Hourani, *History of the Arab People*, 77.

47. Badr, *Masiḥiyya ʿabr tarīkhihā fī al-Mashriq*, 259–60; Lewis, *Middle East*, 61.

witnessed many changes before Islam. They were impacted mainly by the cultures surrounding Arabia to the north, south, or east. In their political and social life, Arabs were scattered and isolated generally. They lacked a native power to unite them and to spread their territory outside of Arabia. The changing political powers in the Middle East prepared the way for Arabs to find their place in history. When Islam came, they were united and expanded out into the world of their time. In religion, the Arabs were divided between their own pagan religions and the religions of other people around them. Islam brought a unifying force, providing one religion, one prophet, and one state.

BIBLIOGRAPHY

Alī, Jawād. *Al-Mufaṣṣal fī Adyān al-'Arab qabla al-Islām* (The Detailed in the Religions of the Arabs before Islam). Cairo: Dar Al Shoaea, 2004.

Amien, Ahmad. *Fajr El Islam* (The Dawn of Islam). Cairo: Al- hayaa Al msryah al-aamah lel kitab, 1996.

Badr, Habib, ed. *Masihiyah 'abr tarikhiha fi al-Mashriq* (Christianity: A History in the Middle East). Beirut: Middle East Council of Churches, 2001.

Chapman, Colin. *Cross and Crescent: Responding to the Challenge of Islam*. Nottingham: InterVarsity, 2007.

Al-Tamīmī, Rafīq. Jaw al-Jazīra al-ʿArabiyya wa-Ātharuhu ʿalā al-Hijrāt al-Sāmiyya (The Climate of the Arabian Peninsula and Its Effect of the Semitic Migrations). Cairo: Al Muqtataf, 1944.

Griffith, Sidney H. *The Church in the Shadow of the Mosque: Christians and Muslims in the World of Islam*. Princeton, NJ: Princeton University Press, 2008.

Hitti, Philip K. *History of the Arab*. London: Macmillan, 1960.

———. *The Near East in History: A 5000 Year Story*. Princeton, NJ: D. Van Mostrand, 1961.

Hourani, Albert. *A History of The Arab Peoples*. London: Faber, 1991.

Hoyland, Robert G. *Arabia and the Arabs: From the Bronze Age to the Coming of Islam*. London: Routledge, 2001.

Lewis, Bernard. *The Middle East*. London: Phoenix, 1995.

Payne, Robert. *The History of Islam*. New York: Barnes and Noble, 1995.

Zwemer, M. Samuel. *The Influence of Animism on Islam*. London: Central Board of Missions, 1920.

2

Islam and Judaism

ISSA DIAB

It is agreed among scholars of Islam and Judaism who accept historical criticism that these two religions are very convergent and have a large number of points in common. This, in our opinion, does not contradict the issue of belief in revelation, as the latter may take different paths and can be understood in different ways. In this chapter, we will attempt to demonstrate this convergence through the investigation of the emergence of Islam in a religious context in which Judaism was widely present. Then we'll study both Judaism and Islam, showing the points of similarity and difference in terms of theoretical concepts, practices, and legislation.

THE JEWISH PRESENCE IN THE ARABIAN PENINSULA ON THE EVE OF ISLAM

The Qur'an, Ḥadith, and Sunnah, as well as traditional Islamic historiography, attest to the presence of Jews in the Arabian Peninsula long before the advent of Islam. This presence was especially concentrated in Yemen and around Yathrib (Medina). Scholars indicate that this Jewish presence was the result of successive Jewish migrations from both their homeland and the land to which they were exiled (Babylon), in addition to the Arabs who converted to Judaism. There were several waves of Jewish migration to Arabia:

1. After the collapse of the kingdom of Judah in 586 BCE.
2. After the Roman conquest of Judea.
3. After the Jewish rebellion in 66 CE and the destruction of Jerusalem by Titus in 70 CE, the exiles found home in the desert.
4. After the Bar Kochba Revolt in 135 CE, survivors sought religious freedom in the Arabian desert rather than live under the Roman rule.
5. After Ghassanid oppression in Syria, there was a wave of immigration, circa 300 CE, by people known in Islamic literature as Banū Aws and Banū Khazraj.
6. After the rise of the Himyarite kingdom around 380 CE, migration from Judea to the southern Arabian Peninsula to support them.

Sanaite Jews have a tradition that their ancestors settled in Yemen forty-two years before the destruction of the first temple. According to Jeremiah, some seventy-five thousand Jews, including priests and Levites, went to Yemen.[1] The Banū Habban of southern Yemen have a tradition that they are the descendants of the Judeans who settled in the region before the destruction of the second temple. These Judeans are said to have belonged to a brigade sent by King Herod to aid the Roman legions fighting in the region.[2] By the end of the fifth century, the Banū Aws and the Banū Khazraj had become rulers of Yathrib. According of Sirah, in about 400 CE, Himyarite King Tubba Abū Karib As'ad al-Kāmil (385–420 CE),[3] a convert to Judaism, led military expeditions into central Arabia and expanded his empire to encompass most of the Arabian Peninsula.[4]

The relationship between the Himyarite kings and the polytheistic Arab tribes was strengthened when, under the royal permission of Abū Karib As'ad al-Kāmil, Quṣayy ibn Kilāb (400–480 CE) rebuilt the Ka'ba from a state of decay and had the Arabs al-Kahinan (Cohanim) build their homes there.

1. Seri and Ben-David, *Journey to Yemen and Its Jews*, 43.
2. Blady, *Jewish Communities in Exotic Places*, 32.
3. Ibn Hishām, I, 26–27.
4. Lane, *Traditional Mu'tazilite Qur'an Commentary*.

Jewish tribes played an important role during the rise of Islam. Muhammad had extensive contact with Jewish tribes, both urban and nomadic. Muhammad viewed Christians and Jews (both of whom he referred to as the "People of the Book") as natural allies, sharing the fundamental tenets of his teachings. At the end of 622 CE, Shallum ben Hushiel[5] went to visit Muhammad in Medina and offered his submission (desiring conversion to Islam).

In the Constitution of Medina,[6] Jews were given equality with Muslims in return for their political loyalty[7] and were allowed to practice their own culture and religion. A significant account symbolizing interfaith harmony between early Muslims and Jews is that of Rabbi Mukhayriq. The Rabbi was from Banū Nadir and fought alongside the Muslims at the Battle of Uhud and bequeathed all his wealth to Muhammad in the event of his death. He was later called by Muhammad "the best of the Jews."[8]

JUDAISM AND MUHAMMAD

In order to identify the Jewish influence that contributed to the formation of the religious thoughts of Muhammad before and after the launch of the Islam, two issues must be explored: his religious background and his sermons that are included in the Qur'an.

RELIGIOUS BACKGROUND OF MUHAMMAD

Muhammad grew up in an extremely diverse religious context. Religion in pre-Islamic Arabia included indigenous Arabian polytheism, ancient Semitic religions, Christianity, Judaism, Mandaeism, Hanīfism, and Iranian religions such as Zoroastrianism and Manichaeism. Arab polytheism, the dominant belief system, was based on the belief in deities and

5. Also known as "Salman al-Farsi," "Shallum the Persian," "Salman the Good," "Abu Bakr al-Chaliva al-Saddiq," "Hanamel the 37th Exilarch," son of the Exilarch Hushiel.

6. The constitution of Medina (ṣaḥīfat al-Madīnah) is the modern name given to a document believed to have been written in 622–624 CE. However, no copy of the document has ever been found. And there is no mention of the existence of such a document until the beginning of the 800s. The traditional Islamic account of this document is as follows: it was written in the name of the Prophet Muhammad shortly after his arrival in Medina in 622 CE (or 1 AH), following the Hijra of Mecca.

7. Esposito, *Islam*, 17; Neusner, *God's Rule*, 153.

8. ʿUmarī, *Madīnan Society at the Time of the Prophet*, 62; Mazuz, *Religious and Spiritual Life of the Jews of Medina*, 16.

other supernatural beings such as the djinn. Gods and goddesses were worshipped in local shrines, such as the Ka'ba in Mecca. According to Islamic traditional sources, Muhammad was born around the year 570 CE in the Banū Hāshim clan, a branch of the powerful Quraysh. They were the ruling tribe of Mecca and guarded its most sacred shrine, the Ka'ba.

The traditional groups that traded in Mecca held many different religious beliefs. The city was a forum of many vices and activities associated with trade, travel, and metropolitan business. To escape the activities of Mecca, Muhammad would often seek the solitude of the mountains, where he could contemplate and think. Muhammad performed many acts of piety (called Taḥannuth),[9] like what the monotheistic Hunafa did.[10]

In the traditional story, Muhammad was in close contact with a Christian sect, later identified as Nestorian, Docetic, or Ebionite, through a Nasrani priest, Waraqa ben Nawfal, who blessed his marriage with Khadija. According to the work of Joseph Azzi, Waraqa ben Nawfal was one of the main inspirations of Meccan Islam and Muhammad might have been a Judeo-Christian of Ebonite inspiration.[11] For Van Reeth, though, it would be a "mistake to want to reduce the origins of Islam to a single community, be it Judeo-Christianity, Elkasaism, Manichaeism or others." Indeed, current research has shown a diversity and multiplicity of influences on nascent Islam.[12] Whatever the case, all these Christian sects that were scattered in the Arabian Peninsula at the time of Muhammad were greatly influenced by Judaism. That is why they acquired a general name: Judeo-Christianity.

JUDAISM AND THE QUR'AN

The Qur'an has passages that talk about Jews, their books, their history, and their beliefs, as well as reactions to their religion. Some of these passages resemble sections of the Hebrew Bible, Jewish writings between the two Testaments, the Midrashim, and the Talmud.[13] It goes without saying that the reason for this is the Jewish presence in the Arabian Peninsula on

9. Kister, "Al-Taḥannuth," 223–36.
10. Tillier and Thierry, «Muhammad à l'assassinat de 'Alî,» 80.
11. Azzi, *Prêtre et le prophète*, 303.
12. Reeth, «Courants 'judéo-chrétiens,'» 427ff.
13. Diab, *Bible qui est dans le Coran.*

the eve of the advent of Islam, and Muhammad's relationship with Jews and Judeo-Christians.

Muslim scholars generally report that pre-Islamic Arabia was polytheistic,[14] a point of view overestimated by the sīra.[15] However, according to Robin, the context of the Qur'an is that of the debates on monotheistic faiths,[16] the oldest and most prominent of which was Jewish monotheism. Robin adds that "the image of an Arabia on the eve of Islam dominated by paganism has no real historical foundation."[17]

Whatever the approach to the origins of Islam, the presence of Jewish or Christian elements in the Qur'an and their influences on the nascent Islam are widely accepted as fact. Herbert Berg asserts, "Attempting to isolate the origins of Islam from the culture that spawned it inhibits our understanding. Islam was not an isolated cult, as the Qur'an itself testifies."[18] Muhammad himself was undeniably in contact with Christians and Jews. The latter even welcomed him into their community in Yathrib (Medina) when he was expelled from Mecca in 622 CE. This probably partly explains the biblical references present in the Qur'an. In addition to taking up numerous themes from the Bible (both the Hebrew Bible and New Testament), the Qur'an refers to the entire monotheistic corpus, such as rabbinic texts (the Mishnah), the Talmud (Shabbat 88),[19] Christian apocrypha (the childhood of Jesus, for example), and Jewish apocrypha (the Testament of Moses).[20]

Judaism and Jews are very often mentioned in the Qur'an. Thus, many Qur'anic passages come from biblical episodes. Nevertheless, the stories are often more related to post-biblical stories and interpretations (midrash) than to the Bible itself. The Qur'an paraphrases more than it quotes the Hebrew Bible. Some authors see it as a mark of orality; others associate it with the ambivalence of Islam toward Judaism. Thus, "faith, law and public and private rights are extremely present and drawn from the Hebrew Bible, like other Jewish sources."[21]

14. Robin, «L'Arabie préislamique,» 74ff.
15. Donner, " Historical Context," 23 ff.
16. Lindstedt, "Pre-Islamic Arabia and Early Islam," 159ff.
17. Robin, «L'Arabie préislamique,» 74ff, note 4.
18. Berg, "Islamic Origins and the Qur'an," 51ff.
19. Gobillot, «L'abrogation (nâsihk et mansûhk) dans le Coran.»
20. Cuypers, «Sourate 81, 'L'obscurcissement.'»
21. Bar-Asher, «Judaïsme et le Coran,» 295ff.

Muslim legal precepts were forged in a context marked by Judaism and sometimes illustrate the changing attitude of nascent Islam toward Judaism. There is a considerable similarity between the rituals of prayer and fasting in both religions, and the Qur'an often also uses religious terminology foreign to the Arabic language.

The Qur'an presents the biographies of the prophets in a very brief way. Except for Joseph and Moses, the stories of the prophets cannot be reconstructed from the Qur'an alone: one must return to the Hebrew Bible or pseudo-Jewish writings. This is because the Qur'an chooses sporadic incidents or episodes scattered in separate surahs. The short method that the Qur'an followed when presenting the biographies of the prophets probably indicates that it was addressing an audience familiar with these stories. This audience may have been Arab Jews, or Arabs who knew these stories because of they were widespread.

How can we explain the existence of many references, implicit and explicit, made to biblical texts by the Qur'an? According to the Islamic perspective, the Qur'an is a return to the sources, an ultimate confirmation of the scriptures already revealed previously (the Torah/Bible), from which the Jews and Christians have moved away.[22]

MUHAMMAD'S CONFLICTS WITH THE JEWS

During Muhammad's proselytizing in Mecca, he viewed Christians and Jews, both of whom he called the "People of the Book," as natural allies. Because they shared the fundamental tenets of his teachings, he anticipated their acceptance and support. The first Muslims, like Jews, prayed toward Jerusalem.[23] At the height of the Muslim persecution in Mecca, Muhammad was offered the position of arbiter in the highly diverse city of Medina, or Yathrib, which had a large Jewish community.[24] While the Prophet's biography says that it was the Yathribis who invited Muhammad to move to their city and settle there, choosing to move to Yathrib was a strategic decision that Muhammad made for religious, economic, and political reasons. With his high intelligence, Muhammad saw that if he controlled Yathrib and its tribes, he would be able to secure the material resources necessary to extend his daʿwa.

22. Nöldeke, *Geschichte des Qorâns*.

23. Esposito, *Islam*, 17.

24. Armstrong, "Muhammad."

Many Medinans converted to the Meccan immigrant faith before and after Muhammad's emigration, but only a few came from a Jewish background as most of the Jewish community rejected Muhammad's prophethood.[25] Their opposition may well have been for political as well as religious reasons.[26] According to Montgomery Watt, Jews would normally be unwilling to admit that a non-Jew could be a prophet.[27] Mark Cohen adds that Muhammad appeared centuries after the cessation of biblical prophecy and wrote his message in verbiage foreign to Judaism in both format and rhetoric.[28]

As Muhammad taught of the new *Islamic* prophets, such as Adam, Lot, and Jesus, his message was identical to those of Abraham and Moses. Still, Jews were able to make some Muslims doubt his prophecy. Judaism does not list Adam, Lot, or Jesus as prophets. In fact, the Talmud (Sanhedrin 11a) states that Haggai, Zechariah, and Malachi were the last prophets, all of whom lived in the sixth century BCE, at the end of the seventy-year Babylonian exile and the restoration, and currently only the "Bath qol" (בת קול, lit. daughter of a voice, "voice of God") exists. The Jews, according to Watt, could argue that "certain passages in the Qur'an contradicted their ancient scriptures."[29] Watt also states that many Jews had close ties to Abd-Allah ibn Ubayy,[30] "the potential prince of Medina," who "but for the arrival of Muhammad"[31] would have become the chief arbiter of the community. The Jews might have hoped for greater influence if Ubayy had become a ruler.[32] Watt writes that the Islamic response to these criticisms was as follows:

> The Qur'ān met these intellectual criticisms by developing the conception of the religion of Abraham. While the knowledge of Abraham came from the Old Testament and material based on that, Abraham could be regarded as the ancestor of the Arabs through Ishmael. It was also an undeniable fact that he was not a Jew or Christian, since the Jews are either to be taken as the followers of Moses or as the descendants of Abraham's grandson,

25. Esposito, *Islam*, 17.
26. Endress, *Islam*, 29.
27. Holt, Lambton, and Lewis, eds., *Cambridge History of Islam*, 43–44.
28. Cohen, *Under Crescent and Cross*, 23.
29. Holt, Lambton, and Lewis, eds., *Cambridge History of Islam*, 43–44.
30. Holt, Lambton, and Lewis, eds., *Cambridge History of Islam*, 43–44.
31. Holt, Lambton, and Lewis, eds., *Cambridge History of Islam*, 40.
32. Holt, Lambton, and Lewis, eds., *Cambridge History of Islam*, 43–44.

> Jacob. At the same time Abraham had stood for the worship of God alone. The Qur'ān therefore claimed that it was restoring the pure monotheism of Abraham which had been corrupted in various, clearly specified ways by Jews, and Christians.[33]

This opinion of Watt is based on the content of surah 3, Āl-Īmran 67. Watt states that the accusation of altering the scriptures may mean nothing more than giving false interpretations to certain passages. Although in contemporary Islam this is considered a textual corruption, in previous revealed books this corruption is called *taḥrīf* (alteration).

The Qur'an also stated that it was not a surprise to see the Jews rejecting Muhammad, especially considering what had been done to most of the prophets mentioned in the Jewish scriptures. Watt asserts that the Qur'an "also criticized Jewish exaggerations of their claim to be the chosen people"[34] and objected to the alleged assertion of the Jews of Medina that "they alone had true knowledge of God."[35] The Qur'an also criticized Jews for believing that Ezra was the Son of God, a claim not attested in either Jewish or other extra-Qur'anic sources.[36] Michael Cook considers the accusation of regarding Ezra as the Son of God as petty or obscure.[37] The *Encyclopaedia Judaica* article on Ezra says: "Muhammed claims (surah 9:30) that in the opinion of the Jews ʿUzayr (Ezra) is the son of God. These words are enigmatic because no such opinion is found among the Jews, even though Ezra was chosen for special appreciation."[38]

After the Jews' rejection of Muhammad as a prophet and the hope of their joining him was lost, relations began to deteriorate. This widened the gap between Muhammad and the Jews. Among the actions that indicate this distance is the fact that Muhammad changed the direction of prayer from Jerusalem to Mecca. In the Constitution of Medina, Jews were given equality with Muslims in return for political loyalty.[39] Afterwards, Badr and Uhud, the Banū Qainuqā' and Banū Nadir, respectively, were expelled with their families and property from Medina. According to the *Jewish Encyclopaedia*, "Muhammad became increasingly hostile to the Jews over time. He grew to perceive that there were irreconcilable

33. Holt, Lambton, and Lewis, eds., *Cambridge History of Islam*, 43–44.
34. Watt, *Muhammad: Prophet and Statesman*, 116.
35. Watt, *Muslim-Christian Encounters*, 14.
36. Zebiri, "Qur'an and Polemics."
37. Cook, *Muhammad*, 34.
38. See Sanhedrin 21b- sefaria; Yevomos—64a–86b.
39. Esposito, *Islam*, 17; Neusner, *God's Rule*, 153.

differences between their religion and his, especially when the belief in his prophetic mission became the criterion of a true Muslim."[40]

The Jewish community challenged "the way in which the Qur'an appropriated Biblical accounts and personages; for instance, its making Abraham an Arab and the founder of the Ka'bah at Mecca."[41] Therefore, Muhammad "accused them of intentionally concealing its true meaning or of entirely misunderstanding it."[42] It is true that the Qur'an does not explicitly state that Abraham was an Arab, but the biography makes him the great-grandfather of the Arabs through Ishmael, and the Qur'an considers him a Muslim.

THE COMMON AND DIVERSE ISSUES BETWEEN ISLAM AND JUDAISM

There are many shared aspects between Judaism and Islam; Islam was strongly influenced by Judaism in its fundamental religious outlook, structure, jurisprudence, and practice.[43] Because of this similarity, as well as through the influence of Islamic culture and philosophy on the Jewish populations in the Muslim world, there has been considerable and continued physical, theological, and political overlap between the two faiths in the subsequent 1,400 years.

Both Are Semitic Religions

Israelite Jews and Arab Muslims are ethnically classified as "Semitic peoples."[44] The terminology is now largely obsolete outside the grouping "Semitic languages" in linguistics.[45] Modern historians confirm the affinity of ancient Hebrews and Arabs based on characteristics that are usually transmitted from parent to child, such as genes and habits, with

40. Singer, ed., "Muhammad."

41. Singer, ed., "Muhammad."

42. Singer, ed., "Muhammad."

43. Prager and Telushkin, *Why the Jews?*, 110–26.

44. A racialist concept derived from biblical accounts of the origins of the cultures known to the ancient Hebrews. First used in the 1770s by members of the Göttingen School of History, this biblical terminology for race was derived from Shem (Hebrew: שֵׁם), one of the three sons of Noah in the book of Genesis (ch. 10). See Baasten, "Note on the History of 'Semitic,'" 57–73.

45. Lewis, *Semites and Anti-Semites*.

the most well-studied criterion being language. Similarities between Semitic languages (including Hebrew and Arabic) and their differences with those spoken by other adjacent people confirm the common origin of Hebrews and Arabs among other Semitic nations.[46] The notion that some languages may be related to other languages was by no means new. Already in ancient times Jewish scholars were aware of the kinship between Hebrew and Aramaic; in medieval times they were able to perceive and even make use of the similarities in their studies of grammar and lexicography.

Language is the most powerful means of communication, a vehicle of expression of cultural values and aspirations, and the instrument of conserving culture. Every religion has a dominant language in which it is formed. This language has an impact on the formulation of religious concepts. Convergent languages make the religious concepts of their religions convergent. As such, language is important to developing and preserving the identity of a particular group or community. A linguistic conflict can play a role in areligious conflict and be used to manipulate certain groups. Generally, as language changes, religion changes too. This may not be the case with Islam for there is a direct relationship between the Arabic language and Islam. The Qur'an and the Hadith are in Arabic, and this has resulted in Arabic being given significant prominence in the study of Islam with the aim of protecting the Qur'an's message from being wrongfully understood.[47]

Both Are Abrahamic

The three major monotheistic religions of Judaism, Christianity, and Islam, alongside the Bahá'í faith, Samaritanism, Druzism, and Rastafarianism, are all regarded as Abrahamic religions due to their shared worship of God (referred to as *Yahweh* in Hebrew and as *Allah* in Arabic), who, these traditions claim, revealed himself to Abraham.[48] Abrahamic religions share the same distinguishing features:[49]

- All of them originated from ancient Semitic religions in the geographical region of the Middle East.

46. *Religion of Semites*, ch. 1.
47. Balraj, Singh, and Harina Abd Manan, unspecified article, 1218.
48. Abulafia, *Abrahamic Religions.*
49. Bremer, "Abrahamic Religions," 19–20.

- All of their theological traditions are to some extent influenced by the depiction of the God of Israel in the Hebrew Bible.
- All of them trace their roots to Abraham as a common patriarch.[50]

The Catholic French scholar of Islam Louis Massignon stated that the phrase "Abrahamic religion" means that all these religions come from one spiritual source.[51] God's promise in Genesis 15:4–8 regarding Abraham's heirs became paradigmatic for Jews, who speak of him as "our father Abraham" (*Avraham Avinu*). With the emergence of Christianity, Paul the apostle, in Romans 4:11–12, likewise referred to Abraham as the "father of all" those who have faith, circumcised or uncircumcised. Islam likewise conceived itself as the religion of Abraham.[52] All the major Abrahamic religions claim direct lineage to Abraham:

- Abraham is recorded in the Torah as the ancestor of the Israelites through his son Isaac, born to Sarah through a promise made to both of them (Genesis 17:16).
- Christians affirm the ancestral origin of Jesus in Abraham; Jesus was descended from Abraham (Matthew 1:1–17). But Paul related Christianity with Abraham by stating that since Abraham believed in Christ, Christians are children of Abraham (Romans 4).
- Muhammad, as an Arab, is believed by Muslims to be descended from Abraham's son Ishmael, through Hagar. Jewish tradition also equates the descendants of Ishmael, Ishmaelites, with Arabs, while the descendants of Isaac by Jacob, who was also later known as Israel, are the Israelites.[53]
- Jews, children of Israel, based on "holy texts," claim that the twelve tribes are the posterity of Abraham, through Isaac. Muslims, based on traditional lineage, claim that Prophet Muhammad is a descendant of Abraham.
- Judaism and Islam are known as "Abrahamic religions." The firstborn son of Abraham, Ishmael, is considered by Muslims to be

50. Hughes, *Abrahamic Religions*, 15–33; Christiano et al., "Excursus on the History of Religions," 254–55.

51. Massignon, "Trois prières d'Abraham," 20–23.

52. Levenson, *Inheriting Abraham*, 178–79.

53. Ṣaḥīḥ al-Bukhārī, book 55, Hadīth no. 584; book 56, Hadīth no. 710.

father of the Arabs. Abraham's second son, Isaac, is considered the father of the Hebrews.

- For Muslims, Ibrahīm (Abraham) is considered an important prophet of Islam and the ancestor of Muhammad through Ishmael, son of Hagar. In Islamic tradition, Isaac is viewed as the grandfather of all Israelites and the promised son of Abraham from his barren wife Sarah.

Both Are Religions of a Book

Judaism and Islam are classified among scriptural religions, in that they rely on a holy book believed to be inspired by God. "Religions of the book" is a common expression to designate mainly, but not only, the Abrahamic religions, Judaism, Christianity, and Islam. This expression underlines the particularity of these religions being formed around a book. It comes from the Qur'anic formula "Ahl al-Kitāb" ("People of the Book"), designating Jews and Christians. For the Qur'an, "the Book" is supposed to come from a mother, the "Mother of the Book" (Āl-'Imrān 3:7 and Ar-Ra'd 13:39), a sort of celestial womb where the Divine Word has always rested.

Judaism and Islam have two types of reference books: the foundational book, and the tradition collected in one book. In Judaism, the Hebrew Bible (including the written Torah) is the legal reference for everything related to faith, worship, and rituals. Next to it is the Talmud, which is an entire collection of Jewish traditions throughout the ages. In Islam, the Qur'an is the supreme reference for everything related to faith, worship, and practice. Muslims then rely on the Sunnah, which is composed of Sirah and Hadith, the sayings and acts of the Prophet. The Islamic hadith and Jewish Talmud have also often been compared as authoritative extracanonical texts that were originally oral transmissions for generations before being committed to writing.[54]

Jews and Muslims believe in the divine source of their scriptures; they believe that it was revealed to them by a prophet. The Jews believe that God revealed the Torah on Mount Horeb (or Sinai), where Moses received it. In the Jewish tradition there is a teaching that God revealed the

54. Freedman, *Talmud*, 58; Firestone, *Children of Abraham*, 42–43; Satlow, *Creating Judaism*, 195.

Torah to Moses by means of angels.[55] Muslims believe that God revealed the Qur'an to the Muhammad. The first revelation came to the Prophet while he was on Mount Arafat in Mecca and the angel Gabriel was the mediator of that revelation. Jews and Muslims believe in literal revelation (*tanzīl*), and that God, with his power, has preserved these books unchanged over generations. One of the effects of believing in scriptures inspired by God is that Judaism and Islam sanctify the Word. Sometimes it is an identification between God and his Word. From here came the Hanbali belief in Islam in the eternity of the Qur'an, and belief in the eternity of the Torah in some Jewish branches.[56]

The narrative similarities between the Torah and Qur'an are many. There is a similarity in the texts themselves, since many characters in the Hebrew Bible and their stories are contained in the Qur'an, although in different and abbreviated forms. The Mosaic law is the heart of the Torah, whereas the Islamic Sharia is the heart of the Qur'an; there is a similarity between the two laws. These similarities are especially seen in what is permissible or forbidden in terms of food, drinks, dress, healthy habits, marital relations, and degrees of kinship allowed in marriage. Narrative similarities between Jewish texts and the hadith have also been noted. For example, both state that Potiphar's wife was named Zuleika.

55. "In reading the Bible's account of the giving of the Torah at Mount Sinai, we observe that there were three principal participants in that event: God, Moses, and the people of Israel. However, Jewish tradition added yet another important role to the cast: the angels. The Midrash, Talmud and liturgical poems populated the Sinai landscape with swarms of angels who heightened the drama of that memorable occasion. Our ancient sages found support for this motif in the words of Scripture itself. In Moses' final words at the end of Deuteronomy he sang of how 'the Lord came from Sinai . . . and he came with myriads of holy ones. From his right hand went a fiery law for them.' A venerable tradition common to rabbinic interpreters and to the early Jewish Greek and Aramaic translations understood that those 'holy ones' were hosts of angels who were present at the Torah's revelation. A similar conclusion was inferred from Psalm 68:18: 'The chariots of God are twenty thousand, even thousands of angels. The Lord is among them, as in Sinai, in the holy place.'" Segal, "Moses vs. Angels," 11.

56. Rambam writes: "It is clear and explicit in the Torah, that the Torah is an eternal commandment; it is not subject to change nor subtraction nor addition." Elsewhere in Mishneh Torah he clarifies this principle: "All the books of the prophets (Nevi'im) and all the Holy Writings (Kesuvim) will be dissolved in the days of Mashiach, except for the Book of Esther, which will remain—like the Five Books of the Chumash and like the legal rulings (halachos) of the Oral Law, which will never be revoked." (Hilchos Yesodei HaTorah 9:1; Hilchos Megillah 2:18.). https://jewsforjudaism.org/knowledge/articles/eternity-torah-mitzvos/.

SIMILARITIES IN BELIEFS

It is only natural that there are many similarities between Islam and Judaism as they emerged in the same region and share a patriarch, and Islam was influenced at its inception by the Jewish context in which it developed. Here are many commonalities between Judaism and Islam; Islam has been strongly influenced by Judaism in its fundamental religious outlook, structure, jurisprudence, and practice.[57]

Both Are Purely Monotheistic

Though Judaism is the world's oldest monotheistic religion, all three major monotheistic religions believe in God the creator, one who rules the universe, judges, punishes, and forgives. The monotheistic deity is considered omniscient and omnipotent. He is incomprehensible; hence he cannot be depicted in any form. The belief in these religions is that the one God revealed himself through ancient prophets. The history of biblical monotheism is not a linear history. Rather, it is a process of maturation, the fruit of a sum of influences, traditions, and events that led to the development of the expression of an original, regional, monotheistic faith.[58] In comparison, the religion of Islam, which appeared some twelve centuries later, was immediately more directive, and more explicit in affirming the sole existence of the one God and in criticizing polytheism. The "Shahadah" (literally translated "testimony;" i.e., the declaration of faith in Allah and recognition of Mohammad as his prophet) denies any other form of divinity. The Qur'an contains verses which affirm monotheism. One of its surahs (chapters) bears the title of al-Ikhlās, pure monotheism.

Jewish and Islamic monotheism are unitary; that is to say, they reject the existence of interpersonal relationships within God. On the other hand, Christian monotheism is Trinitarian, meaning that God is a relational God and that there are relations that unite the Father, Son, and Holy Spirit. Islam and Judaism reject the doctrine of the incarnation and the notion of a personal God as anthropomorphic, because it is seen to be demeaning to the transcendence of God. In Judaism and Islam, God is perceived as unique, perfect, and completely infinite in all his attributes,

57. Prager and Telushkin, *Why the Jews?*, 110–26.

58. Lemaire, "L'émergence du monothéisme en Israël avant l'Exil," 90–101.

having no partner or equal, being the sole creator of everything in existence.[59] God is never portrayed in any image.[60] Judaism and Islam strictly prohibit anthropomorphism or idolatry in any form, especially in relation to God. Sunni Islam prohibits all kinds of anthropomorphism of the prophets as well and considers reverence of the saints in any way to be an affront to the lordship of God.

Islam puts a heavy emphasis on the conceptualization of God as strictly singular (*tawḥīd*).[61] He is considered to be unique (*wāhid*) and inherently one (*aḥad*), all-merciful, and omnipotent. According to the Qur'an, there are ninety-nine names of God (*al-asma al-husna*, lit. "the best names"), each of which evokes a distinct characteristic of God.

Muslims believe that Allah is the same God worshipped by members of the Abrahamic religions that preceded Islam, i.e., Judaism and Christianity (al-ꜥankabūt 29:46).[62] Similarly to Jews, Muslims explicitly reject the divinity of Jesus and don't believe in him as God incarnated or the Son of God. Instead, they consider him a human prophet and the promised Messiah sent by God, beliefs that the Jews do not share.

Islam's Five Pillars and Six Pillars of Faith and the Jewish Faith

The five pillars of Islam are the foundations of Muslim faith. They are the Shahadah (testimony, declaration of faith in Allah and recognition of Mohammad as his prophet), Salah (prayer), Zakāt (alms), Sawm (fasting) and Hajj (pilgrimage to Mecca). Each pillar has its similar one in Judaism. In the Shahadah (testimony), Muslims recite this testimony of faith many times a day: "There is no god but Allah, and Muhammad is the prophet of Allah." It is similar to the Jewish shemā'; Jews recite this testimony of faith: "Listen Yisrael, HaShem is our God, HaShem is One." (Deuteronomy 6:4). As for the Salah, Muslims pray five times a day; Jews pray three times a day. As for alms, Muslims are required to give zakat (al-Baqarah 2: 42, 83, 110, 177, 277; al-Mā'idah 5:12; al-An'ām 6:141); Shi'ah Muslims also pay al-khoms (the fifth, 20 percent) of their yearly savings to charity (al-Moujādalah 13:58; al-Muzammil 20:73; al-Moumtahanah 60:20); Muslims are required to pay other alms when it is needed (at-Tawbah

59. Lebens, "Is God a Person?," 90–95; Grossman and Sommer, "GOD," 294–97.

60. Leone, "Smashing Idols," 30–56.

61. Gardet, "Allāh."

62. Peters, *Islam*, 4.

9:160; al-Thāriāt 51:16; al-Maʿārij 70:25; etc.). Jews are required to pay the tithe, the tzedaqah (charity), 10 percent of their yearly income to charity (Numbers 18:21, 25–28; Deuteronomy 12:6, 18, 19; 14:22–29; 16:16). As for fasting, Muslims fast from sunrise to sunset during the holy month of Ramadan (al-Baqarah 2:183–85); Jews fast from sunset to sunset on fast days like Yom Kippur, the Day of Atonement. As to the Hajj (pilgrimage), Muslims must go for pilgrimage to Mecca at least once in their life (al-Baqarah 2:196–20; Āl-ʿImrān 3:96–97). The Arabic word *Hajj* comes from the root meaning "circle," as Muslims circle the Ka'ba in Mecca. The Jewish pilgrimage holidays are pessāh (Passover), Sukkot (tents), and Shavuot (weeks) (Exodus 34:14, 23–24; Deuteronomy 16:16; 31:11).

The pillars of faith in Islam can be broken into the following six beliefs:

1. Belief in the existence and unicity of Allah. To believe in Allah is to believe that there is only one God worthy of worship, with no partner or son. This concept is known as tawḥīd.
2. Belief in the existence of angels who were created from light before human beings for the purpose of worshipping Allah. They keep a record of our deeds. Some of the other duties of angles include blowing the trumpet on judgment day, taking people's souls (i.e., the angel of death), as well as being keepers of heaven and hell.
3. Belief in the books of Allah. The books of Allah were delivered to the nations by messengers. Allah revealed these books to his messengers as a form of guidance and proof for mankind. The books that were sent and known to mankind are:
    - The Scrolls (Ṣuḥūf) of Ibrahim
    - The Psalms (Zabūr) of Dawūd (David)
    - The Tawrat (Torah) that Allah revealed to the Prophet Musa (Moses)
    - The Gospel (Injīl) that Allah revealed to the Prophet ʿIsā (Jesus)
    - The Qur'an which was sent to the last Prophet Muhammad. The Qur'an is the final revelation; it abrogates all the other previous books.
4. Belief in Allah's messengers and that Muhammad is the last of them. Most of the messengers of Allah were sent to a specific nation, except the Prophet Muhammad, who was sent to guide all of mankind.

5. Belief in the Day of Judgment. Allah created men and jinn to worship him and promised paradise as a reward to those who obey him and his messengers but hellfire to those who disobey him. This will happen after resurrection.
6. Belief in the Qaḍā' and Qadar (Doom and Divine Decree). Doom (Qaḍā') is the general decree of Allah that every human shall die, whereas a divine decree (Qadar) is a particular decree of Allah (or the execution of Qaḍā') that a certain person is to die at a particular time and place. Hence, holding this belief entails believing that Allah has created everything and has foreordained its proper measure.

All of these Islamic beliefs are found in Judaism: belief in God, belief in angels, belief in books, belief in the prophets (the second part of the Hebrew Bible is specified to the prophets), belief in the Last Day (references to resurrection and judgment are found in Daniel 12), and belief in predestination.

There is a shared belief in Islam and Judaism that the Luz bone does not decay and that the body will be rebuilt from it at the time of resurrection.[63] It is a small bone in the body at the base of the spinal column and is known by differing traditions as either the coccyx or the seventh cervical vertebra. Muslim books refer to this bone as "'Ajbu al-Dhanab." In Jewish tradition, when asked by Hadrian as to how man will be revived in the world to come, Rabbi Joshua Ben Hananiah replied, "From Luz, in the back-bone."[64]

Similarities in Religious Law

The two religions share not only central practices of fasting and almsgiving, but also dietary laws and other aspects of ritual purity. Under strict dietary laws, lawful food is called "kosher" in Judaism and "ḥalāl" in Islam. Kosher foods are prepared in accordance with traditional Jewish laws. Ḥalāl foods are made with ingredients permitted under Islamic

63. "Imam Muslim relates in his *Ṣaḥīḥ* from Abu Hurayra that the messenger of God said, 'the dust consumes every human, except the coccyx, from which he was created and in which he will be built (again on the day of Resurrection). The traditional relaying of Bukhārī: every part of man will decay except his coccyx, upon which the creature is built. And according to Aḥmad Ibn Ḥanbal and Abū Yaʿlā and al-Ḥākim: the dust eats all of mankind, except his coccyx."

64. Wisnefsky, ed., *From the teachings of Rabbi Yitzchak Luria.*

law, as defined by the Qur'an. On a kosher diet, foods classified as meat cannot be served at the same meal as foods classified as dairy (Exodus 23:19, 26, 34; Deuteronomy 14:21). Halal diets don't have any rules regarding the food pairings. Halal diets restrict alcohol, pork, foods that contain blood, and meat from certain types of animals (al-Mā'idah 5:3; an-Nahl 16:67). Kosher diets also limit pork, shellfish, and meat from specific animals and animal parts (Leviticus 7:22–27; ch. 11). Kosher meat must be butchered by a *shohet* and soaked before cooking. Halal meat must be butchered in a specific way, and ought to be healthy at the time of slaughter. The name of Allah must also be invoked at the time of slaughter for the meat to be considered halal (al-An'ām 6:121). Halal restrictions are similar to a subset of kashrut food laws, so that all kosher food is considered halal, while not all halal food is kosher. Halal laws, for example, do not prohibit the mixing of milk and meat or the consumption of shellfish, which are prohibited by kosher laws, except for the Shia belief that shellfish, mussels, and fruit sea bass and similar fish without scales are not considered halal.

The sacred texts of both religions prohibit homosexuality (Leviticus 18:22; 20:13; Deuteronomy 23:18), prohibit human sexual relations outside marriage,[65] and impose abstinence during the wife's menstruation (Leviticus 15:19–30). In Islam, wives are not permitted to pray or to fast during their menstruation.[66]

Both religions practice male circumcision as a religious duty. Male circumcision is compulsory for Jews and is commonly practiced among Muslims. In Judaism, the book of Genesis (17:10–13) mentions that God issues a command to Abraham that every male child shall be circumcised. The practice is known as *brit milah* (Covenant of Circumcision) and it is performed on the eighth day after the birth of a baby boy, as instructed in the book of Leviticus (12:3). It is regarded as a sign of God's covenant with Israel. In Islam, Islamic scholars differ over whether circumcision is compulsory for Muslim males: some regard it as obligatory, whereas others view it as an act to be recommended. It is carried out to maintain hygiene, and Muslim boys are usually circumcised before they reach

65. Maududi, " Meaning of the Quran, Volume 3," note 7–1.

66. "It is not permissible for a woman to pray during her menstrual period, because of what he said to Fāṭima bint Abī Ḥabīsh, 'When menstruation comes, then stop praying.'" Also narrated by him: "It is not permissible for a woman to fast during her menstrual period," and it was said that the wisdom behind that is because her body is weak during menstruation, it should not be enjoined upon her. See al-Bukhārī, Kitāb al-Wuḍūᶜ, 1/204.

puberty. Circumcision is not mentioned in the Qur'an, but Muhammad spoke about the practice.[67]

CONCLUSION

In this chapter, we briefly described Islam and Judaism and discussed the similarities and divergences between them from both historical and theological perspectives. We explained the Jewish influence on the emergence of Islamic thought, which resulted in an establishment of harmonious relations between the two religions.

The Slovenian philosopher Slavoj Žižek argued that the term "Judeo-Muslim" to describe Middle Eastern culture versus Western Christian culture would be more appropriate nowadays,[68] thus claiming reduced influence of Jewish culture on the Western world because of the historical persecution and exclusion of the Jewish minority. Still, there are also different perspectives on Jewish contributions and influence that would differ from Žižek's.[69]

Even though Islam and Judaism are two very close religions, this closeness is not cultivated in the Middle East due to tense political issues. Many common points, even those disputed, require deep research in workshops and conferences held between the two parties with the aim of emphasizing this closeness. Moreover, this joint scientific research could extend to other aspects of public life and may be one of the tools used to make peace in the region.

67. Abu-Sahlieh, "To Mutilate in the Name of Jehovah or Allah," 575–622; Abu-Sahlieh, "Islamic Law and the Issue of Male and Female Circumcision," 73–101.

68. Zizek, "Glance into the Archives of Islam."

69. "Jewish Nobel Prize Winners."

BIBLIOGRAPHY

Abul Ala Maududi Sayyid. *The Meaning of the Quran*. Vol. 3. N.p.: Islamic Publications, 2000.

Abulafia, Anna Sapir. *The Abrahamic Religions*. London: British Library, 2019.

Aldeeb Abu-Sahlieh, Sami A. *Islamic Law and the Issue of Male and Female Circumcision*. Third World Legal Studies, Valparaiso University School of Law, 1995. https://scholar.valpo.edu/cgi/viewcontent.cgi?article=1036&context=twls.

———. "To Mutilate in the Name of Jehovah or Allah: Legitimization of Male and Female Circumcision." *Medicine and Law* 13:7–8 (1994) 575–622.

Al-Shahrastani, Muhammad. *Kitab al-Milal wa al-Nihal*. Piscataway, NJ: Gorgias, 2002.

Armstrong, Karen. "Muhammad." In *Encyclopaedia of Religion*, edited by Lindsay Jones. N.p.: n.p., 2005.

Azzi, Joseph. *Le prêtre et le prophète: Aux sources du Coran*. Maisonneuve & Larose, 2001.

Baasten, Martin. "A Note on the History of 'Semitic.'" In *Hamlet on a Hill: Semitic and Greek Studies Presented to Professor T. Muraoka on the Occasion of His Sixty-fifth Birthday*. Leuven: Peeters, 2003.

Balraj, Belinda Marie, Surjeet Singh, and Masdini Harina Abd Manan. Unspecified article. *International Journal of Academic Research in Business and Social Sciences* 10:11 (2020) 1218.

Ben-David, Naftali, and Shalom Seri. *A Journey to Yemen and Its Jews*. Eeleh BeTamar, 1991.

Berg, Herbert. "Islamic Origins and the Qur'an." In *The Oxford Handbook of Qur'anic Studies*, edited by Mustafa Akram Ali Shah and M. A. Abdel Haleem. Oxford: Oxford University Press, 2020.

Bianquis, Thierry, and Mathieu Tillier. «De Muhammad à l'assassinat de 'Alî.» In *Les débuts du monde musulman, VIIe–Xe siècle. De Muhammad aux dynasties autonomes*, edited by Thierry Bianquis, Pierre Guichard, and Mathieu Tillier. P.U.F./Nouvelle Clio, 2012.

Blady, Ken. *Jewish Communities in Exotic Places*. Northvale, NJ: Jason Aronson, 2000.

Bremer, Thomas S., "Abrahamic Religions." *Formed from This Soil: An Introduction to the Diverse History of Religion in America*. Chichester, West Sussex: Wiley-Blackwell, 2015.

Christiano, Kevin J., Peter Kivisto, and William H. Swatos Jr., eds. "Excursus on the History of Religions." In *Sociology of Religion: Contemporary Developments*. Lanham, MD: Rowman & Littlefield, 2016.

Cohen, Mark R. *Under Crescent and Cross: The Jews in the Middle Ages*. Princeton, NJ: Princeton University Press, 1994.

Cook, Michael. *Muhammad*. Oxford: Oxford University Press, 1983.

Cuypers, Michel. "La sourate 81, 'L'obscurcissement', et le chapitre 10 du Testament de Moïse." *Analyse Rhétorique de La Sourate* 81 (n.d.).

Diab, Issa. *La Bible qui est dans le Coran*. Analyse littéraire et recherche des sources. Université de Marseille, 2022.

Donner, Fr. "The Historical Context." *The Cambridge Companion to the Qur'an*. Cambridge: Cambridge University Press, 2007.

Endress, Gerhard. *Islam*. Columbia University Press,1988.

Esposito, John. *Islam: "The Straight Path."* Oxford: Oxford University Press, 1998.

Firestone, Reuven. *Children of Abraham: An Introduction to Judaism for Muslims.* Hoboken, NJ: KTAV, 2001.

Freedman, Harry. *The Talmud: A Biography: Banned, Censored and Burned: The Book They Couldn't Suppress.* London: Bloomsbury, 2014.

Gardet, Louis. "Allāh." In *Encyclopaedia of Islam*, edited by C. E. Bosworth et al. Vol. 1. 2nd ed. Leiden: Brill, 1960.

Gobillot, Geneviève. "L'abrogation (nâsihk et mansûhk) dans le Coran à la lumière d'une lecture interculturelle et intertextuelle." *Al-Mawâqif*, numéro spécial, actes du premier colloque international sur «Le phénomène religieux, nouvelles lectures des sciences sociales et humaines», Mascara: Publication du Centre Universitaire Mustapha Stanbouli, April 14–15 and 16, 2008.

Holt, Peter, Malcolm, Ann K. S. Lambton, and Lewis Bernard, eds. *The Cambridge History of Islam.* Cambridge: Cambridge University Press, 1978.

Hughes, Aaron W. *Abrahamic Religions: On the Uses and Abuses of History.* New York: Oxford University Press, 2012.

Kister, M. J. "Al-Taḥannuth: An Enquiry into the Meaning of a Term." *Bulletin of the School of Oriental and African Studies* 31:2 (1968) n.p.

Lane, Andrew J. *A Traditional Mu'tazilite Qur'an Commentary: The Kashshaf of Jar Allah Al-zamakhshari (D538/1144)/.* Texts and Studies on the Qur'an. Leiden: Brill, 2005.

Lebens, Samuel. "Is God a Person? Maimonidean and Neo-Maimonidean Perspectives." In *The Divine Nature: Personal and A-Personal Perspectives*, edited by Simon Kittle and Georg Gasser. New York: Routledge, 2022.

Lemaire, André. "L'émergence du monothéisme en Israël avant l'Exil." In *Enquête sur le Dieu unique*, by Thomas C. Römer. N.p.: Bayard, 2010.

Leone, Massimo. "Smashing Idols: A Paradoxical Semiotics." *Signs and Society* 4:1 (Spring 2016) 30–56.

Levenson, Jon Douglas. *Inheriting Abraham: The Legacy of the Patriarch in Judaism, Christianity, and Islam.* Princeton, NJ: Princeton University Press, 2012.

Lindstedt, Ilkka. "Pre-Islamic Arabia and Early Islam." In *Routledge Handbook on Early Islam.* London: Routledge, 2017.

Massignon, Louis. "Les trois prières d'Abraham, père de tous les croyants." *Dieu Vivant* 13 (1949) n.p.

Mazuz, Haggai. *The Religious and Spiritual Life of the Jews of Medina.* Leiden: Brill, 2014.

Neusner, Jacob. *God's Rule: The Politics of World Religions.* Washington, DC: Georgetown University Press, 2003.

Nöldeke, Theodor. *Geschichte des Qorâns.* N.p., 1860. Available at https://openlibrary.org/books/OL25666234M/Geschichte_des_Qor'āns.

Peters, F. E. *Islam: A Guide for Jews and Christians.* Princeton, NJ: Princeton University Press, 2003.

Prager, Dennis, and Joseph Telushkin. *Why the Jews?: The Reason for Antisemitism.* New York: Simon & Schuster, 1983.

Reeth, J. Van. "Les courants 'judéo-chrétiens' et chrétiens orientaux de l'antiquité tardive." In *Le Coran des historiens*, edited by Mohammad Ali Amir-Moezzi, Guillaume Dye, and Paul Neuenkirchen. Paris: Editions du Cerf, 2019.

Robin, Christian. "L'Arabie préislamique." In *Le Coran des Historiens*, edited by Mohammad Ali Amir-Moezzi, Guillaume Dye, and Paul Neuenkirchen. Paris: Editions du Cerf, 2019.

Satlow, Michael. L. *Creating Judaism: History, Tradition, Practice.* Neew York: Columbia University Press, 2006.

Segal, Elieze. "Moses vs. Angels" In *From the Sources.* The Jewish Free Press, Calgary, May 25, 2012.

Seri, S., and N. Ben-David. *A Journey to Yemen and Its Jews.* N.p.: Eeleh BeTamar, 1991.

Singer, I., ed. "Muhammad." In *The Jewish Encyclopedia: A Descriptive Record of the History, Religion, Literature, and Customs of the Jewish People from the Earliest Times to the Present Day.* 12 vols. New York: Funk & Wagnalls, 1901–1906.

Smith, W. Rebertson. *The Religion of Semites.* New York: Schocken, 1972.

Sommer. "God." In *The Oxford Dictionary of the Jewish Religion*, edited by Adele Berlin. Oxford: Oxford University Press, 2011.

Tillier, Mathieu, and Thierry Bianquis. "De Muhammad à l'assassinat de 'Alî." In *Les débuts du monde musulman, VIIe–Xe siècle. De Muhammad aux dynasties autonomes.* Edited by Thierry Bianquis, Pierre Guichard, and Mathieu Tillier. N.p.: P.U.F./Nouvelle Clio, 2012.

'Umarī, Akram Ḍiyā. *Madīnan Society at the Time of the Prophet: Its Characteristics and Organization.* Herndon, VA: International Institute of Islamic Thought, 1991.

Watt, W. Montgomery. *Muhammad: Prophet and Statesman*, 116.

———. *Muslim-Christian Encounters: Perceptions and Misperceptions.* London: Routledge, 1991.

Wisnefsky, Moshe Yaakov, ed. and trans. *From the Teachings of Rabbi Yitzchak Luria.* http://www.yeshshem.com/kabbalah-haari-class-3.htm.

Zebiri, Kate. "The Qur'an and Polemics." In *Encyclopaedia of the Qur'an*, edited by Jane Dammen McAuliffe. Leiden: Brill, 2001.

Zizek, Slavoj. "A Glance into the Archives of Islam." N.d. https://www.lacan.com/zizarchives.htm.

3

Early Christian-Muslim Encounters
Timothy I and al-Mahdī as a Model

ARA BADALIAN

INTRODUCTION

Timothy I, patriarch of the East Syrian Church (780–823 CE),[1] remains one of the most consequential members of the East Syriac literary, ecclesial, and theological traditions. Born in or around 723, Timothy received an excellent education in philosophy and scriptural exegesis. Due to his training, he not only excelled as a theologian in his church, but also achieved renown as a translator of Aristotle and other philosophical texts during the period in Islamic history now known as the Translation Movement.[2] Upon being elected patriarch of the Church of the East, Timothy I reformed its bureaucracy and shored up its internal relations in a period of immense political upheaval. His efforts culminated in a rebirth and expansion of the Church of the East's missionary efforts. But perhaps even more consequential than his work in translation and

1. On the history of the East Syrian Church, one may consult Baumer, *Church of the East.*

2. For more on Timothy's life, world, and his conversation with al-Mahdī, see Penelas, "Contents of an Apologetic Nature," 279; Samir and Nasry, *Patriarch and the Caliph*, xxxvi; Griffith, "Disputing with Islam in Syriac," 3.

ecclesial administration, Timothy is known for representing his people—then the largest Christian denomination in Iraq, if not the world—in dialogue with the Muslim caliph al-Mahdī.[3]

This chapter will summarize and analyze in detail the method through which the Patriarch of the East (*Catholicos*) Timothy I fashioned his theological arguments in his famous dialogue with the Muslim caliph al-Mahdī.[4] I will argue that Timothy provides a model for how to undertake Muslim-Christian dialogue in the contemporary period. The discourse presents all the necessary tools for dialogical success between Christians and Muslims: in particular, mastery of Arabic and Christian (e.g., Syriac) languages, knowledge of the Qur'anic and biblical texts, and the ability to deploy one's arguments in the conceptual idiom of the other.

SURVEY OF THE EARLY CHRISTIAN-MUSLIM ENCOUNTERS

Before summarizing and analyzing the text of Timothy's dialogue, I must first address a preliminary question: why is Timothy and al-Mahdī's discourse *uniquely* exemplary in the long history of medieval Christian-Muslim dialogue? After all, the Islamic conquests and the subsequent increase in conversions from Christianity to Islam triggered the rapid development of Christian apologetic discourses.[5] First, these discourses

3. Abū ʿAbd Allāh Muḥammad ibn ʿAbd Allāh al-Manṣūr (r. 775—785) was the third Abbasid caliph. For information on his life, see Al-Ṭabarī's history, translated in Kennedy, *Al-Manṣūr and Al-Mahdī*. For more information on his reign in respect to religious groups, see Farouk, "Some Observations on the Reign," 251–75.

4. Watt thinks that this dialogue took place in 781. See Watt, *Muslim-Christian Encounters*, 63.

5. I take my categorical classification of these literary productions from Griffith, "Disputing with Islam," 32–33. While by no means an exhaustive list, I provide here a sufficient list of the most significant documents in Christian responses to Islam, which I have consulted in my research and which undergird my comparisons between Timothy's dialogue and other Christian literature in this chapter:

Dialogue between the Antiochian Patriarch John III by a Muslim Emir. The Emir could be ʿUmayr ibn Saʿd al-Anṣarī, and was dated Sunday, May 9, 644. See Suermann, "Old Testament and the Jews," 132–33; Penn, *When Christians First Met Muslims*, 200–208. Griffith mentions three sources that present this report: 1) Nau, "Colloque du patriarche Jean avec l'émir des Agaréens"; 2) Samir, "Qui est l'interlocuteur musulman du patriarche syrien Jean III"; 3) Reinink, "Beginnings of Syriac Apologetic Literature in Response to Islam"; Bertaina, *Christian and Muslim Dialogues*, 87.

Dialogue between a monk of Bēt Ḥalē and an Emir. See Griffith, "Disputing," 41. See also Penn, *Christians*, 212–15; Reinink, "Political Power and Right Religion," 153–69;

were diverse in their genre and tone. The quality and relevance to the modern context, then, vary widely. One early mode of discourse was to propose an apocalyptic understanding of the emergence of Islam. By doing so, Christian authors leveraged biblical accounts such as Daniel's visions, and thus fit Islam squarely into a Christian hermeneutic.[6] An apocalyptic understanding of Islam was just one way in which Christian scholars and communal leaders could express the very real anxiety and duress they and their congregations felt from the Islamic conquests. In the modern context, the anxieties and duress facing both Muslim and Christian communities have changed; apocalypticism is no longer a tenable answer to the problems facing either community regarding the

---

Szilágyi, " Disputation of the Monk Abraham of Tiberias," 90–92.

An Apology for the Christian Faith by an anonymous Palestinian or Sinaitic monk, c. 788. See Swanson, "Apology for the Christian Faith," 40–42.

Treatises of Abū Rā'iṭa al-Takrītī (d. 835): *Proof of the Christian Religion, First Risālah on the Holy Trinity, and Second Risālah on the Incarnation.* See Keating, "Use and Translation of Scripture," 259–60.

Treatise on the Existence of God and the True Religion by Theodore Abu Qurra (c. late eighth century). He was born in the middle of the eighth century, and he was a theologian in the early decades of the ninth. For more biographical information, see Lamoreaux, "Theodore Abu Qurra," 60–62.

The letter of ' Abd al-Masiḥ b. Isḥaq al-Kindī in his answer to ' Abdallah b. ' Isma' il al-Hāshimī. For information on this text and for a translation of it, see Muir, *Apology of Al-Kindī.*

Answers for the Sheikh by an anonymous author, c. 780. See Griffith, "Answers for the Shaykh."

The Book of Proof and the Book of Questions and Answers by ʿAmmār al-Baṣrī, c. ninth century. While Graf considers him a theologian who lived between the tenth and thirteenth centuries, Husseini provides pieces of evidence confirming his existence in the early ninth century and perhaps as a contemporary to both Abu Qurra and Abu Ra'iṭa. See ʿAmmār al-Baṣrī, Kitāb al-Burhān wa Kitāb al-Masā'il wal-Ajwiba [The Book of Proof and the Book of Questions and Answers], 11; Husseini, "Early Christian Explanations of the Trinity," 198; Mikhail, "ʿAmmār al-Baṣrī's Kitab al-Burhān," 31.

Apologetic Treatise by Nonnus of Nisibis (d. 870). See Roey, *Traité apologétique.*

Against the Ṭayyayē by Dionysius Bar Ṣalībī (d. 1171)

Letter to a Muslim Friend by Paul of Antioch (c. twelfth to thirteenth century). See Thomas, "Paul of Antioch's Letter to a Muslim Friend," 203–4. See also Griffith, "Paul of Antioch," 216–19.

Finally, some of the writers who had interactions with Islam and Muslims in either Syriac or Arabic include: Yonan of Tella (seventh century), Athansasius II of Balad (d. 686), Jacob of Edessa (d. 708), Moses bar Kepha (813–903), Yaḥyā bin ʿAdī, Abū Nūḥ al-Anbarī, and Yaḥyā bin al-Baṭrīq. For more information on these figures, see Sako, "Muslim-Christian Dialogue in Syriac Sources," 9. Cf. Sako, *Ḥiwārāt Masīḥiyya-' Islāmiyya: Muqarabāt Lahutiyya bil-ʿArabiyya fī ʿAṣr al-Khilāfat al-' Abbāsiyya* [Christian-Muslim Dialogue: Theological Approaches in Arabic Language in Abbasid Periode], 12.

6. Sako, "Muslim-Christian Dialogue in Syriac Sources," 9.

other. After the expansion and hegemony of Islam, another genre of Christian apologetic discourse sought to theologically "explain" Islam. Some authors portrayed Islam as a punishment for the sins of Christians.[7] Like apocalypticism, this genre attempted to "manage" Islam by binding it to certain historical circumstances. Like apocalypticism, the passage of time makes this genre of limited use in the modern period. Finally, other authors sought to formulate a systematic theological presentation of Christian doctrines, as we see in the work of Theodore Bar Kônî and John of Damascus,[8] in response to the challenges presented by Islam.[9] This approach still bears fruit today, though its connection to Islam remains more indirect, as it exposits the systematic coherence of Christianity outside of conversations with Muslims. In sum, all of these genres reflect the tendency toward apologetics as the mode of theology.[10]

On the other side, several works of Muslim critics challenged Christians or responded to Christian works in varying depth. These are some of the more notable Muslim works that were opposed to Christianity and written before 1000 CE:[11]

1. ʿAlī bin Rabbān al-Ṭabarī in his book *Refutation on the Types of Christians*[12]

2. Al-Jāḥiẓ, in his work *al-Mukhtār fī'l-Radd ʿAlā al-Naṣārā*, in addition to another work titled *al-Risālah al-ʿAṣaliyya*[13]

---

7. Sako, "Muslim-Christian Dialogue in Syriac Sources," 36.

8. On St. John of Damascus and his *Heresy of the Ishmaelites*, see Sahas, *Byzantium and Islam Collected Studies*, 358; Janosik, *John of Damascus*, 22–23. For Theodore and his *Scholion*, see See Samir, "Prophet Muḥammad as Seen by Timothy I," 75; Butts, "Theodore Bar Kôni, Scholion, Mēmra 10"; "Theodoros bar Kônî."

9. Bar Kônî's themes deal with the same polemical themes that recur today: Christ, his divine Sonship, the cross, and the Trinity (38–39). It can be found the polemical approach in bar Kônî's *Scholion* c. 10, which was directed against Muslims, who called them Ḥanpē (pagans). Sako, "Muslim-Christian Dialogue in Syriac Sources," 38.

10. Sako, "Muslim-Christian Dialogue in Syriac Sources," 39.

11. Al-Laffi mentions several sources that frame Muslim thinkers' interaction with Christianity. See al-Laffi, *Dirasat al-ʿAqāʾid al-Naṣraniyyah*, 77–82. See also Thomas, "Christian Theologians and New Questions," 257.

12. Al-Ṭabarī, *Al-Radd ʿAlā ʾAṣnaf Al-Naṣārā*, 16–17. See also Brockelmann, *Geschichte der Arabischen Litteratur*; Watt, *Muslim-Christian*, 65.

13. Al-Jāḥiẓ, *Al-Mukhtār fi al-Radd ʿAlā al-Naṣārā*, 12. See also Watt, *Muslim-Christian*, 65.

3. Abu l-Huḍhayl al-ʿAllāf (d. 840 CE), who wrote his book *Kitab ʿ Ala ʿ Ammar al-Baṣri fī'l-Radd ʿ Alā al-Naṣārā* in response to ʿAmmar[14]
4. Ḍirār ibn ʿAmr (728–815 CE)[15]
5. Al-Qāsim bin Ibrahim al-Rissī (785–860 CE), in his great collection[16]
6. Abū Yūsuf Yaʿqūb b. Isḥāq al-Kindī's treatise, *Refutation of the Christians*, is missing, but we can identify it through Yaḥyā bin ʿAdī's response to it.[17]
7. Al-Naẓẓām (d. 835–845 CE)[18]
8. Muḥammad ibn Saḥnūn (817–870 CE), who has several works, including *Kitāb al-Imān wa'l-Radd ʿ Alā Ahl al-Shirk*[19]
9. Al-Ḥasān bin Ayyūb, whose sayings are preserved in *Kitab al-Jawāb al-Ṣaḥīḥ li-man Baddala Dīn al-Masīḥ*[20]
10. Abū ʿĪsā Muḥammad b. Hārūn al-Warrāq, in his work *Radd ʿ Ala al-Thalāthah Firāq min al-Naṣārā*[21]
11. Al-Baqillānī in his book *Kitāb al-Tamhīd*[22]
12. Lastly, there is Ibn Ḥazm's *Kitab al-Fiṣāl*, which criticizes the doctrines of Christians, as well as Jews, Muslim heretical sects, and non-Muslim philosophers.[23]

14. Husseini, "Early," 198. See also Al-Nadīm, *Al-Fiḥrist* [The Index], 5:204; Beaumont, *Christology in Dialogue with Muslims*, 67. Griffith believes that al-Baṣrī is trying to engage in answering Islamic teachings, especially Muʿtazilī doctrines. Griffith, "Ammar al-Basri's Kitab al-Burhan," 169.

15. Husseini, "Early," 208.

16. al-Rissi, *Majmūʿ Kutub wa-Rasā' il al-Imām Al-Qāṣim bin Ibrāhīm al-Rissī* [The Collection of the Books and Treatises of the Imām al- Al-Qāsim bin Ibrāhīm al-Rissī], 10, 76–78.

17. Périer, «Un Traité de Yaḥya ben ʿAdi."

18. Husseini, "Early," 208.

19. Means: "Faith and Refutation of those who associate others with God." See Thomas amd Roggema, eds., *Christian Muslim Relations*, 1:738.

20. Taymiyyah, *Kitāb al-Jawāb al-Ṣaḥīḥ li-man Baddala Dīn al-Masīḥ* [The Book of the Correct Answer for who Changed the Religion of the Messiah], 1:44; 4:88, 96, 158, 164, 170, 179.

21. The source does not exist now, but it is inferred through the reply of Yaḥya ben ʿAdi. *Maqālah fi al-Tawḥīd lil-Shaikh Yaḥya ben ʿAdi* [An Article on Monotheism by Sheikh Yaḥya ben ʿAdi], 53.

22. Al-Baqillānī, *Kitāb al-Tamhīd*, 75–103. See also Watt, *Muslim-Christian*, 65.

23. Watt, *Muslim-Christian*, 65. Although al-Shahrastānī thinks that the correct pronunciation is *Faṣl* and not *Fiṣal*, because it is in singular and not in plural form. See

None of these works—at least, those extant—rise to the level of detail and *mutual* sophistication presented in the dialogue between Timothy I and the caliph. Islamic dialogical texts eventually took the form of criticism directed *against* Christian beliefs and practices, or Christian explanations of them.[24] The reasons for this are perhaps obvious: political power and the pressures to convert disproportionately pressed against Christians. These texts, then, frequently misquote Christian doctrines and responses or take weaker variations of them that they can then reduce *ad absurdum*. While some of these texts, such as ʿAlī al-Ṭabarī's, present a high level knowledge of Christian scriptures and doctrines, their aim is still nevertheless to present the *Islamic* teaching and the *absurdity* of the Christian teaching. As I will show, Timothy's dialogue alone strives to present *both* Christian and Muslim perspectives on any given topic. And while Timothy obviously affirms the Christians perspective, his treatment of Muslim doctrines does not imply that his interlocutor's position is absurd or without merit.

THE MAIN ISSUES IN THE DEBATES

Timothy's dialogue with al-Mahdī centers on several major topics, namely: the validity of the Bible; the logical soundness of the Trinity; the eternal birth of Christ; the divine sonship of the Word of God; the possibility and rationale of the incarnation, crucifixion, resurrection, and ascension; and the evidence for the prophethood of Muhammad.[25] Each topic is posed in series of questions that are always asked by the caliph, al-Mahdī. Timothy's answers to them sometimes span only one question, while at other times his discussion of the topic comprises multiple questions. Furthermore, Timothy's account of the dialogue differs slightly between Arabic and Syriac recensions of the event. The Syriac version that Timothy wrote to his friend, the monk Sergius, sometime after his dialogue with al-Mahdī, is known to us as *Letter 59*.[26] The Arabic versions

Al-Shahrastānī, *Al-Faṣl fī'l-Milāl wal-' Ahwā' wal-Niḥāl* [The Separation in the Religions], 8; Berman, "Biblical Criticism of Ibn Ḥazm the Andalusian."

24. Griffith, "Melkite Arabic Text from Sinai," 277.

25. Sako refers to some of these issues, in addition to others, that constituted a challenge for Muslims. Sako, "Muslim-Christian," 10.

26. Samir and Nasry, *Patriarch*, xxxvi–xxxvii. This Syriac version, which Alphonse Mingana would later translate into English, was a manuscript dating back to the year 1880. Two German and French translations subsequently appeared.

of the dialogue appear in at least six copies, as Samir has noted.[27] Here, I will rely on both the Syriac and Arabic recensions. Below, I will summarize how Timothy answers each of these topics in his dialogue, and identify the salient aspects of his method.

THE AUTHENTICITY OF SCRIPTURES

Timothy's opposition to the concept of corruption of the Scriptures appears in his discussion with al-Mahdī in question 15, in which al-Mahdī accuses Christians of invalidating and changing the prophecies about Muḥammad in the Bible.[28] This accusation appears to have been common at that time. Timothy, like all the church fathers, considers the Holy Scriptures to be infallible, to provide the basis for dogma, and to contain apologetic resources.[29] He strings quotations together in blocks—or *testimonia*—evoking a variety of scriptural citations as evidence for any given Christian doctrine.[30] He tends to adopt the method of historical-typological interpretation common to the East Syrian theological tradition.[31] Thus, he eschewed allegorical interpretation as much as possible.[32] Timothy realizes the importance of employing historical typology in his apologetic method.[33] For example, he uses typology to answer al-Mahdī's question regarding the seeming contradiction between the circumcision of Jesus and the non-circumcision of Christians. Timothy argues that Jesus was circumcised according to Jewish law, but this circumcision was a typology of baptism, after which the need for circumcision was abolished and its significance was transferred to the Christian sacrament.[34]

27. Samir and Nasry, *Patriarch*, xxxvii–xxxix. See also Swanson, "Folly to the Ḥunafa'," 248.

28. Cheikho, *Al-Muḥāwarah*, 136.

29. Timothy used the Syriac Peshitta translation extensively. Hurst, "Syriac Letters of Timothy I (727–823)," 85, 87, 90.

30. Bertaina, "Development of Testimony Collections," 156–57.

31. This method of biblical interpretation was pioneered by Theodore of Mopsuestia, later known in the East Syrian tradition by the honorary title "The Interpreter." For more information on Theodore and this method of exegesis, see Rooy, "Reading the Psalms Historically"; Hovhanessian, *School of Antioch*.

32. Hurst, "Syriac Letters," 86.

33. Hurst, "Syriac Letters," 92.

34. Question 9 in the dialogue. Cheikho, *Al-Muḥāwarah*, 131; Hurst, "Syriac Letters," 92.

Timothy continues his defense of the authenticity and validity of the Christian biblical canon in his answer to al-Mahdī's question about his attitude toward the *prophethood* of Muḥammad.[35] For Timothy, there must be a time limit for the appearance of types and prophecies; that Muhammad has come so long after Christ is an indication for Timothy that it is more likely that the coming of Christ has put an end to the appearance of the prophets who had previously foretold him.[36]

Finally, Timothy addresses the fourfold account of Christ found in the Bible, as al-Mahdī alleges that the differences between these accounts indicates that the Christians' text is corrupted.[37] For al-Mahdī, *al-Injīl*—the gospel—is intuitively *one* coherent scripture.[38] To answer this objection, Timothy recognizes the differences between the Gospels, but he insist that there is no contradiction between them.[39] Timothy also insists on the compatibility between the two Testaments in referring to the fulfillment of the prophecies about Christ, which constitutes the entirety of the Christian doctrines.[40] Rather, their existence is nothing more than the organic compilation of records attesting to Christ's life and divinity. From here, Timothy goes on the offensive. Timothy prompts al-Mahdī to produce the uncorrupted gospel if he is so sure of its existence and likeness.

THE ONENESS AND TRINITY OF GOD

The topic of the oneness and the triunity of God can be found in the dialogue between Timothy and al-Mahdī in questions 6–8.[41] In these questions, Timothy is working against the grain of the traditional Islamic notion that the three hypostases of the Christian Trinity inexorably

35. Hurst, "Syriac Letters," 94.

36. Hurst, "Syriac Letters," 94.

37. Samir refers to the conceptual problem between Timothy and al-Mahdī concerning the meaning of the gospel. Timothy understands the gospel as "the Good News revealed by God himself," while al-Mahdī understands the gospel as a book given by God. Samir and Nasry, *Patriarch*, 105; Cheikho, *Al-Muḥāwarah*, 146; Q23; Hurst, "Syriac Letters," 95.

38. Samir and Nasry, *Patriarch*, 105.

39. Hurst, "Syriac Letters," 96.

40. Hurst, "Syriac Letters," 97; Bertaina, *Christian and Muslim Dialogues*, 156.

41. Cheikho, *Al-Muḥāwarah*, 129–31; Samir and Nasry, *Patriarch*, 12, 14, 16.

terminate in positing three gods.[42] To respond to this notion, Timothy utilizes a traditional patristic analogies (question 6) in which he reviews the union of the Trinitarian persons without separation despite their persistence of the distinction. In the first, Timothy uses the conceptual triad of person, spirit, and word. Just as the caliph conceptually distinguishes all three of these realities in himself, he nevertheless considers himself one. Likewise, then, God, whose Spirit and Word are infinitely greater than our own, is nevertheless one. And while other patristic authors are tempted to supply alternate terms for these concepts (e.g., "will" instead of "spirit"), Timothy's choice is a conscious decision to leverage Qur'anic concepts. For in the Qur'an, God is described as having both a *Word* and *Spirit*.[43] Thus, Timothy has tailored traditional patristic doctrine to an Islamic vocabulary. In the second analogy, Timothy again presents a traditional patristic analogy: the sun disc, its rays, and its heat are all distinct, yet constitutive of the one *being* of the sun.[44]

Timothy then moves on to talk about the eternity of God in question 7. Timothy sets out to prove that God exists eternally with his Word and Spirit, without any separation between them. To support this argument, Timothy relies on Old Testament texts such as Psalm 33:6; 56:4, 10; Isaiah 40:8; John 1:2–4; and Matthew 28:19. In doing so, Timothy seeks to ground the Trinity in the Old Testament and thus demonstrate that divine unity has never been in contradiction to divine triunity.[45]

Once the concept of the Trinity is grounded in this context, Timothy then moves on to consider how the three hypostases are distinct from one another in question 8. It is here that Timothy uses the term *ʾaqānim* (hypostases) for the first time in the text. He again returns to the analogy of the sun, its light, and its heat to illustrate the concept.[46] He also uses an apple as an example, its smell and taste, to show distinction despite its unity.[47]

42. Cheikho, *Al-Muḥāwarah*, 129; Samir and Nasry, *Patriarch*, 12. Norris points out that what al-Mahdī understood in fact represents the stereotypes that Muslims circulate about Christian beliefs. See Norris, "Timothy I of Baghdad," 135.

43. Watt, *Muslim-Christian*, 72.

44. Cheikho, *Al-Muḥāwarah*, 129; Samir and Nasry, *Patriarch*, 12; Watt, *Muslim-Christian*, 72.

45. Samir and Nasry, *Patriarch*, 14.

46. In Arabic, *noor*, although he used the term *rays*, "Shuʿaʿ," previously in Q 6. Cheikho, *Al-Muḥāwarah*, 131.

47. Cheikho, *Al-Muḥāwarah*, 130; Samir and Nasry, *Patriarch*, 14, 16.

With the conceptual infrastructure of the Trinity hypostases constructed, Timothy then turns to the question of the divine economy: namely, the entrance of humanity into the relations of the persons through the incarnation. Timothy makes it clear that both the Father and the Spirit are also united—albeit non-hypostatically—with the humanity of Jesus through the union of the Word with Jesus's humanity.[48] He clarifies his answer with an illustration: the writing process, through which there is a union of the word with the action of writing and the paper/papyrus. While the mind and the soul are not separate from the words being written, they have no direct role in the process of writing.[49]

It is worth noting in this dialogue that the consideration of the Trinity does not touch upon the situation of Mary, as is the Islamic traditional understanding based on Q 5:116, and al-Mahdī does not express any objection regarding the opinion of his interlocutor that the Trinity includes the Father, the Son, and the Holy Spirit.[50]

Although Timothy emphasizes both unity and triunity in the Christian understanding of the Divinity, he believes that the dispute with Muslims is related to the Trinity, as God's unity is taken for granted. Therefore, he elaborates on it extensively.[51] He uses texts from Genesis, the Prophets, and the Gospels to support his opinion.[52]

THE INCARNATION AND SONSHIP OF THE WORD OF GOD

The first five questions in the Timothy-al-Mahdī dialogue cover a major topic that emerges in the Christian-Muslim encounter: the *incarnation*, the *spiritual Sonship* of Christ, his *two natures* (the divine and the human), and his *two births* (the temporal and eternal).[53]

In his confrontation with the Islamic presuppositions that derive from Qur'anic influence, Timothy answers al-Mahdī's questions using the *Testimonia* collection, notably including Psalm 40:6; Hebrews 10:5 in reference to Jesus as the Word of God; and Proverbs 1:9.[54] He also cites

48. Cheikho, *Al-Muḥāwarah*, 131; Samir and Nasry, *Patriarch*, 16.
49. Cheikho, *Al-Muḥāwarah*, 131; Samir and Nasry, *Patriarch*, 16, 85.
50. Watt, *Muslim-Christian*, 64.
51. Hurst, "Syriac Letters," 154–55.
52. Hurst, "Syriac Letters," 162.
53. Cheikho, *Al-Muḥāwarah*, 125–29; Samir, and Nasry, *Patriarch*, 2–13.
54. Bertaina, "Development," 158.

Isaiah 7:14 in a reduced form, followed by Matthew 1:23.[55] Timothy summarizes his conclusion by acknowledging that Christ is the *Word of God*, which appeared in a human person, and he is the *Son of God*, of whom the Holy Scriptures testify, thereby summarizing his Christology.[56]

The use of the title "God's Word" is deliberate, as it has Qur'anic roots (Q 345; 4:171) and would thus be familiar and unobjectionable among Muslims. Thus, Timothy is able to plant his argument that the *Logos* appeared in a human form for human salvation on a solid scriptural ground.[57] In addition, Timothy asserts that Christ's divine Sonship is not physical but eternal in order to assuage concerns that Christ is considered temporally originated. However, he does not delve too deeply into this issue here and is content to state that the pre-eternal generation of the Son cannot be comprehended.[58]

Later in questions 2 and 3, Timothy returns to address the eternal and temporal births of Christ, clarifying that the eternal took place outside of time from God the Father and without separation from him.[59] As for the temporal, he was physically born by the virgin Mary in a specific and known time.[60]

Timothy's answers have raised new questions for al-Mahdī about the nature of that unity between divinity and humanity.[61] Therefore, Timothy replies that although the two essences are present in Christ, they appear as one Christ, one Son, and supports his answer by using examples in some instances, and in others by applying philosophical concepts. One of these is the analogy of the body and soul, which had a near-universal usage across all christological confessions of Timothy's day.[62] Another analogy is that of a king and clothing, which was a popular metaphor among Syriac fathers, such as Ephrem. Relating the analogy to the caliph himself, Timothy notes that al-Mahdī is the same caliph whether he

55. A marginal note appeared in four manuscripts, which referred to it by Samir. Samir and Nasry, *Patriarch*, 6, 8.

56. Cheikho, *Al-Muḥāwarah*, 125; Samir and Nasry, *Patriarch*, 2, 77.

57. Samir and Nasry, *Patriarch*, 2.

58. Cheikho, *Al-Muḥāwarah*, 126.

59. Timothy describes the eternal birth in Q5 as spiritual birth. Samir and Nasry, *Patriarch*, 13, 78, 129.

60. Samir and Nasry, *Patriarch*, 78.

61. Samir and Nasry, *Patriarch*, 81.

62. Hurst, "Syriac Letters," 185. Hurst admits that it is an imperfect analogy to describe the union of divinity and humanity in the person of Christ.

wears royal clothes or any other kind; nevertheless, his choice of royal vestments presents himself to the people in a specific way.[63]

Next, he mentions two other analogies that, according to Hurst, were traditionally used in connection with the Trinity. In fact, part of these analogies relates to the Son, who becomes incarnate: the *tongue* and the *word* are one with the *voice*, as they are clothed by it.[64] This is in addition to the analogy of the *letter* issued by the caliph: it expresses him personally, as he is the owner of the letter, along with all what is written in it, as it expresses his thoughts and stems from his soul, yet it is written down on paper.[65]

At this point, al-Mahdī responds by quoting John 20:17, where Jesus appears to be submissive to God. Here, God is considered superior to Christ, according to al-Mahdī, and what's more, this sense also corroborates the Qur'anic view in Q 3:51. If one accepts this reading of the verse, then there is a contradiction in the Christian belief in the divinity of the Messiah.[66]

THE CRUCIFIXION AND RESURRECTION OF CHRIST

This next section centers around the conversation that addresses the subjects of the crucifixion, death, resurrection, and ascension of Christ, centered in questions 13 and 18–22.

In question 13, al-Mahdī asks why Timothy acknowledges the doctrines that sum up the Nicene Creed, starting with the birth of Christ until his second coming.[67] Timothy answers him with an introduction stressing that this is "the witness of the Scriptures."[68] Here, as he often does, Timothy cites *Testimonia*. He employs several passages about the *signs*, *passion*, *death*, *resurrection*, *ascension*, and *second coming* from the Old Testament in a cumulative manner as a guide for prophecies that have found their fulfillment in the person of Christ.[69] A controversial text that

63. Hurst, "Syriac Letters," 185.

64. Hurst, "Syriac Letters," 186.

65. Hurst, "Syriac Letters," 185–86

66. Samir and Nasry, *Patriarch*, 82.

67. Cheikho, *Al-Muḥāwarah*, 133.

68. It appears verbatim in the Arabic text as follows: "Witness of the Prophets and the Gospel." Samir and Nasry, *Patriarch*, 24, 91.

69. Isaiah 7:14; 35:4–6; 53:5; Psalm 16:10; 68:19; 47:6; Daniel 7:13–14; Bertaina, "Development," 160; Samir and Nasry, *Patriarch*, 26.

comments on the crucifixion, death, and resurrection begins in question 18, about the purpose of prostrating to the cross and the view that it was the cause of death.[70] This controversy continues in the comparison with the Qur'anic narration in Q 4:157.[71] Al-Mahdī emphasizes that Jesus was not crucified, but rather "it was made to appear to them." This dialogue continues until question 22, in which al-Mahdī in logical argument tries to prove his opinion in denying the crucifixion of Christ and rejecting his divinity.[72] Timothy begins his customary use of the *Testimonia* as he constructs his biblical argument, making extensive use of the following texts: Genesis 2:9; Exodus 14:16; 15:20; 17:5–26; Numbers 21:8–9; and John 15:13.[73]

After recounting the biblical argument—and as a reaction to al-Mahdī's question, who cites the Qur'anic text Q 4:157—Timothy uses two other Qur'anic texts and points out that they are from surat ʿIsa.[74] In fact, they are from two suras: Maryam (19):33 and Āl-ʿImrān (3):55. Thus, Timothy relies on texts his interlocutor considers sacred and tries to interpret them in such a way that supports his argument for the crucifixion. He goes directly from the reference to Qur'anic texts to the *Testimonia* and cites many texts from the Scriptures: Psalms 22:17–19; John 19:24; Isaiah 53:15; 50:6; Lamentations 3:4, 30; and Daniel 9:26.[75]

Lastly, he uses a logical argument in his answer to al-Mahdī's question regarding "it was made to appear to them" in questions 19 and 20.[76] He wonders: what is God's purpose in doing this? It shows that God appears as a "deceiver."[77] This also makes Satan able to spoil God's plan, and makes "the prophets to prophesy falsehood."[78]

Timothy proceeds with his logical argument as he traces the argument of al-Mahdī. Al-Mahdī remarks that either it is unreasonable to blame the Jews for having fulfilled the will of Christ in the crucifixion, or Christ was crucified against his will, thereby losing his claim of his

70. Cheikho, *Al-Muḥāwarah*, 140.
71. Cheikho, *Al-Muḥāwarah*, 141.
72. Cheikho, *Al-Muḥāwarah*, 143.
73. Cheikho, *Al-Muḥāwarah*, 140–41; Samir and Nasry, *Patriarch*, 45.
74. Cheikho, *Al-Muḥāwarah*, 141; Samir and Nasry, *Patriarch*, 46.
75. Cheikho, *Al-Muḥāwarah*, 142; Samir and Nasry, *Patriarch*, 48.
76. Cheikho, *Al-Muḥāwarah*, 141–43; Samir and Nasry, *Patriarch*, 46–48.
77. Samir and Nasry, *Patriarch*, 100.
78. "Corrupt the divine economy"; Samir and Nasry, *Patriarch*, 48, 100.

divinity.[79] Timothy, in his treatment of this topic, gives three responses. First, Timothy notes that even though Satan disobeyed God, this does not mean that God is not divine. Second, he notes a similar relationship between God and humans: although humans have disobeyed God, this does not mean that God is no longer God. Third and finally, those who "are fighting for the sake of God," that is, being killed by their enemies for their faith, do not die according to their own desires, but because of the unjustified animus of their killers.[80] In all three responses, then, Timothy is demonstrating how God's creatures can disobey his will even as God accomplishes what he desires through their disobedience. Divinity is not synonymous with being obeyed, and is not contingent upon it.

In the Syriac version, Timothy extends his discussion of what divinity entails by addressing why Christ is called a "servant" in scripture. In al-Mahdī's view, Christ's servant status places him squarely among the prophets and firmly on the human side of the God-man divide. Timothy seeks to again demonstrate that divinity is not contingent upon being obeyed through a few approaches. First, Timothy asks the caliph to consider his son. The son of the caliph could be assigned to a military mission and depart to serve in that position. In doing so, Timothy notes, he does not give up his royal sonship; he is still heir to caliphal authority. In the same way, Timothy argues, the use of this title of "servant" by Scripture is a reference to Jesus' human mission.[81] Second, Timothy once again resorts to scriptural citations or *testimonia*—from both the Bible and the Qur'an. He deploys Q 90:1–3 to support his opinion, wherein the Qur'an mysteriously swears by a father and "the one he begot."[82] Timothy, perhaps a bit too conveniently, takes Q 90 as a reference to God; however, his larger point remains valid: namely, the Qur'an in various places affirms a) the likeness of begotten beings to their begetter and b) that Jesus is not *only* one who does not disdain servitude under God, but also a Word and Spirit from God. For Timothy, this mirrors the biblical approach perfectly, wherein Jesus is referred to as "servant" in respect to his humanity and earthly mission, but also as Word, Son of God the Father, the door, the way, and more. For Timothy, Christ cannot be a servant *in his essence*, but a proper understanding of the incarnation allows us to apply titles such as servant that represent his human person rather than his divine

79. Cheikho, *Al-Muḥāwarah*, 143.

80. Samir and Nasry, *Patriarch*, 103.

81. Hurst, "Syriac Letters," 198–99; Mingana, *Apology of Timothy the Patriarch*, 84–85.

82. Hurst, "Syriac Letters," 198–99; Mingana, *Apology*, 85.

personhood.[83] The Qur'an, Timothy I suggests, implies the same belief when its titles for Jesus are understood properly.

THE PROPHETHOOD OF MUḤAMMAD

In the last section of questions 13–16, al-Mahdī poses the question of Muḥammad's prophethood. Al-Mahdī reads the New Testament's mention of the Paraclete, or "Comforter," as a reference to Muḥammad, and thus as evidence for his prophecy in the Christian Scriptures.[84] In doing so, al-Mahdī was tapping into a common Muslim view at the time that can be found in various contemporary sources, such as the prophetic the biography of Ibn ʾIsḥāq.[85] From this belief in Muhammad's attestation, al-Mahdī challenges Timothy to explain how Christians have not rejected Muḥammad with the same stubbornness that Christians attribute to the Jews in their rejection of Jesus. Timothy must explain how Christians have not "abolished," "erased," or "changed" the scriptural testimonies of Muḥammad in the Gospel.[86]

Next, al-Mahdī moves on to ask Timothy whether the Qur'an is from God or not.[87] Again, this question revolves around whether Muhammad and his dispensation (i.e., the Qur'an) are attested to by Scripture. Al-Mahdī points to Isaiah 21:7 as proof that there is a prediction of the coming of Muḥammad and the Qur'an in the Holy Scriptures.[88] The verse in question reads, "A chariot he saw, with two out-riders, one that rode on an ass, and one that rode on a camel; looked long at them, watching them eagerly." The rider of the ass is clear enough in the New Testament as a reference to Jesus; who could be the rider of the camel, if not Muhammad, who came from the Bedouin environment of the desert?[89]

83. Hurst, "Syriac Letters," 200.

84. Cheikho, *Al-Muḥāwarah*, 135; Samir and Nasry, *Patriarch*, 26.

85. Hurst, "Syriac Letters," 211.

86. Cheikho, *Al-Muḥāwarah*, 135; Samir and Nasry, *Patriarch*, 30. The argument of al-Mahdī reflects an Islamic understanding based on Qurʾanic texts (Q 7:157) which al-Mahdī shows that there are a number of texts in the scriptures that have been removed intentionally, which refer to the prophecy of Muḥammad, like Deuteronomy 18:18; Isaiah 21; John 14:16, 26; 15:26; 16:7. Watt, *Muslim-Christian*, 33–34.

87. Cheikho, *Al-Muḥāwarah*, 136; Samir and Nasry, *Patriarch*, 32.

88. Samir and Nasry, *Patriarch*, 97. For a study of this argument in Christian-Muslim relations, consult Zaleski, "Who Is the Man on the Camel?," 49–80.

89. Cf. Matthew 21:5, "Tell the daughter of Sion, Behold, thy king is coming to thee, humbly, riding on an ass, on a colt whose mother has borne the yoke." This is in turn

Similarly in question 25, al-Mahdī quotes from Deuteronomy 18:15, 18 with the same purpose of grounding Muhammad's prophecy in Christian Scriptures, as the Qur'an itself does in 7:157.[90]

The controversy over the prophecy of Muḥammad is framed by two issues: the biblical testimony and how it is interpreted. From the beginning, al-Mahdī argues that the prophecies about Muḥammad were either removed from the Scriptures or received different interpretations.[91] However, this was enough for Timothy to offer his opinion by saying that the Christians could have contented themselves with saying that Muḥammad was not that prophet who was expected to come, in a similar way to the Jews who had previously done the same with Jesus.[92]

Timothy proceeds to dispute al-Mahdī's identification of Muhammad with the biblical Paraclete through an analysis of prooftexts such as John 14:17, 26; 16:13–14. It is not possible for the Johannine Paraclete to be a prior reference to Muḥammad, Timothy argues, due to the mismatch of many elements, such as the Spirit's consubstantial existence with God the Father, its explicit identification as the "Spirit" of God, and the scripture's claim that the Paraclete knows the "deep things of God," which the Qur'an itself admits Muhammad does not know.[93] Thus, Timothy not

inspired by the prophecy of Zechariah 9:9.

90. Cheikho, *Al-Muḥāwarah*, 148; Samir and Nasry, *Patriarch*, 64, 107.

Deuteronomy 18:15, "No, the Lord thy God will raise up for thee a prophet like myself, of thy own race, a brother of thy own; it is to him thou must listen."

Cf. Q 7:157, "those who follow the Apostle, the untaught prophet, whose mention they find written with them in the Torah and the Evangel, who bids them to do what is right and forbids them from what is wrong, makes lawful to them all the good things and forbids them from all vicious things"; 2:129, "'Our Lord, raise amongst them an apostle from among them, who will recite to them Your signs and teach them the Book and wisdom and purify them. Indeed, You are the All-mighty, the All-wise."; Q 9:128, "There has certainly come to you an apostle from among yourselves. Grievous to him is your distress; he has deep concern for you and is most kind and merciful to the faithful."

91. Notably, al-Mahdī does not mention specific Qur'anic accusations of taḥrīf (i.e., scriptural falsification), such as Q 61:6, 2:75, or 5:13, which in their contexts often refer to *the Jews* and not to the Christians.

92. Cheikho, *Al-Muḥāwarah*, 136; Samir and Nasry, *Patriarch*, 95.

93. Beaumont, "ʿAmmār al-Baṣrī on the Alleged Corruption of the Gospels," 243. Timothy mentions them in detail in the text, as they are clarified and explained later by Samir in his book (Samir and Nasry, *Patriarch*, 93–94; Cheikho, *Al-Muḥāwarah*, 135). On the detail of Muhammad not knowing the "deep things of God," he perhaps has in mind Qur'anic verses such as 7:187: "They question you concerning the Hour, when will it set in? Say, 'Its knowledge is only with my Lord: none except Him shall manifest it at its time. It will weigh heavy on the heavens and the earth. It will not overtake you but suddenly.' They ask you as if you were in the know of it. Say, 'Its knowledge is only

only strives to refute al-Mahdī's argument, but attempts to exposit the Paraclete as undeniably referring to the Holy Spirit, one of the persons of the Trinity.

Timothy then transitions to a more aggressive approach in order to refute al-Mahdī's prooftext of Muḥammad in Isaiah 21:7, as he seeks to exclude Muḥammad from the line of the prophets. First, Timothy stressed that the prophetic line ends with John the Baptist, according to Matthew 13:11. The purpose of John's coming was to prepare for the coming of Christ, not Muḥammad. Timothy then goes even further by mentioning Christ's warning against accepting *prophets* and *Christs* after him—referring to Matthew 24:11, 24—in order to preclude the possibility that anyone may come after Christ to foretell Muḥammad.[94] With these New Testament glosses in mind, Timothy can then turn to explain the prophecy of Isaiah 21:7. Here, Timothy relies on his Antiochene method of biblical interpretation, which eschewed reading christological typologies into the Old Testament as much as possible. For Timothy, Isaiah is not referring to Christ or Muḥammad, as the Muslim (and some Christian) commentators might assume. Rather, it is a prophecy that is confined to its own historical context, and actually refers to Cyrus the Persian and Darius the Mede as the camel and the donkey riders, respectively.[95] In the same vein, he addresses Deuteronomy 18:15, analyzes it grammatically, and concludes that it is inconsistent with a prophecy about Muḥammad.[96]

Despite his rejection of Muḥammad's prophethood, Timothy is moderate in his dialogue with al-Mahdī. He avoids commenting on the origins of the Qur'an. Furthermore, he professes that Muḥammad "walked in the path of the prophets," even if Timothy cannot consider him to be one. He praises Muhammad for striving to teach the oneness of God to a pagan environment full of the worship of demons and idols.[97] In fact, Timothy does not hesitate to compare Muḥammad to Moses

with Allah, but most people do not know.'"

94. Cheikho, *Al-Muḥāwarah*, 140; Samir and Nasry, *Patriarch*, 42; Bertaina, "Development," 158.

95. Cheikho, *Al-Muḥāwarah*, 138–39; Samir and Nasry, *Patriarch*, 36, 38, 40; Thomas, "Paul of Antioch's," 98.

96. Cheikho, *Al-Muḥāwarah*, 148; Samir and Nasry, *Patriarch*, 66, 107; Thomas, "Paul of Antioch's," 98.

97. This appendix is in Cheikho's manuscript, *Al-Muḥāwarah*, 150–52, but it does not exist in Samir's manuscript, Samir and Nasry, *Patriarch*. Watt, *Muslim-Christian*, 27; Platt, "Church of the East," 94.

and Abraham, and even goes so far as to write that God honored him.[98] Therefore, God is sovereign over the two powerful states at this time: Persia and Rome.[99]Timothy, then, remains faithful to his Christianity and the theological approaches and traditions of his East Syrian heritage in explaining to his interlocutor how he can simultaneously respect Muḥammad while remaining firm in his belief that Islam's prophet is not mentioned in the Christian Scriptures.

FEATURES OF TIMOTHY-AL-MAHDĪ ENCOUNTER

Thus far, I have summarized and analyzed the content of Timothy's responses to the caliph al-Mahdī. But what lessons, then, ought the student of Timothy take from his early and thorough dialogue between Christianity and Islam?

First, dialogue requires frankness. What distinguishes Timothy's dialogue from other early Christian-Muslim engagement is Timothy's commitment to addressing the specific questions that al-Mahdī poses to him in a flexible, calm, and wise manner. Timothy is engaging sensitive questions related to very different understandings of Christianity and Islam. Furthermore, the motives behind Muslim-Christian encounters in the early Abbasid were bound up in politics and power dynamics that made abstract theological discussion a functional impossibility.[100] Timothy's success or failure to defend the Christian faith bore existential consequences for him and his people. Timothy's encounter can hardly be called a "dialogue"— a view that Watt holds and this researcher agrees with—because everyone argues about "intellectual structure" in such a way that supports and defends his own faith, and there is no "sharing of religious experience."[101] Griffith also conveys the fears attributed to Timothy that his defensive efforts are of little fruit concerning persuading the interlocutor—and Muslims in general—of the Christian faith and beliefs, and that these efforts will not do much for Christians who rush to convert to Islam.[102]

98. Cheikho, *Al-Muḥāwarah*, 151.

99. Cheikho, *Al-Muḥāwarah*, 152.

100. Harmakaputra, "Muslim-Christian Debates," 443–44.

101. Watt, *Muslim-Christian*, 64.

102. Griffith, *Church in the Shadow of the Mosque*, 48.

Second, understandings of the other reflect highly ethical reactions: the manner of the interaction between the caliph and the patriarch was cordial and respectful. Timothy maintained a high level of respect and appreciation for al-Mahdī. Additionally, Timothy's respectful manner extends to Muḥammad, describing him as walking in the path of the prophets and as honored by God. Finally, he has no problem describing those who "go out to fight for the sake of God" as "martyrs" if they are killed in their efforts.[103] Thus, despite his impartiality and his non-acceptance of the prophethood of Muḥammad or the divine source of the Qur'an, Timothy is open toward Muslims, as he does not use offensive or negative descriptions.[104]

Third, it is necessary to be able to converse in multiple religious traditions competently. The language of Timothy and al-Mahdī's encounter is characterized by the ability of both figures to discuss aspects of the other's religious tradition in a flexible yet concise manner for the purpose of intensifying and developing the arguments in question.[105]

Fourth, Timothy's discourse emphasizes the validity and firmness of the faith. Despite Timothy's impartiality and diplomacy in many instances, he did not hesitate to express his faith, even if it contradicted the viewpoint of al-Mahdī and Islam in general. Rather, he indicated that he would not retreat from his belief, even if it led to his death.[106]

Fifth, it is necessary to know the articulated form of the other—that is, their expressions and understandings of them. Timothy shows that he is adept in the Arabic language and the Islamic perspective on Christian beliefs latent in al-Mahdī's questions. Timothy questions these interpretations, deconstructs them, and then reformulates them to be consistent with the Christian understanding of the events of the New Testament. This method allows Timothy to explain his argument more clearly to his interlocutor.[107]

103. Samir and Nasry, *Patriarch*, 56.

104. Norris, "Timothy I," 135.

105. Bertaina, "Development," 161.

106. Cheikho, *Al-Muḥāwarah*, 152.

107. Swanson, "Folly," 255–56.

CONCLUSION

The Catholicos Timothy's debate with al-Mahdī, in sum, represents a unique and particularly instructive event in the history of Christian engagement with Islam. Timothy's us of positive language, the social status of both participants, and the ways in which their interaction addressed the essential doctrines of Islam and Christian remain a fruitful source of study to this day. In contrast, the most important early Christian-Islamic encounters are defensive in nature and cannot be considered a dialogue in the contemporary sense of the word. While the topics of discussion found in Timothy's dialogue with al-Mahdī also appear in most any prominent Christian-Islamic dialogue or debate of the medieval period, the intensity and depth of their discussion varied widely from one discussion to another. None match the depth and detail one sees in Timothy's discourse.

Indeed, Timothy's dialogue with al-Mahdī demonstrates how dialogue is enhanced by the ability to argue, analyze questions, and employ both Scripture and Qur'anic texts in logical arguments to formulate sound and concise defenses. Firmness of faith need not be mutually exclusive from appreciation and knowledge of the religious other. On the contrary, the meeting between Timothy and al-Mahdī demonstrates that an elevated level of respect and personal appreciation for the religion of each party pushes dialogue forward.

BIBLIOGRAPHY

Al-Baqillānī. *Kitāb al-Tamhīd* (The Book of Preface). Edited by Richard J. McCarthy. Beirut: al-Maktabat al-Sharqiyya, 1957.

ʿAlī bin Rabban Al-Ṭabarī. *Al-Radd ʿAlā ʾAṣnaf Al-Naṣārā* (Refutation on the Types of Christians). Edited by Khalid Muḥammad ʿAbda. Giza: Maktabat al-Nafitha, 2005.

Al-Jāḥiẓ. *Al-Mukhtār fi al-Radd ʿ Alā al-Naṣārā* (The Chosen [Answers] in the Replay on Christians). Edited by Muḥammad A. Al-Sharqawī. Beirut: Dār al-Jīl, 1991.

Al-Qāsim ibn Ibrāhīm al-Rissī,. *Majmūʿ Kutub wa-Rasāʾ il al-Imām Al-Qāṣim ibn Ibrāhīm al-Rissī* (The Collection of the Books and Treatises of the Imām al- Al-Qāsim ibn Ibrāhīm al-Rissī). Edited by Abd al-Kārim Jadban (Sanaʾa: Dār al-Ḥikmat al-Yamāniyya.

Baumer, Christoph. *The Church of the East*. London: I.B. Tauris, 2016.

Beaumont, Ivor Mark. *Christology in Dialogue with Muslims: A Critical Analysis of Christian Presentations of Christ for Muslims from the Ninth and Twentieth Centuries*. Regnum Studies in Mission. Waynesboro, GA: Paternoster, 2005.

Berman, Joshua. "The Biblical Criticism of Ibn Hazm the Andalusian: A Medieval Control for Modern Diachronic Method." *Journal of Biblical Literature* 138:2 (2019) 377–90. https://doi.org/10.1353/jbl.2019.0020.

Bertaina, David. *Christian and Muslim Dialogues: The Religious Uses of a Literary Form in the Early Islamic Middle East*. Gorgias Eastern Christianity Studies 29. Piscataway, NJ: Gorgias, 2011.

———. "The Development of Testimony Collections in Early Christian Apologetics with Islam." In *The Bible in Arab Christianity*, edited by David Thomas, 151–74. Leiden: Brill, 2007.

Brockelmann, Carl. *Geschichte der arabischen litteratur*, 2. Den supplementbänden angepasste aufl. Leiden: Brill, 1943.

Butts, Aaron. "Theodoros bar Kôni." In *Gorgias Encyclopedic Dictionary of the Syriac Heritage*, edited by Sebastian P. Brock et al. Piscataway, NJ: Gorgias, 2011.

———. "Theodore Bar Kôni, Scholion, Mēmra 10." In *Eastern Christianity: A Reader*, 1–14. Grand Rapids: Eerdmans, 2021.

Cheikho, Louis. *Al-Muḥāwarah al-Dānyyah allati Jarat Bayna al-Khālifah al-Maḥdī wa-Ṭimothawus al-Jathalīq* (The Religious Dialogue that Took Place between the Abbasid Caliph Al-Maḥdī and the Christian Nestorian Catholicos Timothy). Trois Traités Anciens de Polémique et de théologie chrétiennes. Beirut: Imprimerie Catholique, 1923.

———. *Ḥiwārāt Masīḥiyya-' Islāmiyya: Muqarabāt Lahutiyya Bil-' Arabiyya Fī ' Aṣr al-Khilāfat al-' Abbāsiyya* [*Christian-Muslim Dialogue: Theological Approaches in Arabic Language in Abbasid Periodo*]. Kirkuk, 2009.

Dionysius bar Ṣalībī. *Dionysius Bar Ṣalībī: A Response to the Arabs*. Corpus Scriptorum Christianorum Orientalium. Scriptores Syri 238. Louvain: Peeters, 2005.

Griffith, Sidney. "Ammar Al-Basri's Kitab al-Burhan: Christian Kalam in the First Abbasid Century." *Muséon (Le) Louvain* 96:1–2 (1983) 145–81.

———. "Answers for the Shaykh: A 'Melkite'Arabic Text from Sinai and the Doctrines of the Trinity and the Incarnation in 'Arab Orthodox'Apologetics." In *The Encounter of Eastern Christianity with Early Islam*, 277–310. Leiden: Brill, 2007.

———. *The Church in the Shadow of the Mosque: Christians and Muslims in the World of Islam*. Princeton, NJ: Princeton University Press, 2008.

———. "Disputing with Islam in Syriac: The Case of the Monk of Bêt Ḥālê and a Muslim Emir." *Hugoye: Journal of Syriac Studies* 3:1 (March 1, 2010) 29–54. https://doi.org/10.31826/hug-2010-030103.

———. "A Melkite Arabic Text from Sinai and the Doctrines of the Trinity and the Incarnation in ʿArab Orthodox Apologetics." In *The Encounter of Eastern Christianity with Islam*, edited by Emmanouela Grypeou, Mark Swanson, and David Thomas, 277–310. Leiden: Brill, 2006.

———. "Paul of Antioch." In *The Orthodox Church in the Arab World, 700–1700: An Anthology of Sources*, edited by Samuel Noble and Alexander Treiger, 216–19. New York: Cornell University Press: 2021.

Harmakaputra, Hans Abdiel. "Muslim-Christian Debates in the Early ʿAbbasid Period: The Cases of Timothy I and Theodore Abu Qurra." *MIQOT* 38:2 (2014) 443–44.

Hurst, Thomas Richard. "The Syriac Letters of Timothy I (727–823): A Study in Christian-Muslim Controversy." PhD diss., Catholic University of America, 1986.

Husseini, Sara Leila. *Early Christian-Muslim Debate on the Unity of God: Three Christian Scholars and Their Engagement with Islamic Thought (9th Century C.E.)*. History of Christian-Muslim Relations 21. Boston : Brill, 2014.

Ibn Ḥazm, ʻAlī ibn Aḥmad. *Kitāb al-faṣl fī al-milal wa al-ahwā' wa al-niḥal.* Bayrūt: Dār al-Ṣādir, 1974.

Ibn Taymiyyah, Taqī al-Dīn. *Kitāb Al-Jawāb al-Ṣaḥīḥ Li-Man Baddala Dīn al-Masīḥ* [*The Book of the Correct Answer for Who Changed the Religion of the Messiah*]. Edited by ʿAlī Ḥasān Naṣir. Vol. 1. 2nd ed. Riyadh: Dār al-ʿAṣimah, 1999.

Janosik, Daniel. *John of Damascus, First Apologist to the Muslims the Trinity and Christian Apologetics in the Early Islamic Period*. Eugene, OR: Pickwick, 2016.

Keating, Sandra. "The Use and Translation of Scripture in the Apologetic Writings of Abū Rā'iṭa Al-Takrītī." In *The Bible in Arab Christianity*, 257–74. Leiden: Brill, 2007.

Kindī, ʻAbd al-Masiḥ al-. *The Apology of al Kindy Written at the Court of al Mâmûn (circa A.H. 215, A.D. 830), in Defence of Christianity against Islam: With an Essay on Its Age and Authorship*. 2nd ed. London: SPCK, 1911.

Lamoreaux, John C. "Theodore Abu Qurra." In *The Orthodox Church in the Arab World, 700–1700: An Anthology of Sources*, edited by Alexander Treiger and Samuel Noble, 60–89. Ithaca, NY: Cornell University Press, 2014.

Mikhail, Wageeh Y. F. "ʿAmmār Al-Baṣrī's Kitab al-Burhān: A Topical and Theological Analysis of Arabic Christian Theology in the Ninth Century." PhD diss., 2013.

Mingana, A., and Rendel Harris. "Woodbrooke Studies: Christian Documents in Syriac, Arabic, and Garshūni, Edited and Translated with a Critical Apparatus. Fasciculus 3: The Apology of Timothy the Patriarch before the Caliph Mahdi." *Bulletin of the John Rylands Library* 12:1 (1928) 137–298. https://doi.org/10.7227/BJRL.12.1.9.

Muḥammad al-Faḍhil al-Laffī. *Dirasat al-ʻAqā'id al-Naṣraniyyah: Manhajiyyat ibn Taymiyyah wa-Raḥmat Allah al-Hindī* (Studying Christian Doctrines: The Methodology of ibn Taymyyah wa-Raḥmat Allah al Hindi). Herndon, VA: International Institute of the Islamic Thought, 2007.

Muḥammad ibn Isḥāq Ibn al-Nadīm. *Kitāb al-Fihrist lil-Nadīm*. 2nd ed., by Reza Tajaddod. Tehran: Marvi Offset, 197.

Nau, François Nicolas. *Un Colloque Du Patriarche Jean Avec l'émir Des Agaréens et Faits Divers Des Années 712 à 716 d'apres Le Ms. Du British Museum Add. 17193*. Imprimerie Nationale, 1915.

Nonnus, of Nisibis. *Traité apologétique,*. Bibliothèque du Muséon 21. Louvain: Bureaux du Muséon, 1948.

Norris, Frederick W. "Timothy I of Baghdad, Catholicos of the East Syrian Church, 780–823: Still a Valuable Model." *International Bulletin of Mission Research* 30:3 (2006) 133–36. https://doi.org/10.1177/239693930603000304.

Omar, Farouk. "Some Observations on the Reign of the 'Abbasid Caliph Al-Mahdi 185/775–169/785." *Arabica* 21:2 (1974) 139–50. https://doi.org/10.1163/157005874X00210.

Penelas, Mayte. "Contents of an Apologetic Nature in Ms. Raqqada 2003/2: Formerly Great Mosque of Kairouan 120/829." In *Eastern Crossroads: Essays on Medieval Christian Legacy*, edited by Juan Pedro Monferrer-Sala. Piscataway, NJ: Gorgias, 2007.

Penn, Michael Philip. *When Christians First Met Muslims: A Sourcebook of the Earliest Syriac Writings on Islam*. Oakland: University of California Press, 2015.

Périer, Augustin. "Un Traité de Yaḥya ben ʿAdi, défence du dogme de la Trinité Contre les Objections d'Al-Kindi." *Revue de L'Orient Chrétien* 2:1 (1920–1921) 3–21.

Platt, Andrew Thomas. "The Church of the East at Three Critical Points in Its History." PhD diss., Catholic University of America, 2017.

Pro Oriente Colloquium Syriacum. *Syriac Churches Encountering Islam: Past Experiences and Future Perspectives.* Pro Oriente Studies in the Syriac Tradition 1. Piscataway, NJ: Gorgias, 2010.

Reinink, Gerrit J. "The Beginnings of Syriac Apologetic Literature in Response to Islam." *Oriens Christianus* 77 (1993) 165–65.

———. "Political Power and Right Religion in the East Syrian Disputation between a Monk of Bēt Ḥālē and an Arab Notable." In *The Encounter of Eastern Christianity with Early Islam*, 153–70. Leiden: Brill, 2007.

Rissi, Al-Qasim bin Ibrahim al-. *Majmūʿ Kutub Wa-Rasā' il al-Imām Al-Qāṣim Bin Ibrāhīm al-Rissī [The Collection of the Books and Treatises of the Imām al- Al-Qāsim Bin Ibrāhīm al-Rissī].* Edited by Abid al-Karim Jadban. Sanaʾa: Dār al-Ḥikmat al-Yamāniyya, n.d.

Sahas, Daniel J. *Byzantium and Islam: Collected Studies on Byzantine-Muslim Encounters.* Boston: Brill, 2021.

Samir, Sami Khalil. "Qui Est l'interlocuteur Musulman Du Patriarche Syrien Jean III (631–648)?" *Han JW Drijvers et Al* (1984) 387–400.

———. "The Prophet Muḥammad as Seen by Timothy I and Other Arab Christian Authors." In *Syrian Christians under Islam: The First Thousand Years*, edited David Thomas, 75–106. Leiden: Brill, 2001.

Samir, Sami Khalil, and Wafik Nasry, eds. and trans. *The Patriarch and the Caliph: An Eighth-Century Dialogue between Timothy I and Al-Mahdi.* Provo, UT: Brigham Young University Press, 2018.

Suermann, H. "The Old Testament and the Jews in the Dialogue between the Jacobite Patriarch John I and 'Umayr Ibn Sa 'd al-Anṣārī." *Eastern Crossroads: Essays on Medieval Christian Legacy*, edited by Juan Pedro Monferrer-Sala, 131–41. Piscataway, NJ: Gorgias 2013.

Swanson, Mark N. "An Apology for the Christian Faith:ةيحيسملادئاقعلايفةيعافدةلاسر." In *The Orthodox Church in the Arab World, 700–1700*, edited by Samuel Noble and Alexander Treiger, 40–59. Ithaca, NY: Cornell University Press, 2014.

———. "'Folly to the Hunafā': The Crucifixion in Early Christian-Muslim Controversy." In *The Encounter of Eastern Christianity with Early Islam*, vol. 5, edited by David Thomas, Emmanouela Grypeou, and Mark N. Swanson. Leiden: Brill, 2006.

Szilágyi, Krisztina. "Chapter 3. The Disputation of the Monk Abraham of Tiberias يناربطلا ميهاربإ بهارلا ةلداجم." In *The Orthodox Church in the Arab World, 700–1700*, edited by Samuel Noble and Alexander Treiger, 90–111. Ithaca, NY: Cornell University Press, 2014.

Thomas, David. "Christian Theologians and New Questions." In *The Encounter of Eastern Christianity with Islam*, edited by Emmanouela Grypeou, Mark Swanson, and David Thomas. Leiden: Brill, 2006.

———. "Paul of Antioch's Letter to a Muslim Friend and the Letter from Cyprus." In *Syrian Christians under Islam, the First Thousand Years*, edited by David Thomas. Leiden: Brill, 2001.

Van Rooy, H. F. "Reading the Psalms Historically. Antiochene Exegesis and a Historical Reading of Psalm 46." *Acta Theologica* 29:2 (2009) 120–34.

Watt, W. Montgomery. *Muslim-Christian Encounters: Perceptions and Misperceptions.* New York: Routledge, 1991.

Yaḥyá ibn ʿAdī. *Maqālah fī al-tawḥīd.* Jūniyah, Lubnān: Rūmah, Īṭāliyā: al-Maktabah al-Būlisīyah; al-Maʿhad al-Bābawī al-Sharqī, 1980.

Zaleski, John. "Who Is the Man on the Camel?: Historical Exegesis of the Hebrew Bible and Christian-Muslim Debate." *Medieval Encounters: Jewish, Christian, and Muslim Culture in Confluence and Dialogue* 26:1 (2020) 49–80.

4

Christian Social Life under Islamic Rule

SAM NWOKORO

This chapter reflects on the social life of Christians under early Islamic rule using the Melkites in Umayyad Syria as a case study. Although helmed by said case study, this chapter hopes to extrapolate on more generally applicable lessons. The focus of this chapter is mainly twofold: a general backdrop and a principal concern. The general backdrop presents a brief exploration of the history of Christian communities under early Islamic rule, particularly examples of schismatic separations and diverse experiences of sociopolitical privileges. The main thrust of this chapter derives largely from a set of rules, postulated to have been typical of legislative exchanges concerning the life of non-Muslims from the eighth century in major cities like the Syrian capital of Damascus. These pledges, which are essentially stipulations, are discussed as highlighting significant modes of lifestyle, expectations, and wealth of Christians as social or religious minority groups under early Islamic *oikumene*. It is hoped that such text-based exploration will enhance our possibilities of knowing what the social life of Christians would have been like during this period, and that it will spur the student of Christian-Muslim relations into further reading and research.

BACKGROUND: THE ARAB CONQUEST AND CHRISTIAN COMMUNITIES IN THE EAST

Christian communities in the East were divided into various confessional groups, based on doctrinal differences, making it difficult to speak of Christians under Arab Islamic rule without having to clarify what confessional group is being referred to. An anecdote, possibly from a later period than the time it testifies, demonstrates this confessional divergence of Christians and how it was reckoned with by the emerging Arab Muslim authorities. The anonymous author of this anecdote, which is preserved in a seventeenth-century manuscript at Saint Petersburg's Institute of Oriental Manuscripts as B1220, claims that during the time of ʿUmar ibn al-Khaṭṭāb (r. 634–44), Christian denominations in Syria came to the caliph to register their confessional communities for state recognition.[1]

After the Jacobites and the Nestorians appeared before the caliph and adopted their respective names, Sophronius, the patriarch of Jerusalem, appeared before the caliph, presenting himself as a Christian (*Naṣārā*), without a confessional or denominational (*ṭāʾifa*) designation.[2] When the caliph insisted that Sophronius adopt a confessional name for his Christian community, the patriarch convened an assembly of priests and monks for a period of fasting and praying, during which it was claimed that Sophronius received a vision to name his confessional group as the people of "the Heavenly King" (*malik al-samāʾ*), and that is how the derivation *al-Malikiyyā* or "the Melkites" came about.[3] This story is hardly otherwise attested. Its main purpose was to correct notions of the Melkites as a confessional group that was fashioned after a pejorative title signifying their allegiance to Byzantine imperial interventions on matters of faith. Despite the need to treat it tentatively, this text helps to highlight how there were various Christian confessional groups under early Islamic rule, such that the idea of not having a sectarian confessional title was odd to the authorities.

Generally, there are three major Christian confessional groups under early Islamic rule: the Jacobites, the Nestorians, and the Melkites. Each of these groups have a historical trajectory that precedes the early Islamic era. In Syria, for instance, there was an additional Christian group

1. Treiger, "Unpublished Texts," 10–20.
2. Treiger, "Unpublished Texts," 17.
3. Treiger, "Unpublished Texts," 16–17.

called the Maronites, whose confessional history was linked to that of the Melkites before a doctrinal schism ensued. The story of the Melkite-Maronite divide is worth a brief trace, highlighting how typical Christian confessional groups formed. Starting from the time of Emperor Heraclius' defeat of Persian forces in 628, the emperor visited Edessa, where, according to Michael the Syrian, he saw and admired the large number of Miaphysites in the city, such that he began to devise ways to convert the Syrian Miaphysites into Chalcedonians.[4] In the Syrian city of Mabbough, Heraclius—as reported by Bar Hebraeus—sought to compel the non-Chalcedonians there to accept Chalcedonianism, although his efforts ultimately failed. Emperor Heraclius' relentless ambition to spread this imperial orthodoxy led to his publishing of the Pact of the Union in June 633, hoping to use it as a document of theological compromise between Chalcedonians and Miaphysites.[5] Five years later, in 638, the *Ekthesis* was published as part of Emperor Heraclius' ban on any theological discussions about the perennially controversial topic of the duality of the wills of Christ, a topic that had been fuelling the doctrinal qualm.[6]

These two documents, the Pact of the Union and the *Ekthesis*, strongly indicate that Emperor Heraclius was interested in uniting the eastern frontier of his empire doctrinally, likely in order to foster an empire bound by a uniform doctrinal creed. However, this imperial project would only create more factions amongst Chalcedonians themselves. This further division began with how, in an attempt to explain the *Ekthesis* and potentially assuage the doubts of Sophronius of Jerusalem, Pope Honorius (625–38) of Rome used the term "a single will," which inadvertently made the *Ekthesis* an imperial sanction for Monotheletism.[7] A long theological dispute was inaugurated from this time between those who stood for the *Ekthesis* and those who preferred an opposite doctrine known as Dyotheletism.

By 680, an imperial ecumenical council was summoned to address this problem, under the pro-Dyothelete Emperor Constantine IV (d. 685). By the end of the sessions in 681, Dyotheletism was upheld as an

4. Text no. 13, §40, n. 323, in Brock, Hoyland, and Palmer, *Seventh Century in the West-Syrian Chronicles*, 140.

5. Booth, *Crisis of Empire*, 205–22.

6. Alexakis, "Before the Lateran Council of 649," 94; Sophronius and Allen, *Sophronius of Jerusalem and Seventh-Century Heresy*, 29.

7. Strickler, "Dispute in Dispute: Revisiting the Disputatio Cum Pyrrho," 248; Hovorun, *Will, Action and Freedom*, 72.

official church doctrine, and Monotheletism was condemned alongside all its proponents.[8] Syrian Dyotheletes came to be known as Melkites, a term cast on them by their doctrinal dissenters for abiding by a doctrinal ruling spearheaded by the Byzantine emperor. Syrian Monotheletes who withdrew to rural settings within the region came to be known as Maronites. This exemplifies how imperial ambitions, as well as peculiar understandings of certain doctrinal matters, bred diverse Christian confessional sects, all of which sought to thrive under the emerging political rule of Arab Muslims.

Consequently, the social life of Christians under early Islamic rule was not homogenous. Different confessional groups had unique historical ties and privileges. As attested in some Christian sources, these historical ties and privileges were sometimes used for the promotion of certain confessional groups at the expense of the others. The confessional group that seemed to have been most fortunate in this regard were the Melkites. The Melkites had a prior ecclesial affiliation to the Byzantine imperial church, and they seemed to have been sociopolitically and ideologically viable in many respects.

Sociopolitically, the Melkites had prominent families, like the Manṣūrs in Damascus, who were involved in the negotiation of the fate of non-Muslims in the city, as well as occupying leading administrative positions. The Melkite historian Eutychius recorded the involvement of Manṣūr in the conquest of Damascus, and that, from the time of the Persian occupation, the main tax official in Damascus was from the Melkite Manṣūr family.[9] Additionally, Arab historians such as Khalifa ibn Khayyat (d. 854), in his *Tārīkh* on the Umayyad dynasty, reported that 'Sarjūn ibn Manṣūr al-Rūmī' was the 'Head of the Dīwān' under Mu'āwiya ibn Abi Sufyan (r. 661–680).[10] This Sarjūn ibn Manṣūr was possibly the son of Manṣūr, the Heraclean tax official; the appellation "'al-Rūmī" affirms that he was a Christian official from the confessional category that we now refer to as Melkite. Melkite elites such as Sarjūn ibn Manṣūr, although polemically reported by non-Melkite sources, were said to have used their political prominence to persecute non-Melkites, thereby showing something of internal antagonism and tension among the various Christian groups. For instance, according to *Chron. Ad. 1234*, Sarjūn ibn Manṣūr had accused Athanasius bar Gūmōyē, who was a tax official under ʿAbd

8. Hovorun, *Will, Action and Freedom*, 86–91.

9. Eutychius, *Das Annalenwerk Des Eutychois von Alexandrien*, 127–28.

10. 'Uṣfūrī, *Khalifa Ibn Khayyat's History on the Umayyad Dynasty*, 89.

al-ʿAzīz (d.705), of siphoning off some of the wealth of the caliph. Caliph ʿAbd Malik (r. 705–715) was said to have punished Athanasius for this allegation, seizing part of his wealth.[11] Similarly, Michael the Syrian reported how the Melkite bishop Bar Qanbara used his political influence to confiscate the Maronite church in Mabbug.[12]

Elite privileges were also useful in the protection of churches, and Melkites had a good number of churches within the city of Damascus. As such, it comes as no surprise that the historian Theophanes reported how Sarjūn ibn Manṣūr intervened when the caliph ʿAbd Malik (r. 705–715) was going to transport pillars of a church to a site of mosque construction.[13] Ideologically, the Melkites had well-educated and well-travelled monks who helped to inspire and communicate their theological convictions. One such well-travelled monk, Anastasius of Sinai, wrote stories and responses that aimed to edify and meet the spiritual needs of ordinary and disenfranchised Melkite believers.[14] Similarly, the well-educated monk and theologian John of Damascus was a theological resource figure for the Melkites, using his education and training to write, refute, and delineate doctrinal boundaries for his confessional community.[15] The Melkites also owned a lucrative bakery that had a yield of up to 230 dinars a year.[16]

Another confessional community with a notable family was the Jacobites. The Jacobite Bar Gumoye family in Edessa could be deemed the Melkite equivalent of the Manṣūrs in Damascus.[17] Like the Manṣūrs in Damascus, the Bar Gumoye family had educated members who assisted in state administration, as did Athanasius Bar Gumoye under the caliph ʿAbd al-ʿAzīz (d. 705) in Kairouan (Egypt). The earlier reported episode between Athanasius and Sarjūn ibn Manṣūr could again suffice as evidence of a malevolent rivalry between leading and influential Christian elites under early Islamic rule. The story has it that after Athanasius had

11. *Chron. Ad.* 1234 trans. text no. 13, §134, in Brock, Hoyland, and Palmer, *Seventh Century in the West-Syrian Chronicles*, 204.

12. Tannous, "In Search of Monotheletism," 35. Cf. Michael I the Syrian, *Chronique de Michel le Syrien*, 4:460–61; Ibrahim, *Edessa-Aleppo Syriac Codex*, 470.

13. Theophanes the Confessor, *Chronicle of Theophanes Confessor*, 510; AM 6183; Hoyland, *Seeing Islam as Others Saw It*, 375.

14. See Papadogiannakis, "Christian Identity in Seventh-Century Byzantium." For some of Anastasius' martyr stories, see Shoemaker, "Anastasius of Sinai."

15. Sahas, *John of Damascus on Islam*; Schadler, *John of Damascus and Islam*; Louth, *St John Damascene*; Chase, *Fathers of the Church*; Awad, *Umayyad Christianity*.

16. Boudier, "L'Église melkite au ixe siècle à travers le conflit.»

17. See Debié, "Christians in the Service of the Caliph."

completed his administrative service in Kairouan and was retiring back to his home country in Edessa, his trip was interrupted while crossing Damascus. This was because the Melkite secretary of the caliph, Sarjūn ibn Manṣūr, had reported Athanasius as having looted the treasury in Kairouan, and as such Athanasius' wealth was partly confiscated by ʿAbd al-Malik.[18] Part of this report has it that Athanasius used his wealth to furnish Jacobite church properties in Edessa, indicating how prominent families used their resources to the benefit of their confessional community. This report demonstrates how Christians sometimes tried to use their proximity to power to outdo members of other confessional groups.

Apart from an institutional or communal perspective, Christian social life under early Islamic rule also involved individual experiences of economic and social hardship. We see this example in martyrological material, which must be treated with extreme caution. For instance, through the martyr stories of Anastasius of Sinai, we encounter Christian slaves like Euphemia of Damascus and George the Black, each of whom were slaves under a Saracen master or mistress. Anastasius wrote these stories to show how courageous Christians who were servants to Muslims could keep identifying with their Christian faith. However, despite his authorial intentions, the stories of these ordinary or non-elite figures highlight something of a social situation where Christians were servants or trade apprentices under Arab Muslims. This provides a balanced view in contrast with the elite narratives. While Christian communities like the Melkites owned a bakery that was leased to Muslims, essentially having such Muslims in their employ, martyr stories provide a plausible example of Christians who served the household or trade ventures of Arab Muslims. Beyond religious and doctrinal categories, Christian-Muslim encounters in the social space also derived from factors of economic import.

Overall, Christian communities under early Islamic rule were highly sectarian in nature. This was rooted in pre-Islamic doctrinal histories. Therefore, Christian social life at the time varied according to confessional life and communal wealth. Equally important is that economic status also shaped the social life of Christians under early Islamic rule.

18. *Chron. Ad.* 1234 trans. text no.13, §134, in Brock, Hoyland, and Palmer, *Seventh Century in the West-Syrian Chronicles*, 204.

TRACING CHRISTIAN SOCIAL LIFE UNDER EARLY ISLAMIC RULE USING DHĪMMĪ REGULATIONS

One of the historical texts that can inform best on the possible nature of the lives of Christians under Muslim rule would be the set of regulations intended for non-Muslims, or the *dhīmmī*. These regulations cannot be seen as completely historical and accurate. However, their evolution has been studied and modern consensus would be that regulations for non-Muslims constitute a historically attested phenomenon that developed at various times and under various circumstances.[19]

We hear about the regulation of non-Muslims the most during the years of consolidation of Arab rule from the eighth century onward. However, the content and grounds for these regulations are often implied to be from the time of the Arab conquest. The assumption would be that when the Arab armies conquered a Christian-majority city, for instance, the Christians were obliged to abide by a set of rules in order to remain in their cities under the new political leaders. Overtime, however, there arose several debates as to what exactly the contents of such agreements were and to what extent they were applicable under new and changing circumstances.

This was certainly the case regarding the Syrian capital of Damascus. Damascene regulations for non-Muslims evolved from the eighth century, when there were various complaints by Christians who felt that the agreement at the time of the conquest was not being upheld by Muslims who were seizing their churches. According to Ibn ʿAsākir, there were at least two such incidents reported during the reign of Al-Awzāʿī (d. 773–734) and Yaḥyā ibn Ḥamza (d. 792) as judges in Damascus.[20]

Since no one knew what the exact content of this treaty was, later Arab Muslim legislative authorities would suggest some and the Christians would also make their own suggestions. Makhūl al-Shāmī (d. 731) was cited by Abū Yūsuf (d. 798) to have said that it was agreed at the time of conquest that churches and synagogues (*biyaʿuhum*) were to be left intact, as long as new ones were not erected.[21] Al-Awzāʿī (d. 773–734)

19. See the following works by Levy-Rubin: "Shurūṭ Umar and Its Alternatives; *Non-Muslims in the Early Islamic Empir*; "Shurūṭ ʿUmar; "Surrender Agreements."

20. Ibn ʿAsākir, *Tāʾrīkh Madīnat Dimashq*, 2:117–18, 354.

21. Zein and El-Wakil, "Khālid b. al-Walīd's Treaty with the People of Damascus," 317, citing Abū Yusuf, Kitāb al-Kharāj, 159. Levy-Rubin, *Non-Muslims in the Early Islamic Empire*, 71–72.

claimed that he was with Ibn Surāqa when Christians from Damascus presented the conquest agreement as proof that their churches were to be protected.[22] Abū Yūsuf (d. 798) claimed that synagogues and churches in the cities and in the metropoles (*amṣār*) at the time of the conquest were not to be destroyed.[23] Ibn al-Mu'allā (d. 899) reported that the caliph 'Umar ibn 'Abd al- 'Azīz (d. 720) had settled a case in which the Christians of Damascus presented the treaty (*al-'uḥud*) regarding the safeguarding of their churches.[24] Muslim jurists came up with recollections and adaptations on how non-Muslim life was to be regulated, based on these emerging debates and divergent recollections of the conquest treaties. Such later recollections leave us with insights and hints on Christian social life under early Islamic rule.

An example of one such recollection was transmitted by a well-known historian, Abū Mikhnaf (d. 774), by the end of the eighth century. Abū Mikhnaf's position represents a more comprehensive example of what a modified stipulation for non-Muslims would have looked like by the end of the eighth and at the start of the ninth century. A full version of Abū Mikhnaf's tradition is preserved and transmitted by Ibn 'Asākir's (d. 1176) *Tā'rīkh Madīnat Dimashq*. This version is presented in a tabular form below with a graph representation of its five main sections.

Table 1. Content of the Pledges in their Respective Units

S/No	**Opening Format: "We will not" (*Lā Na-*)**	Pledge Content: Churches, Monasteries and Church Processions
	we will not	renovate, churches, monastery, cells, and monk houses within the city of Damascus and those around it
	We will not	refurbish anything neither from our destroyed churches nor from those of them located in Muslim neighbourhoods.

22. Ibn 'Asākir, *Tā'rīkh Madīnat Dimashq*, 2:117–18.

23. Abū Yūsuf, *Kitāb al-Kharāj*, p.138, cited in Levy-Rubin, *Non-Muslims in the Early Islamic Empire*, 71.

24. Ibn 'Asākir, *Tā'rīkh Madīnat Dimashq*, 2:273.

	We will not	keep our churches from the Muslims for lodging at night or day. The doors [of our churches] will stay open to passers-by or travelers on foot.
	We will not	host a spy [in our churches or homes] and we shall not conceal anyone who conspires against the Muslim
	We will not	strike our ceremonial sticks (*lā naḍrab binawāqīsinā*) except secretly at the heart of our churches.
	We will not	expose the cross on [our churches].
	We will not	raise our voices in our churches during our prayers or readings
	We will not	process [in public] with our crosses nor our books [in the path of Muslims]
	We will not	go out [processing] on Easter Monday and on Palm Sundays
	We will not	raise our voices regarding our dead, neither will we display fire-torches with regards to our dead in the marketplaces of the Muslims.
S/No	**Opening Format: "We will not" / "We will" (*lā na- / wa 'an na-*)**	**Pledge Content: Religious Practices: Food, Drink, Conversion**
	We will not	go near the Muslims with pigs
	We will not	show *shirk* in the presence of Muslims.
	We will not	cause a Muslim to desire our religion nor bid anyone to it
	We will not	hinder anyone from among our relatives, if he so desires, to enter into Islam
	We will	abide by our religion anywhere we are.
S/No	**Opening Format: "We will not" / "We will" (*lā na- / wa 'an na-*)**	**Pledge Content: Socioreligious Behavior: Dress Codes, Language**
	We will not	imitate the Muslims in apparels, headgear, turban, sandals, hairstyle, and riding gear
	We will not	speak in their language nor shall we name our children with their names
	We will not	teach our children the Qur'ān
	We will not	inscribe on our seal-rings in Arabic

	We will	clip the front-hair of our heads and separate the top of our hair.
	We will	bind belts around our waists.
S/No	**Opening Format: "We will not" / "We will" (*lā na- / wa 'an na-*)**	Pledge Content: Social Gathering and Public Violence
	We will not	mount saddles or bear any form of weapons neither will we make them in our houses.
	We will not	strap swords
	We will not	curse a Muslim and anyone who hits a Muslim breaks his covenant (*'ahādihu*)
	We will not	rise against them (Muslims) in opposition.
	We will	stand up for them from seats if they wish to sit.
	We will	respect the Muslims in their gathering.
S/No	**Opening Format: "We will not" / "We will" (lā *na* -/ *wa 'an na-*)**	**Pledge Content: Hospitality and Trade**
	We will	show them the way
	We will	be hospitable to a traveling Muslim and feed him for three days
	We will not	strike a deal with any Muslim except if the authority in trading is on the Muslim
	We will	not to buy any share of the slave partially owned by a Muslim
	We will not	sell alcohol (*al-khumūr*).

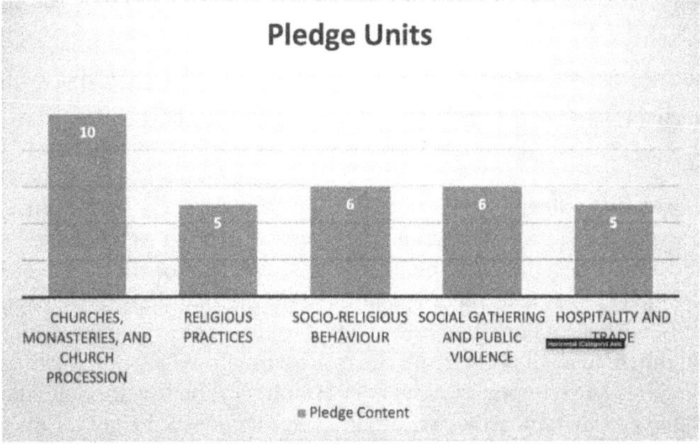

Figure 1. Proportion of Pledge Unit

These regulations are recollected by Abū Mikhnaf as terms of capitulation at the time of the conquest of Damascus. They are portrayed as a letter presented to Abū ʿUbayda ibn al-Jarrāh by the non-Arab (*al-aʿājim*) residents of Damascus and Syria. The letter has three main segments: the opening, the pledged stipulations, and the concluding section. The opening begins with the *fath*ā ("In the name of God, the most merciful") and goes on to indicate how the purpose of the text was a list of pledges by non-Arabs in exchange for protection (*al-amān*) from the Arab Muslim authorities. The concluding section of the text contains an oath of allegiance to the outlined stipulations, mentioning the consequences of a breach and God as witness.[25] Between the opening and the concluding sections, there are thirty-one different pledges. Each of these thirty-one pledges begins either with "We will" (*wa ʿan na-*) or "We will not" (*lā na*).

These thirty-one stipulations are divided into five pledge units. The first unit contains ten pledges regarding churches, monasteries, and church rituals like processions. The second unit contains five pledges outlining religious practices that were deemed acceptable to the Arab Muslims. The third unit contains six pledges regarding dress codes (*ghiyār*) and use of the Arabic language and the Qur'an. The fourth pledge unit contains six different codes on social gatherings and non-violence. The fifth unit contains five pledges regarding hospitality and trade.[26] How might this inform us on the life of Christians under early Islamic rule? Each of these pledge units will be discussed with wider extrapolations on how the pledges therein say a thing or two about the life of Christians, at least in a major city like Damascus, during the years of early Islamic rule in the city.

At this point, it is important to remind the reader that this particular text is a transmitted document attested to have emerged from a particular context, which in this case is the Syrian capital of Damascus. Dwelling on the content of these regulations is more for the purpose of anchoring our discussion on the basis of this textual attestation. It does not

25. "If we seek to alter or breach what we stipulate upon ourselves for you, the things [terms] on which we accept protection, there will be no legal rights [*dhimma*)]for us. It may be acceptable [*ḥall*] if you made for us what is just for the people of rebellion and dissent [*ahl al-maʿānada wa al-shaqāq*]. On these [conditions] grant protection to us and for the people of our community and let us live in your country [*bilādinakum*], which you inherited by the help of the Great and Almighty God. God is witness of that which we oblige to you upon ourselves, let Him be a sufficient witness." Ibn ʿAsākir, *Tāʾrīkh Madīnat Dimashq*, 2:120–21. I thank Prof. Dr. Jens Scheiner for his generous time and very helpful comments during this translation.

26. Ibn ʿAsākir, *Tāʾrīkh Madīnat Dimashq*, 2:120–21.

indicate that all the regulations mentioned are historically certain to have been enacted. Furthermore, these regulations are herein used for very generalized extrapolations for insights into Christian social life within a particular historical context. Consequently, nothing herein contained or extrapolated are intended for political purposes in modern issues of Christian-Muslim encounters.

The first unit contains ten pledges regulating activities around Christian churches and monasteries, including worship and processions. One issue of social import is the third pledge, which says to keep churches available to travelers and wayfarers, some of whom could possibly be Muslim. Why would we have a pledge like this mentioned and to what purpose was it aimed? This might connect to the twenty-eighth pledge, on hospitality to traveling Muslims. It is possible that Christian churches were useful spaces for practical purposes such as lodging for Muslims traveling to cities such as Damascus who had nowhere to stay. Milka Levy-Rubin has pointed out that the early years of Arab Muslim rule warranted migration of Arabs to key cities that had been conquered.[27] Such migration might be for such purposes as the joining of the paid soldiery of the caliphate, which, according to Luke Yarborough, was deemed more reputable than some of the skilled work that Christians occupied, including tax record keeping.[28]

An incident involving Arab strangers who traveled and took over a church for their own volition was reported in Damascus, but this incident does not explicitly mention that the Arabs needed the church space for accommodation. This was reported by Ibn al-Muʿallā to have happened when Yaḥyā ibn Ḥamza was *qāḍī* in Damascus. Ibn al-Muʿallā reported that the Christians from the citadel of Damascus (*qaṣinat Dimashq*) tendered a case before the judge.[29] This was between the Christian religious leaders and some Arabs who were a different group of strangers or migrants (*al-gharbāʾ*).[30] It is possible that immigrant Arab groups would have been interested in a church facility as a place for lodging, as we see how Abū Mikhnaf's (d. 774) transmission later added a legal instruction that the doors of churches stay open to Muslim pedestrians and wayfarers.[31] It is hard to conclude that Christian social experience under early

27. Levy-Rubin, "Shurūṭ Umar and Its Alternatives," 181.

28 For instance, see Yarbrough, *Friends of the Emir*, 32, 83.

29. Ibn ʿAsākir, *Tāʾrīkh Madīnat Dimashq*, 2:354.

30. Ibn ʿAsākir, *Tāʾrīkh Madīnat Dimashq*, 2:354.

31. Ibn ʿAsākir, *Tāʾrīkh Madīnat Dimashq*, 2:120–21.

Islamic rule actually involved the use of churches as lodging for Arab Muslim travelers.

However, since cities like Damascus, from where these pledged restrictions are claimed to have emerged, were Christian cities for a long time, it is reasonable to presume that church buildings were littered across public spaces and that churches were of interest for practical purposes to non-Christians. As a result, it was equally the case that the Christian property for which Christians most frequently appealed based on assumed legal rights of protection or safekeeping—particularly in the face of potential or actual controversies—were churches. Consequently, based on the reports about these appeals for the protection of churches, we can say that early Islamic rule had the administrative and legislative apparatus upon which non-Muslims could draw on, make a case for, and negotiate for what they deemed to be fair and legal. Christians constituted a significant portion of such non-Muslim populace and Christians feature in reports on the use of such appeals.

Another Christian property that was a contact point between Christian communities and Arab Muslims, thereby warranting discussion on the experience of Christians under early Islamic rule, is the monastery. The opening pledge stipulates a regulation not to renovate churches and monasteries among other things. Considering the long history of Christianity in the eastern region prior to Arab Muslim regime, monasteries were bound to be just as common as churches. Monasteries were important sites for Arab Muslim caliphs, who made their lodgings and "villas" around monasteries. Using the Damascene location as a case study once again, there are several Christian monasteries surrounding Damascus that are known to had been visited by Umayyad rulers in the past: Khālid ibn al-Walīd (642) stayed at Dayr Ṣalībā during the siege of Damascus; Yazīd ibn Muʿāwiya ibn ʾAbī Sufyān (d. 683) frequented Dayr Sābur.[32] Jack Tannous also mentioned Dayr al-Hind, Dayr Muḥammad, and Dayr al-Bukht among the monasteries within the environs of Damascus that had been of interest to caliphal figures.[33] Dayr Murrān, however, ranks high in its profile on caliphal visits. Being advantageously located on the slopes of Jabal Qāsiyūn, overseeing the city of Damascus from the north of Paradise Gate (Bāb al-Farādīs), it proved to be a resourceful resort for many caliphs.[34] For instance, Dominique Sourdel mentioned that Yazīd ibn Muʿāwiya

32. Tannous, *Making of the Medieval Middle East*, 384–85.

33. Tannous, *Making of the Medieval Middle East*, 384–85.

34. Sourdel, "Dayr Murrān."

ibn ʾAbī Sufyān (d. 683) had commissioned the development of a river named after him, Nahr Yazīd, for the benefit of the monastic community at Murrān.[35] ʿAbd al-Malik ibn Marwān ibn al-Ḥakam (d. 705), according to al-Balādhurī, made Dayr Murrān his pre-summer lodge.[36] Antoine Borrut mentioned the Dayr Murrān vicinity as a possible burial site for the caliph ʿUmar ibn ʿAbd al-ʿAzīz (d. 720).[37] Sourdel also mentioned that Dayr Murrān was connected to the burial place of al-Walīd I (d. 715) and was the temporary residence of al-Walīd II (d. 744).[38]

The second pledge unit contains five stipulated restrictions regarding desecration and religious conversion. The first two are about desecration with pigs and the theological repulsion of *shirk*, which in basic terms is related to speaking of the incarnation to Muslims.[39] The incarnation and its accompanying doctrine of the Trinity was probably the most theologically assessable debate in public encounters between Christians and Muslims. This can also be seen in how John of Damascus sourced much of his ideas about Islam from an informal public conversational source.

In disproving Muslim notions of the Christian doctrines, John of Damascus used dialogical formats to show the sources of these notions and such formats come in quotes like "we ask/say/remark . . . they answer/call us/accuse us."[40] John of Damascus also introduced the Qur'anic claim about Jesus as a direct speech by Muhammad: "He says that there is one God, creator of all things, who has neither been begotten nor has begotten."[41] This was either a portrayal of popular Islamic confessions that were taking a creedal authority among Muslims or a direct reading of a form of the Qur'an as was accessible to John of Damascus. Qur'anic monotheistic assertions similar to Jewish monotheistic confessions were already alluded to in the writings of authors like Anastasius of Sinai (d. 700), such that by the time of John of Damascus, these assertions would

35. Sourdel, "Day Murrān."

36. Balādhurī, *Anonyme Arabische Chronik*, 200. See also Bacharach, "Marwanid Umayyad Building Activities," 38; Kennedy, *Prophet and the Age of the Caliphates*, 96.

37. Borrut, *Entre MéMoire et Pouvoir*, 304–5.

38. Sourdel, "Dayr Murrān."

39. *Shirk* is simply explained as the Islamic accusation of ascribing the unlikely property of childbearing to God. Early Qur'anic citations attached to Christian claims of Jesus as the begotten son of God cites passages like *Sūrat al-nisa'*ā Q.4:171; see ʿAmr al-Ghaṭafānī, *Kitāb Al-Taḥrīsh*, 42.

40. Chase, *Fathers of the Church*, 37:154ff.

41. Chase, *Fathers of the Church*, 37:153.

have been indicative of aspects of the Islamic faith, including forms of its inscriptions on the Dome of the Rock.[42]

This highlights how Christian social encounters were quite possibly dotted with basic levels of theological exchanges, some of which could have derived from common scriptural understandings or even architectural inscriptions. In the same vein, the idea of common theological interactions is somewhat linked to the adoption of religious identities. This is seen in how the last three stipulations in the second pledge unit have to do with the crossing of religious boundary lines, with the Christians promising not to make converts out of the Muslim, as well as not hindering a Christian who wishes to turn to Islam.

Although we should not be quick to describe this idea of switching religious identity as conversion, especially in the way we understand the word today, we can get a sense of how people's religious identity was defined by typical externalities. A list of these emerges from the sixteenth to the twenty-first stipulations on socioreligious behavior: apparel like headgear, turbans, sandals, and belts; hairstyle; language; and inscriptions. An example connecting religious identity to dress codes is seen in the hagiographical story of a certain Elias of Heliopolis, whose wearing and loosening of his belt (*al-zunnār*), as a Christian servant and apprentice, was tantamount to religious conversion.[43] From this story, in connection with the relevant stipulations, we are inclined to think that a part of Christian-Muslim social encounters during the early years of Islam was the idea that one might be making a statement of religious belonging simply through outward appearance. A final point of extrapolation on the possible nature of Christian social life under early Arab Islamic rule, based on the Abū Mikhnaf transmission, is on hospitality and trade.

The five stipulations of the last pledge unit include practical acts of hospitality and a set of trade ethics. It is hard to glean much from the stipulations on trade. However, we do have evidence of trade agreements between Christians and Muslims. During the time of the Melkite bishop David of Damascus (r. 876–892), Christians in Damascus owned a bakery/oven (*al-furn*), which had an annual lease (*qibālitihi*) of 40 dīnār and was managed by Muslims (*fī yadī al-Muslimīn*).[44] In this instance,

42. See Milwright, "Inscriptions of the Dome of the Rock," 223.

43. Sahner, *Christian Martyrs under Islam*, 57–58. Milka Levy-Rubin has argued that *ghiyār* codes like the wearing of *zunnār* goes back to the time of ʿUmar II. Levy-Rubin, "ʿUmar II's Ghiyār Edict," 158–59.

44. Boudier, "L'Église melkite au ixe siècle à travers le conflit," 68.

the Muslims were business partners with Christians and essentially managed a Christian business outfit on lease. Regarding the set of pledges on hospitality, we see three very practical stipulations: to provide a traveling Muslim with directions, as well as to house and feed them, should the need arise. These pledges depict and anticipate a situation where a traveling or migrant Muslim in a Christian-majority setting might be lost and would need the help of a local to find their way again. Added to this is the pledge to use Christian resources in such settings to meet the needs of any traveler: food and shelter. Like a point earlier made, this leaves us with the imagination that Christian-majority cities, during the early years of Islam, attracted Arab Muslim migrants after the Arab conquest of such cities and that such patterns of migration elicited the need for Christian locals to play the role of good hosts.

CONCLUSION

Based on this information, what set of conclusions might we draw from a general overview about the social life of Christians during the centuries of early Islamic rule? It is important to bear in mind that Christianity was hardly homogenous under early Islamic rule: Christian groups were separately formed along various doctrinal and theological ideologies. All of these Christian confessions hoped to thrive under political regimes, including that of the Arab Muslims. However, some Christian communities stood a better chance of thriving than others. The Christian communities that had elites and monks who were educated enough to work for the Arab Muslim tax registry or to develop theological material stood a greater chance of thriving through political favors and ideological fortifications.

However, a more precise set of insights into the social life of Christians under early Islamic rule is to be gained from regulations intended for non-Muslims, or the *dhīmmī*. These regulations were orchestrated by the need to modify privileges that were granted to non-Muslims who were to live under early Islamic rule. An example of one such modified version of regulations was transmitted by a well-known historian, Abū Mikhnaf (d. 774), dating to the late eighth century. From these regulations we can infer that Christian social experience under early Islamic rule revolved around religious properties and the use of church spaces: while Christian worship places were supposed to have been under the terms of protection at the time of conquests in places like Damascus, disputes arose as to whether some churches were to be retained for Christian use or not. Christian social experience during this time also involved public space theological exchanges, trade, and hospitality.

RECOMMENDED READINGS

Griffith, Sidney H. *The Church in the Shadow of the Mosque: Christians and Muslims in the World of Islam*. Princeton, NJ: Princeton University Press, 2008.
Hoyland, Robert G. *In God's Path: The Arab Conquests and the Creation of an Islamic Empire*. New York: Oxford University Press, 2015.
Sahas, Daniel J. *Byzantium and Islam: Collected Studies on Byzantine-Muslim Encounters*. Leiden: Brill, 2021.
Sahner, Christian C. *Christian Martyrs under Islam: Religious Violence and the Making of the Muslim World*. Princeton, NJ: Princeton University Press, 2018.
Tannous, Jack. *The Making of the Medieval Middle East: Religion, Society, and Simple Believers*. Princeton, NJ: Princeton University Press, 2018.
Yarbrough, Luke B. *Friends of the Emir: Non-Muslim State Officials in Premodern Islamic Thought*. Cambridge Studies in Islamic Civilization. Cambridge: Cambridge University Press, 2019.

BIBLIOGRAPHY

Alexakis, Alexander. "Before the Lateran Council of 649: The Last Days of Herakleios the Emperor and Monotheletism." *AHC* 27/8 (June 1995) 93–101.
Awad, Najib George. *Umayyad Christianity: John of Damascus as a Contextual Example of Identity Formation in Early Islam*. Piscataway, NJ: Gorgias, 2018.
Bacharach, Jere L. "Marwanid Umayyad Building Activities: Speculations on Patronage." *Muqarnas* 13:1 (1996: 27–44.
Balādhurī, Aḥmad ibn Yaḥyá. *Anonyme Arabische Chronik, Band XI, Vermuthlich Das Buch Der Verwandtschaft Und Geschichte Der Adligen*. Leipzig, 1883.
Booth, Phil. *Crisis of Empire: Doctrine and Dissent at the End of Late Antiquity*. Berkeley: University of California Press, 2013.
Borrut, Antoine. *Entre MÉMoire et Pouvoir : L'Espace Syrien Sous Les Derniers Omeyyades et Les Premiers Abbassides (V. 72–193/692–809)*. Leiden: Brill, 2010.
Boudier, Mathilde. "L'Église melkite à l'ixe siècle à travers le conflit entre David de Damas et Siméon d'Antioche. Apports d'un dossier documentaire inédit." *Annales islamologiques* 52 (2018) 45–80.
Brock, Sebastian P., Robert G. Hoyland, and Andrew Palmer. *The Seventh Century in the West-Syrian Chronicles*. Translated Texts for Historians 15. Liverpool: Liverpool University Press, 1993.
Chase, Frederic H., Jr. *The Fathers of the Church: A New Translation: Saint John of Damascus*. Ex Fontibus, 2015.
Debié, Muriel. "Christians in the Service of the Caliph: Through the Looking Glass of Communal Identities." In *Christians and Others in the Umayyad State*, edited

by Antoine Borrut and Fred McGraw Donner. Chicago: Oriental Institute of the University of Chicago, 2016.

ʻAmr al-Ghaṭafānī, Ḍirār ibn. *Kitāb Al-Taḥrīsh*. Edited by Hüseyin Hansu and Muḥammad Kaskīn. Al-Ṭabʻah al-Ūlá. Istānbūl, Turkiyā: Sharikat Dār al-Irshād, 2014.

Eutychius. *Das Annalenwerk Des Eutychois von Alexandrien: Ausgewählte Geschichten Und Legenden / Kompiliert von Sa'id Bn Baṭrīq Um 935 A.D.* Edited by Michael Breydy. Corpus Scriptorum Christianorum Orientalium. Scriptores Arabici, v. 471–472, t. 44–45. Leuven: Peeters, 1985.

Hovorun, Cyril. *Will, Action and Freedom: Christological Controversies in the Seventh Century*. Boston: Brill, 2008.

Hoyland, Robert G. *Seeing Islam as Others Saw It: A Survey and Evaluation of Christian, Jewish and Zoroastrian Writings on Early Islam*. Gorgias Islamic Studies 12. Piscataway, NJ: Gorgias, 2019.

Ibn ʻAsākir. *Tāʾrīkh Madīnat Dimashq*. Vol. 2. Beirut, Lebanon: al-Ḥālūyi, 1995.

Ibrāhīm, Gharīghūriyūs Yūḥannā. *The Edessa-Aleppo Syriac Codex of the Chronicle of Michael the Great, Vol. 1 of Texts and Translations of the Chronicle of Michael the Great*. Piscataway, NJ: Gorgias, 2009.

Kennedy, Hugh. *The Prophet and the Age of the Caliphates: The Islamic Near East from the Sixth to the Eleventh Century*. 3rd ed. London: Routledge, 2015.

Levy-Rubin, Milka. *Non-Muslims in the Early Islamic Empire: From Surrender to Coexistence*. Cambridge: Cambridge University Press, 2011.

———. "Shurūṭ Umar and Its Alternatives: The Legal Debate on the Status of the Shurūṭ Dhimmīs." *JSAI* 30 (2005) 170–206.

———. "Shurūṭ ʻUmar: From Early Harbingers to Systematic Enforcement." In *Beyond Religious Borders: Interaction and Intellectual Exchange in the Medieval Islamic World*, edited by David M. Freidenreich and Miriam Goldstein. Philadelphia: University of Pennsylvania Press, 2012.

———. "The Surrender Agreements: Origins and Authenticity." In *The Umayyad World*, edited by Andrew Marsham. Routledge, 2020.

———. "'Umar II's Ghiyār Edict: Between Ideology and Practice." In *Christians and Others in the Umayyad State*, edited by Antoine Borrut and Fred McGraw Donner. Chicago: Oriental Institute of the University of Chicago, 2016.

Louth, John. *St John Damascene: Tradition and Originality in Byzantine Theology*. Oxford: Oxford University Press, 2002.

Michael I the Syrian. *Chronique de Michel le Syrien, Patriarche Jacobite d'Antioche (1166–1199)*. Paris: Ernest Leroux, 1899.

Milwright, Marcus. "The Inscriptions of the Dome of the Rock in Their Historical Context." In *The Dome of the Rock and Its Umayyad Mosaic Inscriptions*, 214–50. Edinburgh: Edinburgh University Press, 2016.

Papadogiannakis, Yannis. "Christian Identity in Seventh-Century Byzantium: The Case of Anastasius of Sinai." In *Motions of Late Antiquity: Essays on Religion, Politics, and Society in Honour of Peter Brown*, edited by Jamie Kreiner and Helmut Reimitz, 249–67. Cultural Encounters in Late Antiquity and the Middle Ages 20. Turnhout: Brepols, 2016. https://doi.org/10.1484/M.CELAMA-EB.5.108248.

Sahas, Daniel J. *John of Damascus on Islam: The "Heresy of the Ishmaelites."* Leiden: Brill, 1972.

Sahner, Christian C. *Christian Martyrs under Islam: Religious Violence and the Making of the Muslim World*. Princeton, NJ: Princeton University Press, 2018.

Schadler, Peter. *John of Damascus and Islam Christian Heresiology and the Intellectual Background to Earliest Christian-Muslim Relations*. History of Christian-Muslim Relations 34. Leiden: Brill, 2018.

Shoemaker, Stephen. "Anastasius of Sinai and the Beginnings of Islam." *Journal of Orthodox Christian Studies* 1:2 (December 19, 2018) 137–54.

Sophronius, Saint, and Pauline Allen. *Sophronius of Jerusalem and Seventh-Century Heresy: The Synodical Letter and Other Documents*. Oxford Early Christian Texts. Oxford: Oxford University Press, 2009.

Sourdel, D. "Dayr Murrān." In *Encyclopaedia of Islam*, edited by P Bearman, Th. Bianquis, C.E. Bowersock, E. van Donzel, and W.P. Heinrichs. 2nd ed. Leiden: Brill, 2012. http://referenceworks.brillonline.com/entries/encyclopaedia-of-islam-2/*-SIM_1777.

Strickler, Ryan W. "A Dispute in Dispute: Revisiting the Disputatio Cum Pyrrho Attributed to Maximus the Confessor (CPG 7698)." *Sacris Erudiri* 56 (January 1, 2017) 243–72.

Tannous, Jack. "In Search of Monotheletism." *Dumbarton Oaks Papers* 68 (2014) 29–67.

———. *The Making of the Medieval Middle East: Religion, Society, and Simple Believers*. Princeton, NJ: Princeton University Press, 2018.

Theophanes the Confessor. *The Chronicle of Theophanes Confessor: Byzantine and Near Eastern History A.D. 284–813*. Oxford: Clarendon, 1997.

Treiger, Alexander. "Unpublished Texts from the Arab Orthodox Tradition (1): On the Origin of the Term 'Melkite' and On the Destruction of the Maryamiyya Cathedrale in Damascus." *Chronos* 29 (2014) 7–37.

ʿUṣfūrī, Khalīfah ibn Khayyāṭ. *Khalifa Ibn Khayyat's History on the Umayyad Dynasty (660–750)*. Edited by Carl Wurtzel and Robert G. Hoyland. Translated Texts for Historians 63. Liverpool: Liverpool University Press, 2015.

Yarbrough, Luke B. *Friends of the Emir: Non-Muslim State Officials in Premodern Islamic Thought*. Cambridge Studies in Islamic Civilization. Cambridge: Cambridge University Press, 2019.

Zein, Ibrahim, and Ahmed El-Wakil. "Khālid b. al-Wālid's Treaty with the People of Damascus: Identifying the Source Document through Shared and Competing Historical Memories." *Journal of Islamic Studies* 31:3 (September 1, 2020) 295–328.

5

Christian Contributions to the Arab Islamic Civilization

ASHOOR YOUSIF

INTRODUCTION

Christianity and Christians have been an integral part of the Middle East and North Africa from the inception of Christianity, contributing to the region's development and thus shaping its history. On the eve of the rise of Islam, Christianity, especially Syriac Christianity, dominated the Fertile Crescent and the peripheries of the Arabian Peninsula, influencing the religious milieu. Strong Christian presence is attested to among the Arab tribes of north Arabia, especially among the Lakhmids and Ghassanids. There were also Christian communities in the Persian Gulf, Yemen, and Najran in southern Arabia, which in turn reached central Arabia by late the sixth or early seventh century.

With the rise of Islam and the formation of the Islamic caliphate in the seventh century, regional Christians, including Syriac-speaking Christians, become part of this new reality. They maintained a demographic majority until the turn of first millennium and participated in the rise and development of the early Arab Islamic civilization. Thus, they shaped its history and heritage in significant ways especially during its Golden Age of the eighth to tenth centuries. In such a context, Christians were scribes, chancery officials, physicians, scientists, philosophers, translators, and statesmen.[1]

Such active Christian participation continued to shape the Arab-Islamic milieu until the late medieval period, especially during the late Syriac Renaissance of the twelfth and thirteenth centuries.[2] With time, Christians' presence dwindled demographically in the Middle East and their impact on the Islamic civilization declined significantly with the collapse of Islamic civilization itself. Despite this decline, their presence continues until today, and their contributions resurged in modern times, especially during the Arab Awakening in the late nineteenth and twentieth centuries. In the new reality, many of the early roles once again witnessed a strong Christian presence, as well as participation in new aspects of their societies.

However, while such active participation continues in the twenty-first century, the demographic decline of Christians in the Middle East indicates that their impact is at risk of diminishing completely, and their legacy will be forgotten permanently. Thus, the Christians' ancient legacy and modern participation in shaping the Arab Islamic world is a valuable and necessary topic to highlight, lest it be neglected and forgotten with time as the Christian presence disperses in certain parts of the Islamic world and continues to diminish in other parts. The impact of the Christian story in the Islamic world, especially the earlier part, has been missing from modern scholarship, or only featured as a peripheral element for decades until recent years.[3]

Although writing about Christian contributions to Arab-Islamic civilization in a comprehensive fashion would require a multivolume work, and definitely a larger literary space than a chapter permits, surveying some of its most significant highlights is a worthy endeavour. This chapter aims to highlight some of the key areas of Christian contributions to the Arab Islamic world, including but not limited to religion, culture, science, and politics. It will cover a wide range of historical periods from the pre-Islamic era to modern times.

1. Griffith, *Church in the Shadow of the Mosque*, 17–20.

2. Griffith, *Church in the Shadow of the Mosque*, 11.

3. Ellis, ed., *Secular Nationalism and Citizenship in Muslim Countries*, 1–26; Rowe, "Middle Eastern Christian as Agent," 472–74.

RELIGIOUS INFLUENCE (SCRIPTURE, THEOLOGY, AND RITUAL)

Syriac-speaking Christians, along with affiliated Arabic-speaking Christians, were among the earliest influences in shaping Islam religiously. Their strong presence predominantly in their homeland of the Fertile Crescent and the peripheries of the Arabian Peninsula created contacts with the tribes and communities of Arabia. By the end of the sixth century, Eastern Christianity had reached the heartland of south and central Arabia, the Hijaz region of Mecca and Yathrib (Median), the birthplace of Islam.[4] Thus, by the time of Muhammad (ca. 570–632), Eastern Christianity, especially in its Syriac and Arabic forms, had a significant presence and influence on the area. There was widespread awareness of its sacred Scripture, ecclesiastical traditions, and theological doctrines among the region's inhabitants.

The earliest Christian contributions to Islam were religious in nature, related both to the areas of dogma and practices. There is evidence for the direct and indirect religious influence of Eastern Christianity in shaping Islamic doctrines and practices.[5] The Qur'an reflects such a reality, with a strong knowledge of Christian Scripture, creeds, liturgy, and practices, especially in its Syriac expressions—a knowledge that is assumed among its audience. It has common scriptural and doctrinal themes with Christianity, and it engages with and reacts to its doctrines and practices. It both endorses and rejects aspects of them, as it speaks and responds to Christians, alternately praising and critiquing them.[6] Notably, scholars have highlighted the influence of the Syriac language on Qur'anic terminology, where Syriac words are found. Hence, Eastern Christian influence on Islam began during the formation of the faith. Such engagements, influence, and similarities were known to early Christians, such as John of Damascus (d. 750),[7] and it led them to see and describe Islam as a Christian heresy, calling it the heresy of the Ishmaelites.

4. Berkey, "Islam," 21; Osman, "Pre-Islamic Arab Converts."

5. Griffith, *Church in the Shadow*, 6–11; Griffith, "Christianity's Historic Roots in the Middle East," 29–60; Jenkins, *Lost History of Christianity*, 37–38; Bowman, "Debt of Islam to Monophysite Syrian Christianity."

6. Islamic sources reflect an awareness of the different Christian traditions like the Melkites, Jacobites, and Nestorians. Although the Qur'an does not name these traditions, it seems to reference them indirectly, noting the divisions among the Christians (Q 6:159).

7. Some modern scholars seem to agree with these views. They argue for a later

After the seventh-century conquests and the establishment of the Islamic caliphate, Christian-Muslim interactions intensified, as Christians lived as subaltern or secondary members in the caliphate.[8] Christian-Muslim interreligious engagements produced theological debates and literary exchanges.[9] In such a context, Christians responded polemically to the Islamic theological critiques. In their responses, Christians utilized their rich apologetic heritage, which was developed over the centuries out of their engagements with non-Christian interlocutors, as well as in their intra-Christian debates.

The earliest Christian apologetic texts of Christian-Muslim dialogues were Syriac works.[10] Two examples include the unknown account of debate of the West Syriac patriarch John Sedra (d. 648)[11] with a Muslim emir in 644, and the early work of the dialogue of the East Syriac monk of Beth Hale with a Muslim noble from the early eighth century. A later work from the same century is the famous debate between the East Syriac patriarch Timothy I (d. 823)[12] and the Abbasid Caliph al-Mahdī (d. 785) in 781.[13] Notably, Timothy also mentions his encounters with other Muslim religious debaters in the royal court, including an Aristotelian philosopher.

Christians also responded to Islam by developing theological treatises in Syriac, Greek, and Arabic that had the Islamic context and/or Muslim audience in mind. The East Syriac Theodore Bar Koni (ca. 792)[14] wrote in his theological training manual, *The Scholion*, a peda-

---

influence in the early-eighth-century context of the Fertile Crescent, proposing a Syrian-Palestine origin for Muhammad, Islam, and the Qur'an as a Christian heretical movement, an argument that has gained some acceptance. Griffith, "Mansur Family and Saint John of Damascus," 38–43; Griffith, *Church in the Shadow*, 40–42; Brock et al., eds., *Gorgias Encyclopedic Dictionary*, 219–20; Thomas and Roggema, eds., *Christian-Muslim Relations*, 1:295–301.

8. Levy-Rubin, *Non-Muslims in the Early Islamic Empire*.

9. For a comprehensive bibliographical survey, see Thomas et al., eds., *Christian-Muslim Relations*, 4 vols.

10. Brock et al., eds., *Gorgias Encyclopedic Dictionary*, 221–22; Griffith, *Church in the Shadow*, 35–38, 45–48; Meri, ed., *Medieval Islamic Civilization*, 393–94.

11. Brock et al., eds., *Gorgias Encyclopedic Dictionary*, 221, 477; Thomas and Roggema, eds. *Christian-Muslim Relations*, 1:782–85.

12. Brock et al., eds., *Gorgias Encyclopedic Dictionary*, 221, 414–15; Thomas and Roggema, eds. *Christian-Muslim Relations*, 1:515–31.

13. For additional examples, see Bertaina, *Christian and Muslim Dialogues*.

14. Brock et al., eds., *Gorgias Encyclopedic Dictionary*, 221, 405–6; Thomas and Roggema, eds. *Christian-Muslim Relations*, 1:343–46.

gogical chapter (chapter 10) that deals with the theological objections of Muslims in the form of a question and answer between a master and a disciple. Other authors would follow, producing a plethora of apologetic treatises, like Nonnus of Nisibis (d. 861),[15] and Dionysius bar Salibi (d. 1171),[16] just to mention two. Many of these Syriac works were translated into Arabic and circulated widely.

At the same time, other Christians, including Syriac-speaking Christians, produced similar works in Arabic.[17] The anonymous Arabic treatise *On the Triune Nature of God* is one of such early works of eighth century that aimed to defend the Trinitarian view of God. Such literary productions continued in later decades by different theologians such as the Melkite Theodore Abu Qurrah (d. ca. 830),[18] the West Syriac Ḥabīb Abū Rā'ita (d. ca. 850),[19] and the East Syriac ʿAmmār al-Baṣrī (fl. ca. 850).[20] Such participation was an ongoing part of Christian interreligious exchange with Muslims for the next few centuries, as is seen in the works of Ḥunayn ibn Iṣḥāq (d. 873),[21] Yaḥyā ibn 'Adī (d. 974),[22] Elias of Nisibis (d. 1046),[23] and Paul of Antioch (fl. 1200),[24] to name few.

The Christian-Muslim theological engagements challenged Islamic religious views, beliefs, and practices, which in turn demanded that Muslims defend their faith. It also helped them to define and refine their own beliefs and theological studies. This led to the formation of Islamic theological views and schools such as the Iraqi school of the Mutazilites in the eighth century. Furthermore, the Christian apologetic responses

15. Brock et al., eds., *Gorgias Encyclopedic Dictionary*, 221, 313; Thomas and Roggema, eds. *Christian-Muslim Relations*, 1:743–45.

16. Brock et al., eds., *Gorgias Encyclopedic Dictionary*, 221, 126–27; Thomas and Mallett, eds. *Christian-Muslim Relations*, 3:665–670.

17. Griffith, *Church in the Shadow*, 53–62.

18. Brock et al., eds., *Gorgias Encyclopedic Dictionary*, 221, 403–405; Thomas and Roggema, eds. *Christian-Muslim Relations*, 1:439–564.

19. Brock et al., eds., *Gorgias Encyclopedic Dictionary*, 221; Thomas and Roggema, eds. *Christian-Muslim Relations*, 1:567–81.

20. Brock et al., eds., *Gorgias Encyclopedic Dictionary*, 221; Thomas and Roggema, eds. *Christian-Muslim Relations*, 1:604–10.

21. Brock et al., eds., *Gorgias Encyclopedic Dictionary*, 221, 205–6; Thomas and Roggema, eds. *Christian-Muslim Relations*, 1:768–79.

22. Brock et al., eds., *Gorgias Encyclopedic Dictionary*, 221, 429–30; Thomas and Mallett, eds. *Christian-Muslim Relations*, 2:390–438.

23. Brock et al., eds., *Gorgias Encyclopedic Dictionary*, 221, 143; Thomas and Mallett, eds. *Christian-Muslim Relations*, 2:727–41.

24. Thomas and Mallett, eds. *Christian-Muslim Relations*, 4:78–82.

to Islamic critiques exposed the Muslims to a well-attested and ancient stock of Christian apologetic arguments and modes of debate that used Greek rational-philosophical augments. Eventually, Muslims needed, acquired, and adopted such tools in their interreligious engagements with Christians and internal debates among Muslims. This led them to create their own dialectic-apologetic reasoning and philosophical theology, *ʿilm al-Kalām*.[25] This is evident in the anti-Christian polemic works of the Muʿtazilī *mutakallimoun* Abū Mūsā al-Murḍār (d. ca. 840), Abū al-Hudhayl al-ʿAllāf (d. ca. 840), Abū ʿIsā al-Warrāq (d. ca. 860), and ʿAbd al-Jabbār (d. 1025), to name a few.[26] Christian interlocutors of the early Islamic era participated in formulating Islamic theology and apology, as well as their diverse schools and intellectual tools.

In addition to theology, Eastern Christian religious practices may also have shaped Islamic religious practices.[27] Christians religious practices were known to early Muslims, either in their immediate context of Arabia or out of the pre-Islamic Arab trade travel and interactions with Christians of the Fertile Crescent region and Ethiopia. Thus, we find that certain Islamic religious practices resemble their Christian counterparts from the inception of Islam.

For example, Eastern Christian prayer styles, especially among the desert fathers, which involved bowing and prostration, resemble the Islamic prayer style of *sujūd* or *rak'a*.[28] Oriental Christian churches have canonical hours of prayer that divide the day into fixed times of prayers at regular intervals. This may have contributed to the defining of the daily Islamic prayer schedule (five prayer times a day).[29] Additionally, having a prayer direction, often toward the east in Eastern Christianity, seems to have impacted the Islamic concept of *qibla*.[30] Given that fasting is another

25. Griffith, *Church in the Shadow*, 18–20, 62–63, 75–92, 106–28; Gutas, *Greek Thought, Arabic Culture*, 69–74; Taylor, "Philosophy," 532–35; Corbin, *History of Islamic Philosophy*, 105–12; Shah, "Trajectories in the Development in Islamic Theology, 438–41; Cook, "Origins of Kalam."

26. Thomas and Roggema, eds. *Christian-Muslim Relations*, 1:544–49, 611–13, 695–701; and Thomas and Mallett, eds., *Christian-Muslim Relations*, 594–10.

27. Jenkins, *Lost History of Christianity*, 37–38.

28. Jenkins, *Lost History of Christianity*, 195; Tottoli, "Muslim Attitudes towards Prostration"; Dalrymple, *From the Holy Mountain*, 105.

29. Heinz, "Origins of Muslim Prayer," 115, 123, 125, 133, 141–42.

30. One should also note the Jewish influence on Islamic prayer rituals. Jews faced Jerusalem in their prayers, which was the direction of early Muslims' prayers before it was changed to Mecca. Further, Muslims, like Jews, have ritual washing (*withu'*) before performing prayers.

shared aspect of Islamic and Christian religious practice, it can be hypothesized that the annual Islamic period of fasting (Ramadan) might be rooted in the annual Christian fast of Lent.[31] Finally, the Islamic idea of *jihad* (i.e., struggle and suffering for God/faith), and more particularly the concept of *shahada* as "dying for God" as well as "declaration of faith," has a clear corollary in Christian thought and language in the terms "witnessing" and "martyrdom," especially in relation to Syriac Christian vocabulary (Syr. *sahedota*).[32]

Notably, the conceptual and linguistic impact of Syriac on Islamic terminology is seen in other terms such as *salat* (prayer), *sabbiḥ* (ascribe glory), *tazakka* (seek purity), *'abd* (worship), *surah* (Syr. *surta*), *furqān* (Syr. *purqana*, salvation), *qar'a* (read), and even *Qur'an*. More importantly, the formulaic Islamic statement in Arabic, the *Bismallah* (*Bism'llah al-Rahman al-Rahim*, "In the name of God, the Merciful, the Compassionate") is most likely derived from the Syriac *Beshma Rahmana Rahim* ("In the name of God, the Merciful, the Beloved").[33]

INTELLECTUAL NON-RELIGIOUS CONTRIBUTION (PHILOSOPHY, MEDICINE, AND OTHER SCIENCES)

The Christian presence within the Islamic milieu created multiple points of contact between Christians and Muslims, resulting in contributions to the society and context around them. This was not limited to religion but included other intellectual fields. The most notable engagement and influence happened in Baghdad during the Golden Age of Islamic civilization in the early Abbasid period of the eighth through eleventh centuries.[34] During these centuries, Christian intellectuals played a crucial role in developing their world, serving as physicians, pharmacists, philosophers, logicians, mathematicians, astrologists, scribes, copyists, and translators, as well as theologians and apologists. Such individuals, especially Syriac-speaking Christians (which included members of the Church of the East [i.e., "Nestorians"] or the Syrian Orthodox Church

31. Jenkins, *Lost History of Christianity*, 37, 194–95; Chandler, *Pilgrims of Christ on the Muslim Road*, 88.

32. Wicker, *Witnesses to Faith*, 25–26.

33. Bowman, "Debt of Islam," 213, 215.

34. Brock et al., eds., *Gorgias Encyclopedic Dictionary*, 221–22; Meri, ed., *Medieval Islamic Civilization*, 826–28; Griffith, *Church in the Shadow*, 17–18, 106–28; Griffith, "Christianity's Historic Roots"; Gutas, *Greek Thought*.

[i.e., "Jacobites"]), were at the heart of the rise of Islamic civilization in this era with rich contributions.

Prominent among the Christian contributions to the advancement of Islamic civilization was their monumental role in the Greco-Arabic translation movement during the eighth to tenth centuries. In this project, mainly Greek, but also Syriac, Pahlavi (Persian), and Sanskrit (Hindu) works from the Hellenistic and Persian worlds were translated by leading Christians into Arabic, either directly or via Syriac. Such a movement not only brought a variety of ancient intellectual heritages into the Islamic world,[35] but also set the ground for new intellectual developments and productions within the Islamic context. This in turn impacted medieval Europe, and then the rest of the modern world in the following centuries.

The involvement of Christians in the Abbasid translation movement was the result of their earlier engagements with the Hellenistic intellectual heritage in their own Greco-Syriac translation movement in the pre-Islamic era.[36] Starting in the fourth century, Syriac-speaking intellectuals translated Greek Christian religious literature, which developed their translation infrastructure and techniques. They also translated nonreligious material from the Hellenistic heritage, including philosophy and medicine, offering a Semitic vocabulary for the Greek terminologies. At the same time, they were producing their own Syriac original works in multiple disciplines, which would be translated into Arabic during the early Abbasid era.[37]

In the pre-Islamic era, Syriac-speaking Christians, who established and were part of multiple schools and centers of learning and translation, such as the School of Nisibis (fifth century),[38] the School of Edessa (fourth

35. It seems that the entire non-literary and non-historical Greek works were translated. This includes astrology, alchemy, and other occult sciences; arithmetic, geometry, astronomy, and music theory; philosophy (metaphysics, ethics, physics, zoology, botany, logic); health sciences (medicine, pharmacology, veterinary sciences); military science; and wisdom literature. Griffith, *Church in the Shadow*, 106–8; Gutas, *Greek Thought*, 1–3. 136–38; Taylor, "Philosophy," 535–40; Brentjes and Morrison, "Sciences in Islamic Societies," 565–71; Bulliet, "Muslim Societies and the Natural World," 213–15; Watt, "Eastward and Westward Transmissions, 63–76.

36. Brock et al., eds., *Gorgias Encyclopedic Dictionary*, 180–81.

37. Brock et al., eds., *Gorgias Encyclopedic Dictionary*, 221–22; Griffith, *Church in the Shadow*, 17–18, 106–28; Griffith, "Christianity's Historic Roots," 29–60; Brock, *Syriac Perspectives on Late Antiquity*, ch. 5, "From Antagonism to Assimilation: Syriac Attitudes to Greek Learning."

38. The early version of the School of Nisibis was founded by Bishop Jacob of Nisibis around 350, then re-established after the permanent closure of the School of Edessa

century),[39] and the School of Jundishapur (third century),[40] played a major role in preserving and disseminating Greek intellectual heritage.[41] These were important learning centers of theology, philosophy, medicine, and other sciences. Some of these had medical care centers (hospitals and hospices), often established and led by Syriac Christians,[42] like the hospital in Edessa[43] and the *bimaristan*[44] of Jundishapur.[45] Other Christian intellectual centers existed throughout the ancient Near East,

---

in 489 by Emperor Zeno (d. 491). It was also closed earlier in 431. Brock et al., eds., *Gorgias Encyclopedic Dictionary*, 311; Reinink, "'Edessa Grew Dim," 77–89; Jenkins, *Lost History of Christianity*, 77–90.

39. The School of Edessa is also known as the School of Persians in Edessa because it was established by Syriac-speaking Christian scholars who were expelled from Nisibis, among them its director, St. Ephraim the Syrian (d. 373), after its capture by the Persians in 363. Yet, an earlier academic center might have existed in Edessa, possibly dating from the second century CE during the rule of Abgar dynasty. Brock et al., eds., *Gorgias Encyclopedic Dictionary*, 139–40; Drijvers, "School of Edessa," 49–59; Ragab, *Medieval Islamic Hospital*, 15–16; Dols, "Origins of the Islamic Hospital," 372.

40. The city was founded by the Sassanian Shah Shahpur I (d. 271) after his victory over the Roman emperor Valerian in 260. He settled Roman captives in it, including Greek physicians. Later, Syriac Christian, Persian, and Indian physicians settled in it, developing its rich medical heritage. Yet, it was Shahpur II (d. 380) who developed its academy. Brock et al., eds., *Gorgias Encyclopedic Dictionary*, 72; Dols, "Origins of the Islamic Hospital," 367–68.

41. Griffith, *Church in the Shadow*, 113; Reinink, "Edessa Grew Dim"; Gutas, *Greek Thought*, 13–14; Ragab, *Medieval Islamic Hospital*, 15–16; Dols, "Origins of the Islamic Hospital," 366–68; Corbin, *History of Islamic Philosophy*, 15; Kessel, "Syriac Medicine," 441; Hunter, "Transmission of Greek Philosophy," 225–41.

42. The connection of the Middle East to medical institutions that provided collective medical care came from the Byzantian context. St. Leontius of Antioch (d. 358) may have been the first person to build a *xenodoocheion*, doing so in the middle of the fourth century. Other followed such as Eustathius of Sebaste (d. 377), St. Basil (d. 379), and John Chrysostom (d. 404). This continued in the followng centuries. Ragab, *Medieval Islamic Hospital*, 12–13; Bonner et al., *Poverty and Charity in Middle Eastern Contexts*; 96; Horden, "Earliest Hospitals in Byzantium," 365–70; Miller, "Byzantine Hospitals," 54–55.

43. St. Ephraim may have established a hospice and medical care center for the poor and homeless in the city around 370. Later, the Syriac bishop Rabbula of Edessa (d. 435) created a permanent hospital there.

44. This is a Persian name, which means "House of Ill," and it was used subsequently by the Arabs for all their teaching hospitals in Baghdad, Damascus, and Cairo. Notably, Michael Dols argues for the lack of evidence of such a center until the Islamic era. Dols, "Origins of the Islamic Hospital"; Ragab, *Medieval Islamic Hospital*, 18–19; Bonner et al., *Poverty and Charity*, 96.

45. The School of Jundishapur also had an astronomical observatory, like one in Kusumapura in northern India.

like in Merv, Nishapur,[46] and Seleucia-Ctesiphon,[47] besides those in Dayr Qunna (south of Baghdad), al-Hira, and Harran (formerly known as Carrhae).[48] Eventually, at the end of the Sassanian period and during the early Islamic era, these schools became important learning centers, which would shape Islamic intellectualism.[49]

In this intellectual environment, Syriac-speaking Christians were heavily influenced by the Greek Hippocratic-Galenic medical and Aristotelian-Neoplatonic philosophical traditions of Athens and Alexandria, a reality that would later shape Islamic intellectualism.[50] In Alexandria, the West Syriac philosopher and theologian John Philoponos (d. ca. 575)[51] studied in the school of the Neoplatonist Ammonius. One of his students was the Edessan West Syriac, and later Melkite priest, physician, and translator Sergius of Resh'ayna (d. 536).[52] He was one of the first links between the Aristotelian-Neoplatonic school of Alexandria and the Syriac-speaking context of North Syria and Mesopotamia. He is known for some of the earliest translations of medicinal, astronomical, and philosophical sources into Syriac[53] as well as the composition of his own works, including in theology.[54]

With time, the number of Syriac Christians who were engaged with Greek intellectual heritage rose significantly while this heritage was neglected in Byzantium, especially after the closing the School of Athens in

46. A medical school was built here by some of the scholars who left Edessa after the closing of its school by Emperor Zeno (d. 491) in 489.

47. The building of hospitals by East-Syriacs continued even in later centuries, such as the one built in Seleucia-Ctesiphon out the raised funds by Patriarch Timothy I (d. 823). It might have been a renovation project of a fifth-century hospital. rock et al., eds., *Gorgias Encyclopedic Dictionary*, 365; Ragab, *Medieval Islamic Hospital*, 16–19; Dols, "Origins of the Islamic Hospital," 374; Bonner et al., *Poverty and Charity*, 96–97; Pormann and Savage-Smith, *Medieval Islamic Medicine*, 21.

48. For Harran see Brock et al., eds., *Gorgias Encyclopedic Dictionary*, 191–92.

49. Khalidi and Dajani, "Facets from the Translation Movement," 569–76.

50. Kessel, "Syriac Medicine," 423, 441; Corbin, *History of Islamic Philosophy*, 15.

51. Brock et al., eds., *Gorgias Encyclopedic Dictionary*, 231.

52. Brock et al., eds., *Gorgias Encyclopedic Dictionary*, 181, 282, 366; Kessel, "Syriac Medicine," 423, 439–41; Corbin, *History of Islamic Philosophy*, 15; Pormann and Savage-Smith, *Medieval Islamic Medicine*, 18–19.

53. He translated Aristotle's *Categories*, Porphyry's *Isagoge*, twenty-six works by Galen, twelve by Hippocrates, and part of the *Geoponica*, an encyclopedia on agriculture compiled by Cassianus Bassus.

54. Christians active translation and preservation the Greek works was also driven by the severing of relations with the Greek context of the Byzantian Empire out of the christological controversies of the fifth century.

529 by Justinian I (d. 565). Among the East Syriac intellectuals, Paul the Philosopher, also known as Paul the Persian (d. ca. 578), was a Christian Aristotelian philosopher.[55] Educated in the School of Nisibis, Paul produced several theological and philosophical works, possibly in Syriac and Middle Persian.[56]

East Syriac physicians,[57] who were influenced by Greek medical heritage,[58] dominated the schools of Middle Eastern academic institutions. This was due to the fact that instruction was in Syriac, cultivating an intellectual environment like that of the ancient Greek schools. Greek works were also translated into Persian (Pahlavi), especially during the sixth century, making available Greek mathematics, astrology, and alchemy.[59] Indian knowledge, especially in mathematics, astronomy, medicine, and surgery,[60] was also brought into this milieu by Christian doctors from India with Indian physicians and texts. Their openness to other sources of knowledge eventually allowed them to integrate the different intellectual traditions, creating their own Syriac heritage. This heritage not only impacted the Persian-Islamic and the Western worlds, but it was also taken to Armenia, Central Asia, and China.[61] Moreover, Syriac in-

55. Paul later converted to Zoroastrianism. Brock et al., eds., *Gorgias Encyclopedic Dictionary*, 324–25; Gutas, *Greek Thoughts*, 20–21; Griffith, *Church in the Shadow*, 110–13; Brock, "From Antagonism to Assimilation," 17–34.

56. His literary production includes one philosophical work dedicated to Shah Khosrow I (d. 578), who was known for his interest in Greek philosophy.

57. Patriarch Timothy I notes in a letter to his friend Sergius, who was a physician and the metropolitan of Khuzistan, that he is sending one of his students to study with him at Jundishapur. Ragab, *Medieval Islamic Hospital*, 18–19. Dols, "Origins of the Islamic Hospital," 368, 373.

58. Mainly, Hippocratic and Galenic-type medicine, which was translated into Syriac. Ragab, *Medieval Islamic Hospital*, 25–26; Dols, "Origins of the Islamic Hospital," 368.

59. Emperor Justinian closed the Platonic Academy at Athens in 529, and after their exile some of its members went to Harran and from there to Jundishapur under the patronage of Shah Khusraw Anushirawan I (d. 579). Notably, during the fourth century, commentaries and teaching notes were added to the Greek classics, which seemed to reach Harran and then Jundishapur, and later survived in Arab translations in Baghdad. Dols, "Origins of the Islamic Hospital," 368.

60. Hindu contributions to surgery might go back to the middle of the first millennium BCE. Hindu medicine seems to have been introduced in Jundishapur by an East Syriac physician from Nishapur called "Burzuyah," who on his return from a journey to India brought back several Indian physicians and medical texts. Ragab, *Medieval Islamic Hospital*, 27–29; Dols, "Origins of the Islamic Hospital," 367–88; Gutas, *Greek Thoughts*, 25–26.

61. Kessel, "Syriac Medicine," 451–52.

tellectuals developed new approaches to empirical experimentation and institutional organization,[62] which later were adopted by the Muslims and then introduced to the West.

With the rise of Islam during the seventh century, the intellectual milieu of the Middle East continued flourishing under active Syriac-speaking Christians. Although at first Muslims were less inclined and engaged in non-religious intellectualism, being occupied with religio-political and socioeconomic concerns of establishing and solidifying the caliphate, their Christian subjects played key roles in building an Islamic intellectual civilization. Slowly, Muslims, like the Umayyads (661–750), started investing in collections of books in the fields of medicine, alchemy, and astrology, without establishing systematic translations of such works. They were more concerned with translating works in the fields of state's administration, bureaucracy, politics, and commerce.[63]

In this milieu, Syriac-speaking Christians kept up their intellectual pursuit of knowledge, especially Greek secular heritage, setting the ground for the later flourishing of Islamic intellectualism.[64] Among them was the West Syriac Severus Sebokht (d. 666/667),[65] who was an astronomer, philosopher, mathematician, and bishop of Qenneshre. He is

62. They organized the hospital in new ways, creating outpatient and inpatient departments and wards for different medical specialties such as general medicine, surgery, orthopaedics, and ophthalmology. For details regarding the organization of the medical faculty, see Johna, "Mesopotamian Schools of Edessa and Jundi-Shapur," 627–30.

63. Greek was the *lingua franca* of commerce and administration in Syro-Palestine during the Byzantine and early Islamic eras until the language reform of Caliph 'Abd al-Malik (d. 705). In this context, Christians who mastered Greek language and bureaucratic and mercantile skills were employed by Muslims, as they previously served the Byzantines, a theme we will examine later. Furthermore, it should be noted that the Umayyads' interest wasn't limited to bureaucracy, but other sciences such as astronomy and medicine. Furthermore, they cared about aspects of social-intellectual developments, such as architecture (examined later), which also resulted in the employment of skilful Christians. Caliph al-Walid I (d. 715) is credited with building a hospital in Damascus (although it may only have been a chartable house) and commissioning some translations of Greek works. Ragab, *Medieval Islamic Hospital*, 22–25; Dols, "Origins of the Islamic Hospital," 378; Gutas, *Greek Thoughts*, 15–16, 23–24; Brentjes and Morrison, "Sciences in Islamic Societies," 589–90; Bonner et al., *Poverty and Charity*, 97; Goodman, "Translation of Greek Materials into Arabic," 480–82; Lyons, *House of Wisdom*, 55–77.

64. Watt, "Syriac Philosophy"; Gutas, *Greek Thoughts*, 15–16, 24; Corbin, *History of Islamic Philosophy*, 14–22; Brock, "From Antagonism to Assimilation," 22–27.

65. Brock et al., eds., *Gorgias Encyclopedic Dictionary*, 181, 368; Watt, "Syriac Philosophy," 422–27; Corbin, *History of Islamic Philosophy*, 15; Jenkins, *Lost History of Christianity*, 78.

credited with translation of philosophical works from Middle Persian to Syriac,[66] and composing works on astronomy and Aristotelian logic.[67] Severus's student was the West Syriac patriarch Athanasius of Balad (d. 686/687),[68] who is known for being a scholar and translator of Greek theological and philosophical works. Further, Bishop Jacob of Edessa (d. 708)[69] was a highly educated friend of Athanasius who wrote on many topics, including a handbook of philosophical terms. A younger West Syriac scholar was George, bishop of the Arabs (d. 724).[70] He was a protégé of Athanasius and friend of Jacob, and revised earlier translations of Aristotle's works.

With the rise of the Abbasids in 750 and the establishment of Baghdad as the caliphate's capital in 762, the center of Islamic civilization gravitated toward Baghdad, ushering the Islamic Golden Age.[71] During this age, the Abbasid caliphs and the entire elite of the society moved from passive to active acceptance and endorsement of Greek heritage, as well as Persian, Indian, and Chinese sources of knowledge, establishing a type of multicultural society.[72] The earliest interest was in the field of astrology.[73] Later, professional needs for administrative secretaries, lawyers, engineers, and fiscal administrators increased the interest in these

66. His translations included works of Paul the Philosopher (the Persian).

67. On astronomy: *Treatise on the Astrolabe* and *Treatise on the Constellations.* On logic: *Treatise on Syllogisms.* He is also known for his engagement in intra-Christian debate with Maronite interlocuters at the court of the Umayyad caliph Mu'awiya around 659.

68. Brock et al., eds., *Gorgias Encyclopedic Dictionary*, 46; Thomas and Mallett, eds., *Christian-Muslim Relations*, 4:157–59; Watt, "Syriac Philosophy," 422–27.

69. Brock et al., eds., *Gorgias Encyclopedic Dictionary*, 432–33; Thomas and Roggema, eds., *Christian-Muslim Relations*, 1:226–33; Watt, "Syriac Philosophy," 422–27; Corbin, *History of Islamic Philosophy*, 15.

70. Brock et al., eds., *Gorgias Encyclopedic Dictionary*, 177–78, 181; Watt, "Syriac Philosophy," 422–27; Corbin, *History of Islamic Philosophy*, 15.

71. The rapid advance in learning and spread of papermaking from China which resulted from prisoners of war captured at the Battle of Talas in 751, significantly contributed to the translation movement. Gutas, *Greek Thoughts*, 13; Brentjes and Morrison, "Sciences in Islamic Societies," 591.

72. During the Umayyads (661–750) reign, Greek to Arabic translation were common, but not on the scale of the Abbasid era, and not in the field of philosophy and science. Goodman, "Translation of Greek Materials," 480–84; Gutas, *Greek Thoughts*, 1–26, 121–35. Taylor, "Philosophy," 535–40; Brentjes and Morrison, "Sciences in Islamic Societies," 565–71; Pormann and Savage-Smith, *Medieval Islamic Medicine*, 24–27.

73. Gutas, *Greek Thoughts*, 108–10.

disciplines' literature,[74] as well as interest in scientific materials and knowledge, especially philosophy and medicine.[75]

Notably, al-Manṣūr (d. 775) is credited with starting and funding the translation movement that lasted for two centuries and employed Christians and others as translators, copyists, and bookbinders.[76] Later caliphs continued the project, such al-Mahdī (d. 785), who is known for commissioning the translation of Greek works, which was partially driven by his interest in interreligious engagements and *'ilm al-Kalām*.[77] Further, Hārūn al-Rashīd (d. 809), who was personally interested in Greek scholarship, sent agents to Byzantium to purchase Greek manuscripts, something his son al-Ma'mūn (d. 833) did as well. Al-Ma'mūn (d. 833), who was the greatest Muslim patron of philosophy and sciences, invested significantly in the translation movement.[78] He further developed the famous *Bayt al-Hikmah* (House of Wisdom)[79] as an academic and translation center.[80] The center also had a hospital or medical center

74. Gutas, *Greek Thoughts*, 110–14.

75. Gutas, *Greek Thoughts*, 115–20; Taylor, "Philosophy," 532–63; Morrison, "Sciences in Islamic Societies," 564–639; Haq, "Occult Sciences and Medicine," 640–67.

76. Predominantly, it was concerned with translating Greek works into Arabic, but it also included Syriac, Pahlavi, and Sanskrit texts. Originally, medicine, mathematics, and astronomy were the dominating disciplines, but soon philosophy and other disciplines were included. Gutas, *Greek Thoughts*, 28–60; Brentjes and Morrison, "Sciences in Islamic Societies," 568–69.

77. Gutas, *Greek Thoughts*, 61–74; Brentjes and Morrison, "Sciences in Islamic Societies," 569.

78. Caliph al-Ma'mūn was influenced by the Mu'tazilite movement, a religious philosophy based on logic and reason that sought to combine Greek philosophy and Islamic doctrine. He is known for initiating an Islamic inquisition (*mihna*) that promoted Mu'tazilite ideology, which might be part of his motive. Goodman, "Translation of Greek Materials into Arabic," 484–85; Brentjes and Morrison, "Sciences in Islamic Societies," 569; Gutas, *Greek Thoughts*, 75–104; Hyman et al., eds. *Philosophy in the Middle Ages*, 215–17.

79. Notably, the House of Wisdom in Bagdad became an inspiration for similar institutions through the Islamic world from the Iberian Peninsula to Central Asia. For example, The Fatimids' House of Wisdom (Cairo, Egypt), the Aghlabids' House of Wisdom (Raqqada, Tunisia), The Umayyads' House of Wisdom (Cordoba, Andalusia), and others. Algeriani and Mohadi, "House of Wisdom," 184–85.

80. The House of Wisdom might have been previously established by al-Mansur or al-Rashid as a house for the caliphal private collection of rare books place known as *Khizanat Kutub al-Hikmah* (Storehouse of the Book of Wisdom), yet it was al-Mamun who developed it into a larger center of translation and learning around 832/833. The name of the center has a Persian origin. Gutas, *Greek Thoughts*, 53–60. Brentjes and Morrison, "Sciences in Islamic Societies," 569; Algeriani and Mohadi, "House of Wisdom," 180–81.

attached to it.[81] The first hospital at the center, though, was possibly built by Harun al-Rashid under East Syriac Christian physician supervision.[82]

In this context,[83] Christians,[84] especially Syriac-speaking Christians, had a prominent role in shaping the Abbasid intellectual milieu.[85] Unfortunately, those Christians are rarely known and their contributions are often seen only as hired service for Muslim patrons, without intellectual interest. Instead, they should be highlighted as intellectuals who participated in the rise of Islamic intellectualism in partnership with Muslim thinkers. Those Christians often produced their own original works, although many of their non-religious writings are lost to us. Among them, the Syriac-speaking Christians excelled in philosophy, medicine, and other sciences, working as translators, authors, teachers, and physicians.

Significantly, Syriac-speaking Christians played a prominent role in the field of medicine within the Abbasid caliphate.[86] The East Syriac Bukhtishu' family, which included eight generations of the physicians from Jundishapur, were the most prominent doctors of the Abbasid caliphs, sultans, and viziers between the eighth and eleventh centuries.[87] The

81. Meri, ed., *Medieval Islamic Civilization*, 451; Algeriani and Mohadi, "House of Wisdom," 183; Hyman et al., *Philosophy in the Middle Ages*, 215–16.

82. Bonner et al., *Poverty and Charity*, 97. Later, the Buyid ruler 'Adud al-Dawlah (d. 983) built al-'Adudyyia Hospital. In Egypt, Muhamdad ibn Tughj al-Ikhshid (d. 946) built a hospital in al-Fustat after 935. The Fatimids of Egypt also built a hospital in their new capital, Cairo, in 994. The Ayyubids, under Salah al-Din (d. 1193) also did the same in 1181. The Mamluk ruler al-Mansure Qalawun (d. 1290) built a new one around 1285. In the Levant, Nur al-Din Zanki (d. 1174) built a hospital in Damascus. Around 1180s there was also one in Homs. Ragab, *Medieval Islamic Hospital*, 1–5, 33–37.

83. The interest taken by the Abbasid caliphs in collecting books was imitated by several wealthy elite members of the society who established large and specialized libraries. Gutas, *Greek Thoughts*, 121–35; Brentjes and Morrison, "Sciences in Islamic Societies," 572–78.

84. Some non-Christian Syriac-speaking Sabian scholars of Harran were involved in this movement such as Thabit ibn Qurra (d. 901), who was another trilingual translator into Arabic, as well as an author. Brock et al., eds., *Gorgias Encyclopedic Dictionary*, 399–400; Goodman, "Translation of Greek Material," 485–86; Corbin, *History of Islamic Philosophy*, 17, 125, 150; Gutas, *Greek Thoughts*, 135.

85. Watt, "Syriac Philosophy," 427–29; Kessel, "Syriac Medicine," 451; Griffith, *Church in the Shadow*, 106–8; Gutas, *Greek Thoughts*, 135–41; Goodman, "Translation of Greek Materials," 477–98; Taylor, "Philosophy," 535–40; Brock, "Two Millennia of Christianity in Iraq," 178–80.

86. Brock et al., eds., *Gorgias Encyclopedic Dictionary*, 221–22, 282–83; Griffith, *Church in the Shadow*, 113–14; Gutas, *Greek Thoughts*, 118.

87. Brock et al., eds., *Gorgias Encyclopedic Dictionary*, 169–70, 221–22, 282; Kessel, "Syriac Medicine," 449; Goodman, "Translation of Greek Materials ," 480; Ragab,

earliest of them was the head of Jundishapur School, Jurjis ibn Bukhtishu (d. 769), whom al-Mansur (d. 775) called in 765 to serve as his personal doctor.[88] His son Bukhtishu II (d. 801), who led the hospital at Jundishapur while his father was in Baghdad, was later summoned to come to Baghdad in 787 to treat al-Hadi (d. 786). Similarly, the grandson, Jibril II ibn Bukhtishu' (d. 827/8), was also called to Baghdad by al-Rāshid (d. 809) to become his doctor and to build and lead the city's first hospital. He also served al-Amīn (d. 819) and al-Ma'mūn (d. 833).[89] Jibril II is credited with composing several works in the field of medicine.[90] One of the last of these physicians was Jibril ibn Bukhtishu' III (d. 1006), who served the Buyid ruler 'Adud al-Dawla (d. 983) in Shiraz. He was even sought out by the Fatimid caliph al-Aziz (d. 996) and asked to settle in Cairo, but he declined. His son, 'Ubaydallah (d. 1058), was the last of this family of physicians. He wrote an Arabic medical-philosophical dictionary, creating a genre that had not existed before.[91]

The Bukhtishu family was not the only East Syriac family that occupied such a role.[92] There was also the Masawayh family, whose most notable member was Yuhanna ibn Masawayh (d. 857),[93] the son of a pharmacist and physician from Jundishapur, called Georgios, and father of the physician Mikhail. Yuhanna served four caliphs[94] and was a director of the hospital in Baghdad and the House of Wisdom, a famous

---

Medieval Islamic Hospital, 27–33; Dols, "Origins of the Islamic Hospital," 368–69; Bonner et al., *Poverty and Charity*, 97–98; Jenkins, *Lost History of Christianity*, 78; Haq, "Occult Sciences and Medicine," 662–63; Pormann, and Savage-Smith, *Medieval Islamic Medicine*, 19.

88. Syriac-speaking Christian doctors served as royal court physicians during the Persian Empire. Goodman, "Translation of Greek Materials," 480; Ragab, *Medieval Islamic Hospital*, 16–20; Dols, "Origins of the Islamic Hospital," 374.

89. Meri, ed., *Medieval Islamic Civilization*, 473.

90. His works are based on commissioned translations of Galen's Greek works. Brock et al., eds., *Gorgias Encyclopedic Dictionary*, 169–70; Ragab, *Medieval Islamic Hospital*, 4–5, 26–27; Dols, "Origins of the Islamic Hospital," 368–69; Elgood, *Medical History of Persia*, 173.

91. Goodman, "Translation of Greek Materials," 480.

92. The famous historian of Arabian medicine Ibn Abi Usaibia (1203–1270) devotes a whole chapter of his book *The Classes of Physicians* to the biographies of Syriac-speaking physicians who flourished during the Abbasid dynasty.

93. He was known in the West as Janus Damascenus or Mesue the Elder. Corbin, *History of Islamic Philosophy*, 16; Ragab, *Medieval Islamic Hospital*, 31; Bonner et al., *Poverty and Charity*, 97; Haq, "Occult Sciences and Medicine," 663.

94. Al-Ma'mūn, al-Mu'tasim, al-Wāthiq, and al-Mutawakkil.

ophthalmologist, and author.[95] In addition to these families, there were notable East Syriac physicians.[96] One such prominent figure is Hunayn ibn Ishaq (d. 873), a student of ibn Masawahy and the physician of al-Mutawakkil (d. 861), whom we will examine later. Furthermore, Ḥunayn's student 'Isa ibn 'Ali (ninth century) was the physician of caliph al-Mu'tamid (d. 892), and is credited with authoring Arabic works in the field of medicine.[97]

In philosophy, Syriac-speaking Christians were a leading force in introducing Greek heritage to the Islamic world. The East Syriac patriarch Timothy I (d. 823) translated Aristotle's *Topics* upon the request of al-Mahdī (d. 785).[98] The translation involved the Christian secretary of the governor of Mosul, Abū Nūḥ, as well as other Greek-speaking Christians.[99] Notably, Timothy highlights that his access to Aristotle's works came from the West Syriac monastery of Mar Matta, possibly using the translation of patriarch Athanasius of Balad (d. 686/687).[100] Al-Mahdī's astrologer and military advisor, the Maronite Theophilus of Edessa (d. 785),[101] wrote several works in Arabic, which were based on Greek sources.[102] His student Stephanus the Philosopher (d. after 800) was known for a treatise on astrology.[103]

Another East Syriac churchman was the metropolitan 'Abdishu' bar Bahriz (fl. ninth century).[104] He was a legal scholar, logician, and translator who is credited with translating Greek works for al-Ma'mūn (d. 833),

95. He was a known for his anatomical works, possibly more than forty in total, including a first systematic treatise on ophthalmology, titled *Daghal al-'ain* (Disorder of the Eye), as well for performing dissections on apes.

96. For a list of medical doctors during the Abbasid era, see Elgood, *Medical History of Persia*, 58–301.

97. Brock et al., eds., *Gorgias Encyclopedic Dictionary*, 53–54. His works were on using animal organs and the science of poisons.

98. Timothy also utilized Greek philosophy when he engaged in an interreligious dialogue with a Muslim Aristotelian philosopher at the court of the caliph.

99. Gutas, *Greek Thoughts*, 61–69.

100. Brock et al., eds., *Gorgias Encyclopedic Dictionary*, 414–15; Watt, "Syriac Philosophy," 424.

101. Thomas and Roggema, eds., *Christian-Muslim Relations*, 1:305–8.

102. Theophilus also translated into Syriac works by Aristotle, Galen, and Homer.

103. Brock et al., eds., *Gorgias Encyclopedic Dictionary*, 409–10.

104. He is known in Arabic sources by his given name, Habib. Like Timothy, he was also an apologist, and wrote a *Treatise on the Unity and Trinity of God*. Brock et al., eds., *Gorgias Encyclopedic Dictionary*, 2–3; Thomas and Roggema, eds., *Christian-Muslim Relations*, 1:550–52.

with commentaries and summaries,[105] as well as translating works from Syriac to Arabic by commission of the Ṭāhirī governor Tahir ibn Ḥusayn (d. 822) and the physician Jibril ibn Bakhtashu'. He also produced his own philosophical treatises, which were commissioned by al-Ma'mūn. Additionally, the Melkite bishop of Harran, Theodore Abū Qurrah (d. ca. 830)[106] was also known for translating philosophical works[107] for Tahir ibn Husayn.[108]

The connection of Christian intellectuals with the Abbasids and their governors, especially that of al-Ma'mūn's and Ṭāhir ibn Ḥusayn's, is further attested to by the East Syriac physician, philosopher, and translator Job of Edessa (d. ca. 835). He served as physician to al-Ma'mūn and Tahir consecutively.[109] He is known for translating Greek medical and philosophical works as well as writing his own works on natural philosophy, anatomy, medicine, and astronomy, to note a few disciplines. His works were known and referenced by later Muslim scientists, such as al-Khwarizmī (d. 833) and al-Rāzī (d. 925).

However, the most notable of the Christian intellectuals of the era is Ḥunayn ibn Isḥāq al-'ibadi (d. 873).[110] He was a philosopher, physician, theologian, and translator who served as the chief doctor of al-Mutawakkil (d. 861) and as head of the House of Wisdom.[111] He was the most productive translator of his era, translating over one hundred works of philosophy, astronomy, mathematics, medicine, magic. and

105. On Aristotle's "Categories" and "On Interpretation."

106. Brock et al., eds., *Gorgias Encyclopedic Dictionary*, 403–5; Thomas and Roggema, eds., *Christian-Muslim Relations*, 1:439–564.

107. Pseudo-Aristotelian treatise *De virtutibus animae*.

108. For all three persons above: Griffith, *Church in the Shadow*, 107, 113; Brock, "Two Letters of the Patriarch Timothy," 233–46; Gutas, *Greek Thoughts*, 61.

109. Brock et al., eds., *Gorgias Encyclopedic Dictionary*, 225–226.

110. The term *al-'ibadi* comes from *'ibad al-Masih* (Servants or Devotee of Christ), which was *nisba* (nickname) of the Christians of the city of Hira, like Hunayn ibn Ishaq. Hunyan is known in the West as Johannitius, a son a pharmacist, who studied in Jundishapur, traveling widely within the caliphate and Byzantium, acquiring knowledge and manuscripts, and mastering four languages: Arabic, Syriac, Greek, and Persian. Brock et al., eds., *Gorgias Encyclopedic Dictionary*, 205–6, 221–22, 282; Thomas and Roggema, eds., *Christian-Muslim Relations* , 1:768–79; Meri, ed., *Medieval Islamic Civilization*, 336–37, 610, 826–28; Watt, "Syriac Philosophy," 427–29; Goodman, "Translation of Greek Materials," 487–91; Taylor, "Philosophy," 535–39; Griffith, *Church in the Shadow*, 119–22; Selin, ed., *Encyclopaedia of the History*, 611.

111. Corbin, *History of Islamic Philosophy*, 15–16.

oneiromancy (the interpretation of dreams).[112] These translations became a main source of future Islamic intellectual developments. He established a method of translation that was widely used afterward, working with other translators such as ʿIsā ibn Yaḥyā[113] and Istifan ibn Basil.[114] His translation school included his son Ishaq (d. 910)[115] and nephew Hubaysh Ibn al-Ḥasan al-A'sam.[116]

Ḥunayn was a prolific author who is credited with writing about thirty-six books, of which more than twenty were in the field of medicine.[117] He is also known for his philosophical works.[118] He has several works on Greek and Syriac grammar and lexicon. Ḥunayn was an active apologist, who produced works in the field of philosophy of religion.[119] He was also in involved in philosophical (Aristotelian logic) Christian-Muslim dialogues with Muslim astronomer Abū ʿIsā Yaḥyā ibn al-Munajjim (d. 888), who corresponded with Hunayn ibn Ishaq, inviting him to embrace Islam. Ḥunayn responded to this invitation by philosophically arguing the case for Christianity.[120] Like Ḥunayn, the Melkite physician,

112. This includes works by Galen, Hippocrates, Plato, Aristotle, Dioscorides, and Ptolemy. Kessel, "Syriac Medicine," 442; Griffith, *Church in the Shadow*, 120.

113. Meri, ed., *Medieval Islamic Civilization*, 826–28.

114. Notably, he is credited with translating Plato's *Timaeus*, Aristotle's *Metaphysics*, and the Bible (the Greek Old Testament—LXX). In the medical field, Hunayn and his translation school translated the entire medical curriculum of Alexandria, which was followed in Jundishapur. He is credited with translating works such as Galen's *Pharmacopoeia*, *Anatomy of the Veins and Arteries*, *Anatomy of the Muscles*, and *Anatomy of the Nerves*. He also translated *Questions on Medicines*, which is taken from Galen's *Art of Physic* as well as *De materia Medica*, which is a pharmaceutical work. Johna, "Hunayn ibn-Ishaq," 497–99; Jaber, "Landscape of Translation Movement."

115. He is known for translating Euclid's *Elements* and Ptolemy's *Almagest*. Meri, ed., *Medieval Islamic Civilization*, 826–28; Watt, "Syriac Philosophy," 427–29.

116. Notably, Hubaysh is also credited with translating Galen's medical works into Syriac, possibly from Greek and Arabic, at the request of the East Syriac physician ibn Masawayh (d. 857), who was Hunayn's previous medical teacher. Brock et al., eds., *Gorgias Encyclopedic Dictionary*, 27–28; Meri, ed., *Medieval Islamic Civilization*, 826–28; Watt, "Syriac Philosophy," 427–29; Cooper, "Isḥāq ibn Ḥunayn," 578.

117. Kessel, "Syriac Medicine," 443–44; Notably, *Book of the Ten Treaties of the Eye* in ophthalmology, *The Rules of Inflexion According to the System of the Greeks* in Arabic grammar.

118. In *Kitāb adab al-falāsifa* (aka *Nawādir al-falāsifa*), he argues for philosophy as way of life, not merely a tool for intellectual inquiry and discourse. Griffith, *Church in the Shadow*, 121.

119. See his work *How to Grasp Religion*, dealing with themes such as "true religion" and "the existence of God."

120. Griffith, *Church in the Shadow*, 86, 120–21.

philosopher, astronomer, mathematician, and translator Qusṭā ibn Lūqā (d. 912/3)[121] is known for his translations,[122] and for authoring more than sixty works.[123] He also engaged in Christian-Muslim dialogues and responded to ibn al-Munajjam's *Letter* to Ḥunayn, addressed to the astronomer's son.[124]

A new generation of Christian intellectuals followed in the tenth century. One of them was the East Syriac philosopher, physician, and theologian Abū Bishr Mattā ibn Yūnus al-Kunnā'ī (d. 940),[125] who is famous for establishing the Baghdad school of Aristotelian philosophy, which included notable Muslims. In addition to translation works, he wrote several philosophical commentaries, which unfortunately are lost now. Likewise, his East Syriac colleague, Yuhanna ibn Haylān (d. 910),[126] was an active philosopher during that time. Abū Bishr's student was the West Syriac Yaḥyā ibn 'Adī al-Takrītī (d. 974),[127] the leading Aristotelian philosopher of Baghdad in the tenth century, who had Muslim students. Yaḥyā was a professional translator, scribe, and bookseller who translated multiple books of logic and philosophy. His publications include more than 130 items in philosophy, logic, metaphysics, ethics, physics, mathematics, and theology.

During this time, the translation movement paved the way to interpretation and composition of new philosophical works, and Yahya became a leading proponent of this movement. With Muslim colleagues, he

121. Qusta is known for his traveling and acquisition of Greek works from the Byzantine Empire, which were translated to Arabic in Baghdad for the library of the caliphate. Thomas and Mallett, eds., *Christian-Muslim Relations*, 2:147–53; Meri, ed., *Medieval Islamic Civilization*, 826–28; Goodman, "Translation of Greek Materials," 491–92; Griffith, *Church in the Shadow*, 120–21; Worrell, "Qusta Ibn Luqa"; Siraisi, *Medicine and the Italian Universities*, 134.

122. These include works in astronomy, mathematics, mechanics, and natural science.

123. His works include commentaries on Euclid and a treatise on the Armillary Sphere. His work *On the Difference between the Spirit and the Soul* was listed in "Books to Be Read" and studied in the Paris Master of Art faculty in thirteenth century. Burns, "Faculty of Arts," 758.

124. Griffith, *Church in the Shadow*, 86, 120–21.

125. Meri, ed., *Medieval Islamic Civilization*, 826–28; Watt, "Syriac Philosophy," 429; Corbin, *History of Islamic Philosophy*, 16, 492.

126. Brock et al., eds., *Gorgias Encyclopedic Dictionary*, 221–22; Griffith, *Church in the Shadow*, 114; Gutas, *Greek Thoughts*, 14.

127. Brock et al., eds., *Gorgias Encyclopedic Dictionary*, 221–22, 429–30; Thomas and Mallett, eds., *Christian-Muslim Relation*, 2:390–438; Meri, ed., *Medieval Islamic Civilization*, 377, 826–28; Watt, "Syriac Philosophy," 429; Corbin, *History of Islamic Philosophy*, 16, 492–93; Griffith, *Church in the Shadow*, 71, 122–25; Taylor, "Philosophy," 539–40.

was a leading defender of the use of reason during a period of conflict between the philosophers and traditional Muslim religious scholars in tenth century. Further, he was a participant in Christian theological discourse and interreligious discussion.[128] Yaḥyā ibn ʿAdī also wrote about public morality, commenting on themes such as sexual abstinence, a life of celibacy, and human happiness. However, he was more of a philosopher and logician than a theologian, devoted to promoting the philosophical life and the value of reason and virtues in life. He explored the idea of how to become *al-Insān al-Kāmil* (perfect human being),[129] seeking to cultivate a sense of common humanity (*al-insāniyyah*) and mutual esteem in his Islamo-Christian milieu.

It is worth noting that medieval Christian thinkers' interest in ethical, moral, and political themes led them to investigate and deal with questions of sadness, happiness, vices, virtues, societal goodness, governance, and harmony, including interreligious relations between different communities in the Islamic world. Such themes that those early Christian intellectuals struggled with would become once again the concern of Christian thinkers in the modern age, as part of the Arab Awakening (al-Nahda) during the nineteenth and twentieth centuries, which will be examined soon.

Another name is the West Syriac theologian, philosopher, and merchant Abū ʿAlī ʿIsā ibn Zurʿa (d. 1008),[130] a student of Ibn ʿAdī. He translated with introductions Greek philosophical works that later Muslims like Ibn Sina (d. 1037) and Ibn Rushd (d. 1198) used, as well as medical works.[131] He wrote some important works on ethics, on the immor-

128. He defended the rationality of Christian doctrines (e.g. the Trinity and the incarnation) in his work *Maqāla fī al-Tawḥīd*. Further, his *Refutation of the Three Sects of the Christians* was a response to Muslim theological critiques such Abū ʿIsā al-Warrāq's (d. c. 862) and Abū Yūsuf ibn Iṣḥaq al-Kindī (d. 866/7) anti-Christian philosophical tracts.

129. See *Reformation of Morals*. He engaged with Christian and Muslim religio-philosophy scholars and ascetics on religion and philosophy.

130. He is known in Latin as Avenzoreth, who traveled to Byzantine for cultural missions. In the West, his contributions are confused sometimes with those of Averroes, Ibn Rushd (d. 1198). Brock et al., eds., *Gorgias Encyclopedic Dictionary*, 429–30; Thomas and Mallett, eds., *Christian-Muslim Relations*, 2:570–74; Meri, ed., *Medieval Islamic Civilization*, 376–77, 826–28; Watt, "Syriac Philosophy," 429; Goodman, "Translation of Greek Materials," 493–94; Taylor, "Philosophy," 539–40; Bertolacci, "Albertus Magnus and 'Avenzoreth,'" especially 376–78.

131. His translations included Aristotelian, pseudo-Aristotelian, Neoplatonic, and Galenic works.

tality of the soul, and on the luminosity of the planets, which did not survive. However, his work in defense of philosophy against the charges of irreligiosity by Muslim scholars of religion has survived.[132] His West Syriac colleague and student, ibn ʿAdi was al-Hasan ibn al-Khammar (d. after 1017),[133] is known for reconciling Christian views with philosophy and applying the latter in service of religion.

A generation younger was the East Syriac priest, theologian, physician, translator, and philosopher Abū al-Faraj ibn al-Ṭayyib (d. 1043),[134] a student of al-Khammar and one of the last members of the translation movement. He worked at the famous ʿAdudiyya Hospital in Baghdad,[135] and served as secretary for two patriarchs. He produced more than forty works in Arabic in a variety of the fields.[136] There was also the Baghdadi physician Ibn Butlan (d. 1066),[137] who produced medical works in Arabic that eventually reached Europe. Like him, the East Syriac Abū ʿAlī Yahyā ibn ʿIsā ibn Jazla al-Baghdādī (d. 1100)[138] authored an influential medical treatise that was translated into Latin in the thirteenth century. Habbatallah ibn Saʿīd ibn al-Tilmidh (d. 1165)[139] was another physician and pharmacist who worked at the ʿAdudiyya Hospital in Baghdad and served al-Mustadī (d. 1180), who complied several medical and pharmaceutical works. Finally, Ibn al-Quff (d. 1286),[140] one of the last Chris-

132. One example is *On the Composite Intellect*. He also produced Christian rational-logical apologetic treatises, some of which were a result of the requests of Muslims and/or responses to their critiques.

133. Thomas and Mallett, eds., *Christian-Muslim Relations*, 2:557–60; Meri, ed., *Medieval Islamic Civilization*, 377, 828; Corbin, *History of Islamic Philosophy*, 16, 493–94.

134. Brock et al., eds., *Gorgias Encyclopedic Dictionary*, 206–7; Thomas and Mallett, eds., *Christian-Muslim Relations*, 2:667–97; Meri, ed., *Medieval Islamic Civilization*, 168; Kessel, "Syriac Medicine," 438; Corbin, *History of Islamic Philosophy*, 16, 494; Taylor, "Philosophy," 539–40.

135. It was built in 987 by the Buyid ruler ʿAdud al-Dawlah (d. 983). Bonner et al., *Poverty and Charity*, 98.

136. Specifically, theology, canon law, medicine, and philosophy. In philosophy, he wrote commentaries on Aristotle's and Porphyry's works, and likewise in medicine, on the works of Hippocrates and Galen. Also, his theological works were many; their impact reached and influenced even Coptic and Ethiopic churches.

137. Kessel, "Syriac Medicine," 438.

138. He later converted to Islam. Meri, ed., *Medieval Islamic Civilization*, 491; Kessel, "Syriac Medicine," 438

139. Cohen claims that he was of Jewish origin. Corbin, *History of Islamic Philosophy*, 177–79; Kessel, "Syriac Medicine," 438.

140. Meri, ed., *Medieval Islamic Civilization*, 347, 783–84; Kessel, "Syriac Medicine," 438.

tian doctors during the late medieval period, contributed to the field of medical surgery.

These Christian intellectuals worked closely with and influenced Muslim thinkers, creating a *Convivencia* in Bagdad, where intellectual interest and passion brought the two communities together, partnering not only in matters of intellectual inquiries, but also in societal concerns such as the ideas of a good life, morality, and virtues. In this context, Muslim scholars such as Abū Yūsuf ibn Isḥāq al-Kindī (d. 865),[141] Abū Bakr ibn Zakariyya al- Rāzī (d. 925),[142] and Abū Naṣr al-Fārābī (d. 950)[143] were students, colleagues, and teachers of Christian intellectuals.[144] For example, al-Fārābī studied with Abū Bishr and Ibn Haylān. At the same time, al-Razī and al-Farabī influenced Yaḥyā ibn ʿAdī. This reciprocal impact of Muslim and Christian thinkers dominated this era and continued later, impacting the next generations of Muslim philosophers like Ibn Sīna (d. 1037),[145] al-Ghazālī (d. 1111),[146] and Ibn Rushd (d. 1198),[147] which in turn shaped the next Christian generation of intellectuals such as Jacob bar Shakko (d. 1241), Bar Hebraeus (d. 1286), and ʿAbdishoʿ bar Brikha (d. 1318) during the later Syriac Renaissance of the eleventh to thirteenth centuries.[148]

During this late Syriac Renaissance, the participation of Christians in the Islamic intellectual civilization continued, not only by what they produced but also through their adoption and learning from the Muslim intellectuals. It is during these centuries that we encounter the West

141. Meri, ed., *Medieval Islamic Civilization*, 431; Corbin, *History of Islamic Philosophy*, 154–58, 364–69; Taylor, "Philosophy," 540–44.

142. Meri, ed., *Medieval Islamic Civilization*, 671–72; Corbin, *History of Islamic Philosophy*, 136–41, 370–77; Taylor, "Philosophy," 44–45.

143. Meri, ed., *Medieval Islamic Civilization*, 247–48; Corbin, *History of Islamic Philosophy*, 158–65, 378–88; Taylor, "Philosophy," 545–48; Hyman et al., *Philosophy in the Middle Ages*, 220–22.

144. Griffith, *Church in the Shadow*, 114–19.

145. Meri, ed., *Medieval Islamic Civilization*, 369–70; Corbin, *History of Islamic Philosophy*, 167–75, 389–404; Taylor, "Philosophy," 548–52; Hyman et al., *Philosophy in the Middle Ages*, 239–43.

146. Meri, ed., *Medieval Islamic Civilization*, 292–93; Corbin, *History of Islamic Philosophy*, 179–86, 424–45; Taylor, "Philosophy," 552–53.

147. Meri, ed., *Medieval Islamic Civilization*, 365–66; Corbin, *History of Islamic Philosophy*, 167–75; Taylor, "Philosophy," 555–60; Hyman et al., *Philosophy in the Middle Ages*, 285–88.

148. Brock et al., eds., *Gorgias Encyclopedic Dictionary*, 350–51.

Syriac Dionysius bar Salibi (d. 1171),[149] a prolific scholar whose works include philosophical treatises.[150] A later scholar of this period was the East Syriac monk and author John bar Zo'bi (twelfth to thirteenth century),[151] who produced a number works on grammar and philosophy. A younger West Syriac student of John was the bishop of the monastery of Mar Matti, Jacob bar Shakko (d. 1241),[152] who wrote on ethics, logic, metaphysics, physics, mathematics, physiology, and music. A final intellectual voice of this era was the West Syriac Gregory Bar Hebraeus (d. 1286).[153] As the most prolific Christian polymath of the era and the son of a physician, he composed over forty Syriac and Arabic works. His authorial corpus covers exegesis, theology, liturgy, historiography, grammar, and jurisprudence, as well as ethics, medicine, pharmacology, astronomy, oneiromancy, psychology, and philosophy, including one work that served as a general compendium of almost all aspects of Aristotelian philosophy.

Notably, later medieval Christian intellectuals like Jacob and Bar Hebraeus are known for their dependency on the Arabic works of Muslim thinkers, especially in the field of philosophy. In his works, Bar Hebraeus was involved in literal translations and paraphrases of Muslims' works into Syriac, as well as a translation of the complete works of Ibn Sina (d. 1037). He later produced a Syriac grammar book based on theories borrowed from Arab grammarians.[154] The adoption and translation of Arabic scientific and grammar works is also notable in the scholarship of metropolitan 'Abdisho' bar Brikha (d. 1318),[155] the last of the East Syriac intellectuals. He wrote in Syriac and Arabic in the fields of church canons, theology, philosophy, and the sciences.

149. Brock et al., eds., *Gorgias Encyclopedic Dictionary*, 126–27; Thomas and Mallett, eds., *Christian-Muslim Relations*, 3:665–70; Watt, "Syriac Philosophy," 429–30.

150. He produced commentaries on biblical books, doctrinal treatises, theological sermons, apologetic works and church canons. He also produced commentaries on Aristotle's and Porphyry's logical works.

151. This is in addition to his theological treatises. Brock et al., eds., *Gorgias Encyclopedic Dictionary*, 440–41; Watt, "Syriac Philosophy," 429–30.

152. This in addition to his theological works. Brock et al., eds., *Gorgias Encyclopedic Dictionary*, 430–31; Thomas and Mallett, eds., *Christian-Muslim Relations*, 4:241–44; Watt, "Syriac Philosophy," 429–30.

153. Brock et al., eds., *Gorgias Encyclopedic Dictionary*, 54–58; Thomas and Mallett, eds., *Christian-Muslim Relations*, 588–609; Watt, "Syriac Philosophy," 429–30.

154. Brock et al., eds., *Gorgias Encyclopedic Dictionary*, 27–28.

155. Brock et al., eds., *Gorgias Encyclopedic Dictionary*, 3–4, 350–51; Thomas and Mallett, eds., *Christian-Muslim Relations*, 4:762–66.

Eventually, Islamic intellectualism and civilization began to decline, especially after the fall of Baghdad in 1258, with a few notable exceptions. The end of the Abbasid caliphate led to the destruction of the House of Wisdom, and, in this context Christian influence, especially that of Syriac-speaking Christians, significantly diminished. The devastation and persecution of Tamerlane's era (r. 1370–1405) eradicated the Christian presence throughout Asia and turned them into an insignificant minority in the Middle East. Yet, their legacy is well attested even among Islamic historians, especially historians of philosophy and sciences.[156]

Regardless of the demise of Islamic civilization, the legacy of the early Christian-Islamic intellectualism reached beyond the Islamic world, fostering and shaping Western civilization. In Al-Andalus, archbishop Raymond of Toledo (d. 1151) sponsored a school to translate Greek and Arabic works into Latin. Such translations were also carried on in other parts of Spain and Italy during the twelfth and thirteenth centuries, benefiting science, philosophy, and theology. This gave birth to the European Renaissance, which produced notable thinkers like Peter Abelard (d. 1142), Thomas Aquinas (d. 1274), Albert the Great (d. 1280), Duns Scotus (d. 1308), and William of Occam (d. 1349). Notably, translations of Eastern Christian theological and apologetic works from the Islamic context further advanced Western theology and apologetics, possibly contributing to Latin interest in and engagements with the Islamic world, like that of Peter the Venerable (d. 1156) and Raymond Llull (d. 1316).[157]

In the modern era, although Muslims constituted the majority of the intellectuals in the Muslim world, indigenous and foreign Christians were major participants in the renewal of intellectual activities, forming a large percentage of the intellectual community.[158] For example, Western physicians within the Ottoman Empire, as well as Greek and Armenian physicians who studied in the West, served at the Ottoman court. Likewise, students of other disciplines (including astronomy, mathematics,

156. The Islamic historian Ibn-al-Qifti (1172–1248), in his description of the medical school at Jundishapur, wrote: "They made rapid progress in the science, developed new methods in the treatment of the disease along pharmacological lines, to the point that their therapy was judged superior to that of the Greeks and Hindus. Furthermore, these physicians adopted the scientific methods of other people and modified them by their own discoveries. They elaborated medical laws and recorded the work that had been developed." Whipple, "Role of The Nestorians."

157. Griffith, *Church in the Shadow*, 127–28.

158. For reference to the Christians see: Brentjes and Morrison, "Sciences in Islamic Societies," 634–35.

geography, and military sciences) who were educated in Western universities contributed to the development of Ottoman civilization. Some were engaged in translating Latin and other Western works into Turkish, while others composed new works, which also shaped the education system in the Ottoman Empire.

CULTURAL IMPACT (LANGUAGE, ARCHITECTURE, AND ART)

Pre-Islamic and post-conquest Arab Christians contributed to the Arabic culture that dominated the Islamic civilization. The cultural contribution started with contributions to the development of Arabic language script in the pre-Islamic era, associated with the Aramaic script of Nabataeans of Petra or with the Syriac script of Lakhmids of Hira and Anbar, possibly from the influence of Christian monks.[159]

The Christian contribution to the development of Arabic writing was complemented by the pre-Islamic Christian contribution to Arabic poetry.[160] Arab Christian poets were a prominent part of this cultural phenomenon. Christian religiocultural motifs, whether biblical or not, populated the literary sphere of poetry with references to the creation, the flood, the day of resurrection, and judgment to frequent mentions of ascetics and monks. This displays a strong similarity to Qur'anic themes and passages.

In this context, Imru' al-Qays al-Kindī (d. 544),[161] stands out as the most prominent example. His poetry is the earliest of the seven *muʿallaqāt* (The Suspended Odes).[162] Another poet was the ruler of the Taghlib tribe, 'Amr ibn Kulthum al-Taghlibī (d. 584/600),[163] whose grandfather, Abū

159. Bloom, "Literary and Oral Cultures," 669–70; Gruendler, *Development of the Arabic Scripts*, 1–2; Senner, ed., *Origins of Writing*, 100; Schmid, "Louis Cheikho," 354–56.

160. Meisami and Starkey, eds., *Encyclopedia of Arabic Literature*, 1:99–100, 406–7; Schmid, "Louis Cheikho," 355–58.

161. He was the son of Huji bin al-Harith, the Kindite monarch, and his mother was from the Christian Taghlibi tribe. Meisami and Starkey, eds., *Encyclopedia of Arabic Literature*, 1:394–95.

162. One of the most common views is that there were seven poems hanging in al-Ka'ba in Mecca. Meisami and Starkey, eds., *Encyclopedia of Arabic Literature*, 1:532–34; Allen, *The Arabic Literary Heritage*, 103.

163. Meisami and Starkey, eds., *Encyclopedia of Arabic Literature*, 1:87–88.

Layla al-Muhalhil ibn Rabīʿa (d. 531),[164] was also a poet and the uncle of Imru' al-Qais. Likewise, the sixth century had al-Nabigha al-Dhubyanī[165] and ʿAdī ibn Zayd al-ʿIbāḍī al-Tamīmī of Hira (d. c. 600).[166] Ibn Zayd was married to Hind, the granddaughter of the Lakhmid ruler, al-Nu'man III ibn al-Mundhir (d. 602),[167] and played a role in his rule. He also served the Sasanian shah Hormizd IV (d. 590) as secretary of Arab affairs. In addition to these, the well-known romantic poet-warrior ʿAntarah ibn Shaddad al-ʿAbsi's (d. 608)[168] poem was part of the *muʿallaqat*.[169]

At the dawn of Islam, there was the younger poet of the *muʿallaqat*, Abu Bashir Maymun ibn Gays al-Aʿsha (d. 629), who was part of the milieu of Christian Hira[170] along with Umayya ibn Abi al-Salt (d. 631),[171] who interacted with early Muslims, such Abu Bakr (d. 634). The rich heritage of Arab Christian poets and Christian Arabic poetic themes continued in the Islamic era. One notable Christian poet of this era was Ghiyath al-Akhtal al-Taghlibi (d. c. 708/10),[172] who was born possibly in Hira. He was a close companion of the Umayyad Yazid I (d. 683) and was part of his court. He later became ʿAbd al-Malik ibn Marwan's (d. 705) and al-Walid I's (d. 715) official court poet and was favored by different Muslim rulers, such al-Hajjāj ibn Yūsuf (d. 714).

Finally, although Muslim poets and other literary authors were often influenced by Islamic motifs, Christian religiocultural themes also influenced them. These included the common scenes of Christian festivals and monasteries and their stereotypical motifs of drinking wine and encountering Christian monks and female lovers.[173] Furthermore, biblical and Qur'anic characters, most prominently Jesus and Mary, feature in Islamic poetry as evidenced in the examples of Persian Muslim poets like Nizami Ganjavi (d. 1209) and Jalal a-Din Rumi (d. 1273). Jesus often

164. Meisami and Starkey, eds., *Encyclopedia of Arabic Literature*, 1:538.

165. Meisami and Starkey, eds., *Encyclopedia of Arabic Literature*, 1:570.

166. Meisami and Starkey, eds., *Encyclopedia of Arabic Literature*, 1:56–57.

167. He is featured with Hind in one of the Arabian Nights tales.

168. He was the son of an Arab freeman and his Abyssinian maid. Meisami and Starkey, eds., *Encyclopedia of Arabic Literature*, 1:93–94.

169. He is featured with his lover ʿAblah in one of the Arabian Nights tales.

170. Meisami and Starkey, eds., *Encyclopedia of Arabic Literature*, 1:107.

171. Meisami and Starkey, eds., *Encyclopedia of Arabic Literature*, 1:793; Osman, "Pre-Islamic Arab Converts," 75.

172. Griffith, "Mansur Family," 31; Meisami and Starkey, eds., *Encyclopedia of Arabic Literature*, 1:67–68.

173. Schimmel, "Jesus and Mary as Poetical Images," 279–90.

appears as the ideal ascetic and mystic, especially among Sufi authors, as they engage with themes of love, mercy, kindness, devotion, and purity of heart, with biblical passages (e.g., the Sermon on the Mount) and apocryphal themes. The ascetic Jesus theme led to the notable Islamic "Desert Sayings" literature, which featured Jesus and anonymous typological monks, such in the works of Ibn al-Mubārak (d. 797), Ibn Ḥanbal (d. 855), and most notably Ibn Abī al-Dunyā (d. 894). Later Muslims kept such literary traditions, including the famous al-Ghazālī (d. 1111), and even as late as in the modern era of al-Nabulusī (d. 1731) and al-Zabidī (d. 1791), to mention a few.[174]

By the modern era, Christian intellectuals, including authors, journalists, and poets, were active participants in the Arabic Renaissance (*al-Nahda*) during the nineteenth and twentieth centuries. This renaissance awakened the Arab culture from its dormant condition that started in the thirteenth century with the fall of Baghdad in 1258. The modern Arab Awakening, which was influenced by contact with the West and the access to the printing press, touched many areas of art and literature, dealing with issues of identity and secularism and shaping modern Arab culture and politics.[175]

The earliest Arabic books, mainly Christian religious ones, were printed in Europe (in Rome and in France). This encouraged the Middle Eastern churches to invest in such technology, leading to the establishment of seventeen printing presses in Lebanon alone during the nineteenth century. The majority of these belonged to churches.[176] The earliest printing press was the Qozhaya Press, in the famous monastery of the Valley of Qadisha in Lebanon, which printed the Psalms in Arabic in 1585. The Greek Melkite patriarchate of Antioch started a press in Aleppo, Syria, which printed Christian religious books in the eighteenth century, which was what the Maronite Press in Aleppo also did during the nineteenth century. The latter also printed secular materials, including printing the first Islamic calendar in 1883. Likewise, the Greek Orthodox

174. Khalidi, "Extracts from *The Muslim Jesus*," 291–300; Khalidi, *Muslim Jesus*, especially 32–43.

175. Sabella, "Christian Contributions," 89–106.

176. The religious contacts between Christians of the Arab world, especially the Middle East, with Europeans in Europe and via missionaries in the region during the age of modernity (sixteenth century onward), introduced Western civilization and technology to the region, including the printing press. This allowed for Christian religious materials to be produced in Arabic, which boosted interest in the Arabic language. Haywood, *Modern Arabic Literature 1800–1970*; Cheikho, *Fan Al Tiba'ah Fil Sharq*.

Printing Press in Beirut published both religious and secular books, as well as a magazine in Arabic by the late nineteenth century. Finally, the American Press in Beirut, which appeared in the nineteenth century, produced Arabic books in a variety of disciplines under the leadership of Fares al-Shidyad (d. 1887), who was one of the founders of *al-Nahda*. Such Christian achievements highlighted the value of the printing press and led to the establishment of first Islamic printing press in 1874 by Abdel Qader al-Qabbani (d. 1935).

Egypt, Palestine, and Iraq also experienced the impact of contact with the West, which led to the spread of printing presses. In Egypt, the Napoleonic campaign brought printing presses and libraries in the late eighteenth century, including printing newspapers with some Arabic articles. In Palestine, the Franciscan Printing Press was established 1846, the Armenian Press in 1848, and the Greek Orthodox Press in 1849. Private Christian presses were also established, like the Doumani Press, established by the Suleiman Doumani in 1892. Alphonse Antoine Alonzo and Jurji Habib Hananiya did likewise, and also established *al-Qudis*, the first Arabic newspaper in Palestine in 1908. In Iraq, the Dominican fathers established a printing press in Mosul in 1860, which published an Arabic translation of the Syriac version of *Kalila Wa Dumna* in 1869. Another church press was the Chaldean Press, established in 1863.

With such technological development, Middle Eastern Christians played a role in the Arab Renaissance through establishing and leading early Arab journalism. In 1854, the Armenian Rizqallah Hassoubnd (d. 1880), from Aleppo, who was fluent in multiple languages, established an Arabic newspaper *Mir'at al-Ajwal* in Istanbul. In Egypt, the Lebanese Bishara and Salim Takla established the daily Egyptian newspaper *al-Ahram* in Alexandria and then Cairo, while in 1877 the Armenian Damascene Adib Ishaq (d. 1886) along with Sālim al-Naqqash founded the weekly newspaper *Misr* in Cairo, the daily newspaper *al-Tijaraj* in Alexandria, and *al-Mahrousah* in 1880. In 1876, Yacoub Sarrouf and Fares Nimr created a scientific, literary, and cultural magazine named *al-Muqrataf* in Beirut. Later, in 1892, Jurji Zeidan founded a cultural monthly magazine, *al-Hilāl*. These papers discussed and promoted key cultural and social issues, ranging from questions about contact with the West to education's impact on progress, to the place and role of women in society, to political issues related to independence.

Notably, Butros al-Bustānī (d. 1883), who was part of the *al-Nahḍa* movement, was the first writer from a family that produced more than twelve influential authors and publishers. He played a key role in the revival of the Arabic language. He mastered many languages and helped American missionaries translate the Bible and Western literature into Arabic. He established a newspaper (*Nafir Suriyya*) and produced a dictionary and an Arabic encyclopedia. He advocated for the education of women as a necessity for the betterment of society in an 1849 publication. The Bustani family was one of a few key Christian families, like the Yazij and Khoury, who were the pioneers of Arab literary and cultural awakening, bringing to the forefront the literary riches of Arabic in their works and awakening the interest of the general population.

Furthermore, Christian educational institutions (schools) had a leading role in the rise of education in the Arab world, and thus contributed to the Awakening. Institutions like Saint Joseph University and American University of Beirut in Lebanon, and Baghdad College (al-Hikma University) in Baghdad, were leaders in developing the Middle East civilization and culture.[177] The Syrian thinker Constantine Zureiq (d. 2000) was a noted Christian intellectual of the modern era who expressed the importance of Arab nationalism. He was the president of the American University of Beirut and sought to transform Arab society, focusing on its current crisis of disunity and lack of collective loyalty, as well as its backwardness in sciences and productivity.[178]

In theatrical art, private Christian schools led the way through adopting European works. Maroun al-Naqqash (d. 1855) might be considered the father of Arab theater, producing for example *al-Bakhīl*, an adaptation of a Western work. He also built the first stage in the Arab world. In Damascus, Aḥmad al-Qabbanī and later the Qabbani family were influenced by al-Naqqash. The previously mentioned Adib Ishaq worked with Maroun's nephew Salim al-Naqqash to produce Arabic plays in Alexandria, as they partnered in publishing newspapers. The Syrian George Abyad (d. 1952) was another star in Egyptian theater, working with Farah Anton (d. 1922) to produce notable works based on European theatrical works. At the same time, the Chaldean-Coptic Naguib Elias al-Rihānī (d. 1949) was the father of Egyptian comedy in theater and film through acting and production. Palestinian Greek Orthodox Christians such as Jamīl Ḥabīb Baḥrī and Naṣrī al-Jawzī added to the wealth of Arab theater in the early twentieth century, particularly through their

177. MacDonnell, *Jesuits by the Tigris*; MacDonnell, "Jesuits of Baghdad."

178. Atiyeh and Oweiss, eds., *Arab Civilization.*

promotion of women in theater, key among them being Asma Touba. Asma was an active member in the Women's Union of Acre before 1948, then moved to Beirut. The Palestinian Lama brothers, Ibrahim and Badr, were enthusiastic about filmmaking, establishing a film company in Egypt in 1930. They made a movie about Saladin in 1941, which in 1963 was the theme of another Lebanese-Egyptian Christian producer, Yousif Shahin (d. 2008). It was Shahin who launched the career of the international actor Omar Sharif (d. 2015).

Finally, the early twentieth century witnessed Arabic Christian migration to the West and to South America. In their diaspora, some were active contributors to the Arab Renaissance. Al-Rabita al-Qalamiya (the Pen League), which was established in 1920 in New York, is one such example. It included important thinkers like Gibran Khalil Gibran (d. 1931), Nasib Arida (d. 1946), Abd al-Masih Haddad (d. 1963), and Mikhail Na'ima (d. 1988), who shaped modern Arab civilization from the diaspora. They were concerned with reviving Arab literary traditions to speak into modern times. Gibran Khalil Gibran was an important writer and poet as well as a philosopher. He wrote both in Arabic and English with notable works such as *The Prophet*. Nasib Arida and Mikhail Na'ima were also authors while Abd al-Masih Haddad was also a journalist, establishing *al-Saeh* in 1912. At the same times, Amin al-Rehani (d. 1940) wrote *The Book of Khalid*, a philosophical work in English. This was the first book in English by an Arab dealing with sectarianism, tribalism, and localism, and promoting Arab nationalism and unity. In South America, a similar group was influenced by the Pen League and established al-'Usbah al-Andalusiah (the Andalusian League). One of its members, Shukrallah al-Jar, along with Michel Ma'alouf, Natheer Zeitoun, and Habib Mas'oud, published the magazine *New Andalus* in 1932, which aimed to highlight and follow the rich heritage of Arabs in Andalusia.

In the fields of art and architecture, Christian architects, craftsmen, and artists directly and indirectly impacted the development of Islamic civilization.[179] Early Islamic architecture, especially religious buildings (i.e.,w mosques), was influenced by Christian churches and shrines, which dominated the landscape of the Fertile Crescent. The most significant early example is the seventh-century Dome of the Rock in Jerusalem, built around 691 by 'Abd al-Mālik ibn Marwān (d. 705).[180] Its design

179. Griffith, "Images, Islam and Christian Icons"; Ragab, *Medieval Islamic Hospital*, 16–19; Gibb, "Arab-Byzantine Relations, esp. 224–25.

180. Griffith, *Church in the Shadow*, 32–33; Ragab, *Medieval Islamic Hospital*,

reflects the Byzantine design of the Holy Sepulchre of Jerusalem, serving as a challenger to it and to the Christian public religiosity in the caliphate by imitating its design on a grander scale and including Qur'anic statements that challenge Christian beliefs.[181]

Christian religious architecture, which was the product of a long history of Christian craftsmanship, was employed by the Muslims in building mosques that sought to imitate and compete with Christian churches in the public space. There are even references that speak of the role of Coptic Christians in renovating al-Kaʿba in Mecca at the dawn of Islam! Clearly, in the Islamic context of the conquered land, such a role was dominant in early periods. The Umayyads ʿAbd al-Mālik (d. 705) and al-Walīd I (d. 715) employed Byzantine artisans in their building projects.[182] From the Abbasid era, one encounters the frescoes of Samarra, painted between 836 and 883, which reflect the Christian workmanship of a priest, who is the subject and signatures of the artist.[183]

Christian influence on Islamic building was not limited to imitation and craftsmanship, but also the result of appropriation of Christian churches as mosques by Muslims.[184] In Damascus, the Cathedral of Saint John the Baptist was transformed into the Umayyad Mosque by al-Walīd I (d. 715) in 706.[185] The famous Great Mosque of Cordoba stands on the site of a Visigoth church.[186] It was rebuilt around 786 by the Umayyads of Al-Andalus, who made Cordoba their caliphate's capital in the eighth century. The Visigoth Christian architectural style is evident in the horseshoe-style arches, which later spread in the Islamic world across North Africa and Egypt. The mosque's dome is decorated by tesserae that came from the Byzantine Empire with Christian craftsmen to install them.

These are not the only examples. Islamic conversion of Christian churches and shrines to mosques continued in later periods. Madrasat

---

24–25; Milwright, "Islamic Art and Architecture," 690–93; Grabar, "*Umayyad* Dome of the Rock," 223–56; Grabar, *Shape of the Holy*, 52–116.

181. Griffith, "Images, Islam, and Christian Icons"; Ragab, *Medieval Islamic Hospital*, 16–19; Gibb, "Arab-Byzantine Relations," esp. 224–25.

182. Ragab, *Medieval Islamic Hospital*, 22.

183. Arnold, *Painting in Islam*, 99.

184. Jenkins, *Lost History of Christianity*, 37–38.

185. The space was part of an ancient pagan *temenos*. Milwright, "Islamic Art and Architecture," 694–96; Ragab, *Medieval Islamic Hospital*, 22.

186. Previously, the church was a temple of the Roman god Janus. It was converted to a church by the Visigoths around 572. Milwright, "Islamic Art and Architecture," 698–99.

al-Halawiyya in Aleppo, which was developed by the Selijuk Nūr al-Dīn Zangī (d. 1174), has an altar, thus reflecting a possible Christian past. Partial influence also manifests itself in having Christian elements in a Muslim religious building, mainly through reusing Christian handiworks in Islamic building. This is often the case with Crusaders' works. For example, Jami'a al-Aqsa (b. 1218/9) has elements from twelfth-century Latin Crusade structures. Madrasa-Mausoleum of Sultan al-Nasir Muhammad (d. 1341) in Cairo has the doors of a Christian Latin church of St. Jean d'Acre in Acre, taken around 1291. Likewise, the Ayyubid *Bab al-Silsila* and the Nahwiyya Madrasa used Crusade pieces.[187]

The most famous of such examples is the Cathedral of Hagia Sophia in Constantinople, which was turned to a mosque by the Ottomans after the fall of Constantinople in 1453. Hagia Sophia inspired other mosques such as the Shehzabed Mosque, the Suleiman Mosque, and the Rustem Pasha Mosque, dominating the Islamic religious landscape of Istanbul and the Ottoman Empire. Such influence peaked in the sixteenth century, when Ottoman architects mastered the technique of building large open spaces with massive domes, like the Suleiman Mosque, built for sultan Suleiman I (d. 1566) by the famous Christian architect Mimar Sinan (d. 1588) from 1550 to 1557. His work was in competition with St. Peter's Basilica in Rome, by Michelangelo (d. 1564), who, with Leonardo da Vinci (d. 1519), was invited by Suleiman I to build a bridge over the Golden Horn.[188]

Finally, although Islam does not have the richness of Christian iconography due to firm iconoclasm, there is occasional influence from Christian religious art. For example, this impact is noted in the depiction of Muhammad's birth in the history of the Ilkhanate vizier, physician, and historian Rashid ad-Din Tabib's (d. 1318) *Jamīᶜ al-Tawārikh*, which reflects depictions of Jesus's nativity, including the angelic presence. The work also includes other biblical scenes, such as the Old Testament patriarch Jacob and the story of Jonah and the whale.[189] Further, Byzantine iconographical influence appears in the references to Jesus' annunciation and birth and of the virgin Mary in *al-Athar al-Baqiyah*.[190] Ayyubid art

187. Hillenbrand, *Crusades: Islamic Perspectives*, 381–90; Rosen-Ayalon, "Art and Architecture," especially 308–9.

188. Milwright, "Islamic Art and Architecture," 702–3.

189. Arnold, *Painting in Islam*, 58.

190. Arnold, *Painting in Islam*, 100.

also depicts Gospel scenes, including images of the infant Jesus and the virgin Mary, which was influenced by Christian regional iconography.[191]

POLITICAL PARTICIPATION (STATE, SOCIETY, AND DIPLOMACY)

In principle, Islamic views and laws prevented non-Muslims from playing a role in the caliphate's civil affairs and politics, while demanding loyalty to the caliphate.[192] Yet, Muslim rulers employed Christians in running the affairs of their kingdoms from the start. The earliest example was the Mansur family, who served both the Byzantines and the Umayyads. The Syriac-speaking Melkite Manṣūr ibn Sargon was a Byzantine financial official and governor of Damascus, who surrendered the city to the Muslims in 635, securing a safety capitulation agreement. His son, Sargon ibn Mansur, served the Umayyads, starting with Mu'awiya I (d. 680), as head of the caliphate's administration and finance and was followed by his son, the famous polymath Yuhanna, St. John of Damascus (d. 750), in these posts until the reform of 'Abd al Mālik (d. 705) in 700, which arabicized the caliphal administration.[193]

The Mansur family were not the only Christians who served the Umayyads; the West Syriac Gumoye family of Edessa was another family that may have worked together with the Mansur family (and competed with them) in Damascus. One of them was Athanasius bar Gumoye, who served 'Abd al-Mālik's younger brother 'Abd al-Aziz (d. 705), the governor of Egypt for twenty-one years. Athanasius was his secretary and in charge of the tributes. He was a rich Christian and had nine hospitals in Edessa. His eldest son ran his private business, while his younger ones held office as their father's assistants.[194] The descendants of the Arab Christian Salihids and Ghassanids were also employed in the Umayyad bureaucracy.[195]

191. Hoffman, "Christian-Islamic Encounters"; Naby and Magdy, "Representation of Virgin Mary."

192. Mitri, "Christians in Arab Politics," 107–20.

193. Brock et al., eds., *Gorgias Encyclopedic Dictionary*, 230–31; Griffith, "Mansur Family," 29–52; Debie, "Christians in the Service of the Caliph," 53–71; Gutas, *Greek Thoughts*, 17–18.

194. Debie, "Christians in the Service of the Caliph."

195. Griffith, "Mansur Family," 53; Gutas, *Greek Thoughts*, 17–18.

Christian clergy were key in dealing with intercaliphate affairs, especially in relation to managing the Christian communities of the caliphate.[196] For example, the West Syriac patriarch Dionysius of Tell-Mahre (d. 845) had strong relationship with al-Ma'mūn (d. 833) and accompanied him in 830/831 to Egypt in effort to negotiate a peaceful outcome to the armed revolt of Copts.[197] The Christians of Andalusia had similar roles, such as in the case of Dulcidio II (c. 921), a bishop of Salamanca, who represented Christian affairs in the Islamic court, as did an unnamed bishop of Seville around 973.[198]

In the Ottoman Empire, skilled Greek Christians who settled in the Phanar part of Istanbul were utilized in the affairs of the caliphate, especially in later periods when the empire was declining and having problems in their foreign relations. By late the seventeenth century, the Phanariot Greek Christians had roles in the Ottoman Porte (i.e., government) and foreign embassies. Thus, Greek Christian families of Constantinople occupied high positions in the empire, serving as secretaries and interpreters for Ottoman officials.

Christian clergy were also participants in the caliphate's international diplomacy.[199] The East Syriac patriarch Timothy I (d. 823) accompanied al-Rashid (d. 809) during his military campaign to the Byzantine frontiers in 799, possibly to participate in negotiations with the Byzantine forces and/or population for a truce and/or surrender agreement. Later, Patriarch Dionysius was one of the recipients of the Nubian prince George I of Makuria, who visited al-Mu'tasim (d. 842) in Baghdad around 837/838 to heal the political tension between the two kingdoms and negotiate a peace treaty.[200] A century later, sometime around 913 or 922, the Abbasid vizir 'Alī ibn 'Isā (d. 946) commissioned the Melkite patriarchs of Jerusalem and Antioch, Leontius I (d. 929) and Elias I (d. 934), to negotiate the conditions of Muslim prisoners in Constantinople.[201]

In Andalusia, bishop Rabi ibn Zayd of Elvira, also known as Recemundus (fl. mid-tenth century), had a position in the court of caliph 'Abd al-Rahman III (d. 961). He was sent on a diplomatic mission by

196. Yousif, "Churchmen and Statesmen," 39.

197. Yousif, "Churchmen and Statesmen," 39.

198. Yousif, "Churchmen and Statesmen," 41.

199. Such roles continued during the Islamic era from the pre-Islamic times of the Sassanians. For the Sassanian period, see Yousif, "Churchmen and Statesmen," 33–37.

200. Yousif, "Churchmen and Statesmen," 39–40.

201. Yousif, "Churchmen and Statesmen," 40

the caliph to Emperor Otto I (d. 973) of the Holy Roman Empire around 956.[202] At the turn of the millennium and within the Fatimid caliphate of Egypt, al-Hakim (d. 1021) sent the Greek patriarch of Jerusalem Orestes (d. 1006) to negotiate with the Byzantian Empire a peace treaty in 1000, while his sister, Sitt al-Mulk (d. 1023), used Patriarch Nicephorus I of Jerusalem (d. 1048) in her diplomacy with Constantinople around 1023 to mend the relationship after al-Hakim's destruction of the Holy Sepulchre of Jerusalem in 1009.[203]

In the modern era, Christian nationalists were an active part of the new political spirit of the Arab world. They wrote against Turkish occupation, contributing to *al-Nahḍa* and the idea of an Arab nation (*Umma*), which later launched Arab nationalistic movements.[204] Such thinkers used cultural-linguistic (rather than ethno-religious) identity markers to promote an inclusive and united modern national state through the idea of citizenship beyond religious identity. In Egypt, Khalil Mutran (d. 1949), a Lebanese Maronite, played a part in the Arab Awakening there, supporting Arab independence. His Arab nationalistic poetry influenced others such as the Greek Catholic poet and linguist Ibrahim al-Yaziji (d. 1906), who also called for an Arab Awakening that started manifesting itself in political revolutions such as that of 1916 in the Hijaz-Levant area and of 1919 in Egypt.

In Syria and Iraq, Christians were active participants in the Baath Party movement, most notably, its founder, the Syriac sociologist and nationalist Michel Aflaq (d. 1989). In Palestine, Christians partnered with Muslims in the twentieth century in their suffering and resistance. George Habash (d. 2008), the founder of the Popular Front for the Liberation of Palestine in 1967, is another example. Habash was influenced by the Syrian thinker Constantine Zureiq, who is credited with coining the term *Nakba* to refer to the outcome of establishing the State of Israel and the expulsion of Palestinians in 1948. Other Christians were key in the formation of the Palestinian National Authority in 1992.

202. Yousif, "Churchmen and Statesmen," 41.

203. Yousif, "Churchmen and Statesmen," 41.

204. Mitri, "Christians in Arab Politics," 107–20.

CONCLUSION

The Christian influence on and contribution to the Arab-Islamic civilization has been monumental from the pre-Islamic era to the modern era, including the long history of the different Islamic caliphates. The Christian contribution shaped the development of this long history religiously, intellectually, culturally, and politically. Throughout their history within the Arab Islamic world, Christians were scholars, physicians, scientists, philosophers, teachers, authors, poets, scribes, translators, journalists, administrators, politicians, and statesmen. Although this rich and long legacy might be known to scholars and specialists, it is often unknown to the general reader, and it is missing from many works on Arab Islamic civilization. Thus, this chapter aims to highlight this history, especially at this moment, which is witnessing a decline in the Christian presence and influence in the homeland of Christianity and Islam and the marginalization of its history.

BIBLIOGRAPHY

Abdel Naby, Heba M. S. and Heba Magdy. "The Representation of Virgin Mary in Islamic Art during the Ayyubid Dynasty (12th–13th Century)." *International Journal of History and Cultural Studies* 4:4 (2018) 20–41.

Adamson, Peter. *The Age of al-Fârâbî: Arabic Philosophy in the Fourth/Tenth Century*. Warburg Institute Colloquia 12. London-Turin: Warburg Institute-Nino Aragno, 2008.

Algeriani, Adel Abdul-Aziz, and Mawloud Mohadi. "The House of Wisdom (Bayt al-Hikmah) and Its Civilizational Impact on Islamic libraries: A Historical Perspective." *Mediterranean Journal of Social Sciences* 8:5 (2017) 179–87.

Allen, Roger. *The Arabic Literary Heritage: The Development of its Genres and Criticism*. Cambridge: Cambridge University Press, 2005.

Arnold, Thomas W. *Painting in Islam: A Study of the Place of Pictorial Art in Muslim Culture*. Piscataway, NJ: Gorgias, 2004.

Atiyeh, George N., and Ibrahim M. Oweiss, eds. *Arab Civilization: Challenges and Responses: Studies in Honor of Dr. Constantine Zurayk*. Albany, NY: SUNY Press, 1988.

Azmi, Khurshid. "Hunain bin Ishaq on Ophthalmic Surgery." *Bulletin of the Indian Institute of History of Medicine* 26 (1996) 69–74.

Bagliani, A. Paravicini, ed. *The Medieval Legends of Philosophers and Scholars*. Micrologus 21. Sismel—Edizioni del Galluzzo, 2013.

Berkey, Jonathan. "Islam." In *The New Cambridge History of Islam*, vol. 4, *Islamic Cultures and Societies to the End of the Eighteenth Century*, edited by Robert Irwin. Cambridge: Cambridge University Press, 2010.

Bertaina, David. *Christian and Muslim Dialogues: The Religious Uses of a Literary Form in the Early Islamic Middle East*. Piscataway, NJ: Gorgias, 2011.

Bertolacci, Amos. "Albertus Magnus and 'Avenzoreth' (Ibn Zurʿa, d. 1008): Legend or Reality?" In *The Medieval Legends of Philosophers and Scholars*, edited by A. Paravicini Bagliani, 369–96. Firenze: Sismel, Edizioni del Galluzzo, 2013.

Bhayro, Siam. "Syriac Botanical and Pharmacological Literature." Paper presented at the 9th International Congress of the Society of Ethnobiology, University of Kent, Canterbury, UK, June 2004.

Bloom, Jonathan M. *Early Islamic Art and Architecture*. London: Routledge, 2016.

———. "Literary and Oral Cultures." In *The New Cambridge History of Islam*, vol. 4, *Islamic Cultures and Societies to the End of the Eighteenth Century*, edited by Robert Irwin, 668–81. Cambridge: Cambridge University Press, 2010.

Bonner, Michael, and Mine Ener, Amy Singer. *Poverty and Charity in Middle Eastern Contexts*. Albany, NY: SUNY Press, 2003.

Borrut, Antoine, and Fred M. Donner, eds. *Christians and Others in the Umayyad State*. Chicago: University of Chicago Press, 2016.

Bowman, John. "The Debt of Islam to Monophysite Syrian Christianity." In *Essays in Honour of Griffithes Wheeler Thatcher 1863–1950*, edited by E. C. B. MacLaurin, 191–216. Sydney: Sydney University Press, 1967.

Brague, Remi. *The Legend of the Middle Ages: Philosophical Explorations of Medieval Christianity, Judaism, and Islam*. Translated by Lydia G. Cochrane. Chicago University Press, 2009.

Brentjes, Sonja, and Robert G. Morrison. "The Sciences in Islamic Societies (750–1800)." In *The New Cambridge History of Islam*, vol. 4, *Islamic Cultures and Societies to the End of the Eighteenth Century*, edited by Robert Irwin, 564–639. Cambridge: Cambridge University Press, 2010.

Brock, Sebastian P. "From Antagonism to Assimilation: Syriac Attitudes to Greek Learning." In *Syriac Perspectives on Late Antiquity*, 17–34. London: Variorum, 1984.

———. "Syriac Culture in the Seventh Century." *ARAM* 1 (1989) 268–80.

———. *Syriac Perspectives on Late Antiquity*. London: Variorum, 1984.

———. "Two Letters of the Patriarch Timothy from the Late Eighth Century on Translations from Greek." *Arabic Sciences and Philosophy* 9 (1999) 233–46.

———. "Two Millennia of Christianity in Iraq." *Islam and Christian-Muslim Relations* 21:2 (March 2010) 175–84.

Brock, Sebastian P., Aaron M. Butts, George A. Kiraz, and Lucas van Rompay, eds. *Gorgias Encyclopedic Dictionary of the Syriac Heritage*. Piscataway, NJ: Gorgias, 2011.

Browne, Edward Granville. *Arabian Medicine: The Fitzpatrick Lectures Delivered at the College of Physicians in November 1919 and November 1920*. Cambridge: Cambridge University Press, 1921.

———. *Islamic Medicine: Fitzpatrick Lectures Delivered at the Royal College of Physicians in 1919–1920*. New Delhi: Goodword, 2002.

Burnett, C. S. F. *Glosses and Commentaries on Aristotelian Logical Texts: The Syriac, Arabic and Medieval Latin Traditions*. London: University of London Press, 1993.

Burns, J. A. "The Faculty of Arts." *The Catholic Encyclopedia*, vol. 1. New York: Robert Appleton, 1907.

Chandler, Paul-Gordon. *Pilgrims of Christ on the Muslim Road: Exploring a New Path between Two Faiths*. Lanham, MD: Cowley, 2008.

Cheikho, Louis. *Fan Al Tiba'ah Fil Sharq, or History of the Art of Printing in the East*. 2nd ed. Beirut: Dar Al Mashreq, 1995.
Cook, Michael. "The Origins of Kalam." *Bulletin of the School of Oriental and African Languages* 43 (1980) 32–43.
Cooper, Glen M. "Isḥāq ibn Ḥunayn: Abū Yaʿqūb Isḥāq ibn Ḥunayn ibn Isḥāq al-ʿIbādī." In *The Biographical Encyclopedia of Astronomers*, edited by Virginia Trimble et al., 578. New York: Springer, 2007.
Corbin, Henry. *History of Islamic Philosophy*. Translated by Liadain Sherrard and Philip Sherrad. London: Kegan Paul, 2001.
Courbage, Youssef, and Philippe Fargues. *Christians and Jews under Islam*. Translatd by Judy Mabro. London: I.B. Tauris, 1997.
Dalrymple, William. *From the Holy Mountain: A Journey in the Shadow of Byzantium*. London: Flamingo, 1998.
Debie, Muriel. "Christians in the Service of the Caliph: Through the Looking Glass of Communal Identities." In *Christians and Others in the Umayyad State*, edited by Antoine Borrut and Fred M. Donner, 53–71. Chicago: University of Chicago Press, 2016.
Dols, Michael W. "The Origins of the Islamic Hospital: Myth and Reality." *Bulletin of the History of Medicine* 61:3 (Fall 1987) 367–90.
Drijvers, J. W., and A. A. McDonald. *Centers of Learning: Learning and Location in Pre-Modern Europe and the Near East*. Leiden: Brill, 1995.
Elgood, Cyril. *A Medical History of Persia and the East Caliphate*. Cambridge: Cambridge University Press, 1951.
Ellis, Kail C., ed. *Secular Nationalism and Citizenship in Muslim Countries: Arab Christians in the Levant*. London: Palgrave Macmillan, 2018.
Esposito, John L. *The Oxford History of Islam*. Oxford: Oxford University Press, 2000.
Fantini, Bernardino. *Western Medical Thought from Antiquity to the Middle Ages*. Cambridge, MA: Harvard University Press, 1998.
Frank, Richard M. "The Science of Kalam." *Arabic Science and Philosophy* 2 (1992) 9–37.
Friedman, Yohanan. *Tolerance and Coercion is Islam: Interfaith Relations in Muslim Tradition*. Cambridge: Cambridge University Press, 2003.
Grabar, Oleg. *The Shape of the Holy: Early Islamic Jerusalem*. Princeton, NJ: Princeton University Press, 1996.
Gibb, Hamilton A. R. "Arab-Byzantine Relations under the Umayyad Caliphate." *Dumbarton Oak Paper* 12 (1958) 219–33.
Goodman, L. E. "The Translation of Greek Materials into Arabic." In *The Cambridge History of Arabic Literature*, vol. 3, *Religion, Learning, and Science in the ' Abbasid Period*, edited by M. J. L. Young, J. D. Latham, and R. B. Serjeant, 477–97. Cambridge: Cambridge University Press, 1990.
Grabar, Oleg. "The *Umayyad* Dome of the Rock in Jerusalem." In *Early Islamic Art and Architecture*, edited by Jonathan M. Bloom, 223–56. New York: Routledge, 2016.
Griffith, Sidney H. "Christianity's Historical Roots in the Middle East: Christians at Home in the 'World of Islam.'" In *Secular Nationalism and Citizenship in Muslim Countries: Arab Christians in the Levant*, edited by Kail C. Ellis, 29–60. Cham, Switzerland: Palgrave Macmillan, 2018.
———. *The Church in the Shadow of the Mosque: Christians and Muslims in the World of Islam*. Princeton, NJ: Princeton University Press, 2008.

———. "Images, Islam and Christian Icons: A Moment in the Christian/Muslim Encounter in Early Islamic Times." In *La Syrie de Byzance à l'Islam: VIIe-VIIIe siècles: actes du colloque international Lyon—Maison de l'Orient méditerranéen, Paris—Institut du monde arabe, 11–15 Septembre 1990*, edited by Pierre Canivet and Jean Paul Rey-Coquais, 121–38. Damas: Institut français de Damas, 1992.

———. "The Mansur Family and Saint John of Damascus: Christians and Muslims in Umayyad Times." In *Christians and Others in the Umayyad State*, edited by Antoine Borrut and Fred M. Donner, 29–51. University of Chicago, 2016.

Gruendler, Beatrice. *The Development of the Arabic Scripts: From the Nabatean Era to the First Islamic Century According to Dated Texts*. Atlanta: Scholars, 1993.

Gutes, Dimitri. *Greek Thoughts, Arabic Culture: The Graeco-Arabic Translation Movement in Baghdad and Early 'Abbasid Society (2nd–4th/8th–10th Centuries)*. London: Routledge, 1998.

———. "Paul the Persian on the Classification of the Parts of Aristotle's Philosophy: A Milestone between Alexandria and Bagdad." *Der Islam* 60 (1983) 231–67.

Hamori, Andras. "A Sampling of Pleasant Civilities: A 4th/10th Century qissa by al-Babbadhi." *Studia Islamica* 95 (2002) 57–69.

Haq, S. Nomanul. "Occult Sciences and Medicine." In *The New Cambridge History of Islam*, vol. 4, *Islamic Cultures and Societies to the End of the Eighteenth Century*, edited by Robert Irwin, 640–67. Cambridge: Cambridge University Press, 2010

Haywood, John A. *Modern Arabic Literature 1800–1970: An Introduction with Extracts in Translation*. Lund: Humphries, 1971.

Heinz, Justin Paul. "The Origins of Muslim Prayer: Sixth and Seventh Century Religious Influences on the Salat Ritual." PhD diss., University of Missouri, 2008.

Hill, Donald. *Islamic Science and Engineering*. Edinburgh: Edinburgh University Press, 1993.

Hillenbrand, Carole. *The Crusades: Islamic Perspectives.*New York: Routledge, 2000.

Hoffman, Eva R. "Christian-Islamic Encounters on Thirteenth-Century Ayyubid Metalwork: Local Culture, Authenticity, and Memory" *University of Chicago Press Journal* 43:2 (2004) 129–42.

Holmes, Catherine, and Judith Waring, eds. *Literacy, Education and Manuscript Transmission in Byzantium and Beyond*. Leiden: Brill, 2022.

Horden, Peregrine. "The Earliest Hospitals in Byzantium, Western Europe, and Islam." *Journal of Interdisciplinary History* 35:3 (2005) 361–89.

Hoyland, Robert. "Late Roman Provincia Arabia, Monophysite Monks and Arab Tribes: A Problem of Centre and Periphery." *Semitica et Classica* 2 (2009) 117–139.

Hyman, Arthur, James J. Walsh, and Thomas Williams, eds. *Philosophy in the Middle Ages: The Christian, Islam, and Jewish Traditions*. 3rd ed. Indianapolis: Hackett, 2010.

Irwin, Robert, ed. *The New Cambridge History of Islam*, vol. 4, *Islamic Cultures and Societies to the End of the Eighteenth Century*. Cambridge: Cambridge University Press, 2010.

Jaber, Fadi. "The Landscape of Translation Movement in the Arab World: From the 7th Century until the Beginning of the 21st Century." *Arab World English Journal* 6:4 (2016) 128–40.

Jenkins, Philip. *The Lost History of Christianity: The Thousand-Year Golden Age of the Church in the Middle East, Africa, and Asia—and How It Died*. New York: HarperOne, 2008.

———. *The New Faces of Christianity: Believing the Bible in the Global South*. Oxford: Oxford University Press, 2006.

Johna, Samir. "Hunayn ibn-Ishaq: A Forgotten Legend." *The American Surgeon* 68:5 (2002) 497–99.

———. "The Mesopotamian Schools of Edessa and Jundi-Shapur: The Roots of Modern Medical Schools." *The American Surgeon* 69:7 (2003) 627–30.

Kessel, Grigory. "Syriac Medicine." In *The Syriac World*, edited by Daniel King, 438–59. New York: Taylor & Francis, 2019.

Khalidi, Hala, and Basma Ahmad Sedk Dajani. "Facets from the Translation Movement in Classic Arab Culture." *Procedia: Social and Behavioral Sciences* 205 (2015) 569–76.

Khalidi, Tarif. *The Muslim Jesus: Sayings and Stories in Islamic Literature*. Cambridge, MA: Harvard University Press, 2003.

Khalifat, Sahban. *Yahyā Ibn 'Adī: The Philosophical Treatises*. Amman: University of Jordan, 1988.

King, Daniel, ed. *The Syriac World*. London: Routledge, 2019.

Kraemer, Joel L. *Humanism in the Renaissance of Islam: The Cultural Revival during the Buyid Age*. Leiden: Brill, 1986.

———. *Philosophy in the Renaissance of Islam: Abū Sulaymān al-Sijistānī and His Circle*. Leiden: Brill, 1986.

Levy-Rubin, Milka. *Non-Muslims in the Early Islamic Empire: From Surrender to Coexistence*. Cambridge: Cambridge University Press, 2011.

Lyons, Jonathan. *The House of Wisdom: How the Arabs transformed Western Civilization*. New York: Bloomsbury, 2009.

MacDonald, A. A., M. W. Twomey, and G. J. Reinink. *Learned Antiquity: Scholarship and Society in the Near East, the Greco-Roman World and the Early Medieval West*. Leuven: Peeters, 2003.

MacDonnell, Joseph. *Jesuits by the Tigris: Men for Others in Baghdad*. Boston: Jesuit Mission, 1994.

———. "The Jesuits of Baghdad: 1932–69." *Fairfield Now: The Magazine of Fairfield University* 26:4 (Fall 2003) 32–35.

Meisami, Julie S., and Paul Starkey, eds. *Encyclopedia of Arabic Literature*. Vol. 1. London: Routledge, 1998.

Meri, Josef W., ed. *Medieval Islamic Civilization: An Encyclopedia*. Vol. 1. London: Routledge, 2006.

Milani, Milad. *Sufism in the Secret History of Persia*. London: Routledge, 2014.

Millar, Fergus. "Christian Monasticism in Roman Arabia at the Birth of Mahomet." *Semitica et Classica* 2 (2009) 97–115.

Miller, Timothy S. "Byzantine Hospitals." *Dumbarton Oaks Papers* 38 (1984) 53–63.

———. "The Knights of Saint John and the Hospitals of the Latin West." *Speculum* 53:4 (1978) 709–33.

Milwright, Marcus. "Islamic Art and Architecture." In *The New Cambridge History of Islam*, vol. 4, *Islamic Cultures and Societies to the End of the Eighteenth Century*, edited by Robert Irwin, 682–742. Cambridge: Cambridge University Press, 2010.

Mitri, Tarek. "Christians in Arab Politics." In *Secular Nationalism and Citizenship in Muslim Countries: Arab Christians in the Levant*, edited by Kail C. Ellis, 107–20. Cham, Switzerland: Palgrave Macmillan, 2018.

Ohlig, Karl-Heinz, and Gerd-R. Puin. *The Hidden Origins of Islam: New Research into Its Early History*. Amherst, NY: Prometheus, 2010.

O'Leary, De Lacy. *How Greek Science Passed to the Arabs*. London: William Clowes, 1957.

O'Mahony, Anthony. "The Contributions of Ancient Christian Communities to the Contemporary Middle East." Paper presented at the Conference on Christianity and Freedom: Historical and Contemporary Perspectives, Rome, Italy, December 13–14, 2013.

Osman, Ghada. "Pre-Islamic Arab Converts to Christianity in Mecca and Medina: An Investigation into the Arabic Sources." *The Muslim World* 95 (2005) 67–80.

———. "'The Sheikh of the Translators': The Translation Methodology of Hunayn ibn Ishaq." *Translation and Interpreting Studies* 7:2 (December 2012) 161–75.

Pacini, Andrea. *Christian Communities in the Arab Middle East: The Challenge of the Future*. Oxford: Clarendon, 1998.

Pormann, Peter, and Emilie Savage-Smith. *Medieval Islamic Medicine*. Washington, DC: Georgetown University Press, 2007.

Porter, Roy. *The Cambridge Illustrated History of Medicine*. Cambridge: Cambridge University Press, 2001.

Prince, Chris. "The Historical Context of Arabic Translation, Learning, and the Libraries of Medieval Andalusia." *Library History* 18:2 (2002) 73–87.

Ragab, Ahmad. *The Medieval Islamic Hospital: Medicine, Religion, and Charity*. Cambridge: Cambridge University Press, 2015.

Reinink, Gerrit J. "'Edessa Grew Dim and Nisibis Shone Forth': The School of Nisibis at the Transition of the Sixth-Seventh Century." In *Centers of Learning: Learning and Location in Pre-Modern Europe and the Near East*, edited by J. W. Drijvers and A. A. McDonald, 77–89. Leiden: Brill, 1995.

Robson, L. C. "Recent Perspectives on Christians in the Modern Arab World." *History Compass* 9:4 (2011) 312–25.

Rosen-Ayalon, Myriam. "Art and Architecture in Ayyubid Jerusalem." *Israel Exploration Journal* 40:4 (1990) 305–14.

Rowe, Paul S. "The Middle Eastern Christian as Agent." *International Journal of Middle East Studies* 42:3 (August 2010) 472–74.

Sabella, Brenard. "Christian Contributions to Art, Culture, and Literature in the Arab-Islamic World," In *Secular Nationalism and Citizenship in Muslim Countries: Arab Christians in the Levant*, edited by Kail C. Ellis, 89–106. Cham, Switzerland: Palgrave Macmillan, 2018.

Sabra, A. I. "The Appropriation and Subsequent Naturalization of Greek Science in Medieval Islam: A Preliminary Statement." *History of Science* 25:3 (1987) 223–43.

Sahas, Daniel J. *John of Damascus on Islam: The "Hersey of Ishmaelites."* Leiden: Brill, 1972.

Sarton, George. *Introduction to the History of Science*. Baltimore: Williams & Wilkins, for the Carnegie Institution of Washington, 1927.

Schimmel, Annemarie. "Jesus and Mary as Poetical Images in Rumu's Verse." In *The Routledge Reader in Christian-Muslim Relations*, edited by Mona Siddiqui, 279–90. New York: Routledge, 2013.

Schmid, Nora K. "Louis Cheikho and the Christianization of Pre-Islamic and Early Islamic Ascetic Poetry." *Philological Encounters* 6 (2021) 339–73.

Selin, Helaine, ed. *Encyclopaedia of the History of Science, Technology, and Medicine in Non-Western Cultures*. N.p.: Springer Science & Business, 2013.

Senner, Wayne M., ed. *The Origins of Writing*. Lincoln: University of Nebraska Press, 1991.

Shah, Mustafa. "Trajectories in the Development in Islamic Theology Thought: The Synthesis of Kalam." *Religion Compass* 1:4 (2007) 430–54.

Siddiqui, Mona, ed. *The Routledge Reader in Christian-Muslim Relations*. London: Routledge, 2013.

Siraisi, Nancy G. *Medicine and the Italian Universities, 1250–1600*. Leiden: Brill Academic, 2001.

Taylor, Richard C. "Philosophy." In *The New Cambridge History of Islam*, vol. 4, *Islamic Cultures and Societies to the End of the Eighteenth Century*, edited by Robert Irwin, 532–63. Cambridge: Cambridge University Press, 2010.

Thomas, David Richard, and Barbara H. Roggema, eds. *Christian-Muslim Relations: A Bibliographical History*, vol. 1, *600–900*. History of Christian-Muslim Relations 11. Leiden: Brill, 2009.

Thomas, David Richard, and Alex Mallett, eds. *Christian-Muslim Relations: A Bibliographical History*, vol. 2, *900–1050*. History of Christian-Muslim Relations 14. Leiden: Brill, 2010.

———. *Christian-Muslim Relations: A Bibliographical History*, vol. 3, *1050–1200*. History of Christian-Muslim Relations 15. Leiden: Brill, 2011.

———. *Christian-Muslim Relations: A Bibliographical History*, vol. 4, *1200–1350*. History of Christian-Muslim Relations 17. Leiden: Brill, 2012.

Tottoli, Roberto. "Muslim Attitudes towards Prostration (*Sujud*)." *Studia Islamica* 88 (1998) 5–34.

Trimble, Virginia, et al., eds. *The Biographical Encyclopedia of Astronomers*. New York: SpringerLink, 2007.

Trimingham, J. Spencer. *Christianity among the Arabs in Pre Islamic Times*. London: Longman, 1979.

Watt, John W. "Eastward and Westward Transmissions of Classical Rhetoric." In *Centers of Learning: Learning and Location in Pre-Modern Europe and the Near East*, edited by J. W. Drijvers and A. A. McDonald, 61–76. Leiden: Brill, 1995.

———. "Syriac Translators and Greek Philosophy in Early Abbasid Iraq." *Journal of the CanAdyān Society for Syriac Studies* 4 (2004) 15–26.

Whipple, Allen. "The Role of the Nestorians as the Connecting Link between Greek and Arabic Medicine." *Annals of Medical History*, n.s., 2 (1936) 446–62.

Wicker, Brian. *Witnesses to Faith?: Martyrdom in Christianity and Islam*. Aldershot, UK: Ashgate, 2006.

Worrell, W. H. "Qusta Ibn Luqa on the Use of the Celestial Globe." *Isis*. 35:4 (1944) 285–93.

Young, M. J. L., J. D. Latham, and R. B. Serjeant, eds. *The Cambridge History of Arabic Literature*, vol. 3, *Religion, Learning, and Science in the ʿAbbasid Period*. Cambridge: Cambridge University Press, 1990.

Yousif, Ashoor. "Churchmen and Statesmen: Christian Ecclesiastical Embassies and Diplomacy for Non-Christian Empires during Late Antiquity and Medieval Period (4th–14th Centuries)." *Journal of the CanAdyān Society for Syriac Studies* 20 (2020) 33–57.

6

Causes of the Decline of the North African Church

MARINA BOTROS

This article will discuss the causes that led to the decline of Christianity in North Africa. It will refer to historical events from the arrival of Christianity in North Africa to the campaign of the Byzantine leader Belisarius in North Africa in 533 CE, which was ordered by the Byzantine emperor Justinian, up until the year 698, which witnessed the weakening of the North African church in light of the spread of Islam. It will also examine the conquest of the capital city of Carthage by the Arab leader Hassan bin al-Nu'man. Geographically, this research is focused on North Africa, the Maghreb, that is, present-day Tunisia, Algeria, and Morocco, as well as the western part of Libya, which was formerly known as Tripolitania.

THE ARRIVAL OF CHRISTIANITY IN NORTH AFRICA

Historical sources do not provide us with much on how Christianity arrived in North Africa or on the emergence of the church in this region. This is due to the scarcity of both literary and archaeological texts regarding these topics. As for the gospel, historians do not agree on how it arrived in North Africa. There are those who believe that the gospel arrived through the church of Alexandria, while others believe that it arrived through the church of Rome. The latter is most likely, given that the fathers of the North African church, such as Tertullian (155–230 CE), Cyprian (208–258 CE), and Augustine (354–430 CE), were influenced by the church of Rome and the writings of its fathers. It is also likely that the spread of Christianity in North Africa and the establishment of its church began in the first century CE and continued during the second century through the spread of the gospel by missionaries and through the writings of the early fathers.[1] Before discussing this matter, it is necessary to examine North African society and how it accepted this new religion.

North African society in this period consisted of three elements: the indigenous Berbers, who lived in the desert and inland; the Phoenicians, who founded the city of Carthage in 814 BCE; and the Romans, who constituted the upper class by virtue of their control over government and administration in North Africa.[2]

The different people groups that formed North African society also resulted in different common languages: Berber, Phoenician, and Latin. In addition to these languages, Greek was the dominant language in liturgical prayers and among church leaders from the first century to the third century CE. After the third century, Latin became the dominant language in the church, in liturgical prayers, in official transactions, and in daily life.[3]

Some believe the gospel arrived in North Africa in the first century through foreign missionaries. This was mentioned by the first historians who referred to the Bible in order to prove their theory, for in the Act of the Apostles it says: "Parthians, Medes and Elamites; residents of Mesopotamia, Judea and Cappadocia, Pontus and Asia, Phrygia and Pamphylia, Egypt and the parts of Libya near Cyrene; visitors from Rome (both Jews and converts to Judaism); Cretans and Arabs—we hear them declaring the wonders of God in our own tongues!"[4]

John Foster mentioned that African Christians also played an important role in spreading the Bible in North Africa during the first century.[5]

1. Neil, *History of Christian Mission*, 37; Kane, *Concise History*, 10; Foster, *First Advance*, 37–41; Daniel, *This Holy Seed*, 58–64; Schaff, *History of the Christian Church*, 1:26–28; Latourette, *History of the Expansion*, 2:97.

2. Boer, *Short History of the Early Church*, 84.

3. Wand, *History of the Early Church*, 79.

4. Acts 2:9–11.

5. Foster, *First Advance*, 37; Daniel, *This Holy Seed*, 64; Schaff, *History of the*

The missionary historian Herbert Kane believes that the church in North Africa established itself without the help of foreign missionaries, and its beginning was in the Libyan city Cyrene, where the Romans conscripted a person named Simon or Simon of Cyrene, the son of the Jewish peasant of Cyrene, forcing him to carry the cross of Jesus.[6] Kane based his theory on what was mentioned in the Gospel of Mark: "A certain man from Cyrene, Simon, the father of Alexander and Rufus, was passing by on his way in from the country, and they forced him to carry the cross."[7]

In addition to this biblical evidence, in the first century Saint Tertullian witnessed the conversion of some Berber tribes, such as the Moors and others, to Christianity before the Romans' conversion. Tertullian believed that converting to Christianity was not an organized effort; that is, evangelization was not a Roman initiative.[8]

John Caldwell Theisen also traced the movement of the first Christian refugees from Jerusalem to North Africa to escape the persecution of the Roman emperor Titus (39–81 CE) in the year 70 CE. According to him, the arrival of Christianity in North Africa in the first century was limited to Cyrene, and it is likely that it had not yet reached Carthage and the rest of North Africa.[9] At the beginning of the second century, Christianity reached Carthage. Boer posits—and he is supported by other historical records and literary sources that confirm what Tertullian recorded—that Christianity was established in Carthage in the second century.[10]

During the first and second centuries, the North African church was characterized by a huge increase in the number of converts to Christianity and the translation of the Bible from Hebrew into Latin. Indeed, Tertullian points to "the spread of Christianity in the Roman world, especially given the fact that there are a large number of Christians in North Africa."[11]

The North African church's internal organization was characterized by a pyramidal structure in the hierarchy of its clergy. We find in the late first century and in the early second century that bishops were called

Christian Church, 1:26–28; Latourette, *History of the Expansion*, 2:97; Neil, *History of Christian Mission*, 37; Kane, *Concise History*, 10.

6. Kane, *Concise History*, 10; Neil, *History of Christian Mission*, 37.

7. Mark 15:21.

8. Tertullian, *Answer to the Jews*, 7, quoted in Daniel, *This Holy Seed*, 64.

9. Thiessen, *Survey of World Mission*, 182.

10. Boer, *Short History*, 25; Gwatkin, *Early Church History to 313*, 237; Wand, *History of the Early Church*, 55–56; Chadwick, *Early Church*, 91; Bruce, *Growing Day*, 33.

11. Tertullian, *Apology*, 37.

"master" and became political rulers or advisors to the ruler.[12] With regard to the Bible, some historians believe that its first translation from Hebrew into Latin appeared in North Africa in the late first century or early second century; it is likely that Tertullian himself translated it.[13]

Despite the massive spread of Christianity in North Africa, it remained limited to the inhabitants of the Latin-speaking coastal cities. For the inhabitants of the inland regions, such as the Berbers and the Phoenicians, conversion to Christianity was rare as previously mentioned.[14] The spread of Christianity also had a clear impact on the church and on the increase in the number of bishops. Every town had its own bishop who managed the affairs of his church and cared for it. Since this time, bishops became part of the church's administrative structure.[15]

Christianity spread in North Africa over two and a half centuries (30–280 CE). This spread resulted in the North African church being subjected to violent waves of persecution, as other churches also experienced. We will examine this in three connected episodes of persecution.

IMPORTANT EVENTS IN THE NORTH AFRICAN CHURCH

Christianity in North Africa suffered from many internal and external problems, as well as various persecutions, which led to certain internal weaknesses. The following examination of some of these events will help in understanding the decline of the North African church.

As a result of the rapid spread of Christianity in North Africa and an increase in the number of converts, Christians were persecuted, tortured, and killed. In Carthage, much persecution took place in the Carthage Amphitheater.[16] The era of Emperor Diocletian is considered one of the most significant periods of persecution, for he issued a decree dismissing all Christian officials in his government and all Christian soldiers in the Roman army. He also issued four decrees specific to North Africa between 303 and 304.[17] The emperor even went so far as to issue a decree requiring Christians to hand over Bibles for burning. Some tried to find

12. Moxom, *From Jerusalem to Nicaea*, 65.

13. Schaff, *History of the Christian Church*, 1:28; Frend, *Rise of Christianity*, 347; Wand, *History of the Early Church*, 79.

14. Frend, *Rise of Christianity*, 129.

15. Elliott-Binns, *Beginning of Western Christendom*, 153.

16. Tertullian, *Apologeticum* 37. 4–5.

17. Lacanitius, *Deaths of the Persecutors*, 11.

ways to avoid giving up their Bibles, such as Minsurius, the bishop of Carthage, who gave up books of heresies rather than the Bible. Others, like Felix, the bishop of the city of Thebeoca, refused to hand over their Bibles and instead chose martyrdom.[18] These responses to the decrees led to internal division within the church and to there being two bishops of North Africa: Caecilianus, who was ordained by the pope in Rome, and Donatus, who refused to recognize Caecilianus as the bishop of Carthage and considered himself to be the sole bishop. Donatus also published his ideas, which were opposed by many bishops, most notably by Augustine, who did his best to eliminate Donatus and his followers along with their antagonistic ideas, which were hostile to the orthodox faith.[19]

However, with the ascension of Emperor Constantine (305–337 CE), Christianity was recognized as a legitimate religion alongside other religions by virtue of the Milan decree, which was issued in 313 CE.[20] The province of North Africa became the safest region of the empire and a place where Romans fleeing Germanic attacks on Rome took refuge. However, this safety did not last as the Vandals, a Germanic tribe, tried to cross the Mediterranean Sea and reach the African coast. While they initially failed, their subsequent attempt in 429 was successful after King Gensrick unified their ranks. They were therefore able to enter Carthage in 439. Thus, a new period for Christianity began in North Africa; since the Vandals were Arians, they persecuted the Catholic Christians.[21] Vandal kings alternated between applying policies of persecution at times and tolerance at other times.[22]

Vandal persecution against Christians began when they forced the Catholic clergy to convert to Arianism, destroyed most church buildings, and confiscated church lands and investments. Most of the Catholic clergy was arrested and exiled to Rome and Naples, and performing Christian rites was prohibited, as was the ringing of church bells.[23] However, the Christians of North Africa upheld their orthodox religion

18. Frend, *Donatist Church*, 15; Merrills, ed., *Vandals, Romans, and Berbers*, 261.

19. Merrills, ed., *Vandals, Romans, and Berbers*, 366.

20. Lactantius, *Deaths of the Persecutors*, 44; Eusebius, *Life of Constantine*, 38; Eusebius, *Ecclesiastical History*, 99.

21. Courtois, *Vandales et l'Afrique*, 176.

22. Courtois, *Vandales et l'Afrique*, 290.

23. Victor Vit., *Hist. pers.*, 3:21, 133; Kidd, *History of the Church*, 374; Daniel, *This Holy Seed*, 399; Victor, *History*, 5; Robertson, *History of the Christian Church*, 455.

and performed their rituals in secret.[24] This situation continued until the year 530, when the Byzantine emperor Justinian decided to recover the imperial lands and church properties from the Vandals and launched a military campaign led by the Byzantine commander Belisarius. At this point, North Africa entered a new period of its history, which we now call the Byzantine Era.[25]

In the Byzantine Era, the Vandals were not the only danger the Byzantines faced in North Africa; the Berbers in the inland regions and their attempted incursions into the Byzantine provinces in the north also posed a threat. However, the Berbers were eventually subdued and given official imperial insignia, their independence and sovereignty were recognized, and they were considered friends of the Byzantine Empire.[26] Emperor Justinian had objectives particular to North Africa, such as reconstructing churches materially, spiritually, and morally, as well as repairing what was ruined by the Vandals. Thus, he interfered in church affairs, issued laws and decrees specific to the church, fought dissident elements (such as Donatism, Jews, and Monophysites), and resolved disputes between bishops. These conflicts were not only characteristic of the Byzantine Era but continued until the North African church began to decline in the late seventh century.[27]

Emperor Justinian had a desire to achieve political and religious stability throughout the empire, to restore the unity of the faith, and to unite the church throughout the whole empire. However, this placidity did not last long: the emperor who provided peace to the Christians is the same one who disturbed them once more by interfering in theological matters. During the period from the Council of Ephesus (430) to the Third Council of Constantinople (680–681), the empire suffered deep divisions resulting from discussions on the nature of Christ, a subject known as Christology.[28]

Emperor Justinian took upon himself the responsibility of resolving centuries-old theological disputes, thereby initiating the interference of the state into church affairs. In 540, the emperor presented a new initiative to address the issue of Monophysitism. In order to confront the theological issues facing him, Emperor Justinian issued the book *The Three*

24. Daniel, *This Holy Seed*, 402.

25. For more details on the Byzantine-Vandal wars, see Procopius, *De bell.*, 3:9, 10–12 (ed. Haury), 1:353–61.

26. Procopius, *De bell.*, 3:25, 3–8, 1:412–13.

27. Courtois, *Grégoire VII et l'Afrique du Nord*, 203.

28. Birnie, *L'Église de l'Orient*, 90–91.

Chapters in a decree in 544. *The Three Chapters* comprised the writings of Justinian condemning the writings of Theodore, the bishop of Mopsuisita, Ibas, the bishop of Edessa, and Theodore, the bishop of Cyrus. He considered them Monophysites and the protagonists of Nestorianism.[29]

In reaction to this decree from Emperor Justinian, the African bishops expressed their rejection of the emperor's opinions on theological matters. The emperor did not expect the African clergy for whom he had fought to be the first bishops to attack him. Nevertheless, Pontianus, one of the bishops, addressed him, saying: "You have no right to interfere in religious and theological matters." While the bishops of the West, that is, Rome, also condemned *The Three Chapters*, their opposition was not as fierce that of the African church.[30] This dissent marked the beginning of a strong resistance from the African clergy, who continued to challenge Byzantine interference and insist on their autonomy in leading their congregations.[31]

The last decade of the sixth century witnessed great efforts by the pope in Rome and the ruler of Africa to curb the heretical and anti-Catholic activity. They insisted on the need to confront them and to conduct a comprehensive survey of all the dioceses in North Africa in order to identify heretics. The most important of these was perhaps the Donatists, which were based in the diocese of Numidia. The pope urged the emperor to enact laws and take measures to restrain heretics, stressing the necessity of dealing with the Donatists.[32] Thus, the emperor issued a set of laws against the Donatists, but they were never implemented in North Africa. This ineffectiveness was likely due to the unwillingness of the imperial government to stir up trouble on new fronts while it was suffering from both religious turmoil and war with the Persians.[33]

The Jews were considered one of the most dangerous groups of heretics because of their hostility toward the imperial authority, especially in North Africa; and once Christianity became the official religion of the empire, laws that were particularly anti-Jewish began to be issued. Emperor Maurice issued several decisions between the years 630–632 to suppress the Jews throughout the empire in general, and in North Africa in particular, and to force Jews to be baptized and convert to

29. Birnie, *L'Églis de l'Orient e*, 91–92.

30. Pontianus, *Ep.* PL, 67, 998; Maas, *Exegesis and Empire*, 63–64.

31. Maas, *Exegesis and Empire*, 63–64.

32. Gregorius I, *Ep. IV*, 32 (CCL 140:223–51).

33. Gregorius I, *Ep. V*, 3 (CCL 140:268).

Christianity. These decisions reflected the mutual hostility between Judaism and Christianity at that time.[34]

At around the middle of the seventh century, Carthage became the epicenter for the controversy surrounding the Monophysites, who emphasized a belief in the one nature of Christ. This was exacerbated by the fact that Carthage had become a refuge for those fleeing Egypt, Syria, and the surrounding regions due to the wars of the Byzantine Empire with the Persians and the Arabs, and the associated political and religious instability of these areas. As a result, Carthage became overrun with religious conflicts over the nature of Christ.[35]

Some emperors tried to ban all theological discussions regarding the nature of Christ throughout the empire between the years 633–681. As a result of these decrees issued by the Byzantine emperors regarding the nature of Christ, waves of protests by the clergy and the people spread in all parts of the empire. These protests were manifested in the participation of the North African bishops in the controversy surrounding the nature of Christ: whether it was one nature or two natures with two wills. They also led the opposition in the Third Council of Constantinople in 680–681.[36]

The church of North Africa corresponded with the church of Rome at various points in time. The North African church had links to the church of Rome from the Christian evangelization in North Africa, throughout the Vandal periods, and during the Byzantine Era, i.e., after 533. This relationship between the two churches also saw mutual interventions: during the issue of *The Three Chapters*, when Pope Harihouri interfered in the affairs of the North African church, and when African bishops participated in the councils of Rome in the seventh century. The nature of the relationship between the churches was also evident in the desire of the pope to control the North African church, and the desire of African bishops to prevent this control.[37]

Regarding the relations between Rome and the church in North Africa during Arab rule, we have reliable sources that show us the regular correspondence between the papacy of Rome and the bishops of Africa. This provides us with information on the relationship between them during and after the Arab conquest of North Africa. At the end of the ninth century, and as indicated by a primary source, the African bishops wrote

34. Theophanes, *Chron.*, AM 6106 (ed. de Boor), 300–301; Sharf, *Byzantine Jewry*, 44.

35. Ostrogorsky, *History of the Byzantine State*, 127.

36. Price and Gaddis, trans., *Acts of the Council of Chalcedon*, 1:55.

37. Markus, *Christianity and Dissent*, 33.

to Pope Phormosus in Rome, asking for his advice on dealing with the disputes that arose between the bishops of the dioceses and the governors of the provinces. This document also indicates the continued presence of more than one bishop in the North African church, which was a phenomenon that began to diminish during Arab rule.[38]

To confirm this, we refer to the letter sent by clergy in Africa in the tenth century that invites Pope Benedict VII to visit Africa in order to consecrate and bless a priest named James, who was elected by the people and other clergy to become the bishop of Carthage. It was necessary for the three episcopal leaders to meet in Carthage in order to consecrate the archbishop of Carthage.[39]

Additionally, news that reached Rome regarding the situation in Carthage in the eleventh century through the letters of Pope Leo IX affirmed the dominance of the diocese of Carthage over the other North African dioceses. He expressed it by virtue of a papal order stating:

> There is no doubt that the Bishop of Carthage, according to us, is second to the great Roman Pontiff, he is the Archbishop of the largest civilization in all Africa, it is impossible for him to lose this privilege to any other African bishop, the privilege that was granted to him by the Holy Apostle Paul, and which he will keep as long as the name of our Lord Jesus Christ is invoked in Rome, whether Carthage would be deserted, or whether it would return to glory, and this clearly derives from the Synod of the venerable Bishops of all the provinces.[40]

Pope Leo IX also emphasized that the archbishop of Carthage was the only bishop in Africa, and that the African church derived its status from the Holy See in Rome. There is no doubt that what was mentioned in the pope's letters presented a symbolic picture of the end of the long history of ecclesiastical relations between Carthage and Africa, during which the church of Africa had autonomy; yet it always derived its episcopal authority from the Holy See in Rome.[41]

Of course, times and circumstances had changed. In the first centuries of Arab rule, the church of Africa and the church of Rome were of equal power, having the same faith derived from Saint Peter the apostle. However, this changed after the eleventh century, when a letter from

38. Flodoardus, *Hist. eccl. Rem.* (PL 135:267); Mesnage, *L'Afrique Chrétienne*, 534.

39. Flodoardus, *Hist. eccl. Rem.* (PL 135:267).

40. Leo IX, *Ep. 84* (PL 143:729).

41. Leo IX, *Ep. 84* (PL 143:730).

Rome—about which we do not have any details—was sent by Pope Gregory VII to Archbishop Kyriakos of Carthage, the last of the Carthaginian African bishops.[42]

Relations between the church of North Africa and the church of Rome were characterized by mutual respect and recognition of authority. The church of Africa recognized the spiritual authority and status of the church of Rome, and the latter confirmed the rightfulness of the church of Africa to manage the internal affairs of the church in matters in which faith was in jeopardy. This is similar to what happened with the pope's interference in the affairs of the episcopate of Numidia, in which there was some deviation from the orthodox faith. The prevalence of Donatism rendered an intervention necessary in order to prevent its further spread, something that the other African bishops may have understood. Thus, the authority and spiritual dominance of the church of Rome over the church of Africa remained appreciated, respected, and welcomed even after the Arab conquest of North Africa.[43]

CAUSES OF THE DECLINE OF CHRISTIANITY IN NORTH AFRICA

The causes that led to the tragic decline of the North African church were numerous and both internal and external. Indeed, the Arab conquest and the spread of Islam were not the main causes behind the decline of the church. The church itself was one of the causes that led to this decline. In the following section we will analyze these causes and their impact on the church.

THE DIRECT CAUSES

The Church's Preoccupation with Donatism

The most important internal, direct cause of the decline of the North African church might be the presence of Donatism. This was one of the most significant problems that affected the church since its founding in the second century and its subsequent spread in North Africa, especially in the diocese of Numidia. The North African church directed all its energy

42. Gregorius VII, *Ep. I*, 23 (PL 148:307–8); *Ep. III*, 19 (PL 148:450).

43. Markus, *Christianity and Dissent*, 34.

towards repelling the danger of Donatism, defending the orthodox faith, and preventing its spread beyond the borders of the diocese of Numidia.[44]

The danger of Donatism was somewhat diminished by virtue of an effort spearheaded by Saint Augustine at the Council of Carthage in 411 that restricted Donatism to the diocese of Numidia. Nevertheless, this ideology remained present within the North African church, weakening its growth and fragmenting its members, who were supposed to be united in the one body of Christ. The activity of the Donatists increased under the Byzantine presence in North Africa, leading to conflicts between bishops, diverting their attention to the internal affairs of the church, and subsequently causing spiritual, moral, and material weakening of the church.[45]

We see that after the spread of Donatism, North Africa was divided into churches that followed the church of Rome and the archbishop of Carthage, or Donatist churches that followed the Donatist bishop in Numidia. However, the entire North African church remained loyal to the Catholic Church. Although Donatism was nothing but a splinter movement from the principles of orthodox Catholicism, it was the cause of the decline of the North African Catholic Church due to the internal division of the Christians in North Africa between true Catholicism and Donatism, which was particular to North Africa.[46]

Christian Paganism

The term "paganism" is commonly used to refer to a variety of widely separated religions that existed during antiquity and the Middle Ages. Some of these pagan religions were the Greco-Roman religions of the Roman Empire, which included the worship of Roman emperors, various mysterious religions, monotheistic religions (such as Neoplatonism and Gnosticism), and the local indigenous ethnic religions that were practiced within the empire. This term was also used during the Middle Ages to refer to religions that were practiced beyond the former Roman Empire, such as Germanic paganism, Egyptian paganism, and Baltic paganism. From the standpoint of the early Christians, these religions were all described as ethnic (or Gentile—"non-Jewish," "Ethnicus" in Greek, "Gentiles" in

44. Frend, *Donatist Church*, 333.
45. Pringle, *Defense of Byzantine Africa*, 74.
46. Frend, *Donatist Church*, 333.

Latin and in Hebrew, later replaced by "paganism") as opposed to Second Temple Judaism by the beginning of the late Middle Ages.[47]

As for North Africa, the church and Christianity were influenced by the worship of local pagan deities by the Berbers, such as Saturn, Baal, and others, which continued in North Africa until the spread of Christianity.[48] Tertullian wrote a warning opposing "idolatry" due to the persecution of the church and Christians by the pagan emperors. He also criticized all the imperial decrees that were issued against Christian worship, pointing out that they were a deviation from the nature of the orthodox Christian faith. What the general governor of Africa was committing against the Christians during their trials was a form of paganism, since they were forced to abandon their religion despite their innocence. It should also be noted that Tertullian himself was a pagan before converting to Christianity. Nevertheless, he accused certain Christians and criticized their adherence to the Roman pagan gods and continued practice of old rituals even after their conversion to Christianity.[49] According to Tertullian and his understanding of Christianity, Christians worshiped the one God, who, though invisible, created the world with his word and power. He also mentioned that Christians used pagan expressions such as "God is great and good," "God's giving," and "willed by God."[50]

Although Christianity in North Africa meant gathering every week to read the Scriptures and every month to meet the needs of poor Christians, the Christians still considered the pagans to be their brothers and felt close to those seeking knowledge of the true God. This is evidence that the Christians allowed paganism to be integrated into Christianity.[51] Most dangerous was when Christians allowed the practice of offering sacrifices to the emperor even though the Bible forbids it. In addition, North African Christians referred to the emperor by the title "Lord," established prayers for him, and asked God to preserve the Roman Empire.[52] Christians were accused of neglecting the offering of sacrifices to the gods and the emperors, and thus causing the natural disasters that befell the country. However, the pagans neglected offering sacrifices because they converted to Christianity. Tertullian emphasized that the natural disasters

47. Rüpke, *Religion of the Romans*, 35.

48. Latourette, *History of the Expansion*, 1:366.

49. Tertullian, *On Idolatry*, in Donaldson, ed., *Ante-Nicene Fathers*, 3:61.

50. Tertullian, *On Idolatry*, in Donaldson, ed., *Ante-Nicene Fathers*, 3:62–63.

51. Tertullian, *On Idolatry*, in Donaldson, ed., *Ante-Nicene Fathers*, 3:65.

52. Tertullian, *On Idolatry*, in Donaldson, ed., *Ante-Nicene Fathers*, 3:66.

occurred due to the Christians' tolerance of the pagan worship and rituals, and he stated that allowing idolatry along with practicing Christian rites and rituals amounted to "adultery and fornication." He also referred to the worship of the "copper serpent" within the church in North Africa.[53]

Later, during the era of Saint Augustine, we notice the continued influence of the pagan heritage on the public celebrations of Christians, including celebrations within the North African church. These influences were manifested by the practice of worshiping martyrs and saints. Augustine remarked that the celebrations and feasts that were held for the martyrs and saints were like the practices and sacrifices that the pagans offered to the gods; there could be no doubt that these celebratory acts expressed the weakness that afflicted the church and the Christians' respect for the old pagan customs.[54]

But how did paganism, and especially allowing its rituals to be practiced within the church, contribute to the acceptance of and conversion to Christianity by the indigenous population? Some believe that because the Romans allowed for the practice of pagan rituals within the church, they hoped to have pagans convert to Christianity simply by entering the church. Incidentally, this is what happened, especially after pagans witnessed the unification of prayer. However, the truth of the matter is that the language difference between the practice of pagan rituals and Christian prayer was always an obstacle for the conversion of these pagans to Christianity. Some Christian clergymen refused this tolerance towards pagans, out of fear for the purity of the Christian faith and out of respect for the martyrs and saints who died at the hands of the pagans.[55] In any case, these measures attracted pagans to devoting themselves to the church and to practicing church rituals, so that even scholars such as Mibiti have opined that Christianity in North Africa became a mixture of inherited apostolic Christianity and pagan African culture.[56]

Moreover, the role played by the bishops and the church leaders in supporting this approach weakened the North African church.[57] As masses of pagans converted to Christianity, they brought with them their pagan customs, beliefs, and traditions. Despite the church's attempts to eliminate these aspects, all efforts were in vain, and paganism remained

53. Tertullian, *On Idolatry*, in Donaldson, ed., *Ante-Nicene Fathers*, 3:67.

54. Schaff, *History of the Christian Church*, 3:429.

55. Jackson, *History of the Christian Church*, 288–89.

56. Mbiti, *Bible and Theology in African Christianity*, 67.

57. Latourette, *History of the Expansion*, 1:330.

influential within Christianity as it had been in its first period in North Africa.[58]

Despite the attempts of the early church fathers during the first five centuries of Christianity in North Africa to eradicate the features and status of pagan worship throughout the region, they failed. Converts had maintained many of their pagan worship rituals alongside Christian rituals even after widespread conversions. Some scholars call this period "the Age of Theological Confusion."[59] Others believe that while there was reportedly widespread conversion of pagans to Christianity within the first century and into the second century CE, it was only what is called "nominal Christianity;" that is, they converted to Christianity in name only while continuing to practice pagan customs such as drinking wine, fornicating, and eating raw meat.[60]

Therefore, the spread of Christianity in North Africa was a period of religious history that was characterized by the intermixing of pagan customs with Christian beliefs. This in turn led to an increase in the number of spiritually weak clergymen. Following the Arab Islamic conquest of North Africa, African Christians converted to Islam without hesitation due to certain similarities between their pagan customs and traditions that were forbidden by Christianity, as well as attraction to Islamic customs such as polygamous marriage and divorce.[61]

There is no doubt that paganism influenced the purity of Christian doctrine and the teachings of the gospel; had it not been for the clergy allowing the syncretism of Christian teachings with pagan beliefs, it would have been possible for Christianity to continue in North Africa alongside the spread of the Islamic religion.

Secularism within the Church

Secularism spread in the North African church during the first five centuries CE. Because most of the land was owned by the church, the clergy became preoccupied with worldly matters related to the management of

58. Frend, *Rise of Christianity*, 558; Daniel, *This Holy Seed*, 371; Boer, *Short History*, 144; Schaff, *History of the Christian Church*, 3:466; Walker, *History of the Christian Church*, 70.

59. Daniel, *This Holy Seed*, 392.

60. Van der Meer, *Augustine the Bishop*, 46.

61. Latourette, *History of the Expansion*, 94.

church land and property.[62] Instead of directing the income of these lands towards building a spiritual church of God, they focused on a material one through the support of the needy, the poor, the sick, the widows, the orphans, the strangers, the destitute, and the elderly. They established charitable institutions, and these funds were exploited and invested in civil projects. Thus, the church lost sight of its mission to evangelize and instead was turned into an institution whose mission, as Saint Augustine puts it, was to raise funds.[63]

Of course, this affected the clergy and distracted them from their primary mission of evangelization and spreading spiritual awareness among the inhabitants of North Africa. Christians in turn abandoned religious matters, only going to church in search of work or in search of rich husbands or wives who owned properties within the church. Thus, the church essentially became a place to achieve material desires.[64]

Despite the increase in the number of Christians within the church, they were not true Christians, for they went to church in search of personal benefit and not for the enrichment of their faith. Additionally, the religious freedom—the discretion regarding their spiritual lives as well as the church funds—that was granted to the Christians by the church changed their ideologies. Thus, it created a confusion regarding Christianity and faith, which were no longer associated with moral standards and supplications to Christ but were rather related to worldly matters. Amid these contrasting currents, the church was unable to withstand the spread of Islam.[65]

It is worth noting that the secular clergy was not a product of this era. Rather, it dates back to the times of Saint Cyprian. When he converted to Christianity, he donated all his lands and money to the church. This act became a tradition for some and was also a reason for much of the lands and wealth of the church. Thus, it resulted in a love for possessions and wealth, in moral corruption, and in straying away from the love of God.[66]

Another reason behind the spread of secularism among the clergy is that the state granted them the right to practice business in addition to being exempt from taxes. This led to unqualified clergy, both priests and bishops. As a result, the clergy enjoyed raising money and bishops were appointed to the provinces. Thus, members of the clergy enjoyed

62. Schaff, *History of the Christian Church*, 3:99.

63. Schaff, *History of the Christian Church*, 3:91.

64. Daniel, *This Holy Seed*, 388.

65. Jackson, *History of the Christian Church*, 567.

66. Jackson, *History of the Christian Church*, 567.

immunity, exemption from taxes, and other privileges like those of any Roman ruler in the Byzantine Empire.[67]

As Van Der Meer has stated, the clergy were unqualified and did not have an education. The ordination of bishops and priests became based on the church's need for them rather than qualifications such as education and mastery of Latin, the language of rituals and worship within the church. Therefore, the unqualified clergy failed to communicate the Word of God or to explain the Bible. Additionally, the bishops exercised judicial power. There evolved a generation of clergy who were unable to perform rituals, to worship, or to take proper care of the Christians in North Africa. This brought changes in quality of the clergy, especially the bishops, and a shift of focus from ecclesiastical polity to civil polity in terms of office rankings.[68]

We can say, then, that the ascension of the unqualified to the ranks of the clergy within the North African church caused it to lose much spirituality and moral superiority, which were its most important characteristics. The nature of the spiritual interpretation of the Bible also deteriorated, and the church clergy lost the spiritual revelation of evangelization. As a result, some of the clergy neglected their role and their dioceses and lost the spiritual blessings that any cleric who is close to God would receive. Hence, it is not surprising that personal disputes emerged between the clergy and the bishops, as they attempted to drive a wedge between each other with the imperial or the papal authorities.[69]

The Collapse of the Internal Organization of the Church

During the first four centuries CE, the North African church was an episcopal church in which the many bishops were organized according to a strict hierarchy. This system began in the first century, and the hierarchical form of this episcopal polity was completed during the times of Saint Cyprian in the middle of the third century.[70] Saint Cyprian stressed the importance of having a system within the church that guarantees the hierarchical rankings of the clergy, including archbishops, bishops, assistant bishops, and priests. He insisted that "the bishop is the church,

67. Codex Theodosianusin *New Eusebius*, 285.

68. Schaff, *History of the Christian Church*, 3:131.

69. Schaff, *History of the Christian Church*, 3:132.

70. Neil, *History of Christian Mission*, 37.

and the church is the bishop." If there were no bishop, there would be no church. Cyprian believed that the bishops carry the Holy Spirit within them. At the same time, he emphasized the necessity of equality between the bishops and that each bishop has the complete freedom to manage the affairs of his church.[71]

During the time when Saint Augustine was the archbishop of Hippo, he had six deacons and three priests in 424, and seven priests including two deacons in 427.[72]

There was also a diminishing number of bishops during the period of Vandal rule in North Africa due to some of them fleeing to Italy and Spain to escape the oppression of the Vandals, while others fled to some monasteries in Libya and Mauritania. African bishops suffered much torture and exclusion from their churches after being destroyed by the Vandals.[73]

The pyramidal structure within the church continued in the Byzantine Era: at the base there was the bishop of the municipality (and it is likely that the churches of the villages were at the base of the pyramid); above him in rank was the bishop of the city; the bishop of the diocese came at the top of the pyramid; and all of them were headed by the archbishop of the church in North Africa. The total number of bishops at this time reached more than five hundred.[74]

It is worth mentioning that the bishops during this era devoted themselves to solving theological problems, abandoning any interest in the affairs of the church and the people, neglecting matters of worship and liturgical prayers, straying away from serving the poor and overseeing charitable projects, and generally neglecting pastoral work. In the early seventh century, the clergy was divided into two groups: the first was immersed in solving theological problems and the other was busy gathering funds. There were also several secular clergies. Undoubtedly, all these matters contributed to the decline of the North African church in the face of the Arab conquest of North Africa.[75]

71. Cyprian, *On the Unity of the Church*, 4–6, in Bettenson, ed., *Documents of the Christian Church*, 101–2.

72. Frend, *Early Church*, 238; Van der Meer, *Augustine the Bishop*, 225; Boer, *Short History*, 134–44; Scahff, *History of the Christian Church*, 2:123–124.

73. Boer, *Short History*, 125.

74. Boer, *Short History*, 134.

75. Boer, *Short History*, 135.

Refraining from Localizing the Bible

Regarding the language of the Bible, after the spread of Christianity in North Africa—specifically in the year 200 CE—the Bible became available in Latin due to the presence of the Romans who spoke Latin. The church played an important role in spreading the Bible throughout the country, and Christians translated it into their local languages such as Coptic, Syriac, and Aramaic, alongside Latin.

For example, Saint Jerome (327–420 CE) translated the Bible and wrote liturgical prayers in Latin. However, he did not use the literary Latin language used in all the holy books, but rather wrote in colloquial Latin so that everyone could read it. Saint Jerome believed that it was easy to write the Word of God in the common everyday language, that the language of religion should be compatible with ordinary human understanding, and that if laypeople did not understand the Word of God in their everyday language, then their faith would have been difficult to acquire, and it would not continue throughout the generations.[76]

One of the most distinct and complex things that happened is that the early church did not translate the Bible into the Arabic nor the Persian language. The clergy was not concerned about translating the Bible into the Himyarite language in Yemen, for example. In these areas, the clergy continued to read the Bible in advanced languages such as Greek and Latin. As a result, common believers lacked a good understanding of the Word of God and became exposed to other doctrinal currents.[77] In North Africa, the clergy were not concerned about translating the Bible from Latin into the language of the indigenous people such as Tamazight or Phoenician, because Latin was the official language of the North African church and the language of the Bible.[78]

As a result, Christian evangelization was weakened, except amongst the few Berbers and Phoenicians, who in turn did not care about translating the Bible into the Phoenician language. Perhaps if there was an Amazigh translation of the Bible, we would have found a thriving Amazigh church in North Africa.[79] We can say, then, that the North Af-

76. Groves, *Planting of Christianity in Africa*, 91.

77. Kane, *Concise History*, 52; Neil, *History of Christian Mission*, 37.

78. Duchesne, *Early History of the Christian Church*, 1:285–86; Kidd, *History of the Church*, 111; Elliott-Binns, *Beginning of Western Christendom*, 159; Boer, *Short History*, 84; Thiessen, *Survey*, 174.

79. Van der Meer, *Augustine the Bishop*, 228.

rican church was closely associated with the Roman church and not with the indigenous people. This was due to reading the Bible and performing the liturgical prayers exclusively in Latin and to the clergy's disregard for the needs of the indigenous landowners of the Berbers. This led to the weakening of evangelization among them and to the decline of the church's role in society in the face of the Arab conquest.[80]

Neglect of Evangelization in the Inlands

The fact that the Bible did not reach the indigenous peoples in North Africa had its impact on the decline of the missionary role of the church. This is similar to what happened in the churches of Egypt, where the church made special efforts through missionaries to reach the upper classes of the population in cities such as Alexandria, while neglecting to show interest in evangelization to the distant regions west of Egypt. Similarly, the church in Carthage did not make significant efforts to reach the Berbers in the far south.[81]

Christian evangelization in North Africa was limited to urban regions as well as coastal regions. In fact, the church did not realize that the majority of North Africans were Berber tribes—thus, the church did not make any effort to accommodate them. Rather, the church held itself as an entity within a Roman colony and it failed to reach the areas established in the interior regions. Despite the easy conversion of pagans to Christianity, the poor efforts made to assimilate these people prevented them from fully embracing Christianity. Even if there was assimilation in the most limited sense, it was only at the social level, and was not religious or within the church. As a result, the indigenous population, especially the Berbers and the Phoenicians in the rural regions, remained ignorant of and largely ignored Christianity.[82]

Despite the rapid spread of Christianity in North Africa during the first three centuries CE, the church that had failed in the Christian evangelization among the Berbers consequently failed in preventing the assimilation of the arriving Muslim Arabs, resulting in many Roman Christians either fleeing to Europe or surrendering to Muslim Arab rule. It would have been possible for the church to persist if it had rectified

80. Latourette, *History of the Expansion* 1:91.

81. Groves, *Planting of Christianity in Africa*, 1:88.

82. Chadwick, *Early Church*, 90–91.

its error and had been interested in Christian evangelization among the indigenous population of the Berbers and the Phoenicians.[83]

Groves confirms this: "The North African Church's lack of seriousness in evangelization and its failure in sharing the orthodox faith with the Berbers were the most important causes of the doom of this Church." The Muslims did the opposite, because even though the Qur'an was not translated into Tamazight or Phoenician, Islam spread among them because the Muslim Arabs succeeded in assimilating them religiously and socially, according to the principle that says: "there is no preference for an Arab over a non-Arab except by piety."[84]

INDIRECT CAUSES

The Invasion of the Vandals and the Persecution of the Church

One of the most important factors that contributed to the decline of the church in North Africa was the invasion of the Arian Vandals, who were hostile to the Apostolic church in Rome, and this hostility is demonstrated in their persecution of the North African church. Catholic bishops and clergy suffered many forms of torture, exile, and imprisonment, while monasteries were dissolved, churches were demolished, and the Vandals seized all the properties of the African church, including lands, buildings, and farms.[85]

With the repeated hostile attempts of the Vandals to impose their Arian beliefs, many literary works by Catholic bishops appeared on the apology of the orthodox faith against Arianism while they were exiled from their churches. Among these works is that of Victor Al-Fati, who wrote the history *Against Persecution* during his exile from his church at the hands of King Honorik in the year 480. It is worth noting that only the works of Victor Al-Fati survive among the writings of these exiled bishops.[86] Despite the violent practices carried out by some Vandal kings toward the churchmen and the bishops in North Africa, King Helidric allowed the return of the bishops from exile. He also allowed church

83. Northcott, *Christianity in Africa*, 57–58.
84. Groves, *Planting of Christianity in Africa*, 8.
85. Duchesne, *Early History of the Christian Church*, 3:432.
86. Courtois, *Vandales et l'Afrique*, 293.

clergy to hold the council in Carthage in 523 and to perform prayers and celebrate holidays.[87]

King Helidric was dethroned in 530—perhaps in part because of his tolerance towards the Catholic clergy. This is supported by the fact that after he was dethroned, the imperial administration in Constantinople took upon itself the task of saving and protecting the Catholic Christians in North Africa from the oppression of the Arian Vandals. They prepared armies to fight and expel them, an effort that was ultimately successful. Catholicism continued to withstand the persecution of Arianism, and the African Catholic bishops did their utmost to maintain the orthodox faith intellectually and spiritually.[88]

Despite the hostile policy of the Vandals toward the church in North Africa in general, and toward the bishops in particular, the orthodox faith within the church was established. This is demonstrated in the production of literary works in the face of Arianism. However, the long period of persecution and exile of the clergy and the destruction of the church by the Vandals sabotaged the efforts to save the Catholic Church and weakened it spiritually, morally, and materially. This persecution was the final blow to the church, which did not withstand the Arab conquest.[89]

The Interference of the Byzantine Emperors in the Affairs of North Africa

After the Byzantine Empire secured North Africa militarily and administratively from the Vandals, and after restoring church properties taken by the Vandals during the reign of the Byzantine emperor Justinian, the emperor sought to interfere in arranging church affairs. Thus, he issued a decree in 534 for the organization of the church, and the land of the Arian clergy were confiscated and offered to the Catholic clergy.

Additionally, Emperor Justinian issued sets of laws from the years 537 to 545, through which the emperor was able to determine who would be the archbishop of the North African church. He began controlling the bishops, raising the status of the bishop of Carthage at one time, and the status of the bishop of Byzacena at another time. He saw himself to be the

87. Possidius, *Life of St. Augustine*, 25; Frend, *Early Church*, 30.

88. Latourette, *History of the Christian Church*, 1:196.

89. Robertson, *History of the Christian Church*, 460.

shadow of Christ on earth and the only one who had the right and the authority to interfere in the affairs of the church.[90]

When the political and administrative situation in the empire calmed down, Emperor Justinian decided to further interfere in the affairs of the North African church by issuing a decree in 545 regarding the "Condemnation of the Three Chapters."[91] This sparked controversy and division among churchmen, as we have seen. There is no doubt that these interferences by the emperor with his laws and decrees contributed to the scattering of the church, created conflicts between the bishops, and contributed to the division of the church from within.[92]

The Interference of the Popes of Rome in the Affairs of the Church

After the Byzantine Empire took control over North Africa and its church, a new period began in the relationship of the North African church (represented by the archbishop of Carthage) and the church of Rome (represented by the pope of Rome). This period saw efforts by the pope to interfere in the affairs of the North African church. Although the clergy rejected all form of interference from the pope in the affairs of their church, this did not prevent the popes attempting to interfere and to control the church. They considered the church in Africa to be the property of the church of Rome.[93]

For example, we find a huge number of letters sent by Pope Gregory with the aim of interfering in the affairs of the church indirectly.[94] The most important of these were his letters to the archbishop of Carthage stressing that no bishop or priest was allowed to visit Rome without his permission or to leave his church without writing directly to the pope. Pope Gregory also pointed out the necessity of dealing with the Donatist bishops and the Jews. In addition, he interfered in the transfer of bishops between the dioceses within Africa, as well as those between Africa and Rome.[95] We have also witnessed the interference of the pope in the issue of *The Three Chapters* when he had sworn to the emperor that he would

90. Devreese, *L'Église d'Afrique*, 144.
91. Grillmeier, *Christ in Christian Tradition*, II/2, 411.
92. Frend, *Rise of Christianity*, 835.
93. Facundus, *Contr. Moc.*, 64.
94. Gregorius I, *Ep. I*, 75 (CCL 140:84).
95. Markus, *Christianity and Dissent*, 33–34.

end this debate. Thus, he ratified the decree condemning *The Three Chapters* and settled the matter by forcing the bishops of North Africa to agree to this decree.[96]

The Theological Issues

In the first six centuries CE, theological differences and schismatic ideas played an important role in the division of the church. This was apparent in the presence of certain fanatical zealots who were hard-liners in applying the orthodox faith and proponents for the continuity and purity of the church. Dissident movements emerged that led to division and weakness within the church until the Arab conquest in the seventh century.[97]

These schisms and theological differences led to divisions between Christians in North Africa and abroad. For example, Donatism succeeded in dividing North Africa into Catholic churches affiliated with the church of Rome and Donatist churches. The issue of *The Three Chapters* also divided the churches into those affiliated with Emperor Justinian, who condemned *The Three Chapters* and excommunicated its writers, and those churches opposed to the emperor's decisions. All of this weakened the strength and the unity of the church.[98]

As a result of these divisions and schisms, clergymen lost purity of thought and belief in theological matters, and instead devoted their efforts to discussions, to the apology of faith, to controversial theological issues, and to convening councils. The North African church became unable to direct its efforts toward the evangelization and communication of the true faith to the indigenous population; it consumed all its energy in the apology of faith and the validity of the gospel. As Cecil Northcott puts it, "the Church has spent its living blood on controversy and internal disagreements."[99]

96. Markus, *Christianity and Dissent*, 35.

97. Gasque, "North Africa Church," 95; Isichei, *History of Christianity in Africa*, 34.

98. Frend, *Donatist Church*, 335.; Schaff, *History of the Christian Church*, 3:360; Neil, *History of Christian Mission*, 38.

99. Northcott, *Christianity*, 57.

A CONCLUSION

It appears that the churchmen played a role in the decline of the church in the face of the Arab conquest because of the clergy's neglect of the church's affairs, their personal conflicts and doctrinal disputes, the pursuit of wealth and the moral corruption, and disregarding the interest of the church. Secondly, this study shows that the interference of the emperor and the archbishop of Rome in the affairs of the North African church and their pursuit of wealth and moral corruption were strong causes of the decline of the church. Thirdly, this study highlights the doctrinal differences and theological controversy raised by Emperor Justinian regarding the issue of *The Three Chapters*, in addition to the continuous spread of Donatism within the North African church, which contributed greatly to its decline in the face of the Arab conquest. And finally, this study confirmed that the Berbers played an important role in supporting the Arabs against the Byzantines, believing that they would provide them better safety and protection.

BIBLIOGRAPHY

The Acts of the Council of Constantinople of 553: With Related Texts on the Three Chapters Controversy. Translated by Richard Price. Liverpool: Liverpool University Press, 2009.

Andrew H. Merrills, ed. *Vandals, Romans, and Berbers*. Aldershot, UK: Ashgate, 2004.

Bettenson, Henry, ed.. *Documents of the Christian Church*. Oxford: Oxford University Press, 2011.

Boer, Harry. *A Short History of the Early Church*. Grand Rapids: Eerdmans, 1978.

Bruce, F. F. *The Growing Day*. London: Paternoster, 1951.

Chadwick, Henry. *The Early Church*. Middlesex, UK: Penguin, 1967.

Courtois, Christian. "Grégoire VII et l'Afrique du Nord. Remarques sur les communautés chrétiennes d'Afrique au XIe siècle." *Revue Historique* 195 (1945) 97–122, 193–226.

———. *Les Vandales Et L'afrique*. Paris: Scientia, 1964.

Daniel, Robin. *This Holy Seed*. Chester, UK: Tamarisk, 1993.

Devreesse Robert. "L'église D'afrique Durant L'occupation Byzantine." *Mélanges D'archéologie et D'histoire* 57 (1940) 143–66.

Donaldson, James, ed. *Ante-Nicene Fathers*. Grand Rapids: Eerdmans, 1986.

Duchesne, L. *Early History of the Christian Church: From Its Foundation to the End of the Fifth Century*. London: J. Murray, 1950.

Elliott-Binns, L. E. *The Beginning of Western Christendom*. London: Lutterworth, 1948.

Foakes-Jackson, F. J. *The History of the Christian Church*. Cambridge: J. Hall, 1924.

Foster, John. *The First Advance*. London: SPCK, 1991.

Frend, W. H. C. *The Donatist Church*. Oxford: Oxford University Press, 1952.

———. *The Rise of Christianity.* Philadelphia: Fortress, 1989.

Gasque, W. Ward. "The North Africa Church." In *The History of Christianity*, edited by Tim Dowley. London: Lion, 1997.

Grillmeier, Alois, and Theresia Hainthaler. *Christ in Christian Tradition.* Mowbray: Westminster John Knox 1995.

Groves. C. P. *The Planting of Christianity in Africa.* Vol. 1. London: Lutterworth, 1948.

Gwatkin, Henry Melvin. *Early Church History to 313 A.D.* London: Macmillan, 1912.

Isichei, Elizabeth. *A History of Christianity in Africa.* London: SPCK, 1995.

Kane, Herbert. *A Concise History of the Christian World Mission.* Grand Rapids: Baker, 1982.

Latourette, K. S. *A History of the Expansion of Christianity.* Vol. 1. New York: Harper and Row, 1971.

Maas, Michael, and Junilius Junilius. *Exegesis and Empire in the Early Byzantine Mediterranean: Junillus Africanus and the Instituta Regularia Divinae Legis.* Tübingen: Mohr Siebeck 2003.

Markus, R. A. "Christianity and Dissent in Roman North Africa: Changing Perspectives in Recent Work." *Studies in Church History* 9 (1972) 21–36.

Mbiti, John S. *Bible and Theology in African Christianity.* Nairobi: Oxford University Press, 1986.

Merrills, Andrew H., ed. *Vandals, Romans and Berbers.* Aldershot: Ashgate, 2004.

Mesnage, J. *L'Afrique Chrétienne.* Évêches et ruines antiques. Paris: E. Leroux, 1912.

Moxom, Philip Stafford. *From Jerusalem to Nicaea: The Church in the First Three Centuries.* Boston: Roberts Bros., 1895.

Neil, Stephen. *A History of Christian Mission.* London: Hodder & Stoughton, 1965.

Northcott, Cecil. *Christianity in Africa.* London: SCM, 1963.

Ostrogorsky, George. *History of the Byzantine State.* New Brunswick, NJ: Rutgers University Press, 1995.

Price, Richard, and Michael Gaddis, trans. *The Acts of the Council of Chalcedon.* Liverpool: Liverpool University Press, 2005.

Pringle, Denys. *The Defense of Byzantine Africa from Justinian to the Arab Conquest: An Account of the Military History and Archaeology of the African Provinces in the Sixth and Seventh Century.* Oxford: British Archaeological Reports, 1981.

Procopius. *Procopius.* Edited by H. B Dewing. MA: Harvard University Press. 1914.

Robertson, James Craigie. *History of the Christian Church.* London: John Murray, 1854.

Rüpke, Jörg. *The Religion of the Romans.* Translated and edited by Richard Gordon. Cambridge: Polity, 2007.

Schaff, Phillip. *History of the Christian Church.* Grand Rapids: Eerdmans, 1989.

Sharf, Andrew, and Mazal Holocaust Collection. *Byzantine Jewry from Justinian to the Fourth Crusade.* London: Schocken, 1971.

Stevenson, James, ed. *A New Eusebius: Documents Illustrating of the History of the Church to A.D. 337.* London: S.PCK, 1957.

Thiessen, John Caldwell. *A Survey of World Mission.* Chicago: Moody, 1961.

Van Der Meer, F. *Augustine the Bishop.* New York: Harper and Row, 1961.

Walker, Williston. *A History of Christian Church.* New York: Scribner, 1918.

Wand, W. C. *A History of the Early Church.* London: Methuen, 1953.

II.

Theology

7

Islamic Christology

JOHN AZUMAH

Jesus and his mother Mary are held in high esteem in Islamic sources.[1] It is even reported that when Muslims captured the Kaʿbah in 630, Muhammad ordered that all the statues there should be destroyed except for those of Mary and Jesus. In fact, right from the beginning, Muhammad saw himself as the immediate successor of Jesus. A tradition reports him as saying, "I am the nearest of mankind to Jesus, son of Mary—on both of whom be peace—because there has been no Prophet between him and me."

WHY STUDY JESUS IN ISLAM?

Some people might wonder why it is necessary to concern ourselves with what people of other faiths, particularly Muslims, have to say about Jesus Christ. Kwame Bediako's astutely responds to this question by saying:

> Strange as it may seem, theological affirmations are meaningful ultimately, not in terms of what adherents say, but in terms of what persons of other faiths understand those affirmations to imply for them. In other words, our Christian affirmations are validated when their credentials and validity are tested not

1. For more information on this topic, see Azumah, "Islamic Christology."

> only in terms of the religious and spiritual universe in which Christians habitually operate, but also—indeed especially—in terms of the religious and spiritual worlds which persons of other faiths inhabit. For it is in those "other worlds" that the true meaning of Jesus Christ becomes apparent and validated. Christian history shows that as Christian faith engages with new cultures, new insights about Jesus Christ emerge.[2]

We are called not only to confess Jesus Christ as Lord and Savior, but also to witness to this truth about him. Our witness, as Bediako points out, stands to be enriched by new insights that can be gained from other points of view. With this in mind, we shall seek to delineate some of the key theological continuities and discontinuities between Islam and Christianity as regards the identity and mission of Jesus.

JESUS' BIRTH

Sixty-four of the ninety-three verses in the Qur'an that speak about Jesus are found in the nativity narratives in surahs 3 and 19. Kenneth Cragg observes that if the Gospels are said to be really passion narratives with extended introductions, "it could well be said that the Jesus cycle in the Qur'an is nativity narrative with attenuated sequel."[3] Maryam, or Mary the mother of Jesus, is greatly honoured in Islam. She is the only woman mentioned by name in the Qur'an (thirty-four times) and a whole chapter (19) is named after her. She is identified as the daughter of Imran, the sister of Aaron (3:35; 19:28),[4] and is described as a chaste woman whom God chose, made pure, and preferred to all the women of creation (3:42). Before her birth, her mother pledged her unborn child to God. She was greatly distressed when she gave birth to a girl and asked that she and her daughter be protected from Satan. Mary was put under the guardianship of Zachariah in the temple, where she was miraculously fed.[5]

The Qur'an contains two accounts of the annunciation of Jesus' coming birth (3:33–49; 19:16–34). In surah 3, God is said to have sent

2. Bediako, "Christianity, Islam," 6.

3. Cragg, *Jesus and the Muslim*, 19.

4. In Numbers 26:59, Amram is the father of Moses, Aaron, and Miriam (or Maryam). This passage suggests that the Qur'an is confusing Miriam the sister of Moses with Mary the mother of Jesus.

5. The apocryphal *Protevangelium* of James contains the story of Mary being fed by angels in the temple.

an angel to Mary, while in surah 19, it was a spirit that was sent to give her the good news. The angel appeared to Mary and addressed her in the following words:

> O Mary! Allah giveth thee glad tidings of a word from Him, whose name is the Messiah, Jesus, son of Mary, illustrious in the world and the Hereafter, and one of those brought near (unto Allah). He will speak unto mankind in his cradle and in his manhood, and he is of the righteous. (3:45–46)

When Mary queried how this was going to be since no man had known her, the angel assured her that God could do anything. Some Muslim exegetes state that the angel then breathed into a slit in Mary's cloak, which she had taken off. When she put it on again, she conceived Jesus. However it was done, Mary conceived and withdrew to a distant place. When the time came, she gave birth under a palm tree and took the child home to her people. She was accused of having brought shame and dishonor to her family. In response, Mary simply pointed to the infant Jesus lying in his cradle, who then spoke the following words:

> Lo! I am the slave of Allah. He hath given me the Scripture and hath appointed me a Prophet, and hath made me blessed wheresoever I may be, and hath enjoined upon me prayer and almsgiving so long as I remain alive, and (hath made me) dutiful toward her who bore me, and hath not made me arrogant, unblest (sic). Peace on me the day I was born, and the day I die, and the day I shall be raised alive! (19:30–33)[6]

JESUS AS SON OF GOD

Although the Qur'an accepts the virgin birth, the incarnation is strongly and repeatedly rejected. His miraculous birth is not considered to prove that he is either the Son of God or God. The Qur'an strongly condemns the very idea and insists that Jesus is no more than a human being and a prophet:

> The Messiah, son of Mary, was no other than a messenger, messengers (the like of whom) had passed away before him. And

6. The Arabic and Syrian versions of the infancy gospels, which are said to have been in circulation in Arabia during the time of Muhammad, also have Jesus speaking from the cradle to announce his identity and mission.

> his mother was a saintly woman. And they both used to eat (earthly) food! (5:75)

In arguing that Jesus is a created being, Muslims cite the angel's words to Mary when she asks how she can have a child while still a virgin. The angel replies that when God wills something he commands it "Be! and it is" (3:47). On the strength of this verse, Muslim theologians insist that Jesus was a creature made by God, the Creator, who has no associate. Muslims also argue that the creation of Adam was even more marvellous than that of Jesus. God created Adam from dust and commanded him into being (3:59). He had no father and no mother, did not have to go through the normal developmental stages of life, and was honored by God, who asked his angels to prostrate themselves before him (i.e., worship him). If unusual birth makes one the Son of God or God, then, Muslims argue, Adam qualifies even more than Jesus!

Mainline Islamic teaching about Jesus is summed up in the following quotations from the Qur'an:

> O People of the Scripture! Do not exaggerate in your religion nor utter aught concerning Allah save the truth. The Messiah, Jesus, son of Mary, was only a messenger of Allah, and His word which He conveyed unto Mary, and a spirit from Him. So, believe in Allah and His messengers, and say not 'Three'. Cease! [It is] better for you! Allah is only One God. Far is it removed from His transcendent majesty that he should have a son. His is all that is in the heavens and all that is in the earth. And Allah is sufficient as Defender. (4:171)

> They surely disbelieve who say: Lo! Allah is the Messiah, son of Mary. The Messiah (himself) said: O Children of Israel, worship Allah, my Lord and your Lord. Lo! whoso ascribeth partners unto Allah, for him Allah hath forbidden Paradise. His abode is the Fire. For evildoers there will be no helpers. (5:72)

Indeed, the Qur'an reports Jesus denying ever instructing his disciples to take him and his mother as gods along with God (5:116).

The Qur'anic denial that Jesus is the Son of God is based on the idea that his conception would have required God to physically take Mary as his wife. The term used for "child" in all except one of the verses denying that God has offspring is *walad*, a word that denotes physical conception. The Qur'an thus asks: "How can He have a child, when there is for Him no consort?" (6:101). In other words, for Allah to have a child, he must take a spouse, and it is not in his nature to do such a thing. Yusuf Ali, one of the leading Qur'anic commentators of the last century, sums up the Islamic position in the following words:

> Begetting a son is a physical act depending on the need of men's animal nature. God Most High is independent of all needs, and it is derogatory to Him to attribute such an act to Him. It is merely a relic of pagan and anthropomorphic superstitions. Such an attribution to God of a material nature, and of the lower animal functions of sex is derogatory to the dignity and glory of God. The belief in God begetting a son is not a question of words or of speculative thought. It is a stupendous blasphemy against God. It lowers God to the level of an animal.[7]

The Islamic position seems to have been influenced by the pre-Islamic Arab belief that God had daughters in the form of female deities, whose intercession was sought. In fact, the Qur'anic denials of God having children were first directed at the pre-Islamic Arabs, who are accused of preferring sons for themselves but assuming that God only has daughters (53:19–22). It appears that these denials are then extended to the Christian teaching about Jesus being the Son of God without a good understanding of what Christians mean by that title. Unfortunately, this position remains the orthodox Muslim teaching regardless of Christian protestations to the contrary.

JESUS AS GOD

The Islamic denial of the deity of Jesus is rooted in core Qur'anic teaching and Islamic beliefs about the oneness of God (*tawḥīd*), his transcendence, and the nature of revelation. The core message of the Qur'an is that Allah is *wāḥid*, the sole divinity. The assertion "Lo! thy Lord is surely One" (37:4) is at the very core of Muhammad's preaching concerning God and is constantly repeated throughout the Qur'an (e.g., "It is inspired in me that your God is One God" [41:6]; see also 2:163). Indeed, belief in the oneness of God forms the cornerstone of the Islamic witness or Shahadah: "I bear witness that there is no God but Allah, and that Muhammad is the Messenger of Allah."

Surah 112 of the Qur'an is the surah of unity (*tawḥīd*) par excellence: it stresses that God alone is the Master, not begetting and not

7. See Troll, "Jesus Christ and Christianity."

begotten, without equal. It asserts the unity of the divine nature, whose intrinsic mystery cannot be fathomed (see also 23:91). God the Creator is unique and totally other; to associate anything or anyone with him constitutes *shirk*, the greatest and unpardonable sin. Consequently, the Christian teaching that God took human form and came to dwell with human beings is both alien and repugnant to Islam. God is absolute and transcendent—the very possibility of *Emmanuel* (God with us) is unthinkable. As long ago as the tenth century, a Muslim scholar expressed this repugnance in his correspondence with a Christian:

> In your error, your ignorance and your presumption in the face of God—Praise and Glory to Him—you still pretend that God came down from His Majesty, His Sovereignty, His Almighty Power, His Light, His Glory, His Force, His Greatness and His Power, even to the point of entering into the womb of a woman in suffocating grief, imperfection, in narrow and dark confines and in pain, that he stayed in her during nine months to come out as do all the sons of Adam, that he was then fed at her breast during two years, behaved as any child does and grew as any other child, year by year, crying, sleeping, eating, drinking, experiencing hunger and thirst during the whole of his life. Well then: who was ruling the heavens and the earth? Who was holding them? Who made laws for them? Who dictated the course of the sun, the moon, the stars, of the night, of the day, and of the winds? Who created? Who gave life and death while Isa was in the womb of his mother and after he came into the world? Praise and Glory to God![8]

However, just as Christians have debated whether Jesus is divine or human and have finally settled on the position that he is fully divine and fully human, so Muslims have debated the nature of the Qur'an. As the literal word of God, is the Qur'an created and therefore not eternal? Or is it uncreated and therefore eternal and divine? The official position, reached in the early tenth century, is that Muslims should believe in the Qur'an as uncreated and eternal "without asking how" (*Bilā Kayf*).

The role of Muhammad in the revelation of the Qur'an is comparable to that of the virgin Mary in Christianity. Just as God chose to reveal his Son through Mary in Christianity, so he chose to reveal his will through the "illiterate" Muhammad. It may be that the issue of the nature

8. Umar's Letter to Leo, cited in Gaudeul, *Encounters and Clashes*, 153.

of revelation is an area in which Christians and Muslims can hope for constructive dialogue on christological questions.

JESUS' MISSION AND MIRACLES

According to the Qur'an, Jesus was no more than a prophet. His mission was primarily to the children of Israel, whereas Muhammad's mission was universal. Jesus was a sign from God for humanity, strengthened by the Holy Spirit (5:110, 2:87). He was taught Scripture by God (3:48).

The content of Jesus' teaching, for example, the Sermon on the Mount, is barely mentioned in the Qur'an. All that is said is that he came to confirm the truth in the Torah and make lawful what was hitherto declared unlawful (3:50; 4:46; 3:93). He came to clarify previous revelations (43:63), enjoin the fear of the one God, and warn against ascribing partners to God (5:72). The religion Jesus established was the same as that of Noah, Abraham, Moses, and subsequently Muhammad—or in other words, Islam (33:7; 42:13). The *injīl* (gospel) given to Jesus contains guidance, light, and admonition (5:46), as well as good tidings about the coming of an "unlettered prophet" (7:157). The gospel and message preached by Jesus have, however, been tampered with and corrupted by successive generations of Christians. Jesus himself prophesied of the coming of a prophet named Ahmad or "the praised one" (61:6). The Gospel of Barnabas, which has been proven beyond any doubt to be a fictitious work produced in Spain in the late sixteenth and early seventeenth century, develops this theme more fully.[9] In this so-called gospel, Jesus predicts the coming of Muhammad by name, and Muhammad, rather than Jesus, is identified as the Messiah. In this case, the Gospel of Barnabas clearly contradicts the Qur'an by referring to Muhammad rather than Jesus as the Messiah. Strangely, it refers to Jesus as "Christ" but reports him denying that he is the Messiah.

Jesus and Mary are the only two people whom the Qur'an describes as sinless (3:36, 46). Islam rejects the concept of original sin, but nevertheless there is a tradition that states that "every son of Adam when newly born is touched (or probably squeezed) by Satan [and infected with sin] . . . it is at this contact that the child utters his first cry."[10] The only exceptions were Mary and Jesus, both of whom were granted the

9. Slomp, "Gospel of Barnabas."

10. Anawati, "Isa."

extraordinary privilege of being preserved from any contact with the devil at the instant of their birth. They are unique, for the Qur'an reports other prophets falling into temptation, sinning, and asking for forgiveness—Adam (7:22–23), Abraham (26:82), Moses (28:16), Jonah (37:142), and Muhammad (3:31; 47:19).

Many traditions abound about Jesus' omniscience and supernatural powers both as a child and an adult. He is the only one, apart from God, with the power to create life (birds) by using clay and breathing life into them (3:49). This tradition about his modeling of birds is found in the apocryphal gospels (the Gospel of Thomas, ch. 2; the Arabic Gospel of the Infancy, chs. 1, 36, 46; and the Armenian Gospel of the Infancy, chs. 18 and 2). Christian apologists have always pointed out that the verb *khalaqa*, used of Jesus' creating birds, is a verb that the Qur'an elsewhere uses exclusively to refer to God's activity. The substance used, clay, is what God used to create the first man, Adam (6:2; 7:12; 28:38). The act of breathing into the birds is similar to the way God breathed into Adam and into Mary. The breath of Jesus, like that of God, has the power to give life. This point should not be dismissed lightly.

The Qur'an acknowledges that Jesus was the only one of all the prophets to be given the power to heal the sick and raise the dead, and says that he performed all these miracles by the permission of God (5:110). Still, it denies that these unique signs of healing and even giving life indicate that Jesus was something more than a prophet. Muslims argue that other prophets, especially Moses, performed even greater miracles than Jesus did. Responding to Christian use of Jesus' miracles as signs of his divinity, a tenth century Muslim noted:

> And if you are to consider Isa as a god only because he raised the dead to life, cured the sick, and accomplished miracles with the permission of God, then (I would answer) that Hazqil [Ezekiel; Ezek. 37] also raised the dead to life, as you can see in your book, thirty-five thousand people . . . many more than were raised by Isa and yet you have not made him into a god.
>
> In the same way Elyas [Elisha] raised to life the son of the old woman as you maintain . . . The miracles of Isa are not superior to those accomplished by Musa in the presence of Pharaoh's magicians . . . And both of them only did what they did with the permission of God, on His order, and in virtue of His Decree, because God decides in His wisdom, and acts with Power.[11]

11. Umar, cited Gaudeul, *Encounters and Clashes*, 154.

On the whole, Muslim commentators regard Jesus' mission as a failure at worst and an unfinished or preparatory task at best. They point out that he never married, achieved military victory over his enemies, or attained temporal power. By contrast, Muhammad "wrought a mighty revolution and made the Arabs master of the then civilized world' whereas Jesus 'could not free his people from the yoke of the Romans."[12]

Jesus' teaching in the Sermon on the Mount is derided as impracticable, unrealistic, and too docile. One Muslim writer describes it as "pathetic and escapist," appeasing the Roman overlords by making virtue out of suffering and oppression and preventing action in this world by offering consolation in the next. He goes on to describe the Sermon on the Mount as "meek and spineless."[13] In other words, Jesus failed to achieve manifest success. But Muslims then must face the problem of explaining how a prophet could be a failure. Does this represent a failure on God's part? In an apparent attempt to resolve this problem, Islam teaches that Jesus will return to earth before the end of the world to accomplish what he could not do in his earlier life. This second coming is known as the "Descension of Jesus"—*nuzūl ʿ Īsá*. This belief is derived from surah 43:61, which talks of Jesus being the "sign of the hour." Tradition has surrounded this rather oblique reference with a mass of detail. Some of these details are as follows: On returning to the earth, Jesus will descend onto the white arcade of the eastern gate at Damascus or (according to another tradition) onto a hill in the Holy Land. His head will be anointed. He will have in his hand a spear with which he will kill the Antichrist (al-Dajjal). Then he will go to Jerusalem at the time when the imam is leading the dawn prayer. The imam will try to give up his place to him, but Jesus will put the imam in front of him and will pray behind him, as prescribed by Muhammad.

Then he will kill all pigs, break the cross, destroy synagogues and churches, and kill all Christians except those who believe in him (following 4:159). Once he has killed the false Messiah, all the Peoples of the Book (Jews and Christians) will believe in him, and there will be only one community (the Islamic umma). Jesus will make justice reign. Peace will be so complete that it will extend even to man's relations with the animals and to the relations among animals. Jesus will remain for forty years, will get married and have children, and will then die. The Muslims will

12. See Zebiri, *Muslims and Christians*, 63–66.

13. See Zebiri, *Muslims and Christians*, 63–66.

arrange his funeral and will bury him at Medina, beside Muhammad.[14] To sum up, Jesus will complete the mission that had been cut short. As a prophet of God, he must not only succeed; he must also be seen to have succeeded.

Contemporary mainstream Muslim writers see the mission of Jesus principally as preserving the Torah and announcing the coming of Muhammad, and regard Islam as a culmination and replacement of whatever he taught. S. H. Nasr, for instance, sees Muhammad as synthesising the elements of faith, law, and the spiritual way as represented by Abraham, Moses, and Jesus respectively.[15] Cragg notes that

> If Jesus . . . supplies Islam with its eschatological perception and goal, Muhammad supplies the historical realism which is wanting in Jesus and precluded by his context. If Islamic traditions need to anticipate a Christ-style future, Jesus needed to anticipate a Muhammad-style future, the one in eternal the other in temporal terms. The Gospel may have it right in the ultimate; but the Qur'an has it right in the concrete.[16]

In talking about the Qur'anic view of Jesus and his mission, however, the Christian theologian Hans Küng rightly observes that "the portrait of Jesus in the Qur'an is all too one-sided, too monotone, and for the most part lacking in content."[17]

JESUS' NAMES AND TITLES

Despite vigorous Qur'anic and Muslim denials that Jesus is divine, the Qur'an gives him a series of honorable titles, some of which strongly hint at divinity. The list below includes most of the names and titles given to Jesus in the Qur'an:

' Īsá is Jesus' personal name, derived from the Syriac version of the Hebrew *Yeshua* or Jesus. It is used twenty-five times in the Qur'an.

Nabī ' Īsá (Prophet Jesus) is the way Muslims commonly refer to Jesus.

14. Anawati, "Isa."
15. Nasr, *Islamic Life and Thought*, 210
16 Cragg, *Jesus and the Muslim*, 53.
17. Küng, "Christianity and World Religions," 89.

Nabī Allāh (Prophet of God) is used only once in the Qur'an with reference to Jesus (19:30–31), even though he is always listed among the prophets.

Rasūl Allāh (Apostle or Messenger of God) is used ten times (e.g., 5:75; 61:6). Jesus is one of, if not the favored or exalted, apostle of God (2:253).

ʿĪsá Ibn Maryam (Son of Mary) is used twenty-three times in the Qur'an. This title, which occurs only once in the New Testament (Mark 6:3), appears five times in the Arabic Gospel of the Infancy and fifteen times in the Syriac version of the same gospel, indicating that early Arab and Syrian Christians referred to Jesus in this way.

ʿAbdallāh (Servant or Slave of God) is used three times (4:172; 19:30; 43:59). It simply means a creature indebted to God.

Al-Masīḥu, (the Messiah) is used eleven times in the Qur'an exclusively for Jesus. In the account of the annunciation, we read that "His name shall be the Messiah, Jesus, Son of Mary" (3:45). However, according to the Qur'an, this title does not make him any different from other prophets, for "the Messiah, son of Mary, was no other than a messenger" (5:75).

Wajīh (outstanding) is the way Jesus is described in 3:45. This word comes from *wajh*, meaning face, and indicates being in the forefront, preeminent, or highly honored.

Muqarrab (drawn near) is also used in 3:45 to describe Jesus' relationship with God. Elsewhere, the same word is used to refer to those who are admitted to Paradise (83:21, 28; 56:88) and to angels (4:172).

Āyah (sign) is the title assigned to Jesus when Gabriel tells Mary of God's intentions: "We are to make him a sign for mankind" (19:21). The word translated "sign" can also be translated as "miracle." It later came to be used to refer to the individual verses in the Qur'an, each of which is considered a miraculous sign from God. Muslim commentators take the "sign" to which Gabriel refers to be Jesus' miraculous conception. Jesus himself is also reported as saying, "I came to you with a sign from your Lord; so, fear God and obey me" (3:50). Here the "sign" may be any of the miracles Jesus performed. In surah 21:90, the use of "sign" is even more expansive: "We made her and her son a sign for the world." One would expect this verse to be interpreted as a reference to the universal scope of Jesus' mission.

Raḥmah (mercy) is another title assigned at the annunciation, when Gabriel explains that Jesus is to be "a mercy from us" (19:21).

Mubārakan (Blessed) is another word applied to Jesus at his birth, where he is said to have spoken from his cradle and announced that God has "made me blessed wheresoever I may be" (19:31).

Āyat Allāh (Sign, Revelation, or Token from God to the world) is used to describe Jesus in 19:21 and 23:50. Traditionally, Muslim commentators have taken it to mean that Jesus is the "Sign of the Hour," and that his second coming and all that he will accomplish then will signal the end of the world.

Kalimatu Allāh (Word of God) is one of most striking titles of Jesus for Christians. The Qur'an uses it when the angel tells Mary: "Allah giveth thee glad tidings of a word from Him, whose name is the Messiah, Jesus, son of Mary" (3:45). Classical Muslim commentators have interpreted this title in various ways: some say that Jesus is the fulfillment of the creating word of God, uttered at the moment of his conception; others that he is the prophet announced in the word of God, received and preached by the earlier messengers; others that he is the word of God because he speaks on behalf of God and thus leads men in the right way; and still others that he is a word of God because he is, in his own person, "good tidings."

Rūḥ Allāh (Spirit of God) is another striking title used for Jesus alone in the Qur'an: "The Messiah, Jesus, son of Mary, was only a messenger of Allah, and His word which He conveyed unto Mary, and a spirit from Him" (4:171).

While Christians may be tempted to interpret some of the names and titles in the preceding list as pointing to the divinity of Christ, Islamic orthodoxy has vehemently insisted that all of them are honorific and that their meaning should be taken at face value. But all human cultures, and especially Semitic and African people, attach deep significance to names and titles. This point is evident not only from the Bible, but also from the practice of several people groups today. Names, surnames, nicknames, and titles are bestowed upon people and places in order to express their significance or some special circumstance relating to them. For instance, names can tell us where someone comes from and, in African cultures, the circumstances under which that person was born. Titles tell us something about what a person has achieved. As an African, I think it requires more faith to take all the names and titles given to Jesus in the Qur'an only at face value than it does to admit that there is something unique and special about him, even among prophets!

JESUS' PASSION

The Qur'anic witness to Jesus' passion is even more problematic than its witness to his birth. It appears to deny either the crucifixion or that Jesus was the one crucified:

> And because of their saying: We slew the Messiah, Jesus, son of Mary, Allah's messenger. They slew him not nor crucified, but it appeared so unto them; and lo! those who disagree concerning it are in doubt thereof; they have no knowledge thereof save pursuit of a conjecture; they slew him not for certain, But Allah took him up unto Himself. Allah was ever Mighty, wise. (4:157–58)

The passage is part of an invective against the Jews, who were apparently boasting about having crucified Jesus. The Qur'an insists that the Jews did not kill Jesus but that it only "appeared so unto them." This part of the verse has been the subject of intense speculation by various Muslim commentators. Almost all agree that a crucifixion did take place but that Jesus was not the victim. So, the questions that have been debated are: firstly, what is meant by "it appeared so unto them" and, secondly, who was the victim? A common Muslim interpretation is that a substitute made to look like Jesus was crucified in his place. This view has tantalizing parallels to the ancient Gnostics' position that a substitute died in place of Jesus, or that only Jesus' body was crucified while the true Jesus within did not suffer.[18] Various Islamic traditions and commentaries suggest the following possibilities:

> God outwitted the Jews and deluded them by making all of Jesus' disciples look like him at the time of his arrest. One of these disciples was then arrested and crucified.

Simon of Cyrene, one of Jesus' disciples, volunteered to take on his likeness and his place on the cross.
Jesus bribed his way out of the cross by promising paradise to one of his disciples (Sergus) who took his place.

God cast the likeness of Jesus on Judas, who was crucified as punishment for his treachery.
God outwitted the Jews by taking Jesus to heaven. To conceal this ascension, the Jews seized an innocent man, crucified him on an isolated hill,

18. Robinson, ed., *Nag Hammadi Library in English*, 245, 332, 334.

and barred anyone from coming to the place until the features of the body had changed beyond recognition.

> Pilate ordered his soldiers to free Jesus Barabbas, but they mistakenly set Jesus of Nazareth free, who then escaped and went to meet with his disciples.[19]

According to the so-called Gospel of Barnabas, Jesus was whisked away to heaven by four angels and his likeness was cast upon Judas, who was then arrested, crucified, and buried by the disciples, under the impression that he was Jesus. Some of the disciples then stole the body and started to spread lies about a resurrection. Jesus pleaded with God in heaven to let him go back and console his mother and disciples and God granted him three days. He then returned under the protection of the same four angels, met his mother and disciples on the Mount of Olives, and explained what had actually happened. He warned them to stop spreading lies about his death and resurrection, after which he was taken back up into heaven.[20]

But these Islamic denials of Jesus' death are complicated by the existence of other Qur'anic verses that allude to his death. The infant Jesus is reported to have said, "Peace on me the day I was born, and the day I die, and the day I shall be raised alive!" (19:33). Zechariah invokes the same blessing on John the Baptist in 19:15, implying a real death and resurrection in each case.

In 3:55, God says to Jesus, "Lo! I am gathering [*mutawaffī ka*] thee and causing thee to ascend unto Me." The verb *tawaffá* is associated with death in the other twenty-five uses of it in the Qur'an, including in 4:157, where it is used to deny that the Jews had killed Jesus. On three occasions, this verb refers to Muhammad's death. In fact, Muhammad, arguing against the divinity of Jesus in a discussion with Christians from Najran, is reported to have asked them: "Do you not know that our Lord is living and does not die, and that Jesus passed away?"[21] In this tradition, Muhammad appears to accept that Jesus died, and in fact uses his death as an argument against Christian claims of Jesus' divinity.

Mainstream Islamic teaching has continued to maintain that all references to the death of Jesus in the Qur'an are eschatological (that is, they refer to his death forty years after his second coming). However, some

19. See Robinson, *Christ in Islam and Christianity*.

20. See excerpts in Gaudeul, *Encounters and Clashes*, 175–78.

21. Guillaume, *Life of Muhammad*, 272.

individual Muslim commentators and writers have acknowledged that 3:55 and 3:48 may refer to a real death of Jesus. Some have said that Jesus died for three hours before being raised, others that he was dead for seven hours. Ibn Kathir (d. 1373) simply said, "God caused him to die for three days, then resurrected him, then raised him."[22]

Mahmoud Ayoub, a Lebanese Shia Muslim living in the United States, is of the opinion that Muslim commentators have not been able to convincingly disprove the crucifixion. On the contrary, they have made the matter even more complicated by introducing the substitution theory. The Qur'an, according to Ayoub, does not deny the crucifixion as a historical event but rather its theological implications. Rather than speaking about a righteous man who was wronged, the Qur'an is speaking about the Word of God who was sent to earth and who returned to God. The denial of the killing of Jesus is thus a denial of the power of men to vanquish and destroy the divine Word, which is forever victorious.[23] Another highly respected contemporary Egyptian Muslim scholar declares:

> The idea of a substitute for Christ is a very crude way of explaining the Qur'anic text. They had a lot to explain to the masses. No cultured Muslim believes in this nowadays. The text is taken to mean that the Jews thought they had killed Christ, but God raised him unto Himself in a way we can leave unexplained among the several mysteries which we have taken for granted on faith alone.[24]

The Aḥmadīya movement claims that Jesus was crucified on the cross, taken down in a coma, and nursed by his disciples in a cave. He is said to have recovered and escaped to India in search of the lost tribe of Israel. He lived in India for 120 years, died, and lies buried in Kashmir. It appears that in order to claim the title Messiah for himself, Ghulam Ahmad (the founder of the movement) had to find a grave for Jesus. Even more important, he wanted to counter the Christian argument that Muhammad is dead and buried in Medina while Jesus is alive with God in heaven.

The stance of the Aḥmadīya movement and much of the Muslim attitude to Jesus seems to be shaped more by Christian claims that Jesus

22. See Robinson, *Christ in Islam and Christianity*, 120–22.

23. Ayoub, "Towards an Islamic Christology."

24. Husain, *City of Wrong*, 222.

is superior to Muhammad than by Qur'anic teaching. At the heart of the Islamic puzzle about the passion of Christ are the contrasting prophetic experiences of Muhammad and Jesus. When the Meccans plotted to kill Muhammad, he escaped, leaving his cousin Ali in his bed to deceive his pursuers. He hid in a cave for three days and then slipped away to Medina. From there, he organized his followers, fought his enemies, and finally captured Mecca. So crucial is the *hijra* in Islam that this event, rather than the birth or death of Muhammad, marks the beginning of the Islamic calendar. When Muslims compare his escape with Jesus' capture in Gethsemane, they see the vindication of Muhammad in his rescue from his enemies and, more importantly, in his victories over them in subsequent battles. The image of a suffering prophet is therefore difficult to reconcile with what Kenneth Cragg calls the "manifest victory" or "success" associated with the prophetic office in Islam. As one key Muslim writer put it, "in the Qur'an, everything is aimed at convincing the Believer that he will experience victory over the forces of evil . . . Islam refuses to accept this tragic image of the Passion. Not simply because it has no place for the dogma of the Redemption, but because the Passion would imply in its eyes that God had failed."[25]

Islamic objections to the passion of Christ are also rooted in contrasting views of what constitutes the human problem and the solution required. According to Christian teaching, Jesus is not just a prophet but also the savior who came to redeem humanity from the power of sin by offering the ultimate sacrifice on the cross. Thus, the doctrine of salvation (soteriology) is intimately associated with Christ's suffering and death. On the other hand, in Islam, the human problem is not sin but ignorance of the will of God. What is needed is therefore a prophet who will bring guidance rather than a savior bringing redemption.

Kenneth Cragg summarises the Islamic objections to the passion of Christ as follows: "It did not, historically; it need not redemptively; and it should not morally happen to Jesus."[26] Historically, it did not happen because the Qur'an denies it. Redemptively, it need not happen because "Islam holds man to be not in need of salvation" but of success, which can be obtained with the right guidance of the law. Morally, it should not, because everyone is responsible for their own sins. Why should a just God hold one person responsible for the sins of another? Moreover, if the

25. Merad, "Christ According to the Qur'a¯n," 14ff.

26. Cragg, *Jesus and the Muslim*, 178; Al-Bajī (1012–1081), in Gaudeul, *Encounters and Clashes*, 182–83.

redemption of humanity from the power of sin is what Jesus set out to achieve through his death on the cross, then he failed because he ended his ministry with only a "few believers" and human beings continue to live under the power of sin. Muslims therefore regard Jesus' death on the cross (if they admit that this did happen) as a pathetic misadventure unworthy of a prophet of God, let alone one believed to be God. As one eleventh-century Muslim apologist put it:

> [Jesus] gave his blood freely, according to what you say, desiring to save mankind from error, and only a small number believed in him. Yet people believed in other Prophets who did not go so far as this . . . Moses, on whom be peace, did not die till a large number believed in him, a great multitude; nor did Muhammad—may God bless him and give him peace—die till a huge number believed in him, who thereby gained possession of the lands and conquered the horizons, and God made him victorious over every religion . . . If Jesus, on whom be peace, knew the Unseen, why did he give his blood through a desire for that which was not accomplished, and from which he gained nothing?[27]

With regard to the person, mission and passion of Christ, in Islam faith and belief take precedence over empirical historical evidence. It is futile to try to convince Muslims that some aspects of Islamic Christology are mistaken because they are not in line with the biblical accounts or empirical evidence. Any such suggestion strikes at the heart of the integrity of the Islamic faith. Making this point, Seyyed Hossein Nasr notes that it is God who revealed the Islamic doctrine of Christ to Muslims. If certain verses of the Qur'an like those of Sūrat Maryam are incorrect, then by what criterion should Muslims accept the rest of the Qur'an? If certain verses of the Qur'an are rejected because of some extrinsic argument or in order to make friends with Christians or achieve world peace or get into the United Nations, or for any other worldly reason, however laudable, then the rest of the Qur'an must also be rejected as the Word of God.[28] Nasr explains further that "even if [the crucifixion] had been recorded on film and thoroughly documented (God forbid), nevertheless the Islamic position would not logically [his emphasis] be destroyed."[29]

27. Al-Bajī (1012–1081), in Gaudeul, *Encounters and Clashes*, 182–83.

28. Nasr, "Response to Hans Küng's Paper," 100.

29. S. H. Nasr's comments during discussions on Küng's "Christianity and World Religions" in *The Muslim World*, 77:2 (April 1987) 124.

The point Nasr is making on behalf of all Muslims is that since the Muslim teaching about Christ is revealed by God and recorded in the Qur'an, it cannot be contested, let alone contradicted. The Qur'an says Jesus was not crucified and no amount of "evidence" can contradict that, since that would amount to questioning the integrity of God and the Qur'an.

JESUS IN MUSLIM TRADITIONS AND DEVOTION

While firmly rejecting the divinity of Jesus, Muslim traditions and devotion seem to have gone far beyond the usual interpretation of the Qur'an in providing detailed accounts of Jesus' birth, physical features, and ministry.

Islamic tradition tells that Mary conceived Jesus at the age of thirteen (others say fifteen). She and her cousin Joseph the carpenter lived and worked in a mosque as water carriers. One day, Mary went to fetch water and God sent Gabriel to her and made him resemble a "handsome young man."[30] And he said to her, "O Mary, truly God hath sent me to you that I may give you a pious child." When Mary said, "I take refuge from you," he said to her, "Verily I am the apostle of thy Lord to give you a pious child." She said, "Shall there be to me a child, and no one has touched me, and I have committed no folly?" He said, "That is true, but thy Lord finds a miracle easy." And he breathed in the opening of her dress, which she had taken off; and when he departed from her, Mary put it on, and so she conceived Jesus.

Joseph and Mary escaped to Egypt because Herod wanted to kill Jesus. While there, he was sent to school but was too clever to be taught by any teacher. He and his mother lived in the house of the ruler of Egypt, and he performed one of his first miracles during the wedding ceremony of the king's son.

The king made a feast and collected all the people of Egypt and fed them for two months. And when it was finished, certain people from Syria came to see him, and he did not know of their coming until they came down upon him. And on that day, he had no drink for them. And when Jesus saw his anxiety on this account, he entered some of the chambers of the ruler in which there were rows of jars, and he passed by them one by one, touching them with his hand; and every time he touched one,

30. Unless otherwise stated, all quotations in this section are taken from Zwemer, *Moslem Christ*, as found in the CD-ROM entitled *The World of Islam: Resources for Understanding Islam* (Colorado Springs, CO: Global Mapping International/Fuller Theological Seminary, 2000).

it was filled with drink, until he came to the last one. And he was at that time twelve years old.

Unlike the Qur'an, which gives no details about Jesus' healings and other miracles, Islamic traditions contain many colorful accounts of dazzling miracles. For example, when Jesus was describing Noah's ark to his disciples, they are said to have responded: "If you had sent us someone who had seen the ark and could describe it to us, we would believe." So, he arose and came to a little hill, and struck it with his hand and took a handful of the earth and said, "This is the grave of Shem, the son of Noah. If you wish, I will raise him for you." They said, "Yes"; and he called upon God by his greatest name, and struck the hill with his staff and said, "Come to life by permission of God." Then Shem, the son of Noah, came forth from his grave, white haired. And he said, "Is this the resurrection day?" Jesus said, "No, but I have called you out in the name of God Most High." Shem had lived five hundred years and he was still young. So, he told them the news of the ark. Then Jesus said to him, "Die"; and he said, "Only on one condition, that God protects me from the agonies of death." Jesus granted his request by permission of God.

Another tradition, recounted by Sayyid Kaʿab, describes Jesus as

> a ruddy man, inclining towards white. His hair was not lank, and He never oiled it. He went barefooted; and He never owned a place, or a change of garments, or property or vesture or provisions, except His daily bread. And whenever the sun began to set, He would kneel and pray until the morning. He was in the habit of healing the sick and the lepers and raising the dead by the will of God. He could tell those about Him what they ate in their houses, and what they laid up against the morrow. He walked on the face of the water on the sea. He had dishevelled hair, and His face was small. He was an ascetic in this world and greatly desirous of the world to come; diligent in serving God. And He was a wanderer in the earth till the Jews sought Him and desired to kill Him. Then God lifted Him up to heaven, and God knows best.[31]

Many Islamic traditions speak highly of Jesus' teaching and portray him not only as a modest self-effacing ascetic but as someone unique and special even amongst prophets. One of the most respected Muslim mystics, Al-Ghazālī (d. 1111), reports a tradition that when Jesus was asked, "Are there any on earth like you?," he answered: "Whoever has prayer for his speech, meditation for his silence, and tears for his vision,

31. See Zwemer, *Moslem Christ*, 56ff.

he is like me."[32] One of the earliest and most famous Sufis, al-Ḥallāj (d. 922), while not speculating about the person of Jesus, was enthralled by the mystery of the cross. His guiding ideal was union with God through an all-absorbing love, a love that could not find expression in enjoyment but only in suffering and the cross. A line from one of his poems reads: "I will die in the religion of the cross. I need go no more to Mecca or Medina." And so he died, crucified as a heretic.

Ibn-ʿArabī (d. 1240), another celebrated Muslim mystic, also speculated about Jesus. He is responsible for popularizing the title "the Seal of Saints" (*Khātim al-Anbiyā'*) for Jesus, which corresponds to Muhammad's title "the Seal of Prophets" (33:40). He argued that Muhammad brought definitive legislative prophecy; Jesus will bring definitive holiness when he returns, sealing all holiness from Adam to the end of time.

Merad Ali, a French Muslim of Algerian origin, is of the view that the classical commentaries "do not shed light on the figure of Christ in the way he deserves." He points out that "everything in the Qur'an points to the fact that Christ is seen as an exceptional event in the history of the world, an event pregnant with exceptional meanings." Merad stresses the aura of mystery surrounding the person of Jesus in the Qur'an: the use of terminology such as "Spirit" and "Word" when referring to him—terms that are used of no one else—and the uniqueness of the miracles attributed to him, in particular those of creation and healing. He accepts that the Qur'an denies Christ's divinity, but finds it significant that "at no time is the term bashar (human being) applied to Christ." Merad ends on an open note, saying that the Qur'an aims "to provoke reflection rather than to furnish final answers."[33]

Coming home to Africa, Amadou Hampâté Bâ (1900–1991), a Malian Muslim mystic and scholar, talks about what he calls "the mysterious link which appears between the Qur'anic name of Jesus and the name by which God has named himself." Bâ uses numerology to calculate the numerical value of the name Allah and the title "Messiah, son of Mary," exclusively given to Jesus in the Qur'an. He concludes:

> Whoever is enlightened by this secret stops being amazed when he hears that Jesus participates, in a certain way, in the Essence of the Divine Being. Are not the Word and the Spirit of a being inevitably a part of him? But, the two expressions "God's Word"

32. Cited in Cragg, *Jesus and the Muslim*, 49.

33. Ali, "Christ According to the Qur'ān," 2–17.

> and "the Spirit of God" were attributed to the Virgin Mary's son by the Qur'an itself . . . I could, without trouble, without prejudice or fear, set myself to listen to the Christian Path and to appreciate, for example, the depth of the Gospel according to John, notably in the first three verses of its prologue: "In the beginning was the Word, the Word was with God, the Word was God. He was in the beginning with God. All things came to be through him, without him nothing came to be."[34]

Before a wrong impression is created that the Muslims mentioned above are Christians in all but name, it has to be said that whatever is said of Jesus in Muslim traditions and devotion, much more is said of Muhammad. The superiority of Muhammad is maintained in every way. In summarising the whole of Islamic Christology, Cragg notes:

> Islam has a great tenderness for Jesus, yet a sharp dissociation from his Christian dimensions. Jesus is the theme at once of acknowledgment and disavowal. Islam finds his nativity miraculous but his Incarnation impossible. His teaching entails suffering, but the one is not perfected in the other. He is highly exalted, but by rescue rather than by victory. He is vindicated, but not by resurrection. His servanthood is understood to disclaim the sonship which is its secret . . . Islam has for him a recognition moving within a non-recognition, a rejectionism on behalf of a deep and reverent esteem.[35]

ISLAMIC CHRISTOLOGY SUMMARIZED

Transcendence

For Muslims, Christology is a nagging theological issue: whether, as Christians contend, it is permissible to speak of God assuming human form and endowed with human qualities without that conflicting with the idea of God as transcendent and omnipotent, of God in the elative as *Allāh-u-akbar* ("God than whom nothing is greater"). The church speaks of God assuming human form as the incarnation, a way of describing God that is explicitly rejected in the Qur'an specifically (surah 112) and by Muslim tradition generally, though Muslim Sūfis complicate the issue to their own advantage.

34. Cited from Gaudeul, *Encounters and Clashes*, 158–59.

35. Cragg, *Jesus and the Muslim*, 278–79.

Servanthood

The Islamic theological view of God requires that God be understood as utterly unlike anything human, created, or finite. Accordingly, the divinity of Jesus is rejected as heretical and naïve. Muslims say that even Jesus shunned the title "Son of God" and instead referred to himself simply as "Son of Man." The view is pressed that ascribing divinity to Jesus lands Christians with problems they can afford to do without, such as speaking of three gods in one. Jesus is not God, Muslims insist, and Christians would do well to keep faith with the witness of all Israel that the Lord God is one God, and there is none beside him (Deuteronomy 6:4; Mark 12:29). Here Muslims close theological ranks with Jews against the Christians.

Attributes

Notwithstanding such strictures against the incarnation, the Qur'anic witness to Jesus remains among the most impressive outside Christianity. Jesus is the "word from God" (*kalimatun min Allāhi*) (3:45; 4:171; 19:34); Jesus is the creative word that God cast into Mary (21:91); Jesus is the Second Adam (3:59); he is called "spirit of God" and "servant of God" (19:30). He is the Messiah (3:45; 4:171); he was endowed with the "true word of God" (*qawl al-ḥaqq*), and the sending of him is a "holy sign" (*āyah*) and "mercy" (*raḥmah*) from God; Jesus brought "divine proofs" (*bayyināt*) and "wisdom" (*ḥikmah*). As a result, God aided him with the "Holy Spirit" (*rūḥ al-qudus*) (2:87; 5:110).

Crucifixion

In a famous and theologically challenging Qur'anic passage, the death and resurrection of Jesus are affirmed explicitly. We tend to lose the significance of the Qur'anic statement in standard English translations, such as Arberry's otherwise impeccable version: "Jesus, I will take thee to Me and will raise thee to Me, and I will purify thee of those who believe not" (3:48). The Arabic is: *qāla allāhu yā ʻ Īsá innī mutawaffīka wa rāfiʻ uka ilayya*. The operative word is the verb *mutawaffīka*, in the sixth form, and means literally "to die"; that is, God receiving back the physical life of Jesus. Several interpretations have been offered for this word but, given the context of Jesus returning to God out of seeming death (4:158), we are on firm ground for inferring physical death as the plain meaning. Such an interpretation casts an ironic light on God's pledge of "purifying Jesus of those who do not believe" that he died and was raised to God. The sense of the death of Jesus seems inescapable here.

Disavowal

Jesus has remained an unresolved question in Muslim theology because elsewhere in the Qur'an we have a repudiation of the claims of those who said that they killed him, for such claims stand in defiance of God's omnipotence and omniscience. Muslims object: how could Jesus' enemies prevail against God's indomitable will and strength? Surah 4:155 puts the objection in direct and robust terms as follows: *wa mā qatalūhu wa mā ṣalabūhu wa lākin shubbiha lahum. . .wa mā qatalūhu yaqīnan* ("yet they did not slay him, neither crucified him, but only a likeness of that was shown to them . . . they did not slay him for certain"). The verse opens a Pandora's box of intractable textual and theological problems, with scholarly debate concentrating on what the preposition "it" of the italicized Arabic for "likeness of it" could be referring to: the victim or his cross? A Docetic view might be at work here, though in that case even a handy optical illusion cannot evade or resolve the challenge of an anonymous victim on the cross. In the eyes of his enemies, a Docetic Jesus (as in "the likeness of it" and "they did not slay him for certain") still came to grief when his earthly ministry ended tragically on the cross. The illusion served the purposes of Jesus' enemies no less effectively, constraining a Muslim writer, for example, to devote a unique, remarkable study to the compelling mystery of Good Friday. Why would God allow even an anonymous but innocent victim to be crucified?

Incarnation

At the core of Islamic teaching is the preservation of divine transcendence or otherness. The Qur'an nevertheless speaks of Jesus as God's "mercy," as God's *raḥmah*, a claim not so alien to how St. Paul described Jesus as God's righteousness (Romans 3:25), the righteousness of eternal redemptive merit, not the righteousness of finite human wisdom (1 Corinthians 1:30, 3:18ff.). By several centuries Gregory of Nyssa (d. c. 395) anticipated and respondd to the issue of the Islamic christological objection by insisting that the transcendent power of God is "the condescension to the weakness of our nature" so that "sublimity is seen in lowliness and yet the loftiness descends not." Divine humility is testimony to divine omnipotence in Gregory of Nyssa's view. To deny that option to God would be to infringe on God's prerogative to be God. *Allāh-u-akbar*, most assuredly.

BIBLIOGRAPHY

Anawati, G. C. "ʿĪsā." *Encyclopaedia of Islam*, edited by P. Bearman et al. 2nd ed. Online ed., 2012. http://dx.doi.org/10.1163/1573-3912_islam_COM_0378.

Ayoub, Mahmoud. "Towards an Islamic Christology, II. The Death of Jesus: Reality or Delusion." *The Muslim World* 70:2 (April 1980) 116–18.

Azumah, John. "Islamic Christology: A Case of Reverential Disavowal." *Journal of African Christian Thought* 8:1 (June 2005) 50–60.

Bediako, Kwame. "Christianity, Islam and the Kingdom of God: Rethinking Their Relationship from an African Perspective."" *Journal of African Christian Thought* 17:2 (December 2004) 3–7.

Cragg, Kenneth. *Jesus and the Muslim: An Exploration*. Oxford: Oneworld, 1999.

Gaudeul, Jean-Marie. *Encounters and Clashes: Islam and Christianity in History*. Vol. 2. Rome: Pontificio Istituto di Studi Arabi e d'Islamistica, 2000.

Guillaume, Alfred, trans. *The Life of Muhammad: A Translation of Ibn Ishaq's Sirat Rasul Allah*. Oxford: Oxford University Press, 1982.

Husain, M. Kamil. *City of Wrong. A Friday in Jerusalem*. Translated by by K. Cragg. Amsterdam: Djambatan, 1964.

Küng, Hans. "Christianity and World Religions: The Dialogue with Islam as One Mode." *The Muslim World* 77:2 (April 1987) 80–95.

Merad, M. Ali. "Christ According to the Qur'an." *Encounter* 69 (November 1980) 306–20.

Nasr, S. H. *Islamic Life and Thought*. London: Allen & Unwin, 1981.

———. "Response to Hans Küng's Paper on Christian-Muslim Dialogue." *The Muslim World* 77:2 (April 1987) 97–105.

Robinson, James M., ed. *The Nag Hammadi Library in English*. New York: Random House, 1977.

Robinson, Neal. *Christ in Islam and Christianity*. London: Macmillan, 1991.

Slomp, Jan. "The Gospel of Barnabas in Recent Research." *Islamochristiana* 23 (1997) 81–109.

Troll, Christian. "Jesus Christ and Christianity in Abdullah Yusuf Ali's English interpretation of the Qur'a¯n." *Islamochristiana* 24 (1998) 93–94.

Zebiri, Kate. *Muslims and Christians Face to Face*. Oxford: Oneworld, 1997.

Zwemer, M. Samuel. *The Moslem Christ: An Essay on the Life, Character and Teachings of Jesus Christ According to the Koran and Orthodox Traditions*. New York: American Tract Society, 1912.

8

The Trinity and The Absolute Oneness of God

IMAD N. SHEHADEH

This study will demonstrate the coherence of the Christian doctrine of the Trinity based on its firm belief in the oneness of God.[1] Two systems of thought about God form the background to this study. The first is *absolute oneness*, which refers to the belief in one necessary and sovereign creator God, without the existence of any other God or any secondary god, and without this oneness being inclusive of any persons in relationship. The concept of absolute oneness is not confined specifically to Islam but is the general belief of a large portion of humanity and is also the conclusion of philosophy. It is also known as "monadic monotheism."

On the other side of the spectrum is *oneness in Trinity*. It shares with absolute oneness the belief in one necessary and sovereign creator God, without the existence of any other God or any secondary god. However, oneness in Trinity goes further than absolute oneness by holding to the

1. A complementary study by this author covers the additional important subjects of the historical predicament of absolute oneness and the harmony of the Trinity with logic. It is entitled "The Integral Foundation of the 'Father-Son' Revelation to the Perfection and Activity of the Divine Attributes," and is sponsored by the Jenkins Center for the Christian Understanding of Islam, at the Southern Baptist Theological Seminary. Both studies are the byproduct of an extended treatment by Imad Shehadeh, *God With Us and Without Us*.

existence of an eternal and active relationship between persons within God's oneness. Accordingly, there is a plurality within oneness without being composed of parts. That being the case, God revealed himself as existing outside of creation in three equal but distinct persons in an eternal relationship, i.e., from eternity past to eternity future, and yet being one in essence. These persons are the Father, Son, and Holy Spirit, whereby each of them is equally God, without separation or confusion, and each is distinct from the other. This is referred to in historical Christianity as the doctrine of the Trinity. Other expressions used throughout history include "triunity," "inclusive and exclusive oneness," "Trinitarian monotheism," or simply "Trinitarianism."

THE NATURE OF THE BIBLICAL LANGUAGE ABOUT ONENESS

The biblical language about oneness reveals insistence on the oneness of God in both Testaments. Yet the Old Testament reveals plurality within oneness, and the New Testament presents peculiar expressions about oneness.[2] Both the Old and New Testaments hold fiercely to the oneness of God. Below are sample verses from both. The following are sample verses from the Old Testament that speak of God as the one and only God:

> [Moses the prophet wrote,] "In the beginning God created the heavens and the earth." (Genesis 1:1)
> [Moses the prophet wrote,] "You shall have no other gods before Me." (Exodus 20:3)
> [Moses the prophet wrote,] "To you it was shown that you might know that the LORD, He is God; there is no other besides Him." (Deuteronomy 4:35)
> [Moses the prophet wrote of the Lord speaking,] "See now that I, I am He, and there is no god besides Me." (Deuteronomy 32:39a)
> [Moses the prophet wrote,] "Hear, O Israel! The LORD is our God, the LORD is one." (Deuteronomy 6:4)
> [David wrote,] "The heavens are telling of the glory of God; and their expanse is declaring the work of His hands." (Psalms 19:1)
> [Solomon wrote,] "The conclusion, when all has been heard, is: fear God and keep His commandments, because this applies to every person." (Ecclesiastes 12:13)

2. For further examination, see Shehadeh, *God With Us*, 45–57, 201–10.

> [Isaiah the prophet wrote of God speaking,] "They will make supplication to you [Israel]: 'Surely, God is with you, and there is none else, no other God.'" (Isaiah 45:14b)
> [Isaiah the prophet wrote of God speaking,] "I am God, and there is no other; I am God, and there is no one like Me." (Isaiah 46:9b)

THE TESTIMONY OF THE NEW TESTAMENT ABOUT THE ONE AND ONLY GOD

The following are sample verses from the New Testament that speak of God as the one and only God:

> 29 Jesus answered, "The foremost [commandment] is, 'hear O Israel! The Lord our God is one Lord; 30 And you shall love the Lord your God will all your heart, and will all your soul, and with all your mind, and with all your strength . . . 32 The scribe said to Him, "Right, Teacher; You have truly stated that He is one, and there is no one else besides him." (Mark 12:29–30, 32)
> 1 Jesus spoke these things . . . , 3"This is eternal life, that they may know You, the only true God, and Jesus Christ whom You have sent." (John 17:1–3)
> [Luke wrote of the apostle Paul's words,] "24 The God who made the world and all things in it, since He is Lord of heaven and earth, does not dwell in temples made with hands; 25 nor is He served by human hands, as though He needed anything, since He Himself gives to all people life and breath and all things; 26 and He made from one man every nation of mankind to live on all the face of the earth, having determined their appointed times and the boundaries of their habitation, 27 that they would seek God, if perhaps they might grope for Him and find Him, though He is not far from each one of us." (Acts 17:24–27)
> [The apostle Paul wrote,] "18 For the wrath of God is revealed from heaven against all ungodliness and unrighteousness of men who suppress the truth in unrighteousness, 19 because that which is known about God is evident within them; for God made it evident to them. 20 For since the creation of the world His invisible attributes, His eternal power and divine nature, have been clearly seen, being understood through what has been made, so that they are without excuse." (Romans 1:18–20)
> [The apostle Paul wrote,] "4. . . We know that there is no such thing as an idol in the world, and that there is no God but one . . . 6 For us there is but one God, the Father, from whom are all things,

> and we exist for Him; and one Lord, Jesus Christ, by whom are all things, and we exist through Him." (1 Corinthians 8:4b, 6)
>
> [The apostle Paul wrote,] "3 Being diligent to preserve the unity of the Spirit in the bond of peace. 4 There is one body and one Spirit, just as also you were called in one hope of your calling; 5 one Lord, one faith, one baptism, 6 one God and Father of all who is over all and through all and in all." (Ephesians 4:3–6)
>
> [The apostle James wrote,] "You believe that God is one. You do well." (James 2:19a)

PLURALITY WITHIN ONENESS IN THE OLD TESTAMENT

Although the Old Testament clings tenaciously to the oneness of God, careful examination of the Old Testament proves that there is plurality within God's oneness. This in turn prepares for the full revelation of the Trinity in the New Testament. This plurality in unity in the Old Testament manifests itself in several ways. Some notable expressions that appear, which will be examined in more detail below, are as follows: in the meaning of the word "one"; in some of the names and titles of the Lord; in divine discourse; and in the appearance of the Angel of the Lord.

THE MEANING OF "ONE"

The Torah declares God's oneness and man's relationship to him in what is called the "Shema": "4Hear, O Israel! The LORD is our God, the LORD is one! 5And you shall love the LORD your God with all your heart and with all your soul and with all your might" (Deuteronomy 6:4–5). To say that God is "one" does not exhaust the meaning of the word so as to mean one and not two.[3] An examination of the word "one" points to a plurality within oneness as evidenced by several reasons.

First, Deuteronomy 6:4 uses the singular *YHWH* with the plural *Elohim* so that the Shema states, "*YHWH* [singular] our God [plural], *YHWH* [singular] is one [singular]."[4]

3. Cf. Knight, *Biblical Approach*, 17.

4. The word "Lord" in many English Bibles reflects the word יְהוָה (*YHWH*). The word אֱלֹהֵינוּ (*elohaynu*), meaning "our God," is from the plural אֱלֹהִים (*elohim*) in construct (so the last mem is dropped) plus the first common plural personal pronoun.

Second, the word used in Deuteronomy 6:4 for "one" is a special word in that it may be used for one without plurality as in "one man" (Genesis 42:13),[5] and may also be used to refer to one with plurality, as in "there was evening and there was morning, one day" (Genesis 1:5); "For this reason a man shall leave his father and his mother, and be joined to his wife; and they shall become one flesh" (Genesis 2:24); "Then the LORD God said, 'Behold, the man has become like one of Us'" (Genesis 3:22a). Moses could have used another word meaning "only one" to signify oneness in the sense of absolute oneness but he did not.[6] This word is used in the expressions "take now thine only son" (Genesis 22:2) and "my only one" (Psalms 22:20; 35:17; personal translation).

Third, the word for "one" used in Deuteronomy 6:4 is an adjectival form related to the word meaning "to unite" (as in "unite my heart to fear your name," Psalms 86:11b), and to the word "together" (as in "the two of them walked on together," Genesis 22:8b), both of which have the idea of uniting into one.[7] Thus the word for "one" in Deuteronomy 6:4 clearly conveys a unity brought about by the joining of separate elements together.

Fourth, faith in *YHWH* as one is not only required in Israel's confession from the beginning, but it is also required in the last days: "In that day the LORD will be the only one, and His name the only one" (Zechariah 149b).[8] Eugene Merrill perceptively points out that since Deuteronomy 6:4 is used in Israel's repeated confession of its faith, it is highly justifiable to lay more weight on the etymological use of "one" of Deuteronomy 6:4 to arrive at its theological significance. It shows that the uniqueness of God is in that he is one in one sense, and yet there is also plurality in this oneness in another sense. He asserts,

> In Deuteronomy 6:4, a statement highly charged with theoretical content in light of its confessional character, it is not at all unreasonable to assume that the historical, etymological meaning is in view. This is particularly likely given the divine intentionality—namely, the selection of a theologically loaded term

5. The word for "one" is אֶחָד (*eḥad*).

6. The word for "only one" is יָחִיד (*yaḥīd*).

7. The word one אֶחָד (*eyhad*) is an adjectival form related to יַחֵד (*yhad*), meaning "to be united," and the word יַחְדָּו (*yaḥdo*), meaning "together" (cf. Brown, Driver, and Briggs, eds., s.v. "3–402 ",יַחֵד. It is cognate with Arabic وحّد (*waḥada*) and توحيد (*tawḥīd*), meaning "to make one" or "to unite."

8. The Hebrew text reads: יִהְיֶה יְהוָה אֶחָד וּשְׁמוֹ אֶחָד: (*YHWH YHWH Ehad washmo eḥad*

> to convey at once the uniqueness and solitariness of the Lord and the multi-personality of the Godhead.[9]

IN THE NAMES AND TITLES OF GOD

A name in the Bible points to the nature of the personality carrying the name and its characteristics.[10] This applies to both man and God. In regard to man, the name stands for the uniqueness of the person, or is related to a peculiar event surrounding his/her birth, or a change in their personality or circumstances. In the same way, the names and titles of God express his nature, personality, and actions with mankind. Some of the most significant names and titles that express plurality in oneness include: *Elohim*, *Adonai*, and *Panim*.

Elohim

The term *Elohim* for God is more of an appellative than a name.[11] It is plural in form and yet in most of its usage it refers to the one God. It is similar in its usage in referring to the "waters" and to the "heavens."[12] Water can be thought of as drops of rain, or oceans, and yet it is all one mass of water. Similarly, heaven can be thought of as several layers: the sky that is beheld, the outer space, or the heavenly abode. In all the mysteries of the components of heaven it still belongs to the large class of "heaven." The word *Elohim* acts in a similar way. Though it is plural in form, it is often used with a singular verb (cf. Genesis 1:1). While there are singular names for God, the term *Elohim* is used many times more to reveal an aspect of God, in that while he is one, he is simultaneously more than one.[13]

Many languages, including Greek, have no word that could exactly translate *Elohim*. Commenting on the Septuagint translation of the word, Knight affirms,

9. Merrill, "Is the Doctrine of the Trinity Implied," 124.

10. For a fuller treatment of the phenomena of "name," see Knight, *Biblical Approach*, 10–14; Ross, "4:147 ",שֵׁם.

11. Cf. Ringgren, "אֱלֹהִים," 267–84.

12. Both of these terms are referred to in the plural מַיִם (*mayīm*) and שָׁמַיִם (*shamayīm*), respectively.

13. Examples of other names of God used less times that *Elohim* are the following: אֵל (*el*), אֱלוֹהַּ (*eloah*), גִּבּוֹר (*gibor*), שַׁדַּי (*shadai*).

> Translated in Alexandria as it was, and reflecting as it does the philosophical-speculative approach of the Greek-speaking world, the LXX was unable to appreciate the need for a word that is both singular and plural at the same time.[14]

This general difficulty in translating *Elohim* in many of the languages of the world is relieved by the progress of revelation of plurality in oneness leading climactically to the doctrine of the Trinity.

Adonai

It is well known that the Hebrews, out of reverence for God, did not pronounce the sacred Tetragrammaton, *YHWH*. Instead, they would pronounce the word *Adonai*, meaning "lord." However, this name is in the plural and not the singular.[15] So the word *Adonai* is literally "my lords," where "lords" functions in the same way as *Elohim*. This is further evidence that the Hebrews understood the nature of God as plurality in oneness.[16]

Panim

The word *Panim* refers to the presence of the Lord, but is joined with verbs, not only in the plural, but also in the singular.[17] For example, Exodus 33:14 may be translated literally as "my faces go before you and I will give you rest."[18] It must be observed that, though the terms "faces" and "go" are in the plural, the expression "I will give you rest" is in the singular. Again, plurality in oneness is evident.

14. Knight, *Biblical Approach*, 20.

15. The word *Adonai* is אֲדֹנַי, meaning "my lords," and is composed of the plural אֲדֹנִים (*adonīm*), meaning "lords," from the root אָדוֹן (*adōn*), meaning "lord," with the first-person pronoun. אֲדֹנִים (*adonim*) is dropped from being in construct.

16. Knight, *Biblical Approach*, 19.

17. The word *panai* (פָּנַי)means "my faces" and is composed of the plural פָּנִים (*panīm*), meaning "lords," from the root פָּנֶה (*panah*), meaning "lord," with the first-person pronoun. פָּנִים (*panīm*) is dropped from being in construct.

18. The text of Exodus 33:14 is: פָּנַי יֵלֵכוּ וַהֲנִחֹתִי לָךְ (*panai yilkhu whanikhoti lakh*).

IN DIVINE CONVERSATIONS

The Scriptures reveal that God speaks of himself using the plural language such as: "let Us make man in Our image, according to Our likeness" (Genesis 1:26a); "Behold, the man has become like one of Us" (Genesis 3:22a); "Let Us go down and there confuse their language" (11:7a); "the LORD said to my Lord" (Psalms 110:1a); "Whom shall I send, and who will go for Us?" (Isaiah 6:8b).

The use of the plural in this divine conversation is not an expression of the majesty of the speaker. This is supported by several factors. First, the use of the plural to magnify self was not used in this time.[19] Men of power used the first-person singular to speak of themselves. For example, Pharaoh said to Joseph, "In my dream, behold, I was standing on the bank of the Nile" (Genesis 41:17). Nebuchadnezzar, the king of Babylon, likewise said to Daniel, "I, Nebuchadnezzar, was at ease in my house and flourishing in my palace" (Daniel 4:4). Second, God often uses the first-person singular to speak of himself. For example, God said to Abraham, "I am a shield to you" (Genesis 15:1b),; and he spoke of himself declaring, "I am the LORD, and there is no other" (Isaiah 45:6b). However, he also alternates between the singular and the plural in other instances. For example, "Whom shall *I* send, and who will go for *Us*?" (Isaiah 6:8b, emphasis added). Samaan observes that it is unlikely that God would use expressions not familiar to people.[20] When he used the plural with the singular, he was indicating plurality in oneness. Third, God does not need to magnify himself through the unusual use of language, for "He who is great with all greatness does not resort to making Himself great."[21]

IN THE APPEARANCE OF THE ANGEL OF THE LORD

A most amazing phenomena that the Pentateuch records is that of the appearance of the angel of the Lord.[22] Beginning with the Pentateuch, revelation is made of this mysterious phenomenon, which reflects diversity

19. The Arab philosopher, Awad Samaan, gives several examples that show that plural of majesty was not used in or outside the Bible during the time of its writing. See Samaan, *Allah: Dhātuhu wa-Nūʿ Waḥdaniyyatihi* [God: His Essence and the Kind of His Oneness], 20–25.

20. Samaan, *Allah: Dhātuhu wa-Nūʿ Waḥdaniyyatihi* [God], 23, 21.

21. Samaan, *Allah: Dhātuhu wa-Nūʿ Waḥdaniyyatihi* [God], 21.

22. The word "Lord" is mostly a translation of יְהוָה (YHWH).

in oneness. The angel of the Lord is God himself, as well as the messenger of God, as evident in the following passages.

The Encounter with Hagar

The angel of the Lord, first mentioned in Genesis 16, is identified as God himself:

> 7 Now the angel of the LORD found her by a spring of water in the wilderness. . . 13 Then she called the name of the LORD who spoke to her, "You are a God who sees." (Genesis 16:7a, 13a)

This phenomenon of introducing the angel of the Lord as the Lord himself is repeated (Genesis 22:11–12; 31:11, 13; 48:16; Jude 6:11, 16, 22; 13:22–23).

In the Visit to Abraham

In Genesis 18, a visit by three men is recorded as having come to see Abraham at the great trees of Mamre (cf. 13:18; 14:13). But the chapter begins by indicating that it was the Lord himself who appeared to Abraham. The verb "appeared" in the expression "The LORD appeared to him" (18:1) points to the appearance as an initiative of God himself (cf. 12:7).[23] The text continues to speak of the Lord (18:13, 17, 20, 22, 26, 33). The other two visitors are introduced as angels (cf. 19:1). This visit no doubt reflects the intimate fellowship that occurred when the Lord desires to confirm his promises. Upon seeing them, Abraham runs to meet them, and bows down to them to the ground, a clear act of worship (18:2). He begs the Lord to stay (vv. 4–5), hurries to tell Sarah to prepare a meal (vv. 6–7), and stands while they eat (v. 8). Though there are three personalities, the text alternates between the singular and the plural, ending with the Lord himself, who departs (18:33).[24] At the same time, the passage clearly differentiates between the Lord and his two companions (cf. 18:22; 19:1). Furthermore, while Genesis 19 speaks of two angels (v. 1) who are sent by YHWH (v. 13), the Masoretic Text goes on to present Lot as speaking to the two in the singular (19:18–19, 21). In spite of this,

23. The verb for "appeared," וַיֵּרָא ("vayera"), is niphal preterite 3ms + w consecutive.

24. Knight observes that the LXX of Genesis 18:9 uses the singular in Greek while the MT maintains the plural. Cf. Knight, *Biblical Approach*, 25.

this text of Genesis 18–19 does not connect these three personalities with the three persons of the Trinity, but only shows the concept of plurality in oneness.

At the Offering of Isaac

In Genesis 22:9–18, the angel who converses with Abraham is presented as the mouthpiece of God, yet the angel speaks as if he were God himself. Likewise, Abraham regards this experience as an encounter with God himself: "Abraham called the name of that place The LORD Will Provide, as it is said to this day, 'On the mount of the LORD it will be provided'" (22:14).

In the Experience of Jacob

In an amazing story, Genesis 32:24–30 speaks of Jacob wrestling with a man. But it becomes clear that this is greater than a man. This began to be revealed when the man touched Jacob and dislocated the socket of his thigh. This led Jacob to ask the visitor to bless him, and he called the place "Paniel," meaning "the face of God."[25] Jacob then stated, "I have seen God face to face, yet my life has been preserved" (32:30).

In the Experience of Moses

In Exodus 3:2, it is the angel of the Lord that appears to Moses, but he is identified as *YHWH* and *Elohim* in 3:4.

In the Journey of the People in the Wilderness

In the journey of the Israelites in the wilderness, it was God—who is sometimes referred to as *YHWH* and sometimes as *Elohim*—who led the people (Exodus 13:21; 14:24). The angel of the Lord is also mentioned as the one who led the people (Exodus 14:19; Numbers 20:16). The text introduces the angel of the Lord or the angel of God as different from the Lord or God, and then returns and refers to him as God or the Lord himself.

25. The word is פְּנִיאֵל (Peniel).

THE ANGEL OF THE LORD

It is clear that the Torah leaves the text vague and awaits a future revelation, fulfilled ultimately in the New Testament. However, several conclusions can be made about the appearances of the angel of the Lord in the Old Testament.

First, according to the commentator Derek Kidner, the oneness of God is not a rigid oneness. From the very beginning of God's revelation of himself, though God insists on his oneness, he also refers to a wondrous plurality within this oneness. Kidner states,

> We may note the occasional indications, in the terms "the angel of the Lord" or "of God" and "the Spirit of God," that God's unity is not monolithic. A study of "the Angel of the Lord" passages . . . leaves no room for doubt that the term denotes God Himself as seen in human form.[26]

Secondly, there is a difference between the presence of God and seeing God. His presence is real every time, but experiences of seeing him are diverse and indirect.[27] In the appearance of the Lord's angel, seeing God is through the mediation of an angelic form, a quasi-human being. With this mediation, there is a real presence of the Lord himself. The Old Testament avoids mediation without real presence and real presence without mediation, while the biblical balance introduces both at the same time. This is an indication of the coming time in which believers see God directly in the person of Jesus Christ.

Third, Kidner states that the word for "angel," which has the meaning of "messenger" or "sender," indicates that the invisible God becomes visible, and that the sending God is at the same time the sent God. This mystery fades and is explained in the New Testament. Kidner writes,

> What should be added is the "Angel," by its meaning "messenger," implies that God, made visible, is at the same time God sent. In the Old Testament nothing is made of this paradox, but it should not surprise us that the apparent absurdity disappears in the New Testament.[28]

26. Kidner, *Genesis*, 33–34.

27. Cf. Exodus 33:12–17, 20; Deuteronomy 4:12; Psalm 97:2–6; 1 Timothy 1:17; 6:16; 1 John 4:12.

28. Kidner, *Genesis*, 33–34.

Fourth, as Kidner also states, just as the expression "the Spirit of God" in the Old Testament awaited full revelation on the Day of Pentecost, so the angel of the Lord as an expression of the Lord himself, will be revealed in its full meaning in him whom the Father sent to the world, the eternal Son.[29]

Fifth, all that is stated above indicates that the expression "angel of the Lord" is a functional expression that is occupied not by one person, but by a number of personalities according to God's will.

PECULIAR NEW TESTAMENT EXPRESSIONS ABOUT ONENESS

The New Testament speaks of God in the same way as the Old Testament. However, it adds a revelation of God's penetration to complement the appearances of the Old Testament as well as to vindicate his attributes and fulfill his promises. Thus, the appearance that was intermittent became permanent, and what these appearances indicated became promises fulfilled. This took place climactically through the incarnation and redemption in Christ.

However, it is necessary to observe that though the New Testament explains in detail how the incarnation and redemption were accomplished through the new revelation of the Father, Son, and Holy Spirit, it nevertheless includes many expressions that point to the incarnation and redemption as being the work of God without emphasizing the work of the Son or the Holy Spirit, and often without directly mentioning them.

Using the same expression "God" of the only God of whom there is no other, and in a startling way, the New Testament points to God's involvement in the human condition, the revelation of the gospel of God for the joy of humanity, the salvation of God for all peoples, the appearance of God in the flesh, the work of the grace and mercy of God, the manifestation of the righteousness of God, the hope of the fulfillment of the word of God, ownership of the universal church of God, and the work of the local churches of God. All this is without immediate explanation of how these works of God came to be. The following are sample verses:

29. Kidner, *Genesis*, 33–34.

God's Involvement in the Human Condition

"Behold, the virgin shall be with child and shall bear a Son, and they shall call His name Immanuel," which translated means, "God with us." (Matthew 1:23)
What then shall we say to these things? If God is for us, who is against us? (Romans 8:31)

The Gospel of God for the Joy of Humanity:

I preached the gospel of God to you without charge. (2 Corinthians 11:7b)
2 We had the boldness in our God to speak to you the gospel of God amid much opposition . . . 8 Having so fond an affection for you, we were well-pleased to impart to you not only the gospel of God but also our own lives, because you had become very dear to us. 9 For you recall, brethren, our labor and hardship, how working night and day so as not to be a burden to any of you, we proclaimed to you the gospel of God. (1 Thessalonians 2:2b, 8–9)
According to the glorious gospel of the blessed God, with which I have been entrusted. (1 Timothy 1:11)
For it is time for judgment to begin with the household of God; and if it begins with us first, what will be the outcome for those who do not obey the gospel of God? (1 Peter 4:17)
In the days of the voice of the seventh angel, when he is about to sound, then the mystery of God is finished, as He preached [proclaimed the gospel] to His servants the prophets. (Revelation 10:7)

The Salvation of God to All Peoples

Glory to God in the highest, and on earth peace among men with whom He is pleased. (Luke 2:14)
Therefore let it be known to you that this salvation of God has been sent to the Gentiles; they will also listen. (Acts 28:28)
2 In hope of eternal life, which God, who does not lie, promised before the ages began. 3 But now in his own time he has made his message evident through the preaching I was entrusted with according to the command of God our Savior. (Titus 1:2–3)
The kindness of God our Savior and His love for mankind appeared. (Titus 3:4b).

The Appearance of God in the Flesh

> By common confession, great is the mystery of godliness: [God] who was revealed in the flesh, was vindicated in the Spirit, seen by angels, proclaimed among the nations, believed on in the world, taken up in glory. (1 Timothy 3:16)[30]

The Work of God's Grace and Mercy

> And now I commend you to God and to the word of His grace, which is able to build you up and to give you the inheritance among all those who are sanctified. (Acts 20:32)
> 22 What if God, although willing to demonstrate His wrath and to make His power known, endured with much patience vessels of wrath prepared for destruction? 23 And He did so to make known the riches of His glory upon vessels of mercy, which He prepared beforehand for glory, 24 even us, whom He also called, not from among Jews only, but also from among Gentiles. (Romans 9:22–24)
> [After the teaching on justification and regeneration:] 32 For God has shut up all in disobedience so that He may show mercy to all. 33 Oh, the depth of the riches both of the wisdom and knowledge of God! How unsearchable are His judgments and unfathomable His ways. (Romans 11:32–33)
> For the grace of God has appeared, bringing salvation to all men. (Titus 2:11)
> This is the true grace of God. Stand firm in it. (1 Peter 5:12b)

The Manifestation of the Righteousness of God

> But now apart from the Law the righteousness of God has been manifested, being witnessed by the Law and the Prophets. (Romans 3:21)

30. The reading of the Byzantine text of 1 Timothy 3:16 along with a few other witnesses is θεός rather than ὅς. However, the relative pronoun ὅς has earlier and stronger support. "Externally, there is no question as to what should be considered original: The Alexandrian and Western traditions are decidedly in favor of ὅς. Internally, the evidence is even stronger. What scribe would change θεός to ὅς intentionally?" (*NET Bible* notes). Nevertheless, the relative pronoun must point to a referent, and the immediate prior context clearly refers to God: "the household of God" and "the church of the living God." Thus, the passage intends to point to Christ as God appearing in the flesh. This is why some scribes added the word "God" in the transcription of some manuscripts.

Indeed God who will justify the circumcised by faith and the uncircumcised through faith is one. (Romans 3:30)

The Hope of the Fulfillment of the Word of God

And now I am standing trial for the hope of the promise made by God to our fathers. (Acts 26:6)
5 The hope laid up for you in heaven, of which you previously heard in the word of truth, the gospel 6 which has come to you, just as in all the world also it is constantly bearing fruit and increasing, even as it has been doing in you also since the day you heard of it and understood the grace of God in truth. (Colossians 1:5–6)
For this reason we also constantly thank God that when you received the word of God which you heard from us, you accepted it not as the word of men, but for what it really is, the word of God, which also performs its work in you who believe. (1Thessalonians 2:13)
For it is for this we labor and strive, because we have fixed our hope on the living God, who is the Savior of all men, especially of believers. (1 Timothy 4:10)

Ownership of the Universal Church of God

Is purchased by his blood: "Be on guard for yourselves and for all the flock, among which the Holy Spirit has made you overseers, to shepherd the church of God which He purchased with His own blood" (Acts 20:28b).[31]
Locally centralized: "To the church of God which is at Corinth . . . in every place" (1 Corinthians 1:2; also 2 Corinthians 1:1).
Responsibility to care for it and not offend it: "If a man does not know how to manage his own household, how will he take care of the church of God?" (1 Timothy 3:5); "Give no offense . . . to the church of God" (1 Corinthians 10:32).

31. This verse makes a strong declaration about the blood used in purchasing the church. The phraie τὴν ἐκκλησίαν τοῦ θεοῦ, ἣν περιεποιήσατο διὰ τοῦ αἵματος τοῦ ἰδίου (*tane eklessia tu theou, hane perepoiesato dia tu haimatos tu idieu*) is considered here to be the correct reading. The translation "with his own blood" appears in the major English translations, and is the one adopted here. However, it is possible to translate the last part of the verse in various other ways. For further analysis, see Shehadeh, *God With Us*, 53–55; See also Metzger, *Textual Commentary*, 425; *NET Bible*, 2nd ed., notes on Acts 20:28; Harris, *Jesus as God*, 137.

Can be persecuted: "For I am the least of the apostles, and not fit to be called an apostle, because I persecuted the church of God" (1 Corinthians 15:9; also Galatians 1:13).
It is the house of God where the truth is: "Know how one ought to conduct himself in the household of God, which is the church of the living God, the pillar and support of the truth" (1 Timothy 3:15b).

The Work of the Local Churches of God

Must avoid the practice of contentiousness in it: "But if one is inclined to be contentious, we have no other practice, nor have the churches of God" (1 Corinthians 11:16).
Can experience persecutions and afflictions: "Therefore, we ourselves speak proudly of you among the churches of God for your perseverance and faith in the midst of all your persecutions and afflictions which you endure" (2 Thessalonians 1:4).

The Sovereignty of God

> 26 The last enemy that will be abolished is death. 27 For He [i.e., God the Father] has put all things in subjection under his [i.e., the Son's] feet. But when He says, "All things are put in subjection," it is evident that He is excepted who put all things in subjection to Him. 28 When all things are subjected to Him, then the Son Himself also will be subjected to the One who subjected all things to Him, so that God may be all in all. (1 Corinthians 15:26–28)
> 2 And I saw the holy city, new Jerusalem, coming down out of heaven from God, made ready as a bride adorned for her husband. 3 And I heard a loud voice from the throne, saying, "Behold, the tabernacle of God is among men, and He will dwell among them, and they shall be His people, and God Himself will be among them." (Revelation 21:2–3; see also 21:10–11; 22:18–19)

In all the examples above from the Old and New Testaments, the Bible declares that the one and only God penetrates creation in a specific way and in a specific time and place. This he accomplishes in his gospel, his salvation, his appearance in the flesh, his grace, his mercy, his manifestation of righteousness, his fulfillment of his word, and for the benefit of his church. All this was fulfilled through the work of the Father, Son, and Holy Spirit, which is hidden latently in some texts of the Bible but is revealed clearly in other texts. All of this is for the glory of the one and only true God in his beautiful nature.

On this basis, the Christian believer in oneness in Trinity may use "God" to state the following: "God created me, then God became a man like me. God took my place by bearing the penalty of my sins through his death on the cross and rose from the dead victoriously. He then gave me new life and now he lives in me."

THE INEVITABILITY OF THE ETERNAL ACTIVITY OF PERSONS WITHIN ONENESS

In contrast to absolute oneness, the biblical revelation of oneness in Trinity presents the eternal activity of persons within oneness outside creation as the foundation for their manifestation in creation. This is examined here beginning with a treatment of the challenge to this concept.[32]

The Challenge to the Concept

Some consider a probe into the activity of God outside creation to be outside the realm of human inquiry. They insist that talk about God should be limited to what he revealed in his actions in history. There is a continual appeal even from some of the finest theologians to avoid endeavoring to know God in himself outside creation. Some believe that the Scriptures do not present the doctrine of the immanent Trinity (God's activity in himself), but only of the economic Trinity (God's activity in creation).[33] Appealing to the "hiddenness" of God as his divine prerogative, Robert Jensen asserts that honoring God comes by abstaining from such a quest:

> We can honor and obey the divine majesty of God "in himself" only by refraining from the religious quest for God "in himself" beyond his temporal revelation, only by truly obeying the Socratic motto "Quae supra nos, nihil ad nos" (What is above us is none of our business).[34]

32. For further treatment, see Shehadeh, *God With Us*, 107–9, 133–48, 170–72, 213–22.

33. Karl Rahner speaks of claims by those who insist that the Bible speaks only of God's activity in creation and makes an excellent case for God's activity in himself. Rahner, *Trinity*, 22.

34. Jensen, *Triune Identity*, 27.

However, contrary to the above opinions, the pursuit of understanding the activity of God's attributes in himself without creation is legitimate, logical, and holy. First, to begin with, belief in the Trinity means belief in the eternal activity of God independent of creation. This activity of God is a necessity presupposed in Christian theology.

Second, God revealed his desire to be known and trusted. When Moses asked the Lord to see his glory, the Lord answered him by revealing that seeing his glory is chiefly in knowing his true attributes:

> 5 The LORD descended in the cloud and stood there with him as He called upon the name of the LORD. 6 Then the LORD passed by in front of him and proclaimed, 'The LORD, the LORD God, compassionate and gracious, slow to anger, and abounding in lovingkindness and truth; 7 who keeps lovingkindness for thousands, who forgives iniquity, transgression and sin; yet he will by no means leave the guilty unpunished. (Exodus 34:5–7a)

Austin Surls effectively demonstrates how the words of Exodus 34:6–7 were repeated or alluded to for hundreds of years throughout Israel's history by Moses, Solomon, Hezekiah, Daniel, Nehemiah, Joel, Jonah, Micah, Jeremiah, Nahum, Psalms and Proverbs.[35] The words of Exodus 34:6–7 were also used to introduce the incarnate Christ (John 1:14–16).

Third, it is unreasonable for God to reveal his attributes and then prevent people from experiencing them. Rather, it is God's pleasure for his people to know him, and it grieves him when they do not: "'Let him who boasts boast of this, that he understands and knows Me, that I am the LORD who exercises lovingkindness, justice and righteousness on earth; for I delight in these things' declares the LORD" (Jeremiah 9:24).

Fourth, there are serious dangers in separating the works of God inside creation from the truth about his nature independent of creation. Among these dangers is impairing humanity's knowledge of what is real and objective about God as he is in himself. The theologian Carl Henry states that separating the divine essence from the divine attributes deprives the essence of content and meaning, as occurs in absolute oneness:

> Divine essence and attributes are integral to each other. God is not a substance essentially distinguished from his psychic properties or attributes. Such a notion would reduce divine essence to a barren concept, a postulation devoid of content and

35. For an excellent treatment of quotations and allusions of Exodus 34:6–7 in the Old Testament, see Surls, "Verbal Echoes of Exodus 34:6–7."

> meaning. . . The view that divine attributes are completely separate or distinct functions in the nature of God and more or less independent of his essence, reflects the notion of an underlying substance, a notion that influenced even Islamic philosophy.[36]

Karl Barth asserts that this matter is not merely an academic triviality but is rather concerned with whether the attributes really occur in God or are merely in man's imagined knowledge of God.[37]

Fifth, and in a similar fashion to Barth, Schwöbel stresses that separating the works of God in history from his nature outside history would mean that his works in history would not reveal anything about God in himself. Thus, Schwöbel argues, the importance of God's action in creation are in danger of being diminished, as there would be no influence of the nature of God on his works in history, thereby depriving it of both meaning and benefit.[38]

Sixth, the Bible shows that God did reveal the reality of an eternal activity in himself apart from creation. For while the Bible insists on the oneness of God, it also insists on the presence of plurality of active persons within this oneness, beginning from the Old Testament and extending into the New Testament.

Seventh, as the Arab philosopher Ammar Al Basri asserts, to ascribe an attribute to God only to then deny its activity has the result of negating what was originally ascribed. This would imply that there is lying in the attribute proclaimed.[39]

Eighth, limiting the work of God's attributes until after creation means that his eternal activity is dependent on the existence of creation. This means that his eternal attributes are limited to be within what is contingent. However, this is impossible because the Creator does not depend on creation, and the necessary being does not depend on what is contingent but rather the opposite.

Ninth, confining the work of God's attributes post-creation implies change in him. For if God's attributes were potential and not active without creation, this means that becoming active after creation implied a certain change in his nature. This goes against his immutability.[40]

36. Henry, *God Who Stands and Stays*, 130.

37. Barth, *Gottingen Dogmatics*, 378.

38. Schwöbel, *Trinitarian Theology Today*, 6–7.

39. This is what the Arab philosopher Ammar Al Basri, from the ninth century, asserted. See Al Basri, *Kitāb al-Burhān* [The Book of Evidence], 47–48.

40. This is clarified by the Christian philosopher Awad Samaan (see الله، ذاته ونوع

Tenth, limiting the activity of the attributes of God to after creation implies his imperfection. If, for example, the attribute of knowledge did not become active until after creation, this would mean that God was ignorant of something before creation. But this is impossible and contrary to the nature of God who is omniscient. There is no time that God did not practice his knowledge, holiness, justice, goodness, etc.[41]

The Unavoidable Question

Behind the difference between God's absolute oneness and God's oneness in Trinity of Christianity lies a question that cannot be avoided. It is the question behind every question related to the nature of God. It is also a theological inquiry that all religions and faiths must answer. The question is: how can the attributes of God be active eternally apart from the existence of creation without God existing in relationship?

The question can be explained using the example of love: if love is one of God's eternal attributes, this requires the presence of the lover and the one loved (or beloved), in addition to love itself. Simply, how can love be active eternally without a relationship?

If the object of God's love is outside of himself, this leads to two options. The first option is that God is in relationship with another eternal being like himself. But this is rejected because it opens the door to polytheism. There is only one God with no partners. The second option would be that God is in an eternal relationship with creation. However, this is rejected as well because it makes creation eternal like God, and it also causes the necessary being (God) to be dependent on what is contingent (creation).

Returning to the example of love, if the object of God's love is within himself, this leads to two conclusions. The first is God being compound. This conclusion is rejected at once because of God's simplicity, i.e., he is not divisible and is not made up of parts. The second and last conclusion is plurality in unity, or that God exists in a relationship within himself, implying at least a duality in his one essence. Since God is independent of

وحدانيته [God, his essence and his kind of unity], 8; also Samaan, *Allah bayna Falsafa wa-Masīḥīyya* [God, between philosophy and Christianity], 56.

41. Awad Samaan expresses the same thoughts in Samaan, *Allah bayna Falsafa wa-Masīḥīyya* [God, between philosophy and Christianity], 58.

anything outside of himself, the three elements (lover, beloved, and love) must exist in himself eternally. The same applies to all moral attributes.[42]

The Unavoidable Relationship

If the activity of God's attributes is eternal, this presupposes the existence of a relationship between real persons. This is supported by several factors.

First, the existence of a personality is not philosophically confined only to existence but also to existence in relationship. This means that there are two necessary elements required for the existence of a person. The first is existence, and the second is existence in relationship.[43] Therefore, John Zizioulas asserts that these two elements are identical, so that the principle of "existence in relationship" is the only principle that gives a personality the meaning to its existence, otherwise there would be no personality. For "to be and to be in relation becomes identical . . . It is only in relationship that identity appears as having an ontological significance."[44] Personality becomes evident in relationship.

Second, God loves not because he can love as a decision of his will but because he is love in his nature, and he is love in his nature because he loves from eternity, and he does so because he is in relationship.[45] This is fair and sound reason. There is no other conclusion.

Third, the relationship would be deficient and lacking if it was restricted to a relationship with the self, as in saying that a person loves himself or God loves himself. For a relationship requires an activity between subject and object that are distinct from one another. This applies to people as well as to God but without God being composite. For it is impossible in a reciprocal relationship for the subject to be an object at the same time. Furthermore, confining relationship to the self lacks expression outside of the self and restricts it to caring for self only, which would pollute the purity of moral attributes. Using the example of love, the theologian Schelling asserts that love does not seek what is its own

42. As MacDonald puts it, to say that God is knower must mean that he either knows something within himself, implying duality, or that he knows something outside himself, implying dependence. MacDonald, "God—a Unit or a Unity?," 13.

43. Zizioulas, *Being as Communion*, 83–84. Cf. Schelling, *Ages of the World*, 96–97; Athanasius, "Four Discourses against the Arains" (*NPNF*2, 6:20, 88).

44. Zizioulas, *Being as Communion*, 83–84.

45. Cf. Glaser, "Concept of Relationship," 58.

and that its presence alone without a relationship between distinct persons deprives from the principle of personality and is rather the opposite of the meaning of personality.[46] Richard of St. Victor asserts similarly that if God were one personality, he would not experience sharing the richness of what he owns, and this would deprive him of pleasure forever.[47]

Fourth, there must be a reciprocal and equal interaction in thought, will, purpose, emotion, and holiness between the persons. Chafer writes,

> In the case of the exercise of the attributes which are moral, both the agent and the object must exhibit intelligence, consciousness, and moral agency. In the experience of communion, the necessity is as much on the object as it is on the agent, that there shall be similarity of thought, disposition, will, purpose, and affection. If the agent is a person, the object must be a person also; whatever pertains to Deity is of necessity eternal.[48]

Fifth, if the attributes of God are eternal, the persons must also be eternal. The perfection of the relationship requires that every person equally loves and accepts love eternally. Each equally understands and enjoys the other person eternally. The will of one person agrees equally with the will of the other person eternally.

Perfection Guaranteed through Oneness

The Trinity preserves the plurality of personalities in God on the one hand but also the oneness of God on the other. For it is a oneness that joins persons and guarantees the perfection of the attributes. This is made evident by several factors.

First, a perfect relationship requires perfection of attributes. The presence of an eternal relationship requires the attributes to be perfect, without any deficiency and without any impurity. For the presence of any deficiency or any impurity in any of the attributes destroys the relationship. Therefore, the attributes of God must stem from his unchanging nature and not from a capricious will.

Second, the perfection of attributes requires eternality. The activity of the attributes must be without beginning or end and not temporary. Perfection requires eternality.

46. Schelling, *Ages of the World*, 96–97.

47. Richard of St. Victor, *Book Three of the Trinity*, 387f.

48. Chafer, *Chafer, Systematic Theology*, 1:293; cf. Berkhof, *Systematic Theology*, 84–85.

Third, eternality requires oneness. The guarantee of the eternality of attributes is oneness because oneness means the absence of any deficiency or impurity in the attributes active in the eternal relationship. So, the perfection of attributes requires oneness.

Fourth, oneness requires perfection of attributes. As the perfection of attributes requires oneness, likewise oneness requires the perfection of attributes; i.e., the activity of the attributes between the persons must be fully operational and in harmony, without independence from each other—and all this eternally. Anything other than that not only destroys the relationship; it also destroys the oneness. So, the oneness of God means the infinite perfection of all his attributes.

THE LESSONS FROM DANGEROUSLY REJECTING A RELATIONSHIP WITHIN ONENESS

There is great danger in rejecting a relationship within oneness. This was illustrated in the historical predicament that absolute oneness faced during the eighth century CE between two Arab philosophies in their attempt to answer the question of how the attributes of God can be active eternally without God existing in relationship. This is dealt with elsewhere in detail.[49] To summarize, according to absolute oneness, God's attributes of action stem from his will and are manifested in power. Also, describing God in human attributes is seen as unrelated to God. In addition, attributes of action are seen as separate from attributes of essence, and attributes of essence cannot be known or understood. As a result, there is a wavering content of faith and no basis for a personal relationship with God.

In contrast, oneness in Trinity proclaims an eternal relationship in God. Accordingly, attributes of action stem from his nature and are manifested in being equal and in harmony. Also, describing God in human attributes comes from man being in the image of God. In addition, attributes of action stem from attributes of essence, and attributes of essence can be known and understood. As a result, there is a steadfast content of faith and an abiding basis for a personal relationship with God.

49. For a fuller treatment, see Shehadeh, *God With Us*, ch. 6, "The Historical Conflict of Absolute Oneness."

CONCLUSION

This study demonstrated the coherence of the Christian doctrine of the Trinity within its firm belief in the oneness of God. It embarked with a challenge to consider deeper truths about this oneness as revealed in the Bible. It then moved to examine the nature of the biblical language about oneness, from the insistence on the oneness of God in both Testaments, to the plurality within oneness in the Old Testament, to the unique New Testament expressions about oneness. This study ended by demonstrating the inevitability of the eternal activity of persons within oneness, moving from oneness to plurality and back to oneness, thereby guaranteeing the perfection of God's attributes.

One cannot speak of God's attributes and actions in history and at the same time reject any revelation of God about his inner nature. If God does not exist eternally in an active relationship in himself, it leads to depriving humanity of any knowledge of him. And if God cannot be known, this means that he cannot enter into a relationship with humanity. In short, lack of relationship in God would result in humanity's lack of relationship with God.

Humanity must be thankful that God has revealed deeper truths about the eternal activity of a relationship within his oneness. They are invited into this relationship of growing trust in the perfection, equality, and harmony of all God's attributes. It is a journey away from dealing with the Trinity as a problem to be solved and into a beauty to be discovered.

BIBLIOGRAPHY

Arabic Sources

ᵉAmmār al-Baṣrī, *Kitāb al-Burhān*, ed., Michel Hayek (Beirut, Lebanon: Dār al-Mashriq, 1993)

Samᵉān, ᵉAwaḍ. *Allah bayna al-Falsafa wa'l-Masīḥiyya*. Stuttgart, Germany: Nadā' al-Rajā'.

———. *Allah: Dhātuhu wa-Nawᵉ Waḥdaniyyatihi*. Stuttgart, Germany: Nadā' al-Rajā'.

Shaḥadah, ᵉImād . *Allah Maᵉna wa min Dūninā: al-Ḥatmiyya wa'l-Jamāl wa'l-Quwwa lil-Waḥdaniyyati bi-Thalūthin Muqābil al-Waḥdaniyyati al-Muṭlaqati*. Dār Manhal al-Ḥiyāt fī Lubnān and Dār al- Hayʾat al-Injīlīyya lil-Nashr wa'l- tawzīʿ, 2020.

English Sources

Athanasius. "Four Discourses against the Arains." In *Nicene and Post-Nicene Fathers*, 2nd ser., edited by Philip Schaff and Henry Wace, vol. 4. New York: Christian Literature, 1892.

Barth, Karl. *The Gottingen Dogmatics. Introduction in the Christian Religion*. Vol. 1. Grand Rapids: Eerdmans, 1991.

Berkhof, Louis. *Systematic Theology*. Grand Rapids: Eerdmans, 1982.

Brown, Francis, S. R. Driver, and Charles A. Briggs, eds. *Enhanced Brown-Driver-Briggs Hebrew and English Lexicon*. Electronic ed. Oak Harbor, WA: Logos Research, 2000.

Chafer, Lewis Sperry. *Chafer Systematic Theology*. Vol. 1. Dallas: Dallas Seminary Press, 1980.

Cross, F. L., and E. A. Livingstone, eds. *The Oxford Dictionary of the Christian Church*. 3rd rev. ed. Oxford: Oxford University Press, 2005.

Geisler, Norman L., and Paul D. Feinberg. I*ntroduction to Philosophy: A Christian Perspective*. Grand Rapids: Baker, 1999.

Glaser, Ida. "The Concept of Relationship as a Key to the Comparative Understanding of Christianity and Islam." *Themelios* 11 (1986) 57–60.

Hastings, James, J. A. Selbie, and J. C. Lambert. *Dictionary of the Apostolic Church*. New York: Scribner, 1951–1954.

Harris, Murray J. *Jesus as God: The New Testament Use of Theos in Reference to Jesus*. Grand Rapids: Baker, 1992.

Henry, Carl F. H. *God Who Stands and Stays*. Vol. 5 of *God, Revelation and Authority*. Waco, TX: Word, 1982.

Jensen, Robert W. *The Triune Identity: God According to the Gospel*. Philadelphia: Fortress, 1982.

Keller, Timothy. *The Timothy Keller Sermon Archive*. New York City: Redeemer Presbyterian Church, 2013. Hypertexted and formatted by Logos Electronic Library.

Kidner, Derek. *Genesis*. Tyndale Old Testament Commentary. Downers Grove, IL: InterVarsity, 1973.

Knight, G. A. F. *A Biblical Approach to the Doctrine of the Trinity*. Edinburgh: Tweedale Court, 1953.

Louw, J. P., and E. A. Nida. *Greek-English lexicon of the New Testament: Based on Semantic Domains*. New York: United Bible Societies, 1989.

MacDonald, Duncan Black. "God—a Unit or a Unity?" *Moslem World* 3 (1913).

Merrill, Eugene H. "Is the Doctrine of the Trinity Implied in the Genesis Creation Account?" in *The Genesis Debate*, edited by Ron Youngblood. New York: Thomas Nelson, 1986.

Metzger, Bruce M. *A Textual Commentary on the Greek New Testament*. 2nd ed. Stuttgart: Deutsche Bibelgesellschaft, 1994.

The NET Bible Second Edition Notes (NET Notes). Nashville: Thomas Nelson, 2019.

Prestige, G. L. *God in Patristic Thought*. London: SPCK, 1952.

Rahner, Karl. *The Trinity*. Translated by Joseph Donceel. New York: Seabury, 1974.

Richard of St Victor. *Book Three of the Trinity*. Translated by Grover A. Zinn. New York: Paulist, 1979.

Ringgren, Helmer. "אֱלֹהִים." In *Theological Dictionary of the Old Testament*, edited by G. Johannes Botterweck and Helmer Ringgren, translated by John T. Willis, 267–84. Grand Rapids: Eerdmans, 1986.

Ross, Allen P. "שֵׁם." In *New International Dictionary of Old Testament Theology and Exegesis*, edited by Villen A. VanGemeren, 4:147. Grand Rapids: Zondervan, 1997.

Schelling, Friedrich. *The Ages of the World*. Translated by Fredrick de Wolfe Bolman Jr. New York: Columbia University Press, 1942.

Schwöbel, Christoph. *Trinitarian Theology Today: Essays on Divine Being and Act*. Edinburgh: T. & T. Clark, 1995.

Shehadeh, Imad. *God With Us and Without Us*, vols. 1 and 2, *The Beauty and Power of Oneness in Trinity verses Absolute Oneness*. Carlisle: Langham Global Library, 2020.

Surls, Austin. *Making Sense of the Divine Name in the Book of Exodus: From Etymology to Literary Onomastics*. Bulletin for Biblical Research Supplement 17. Winona Lake, IN: Eisenbrauns, 2017.

Thayer, Joseph Henry. *Thayer's Greek-English Lexicon of the New Testament*. Grand Rapids: Baker, 1977. Electronically version, OakTree Software.

Weinandy, Thomas G. *Does God Change?* Still River, MA: St Bede's, 1985.

———. *Does God Suffer?* Notre Dame, IN: University of Notre Dame Press, 2000.

Zizioulas, John D. *Being as Communion*. Crestwood, NY: St. Vladimir's Seminary Press, 1997.

9

Sin and Salvation in Islam and Christianity

A Catholic Perspective

COSMAS SARBAH

In order to understand the nature of salvation in Islam, one has to know how sin is defined within the Islamic context. In Islam, to sin is to disobey God. Sin is the violation of the divinely established rules as given by God's prophets. There are two main aspects to sin: sin of omission and sin of commission. One commits the sin of omission by refusing to do what God has commanded. On the other hand, one commits the sin of commission by doing what God has forbidden. A believer should avoid both types of sins. It is clear that in Islamic religious thought, sin comes about as a result of the misuse of human freedom. Sin is the work of Satan, who is considered the worst enemy of humankind. Satan and his agents attempt to mislead human beings through temptation. The story of the first human beings ever created by God—Adam and Eve—in the garden of Eden (Genesis 2:30–39) is depicted in the Qur'an as a paradigm of human weakness and vulnerability in the face of Satan's various attempts to mislead humanity.

Sin has effects on humanity, both personally and collectively. From the Qur'an and the Ḥadith, we learn that sin brings anxiety, loneliness, physical and spiritual harm, degradation, and alienation both to the individual and the people around them. Sin multiplies over time and incurs punishment to people in this life and/or in the life to come. Obedience to the laws of God, on the other hand, brings goodness and peace, harmony and prosperity, physical, and spiritual well-being, as well as blessings for God's people in this life and in the life to come.

ABSENCE OF ORIGINAL SIN

Largely, Muslims acknowledge that the human being is flawed even before they choose to sin. However, they do not entirely accept the doctrine of the original sin, which is associated with the fall of Adam and Eve. Muslims admit that Adam and Ḥawā' (Eve) broke the command of God and so they were banished from heaven. However, they do not accept that the sin of Adam and Eve changed their nature. In his banishment, Adam completely retained his original nature. He remained obedient to God on earth.[1]

Muslims also believe that Adam's sin had no negative effect on his descendants. Thus, a human being is conceived and born pure and innocent; it is recorded in Muslim tradition that the Prophet Muḥammad said, "No child is born except in a state of natural purity (*fiṭrah*) and then his parent makes him Jewish, Christian, or Magian."[2] Therefore, in Islam, all humans are born good and remain good until they give in to sin by breaking God's law.

According to Ron Rhodes, the disobedience of the first parents (Adam and Eve) was their own personal sin. They were forgiven when they repented and asked for forgiveness. As a prophet of God, Adam could not have engaged in a grave sin. Otherwise, he would not have been entrusted with the significant task of bringing God's message to all his subjects.[3] For Muslims, Adam only made a mistake by refusing to adhere to the laws of God, and Adam's atonement for his sin was accepted by God.[4] In addition, according to Muslims, humans commit sins because they are weak and forgetful, not because they have an inherited or original sin nature. According to Qur'anic teaching, Adam

1. Rhodes, *10 Things You Need to Know*, 74.
2. al-Bukhārī, 4775.
3. Rhodes, *10 Things You Need to Know*, 74.
4. Rhodes, *10 Things You Need to Know*, 74.

repented of his sin, God forgave him, chose him as prophet, and guided him in his ways.[5]

REPENTANCE

Sin and its impact on humanity is overcome by repentance (*tawbah*). Muḥammad once said, "one who repents from sin is like one without sin."[6] True repentance, however, comes from a sincere heart. The repentant person is considered a "returnee" to God, and his return brings joy to God. God is most forgiving and merciful (*Ghafūr wa Raḥīm*). God loves to forgive. He says in the Qur'an:

> "O My servants who have transgressed against their souls! Do not despair of Allah's mercy, for Allah forgives all sins. He is indeed Oft-forgiving, Most merciful." (39:53)

Thus, according to the Qur'an, punishment as a result of sin is not the necessary and unavoidable consequence of sin. Humans may or may not be punished, and it is not always the case that they face punishment for their sins. Sin, no matter its intensity, is forgiven by the mercy of God (39:53). Thus, God is not bound to punish (4:147). However, this does not in any way degrade the justice of God. The justice of God in Islam means that God does not ignore the righteousness of the righteous. It does not mean that Allah has no power to pardon and forgive.

NATURE OF SALVATION

A thorough study of the Qur'an reveals two aspects of salvation that are key in Islam. First, there is salvation from evil, harm, difficulties, and, eventually, from hell. Second, there is salvation to goodness, virtue, well-being, felicity, and success, culminating in the bliss and eternal happiness in heaven.[7] Salvation can be temporal and permanent. Temporal salvation is attained here on earth, and the fruits of temporal salvation are realized here in this life. When an individual or group repents and asks for Allah's forgiveness, a transformation in their personality takes place—this is salvation. Salvation is a return to God and repentance is the

5. Thackston, trans., *Tales of the Prophets of al-Kisā'ī*, 59.
6. Ibn Majah, *Sunan Ibn Majah*, book 37, hadith 4250.
7. Siddiqi, "Salvation in Islamic Perspective," 1.

first stage on this road to salvation. The road or path to salvation is called the *Sharī' ah*. When an individual or community follows the *Sharī' ah*, they establish justice and equilibrium in this world and develop a relationship with God. In doing so, they work their way towards salvation. The kingdom of God is realized here in this world before it is realized in the hereafter. Salvation in this world is the work of human beings. It is God's demand from us that we must work to reform and transform this world in order to bring justice, peace, harmony, and goodness to all the inhabitants of this earth. For this reason, God demands us to live according to his rules and commands us to establish a system based on these rules. The *Sharī' ah* makes available to us the first fruits of salvation in this world, here and now.

However, salvation in Islam is not only here on this earth. There is also eternal salvation. The eternal salvation will be in the hereafter, when everyone will be saved from all pain, grief, and death, and instead will find eternal bliss in the presence of God. Righteousness in this world has a bearing on the salvation in the hereafter, but we must keep in mind that eternal salvation is the act of God alone. No one is capable of saving anyone but God. No one can save himself or others. Even prophets and the most righteous people cannot save themselves or others. Thus, to acknowledge a savior other than God is blasphemy and a grave sin. Islam emphasizes righteousness and living according to the rules and laws of God, but even righteousness cannot save a person. It is also a blasphemy to believe that one's righteousness can save him in the hereafter. Thus, the Qur'an indicates: "Were it not for Allah's grace and mercy and mercy on you all, none of you would have become purified; but Allah purifies whom He pleases. And Allah hears and knows all" (24:21). The Prophet of Islam also explained the same point in one of his sayings:

> "Do good deeds properly, sincerely and moderately and rejoice, for no one's deeds will put him in paradise. People asked him: 'Not even you, O Messenger of Allah?' He replied: 'Not even me unless Allah bestows his pardon and mercy on me."[8]

Although salvation is completely an act of and gift from God, human effort is deemed necessary. God has the power to forgive even the worst sinner, but God's power also operates through his wisdom. God, in his wisdom, will not treat the righteous and the sinners alike. The Qur'an

8. Bukhārī, *Ṣaḥīḥ al-Bukhārī*, hadith 5673.

says: "Shall we then treat the people of faith like the people of sin? What is the matter with you? How do you judge?" (68:35–36).

SIN AND SALVATION IN CHRISTIANITY

The Original Sin and Human Condition

Various religious traditions have, over the years, attempted to explain the human inclination to sin in many ways. The Christian response to the human inclination to sin is found in the doctrine of original sin. Original sin is a state into which all human beings are born. It is essentially a state of alienation from God, which is the result of the fall of Adam. The doctrine claims that God endowed the first human beings (Adam and Eve) with privileges that their descendants were to inherit. These privileges essentially include a life in free submission to God and the gravitation to the good upheld by God's law. They were also liable neither to death, nor to toil and pain, nor even to wickedness. But Adam and Eve lost these privileges not only for themselves when they sinned, but also for their descendants. They, and their successors, became liable to sin, pain, toil, and death.[9] Humanity forfeited that moral equilibrium, the propensity to submit to and to live in good relationship with God, which was the original endowment of the human race.[10]

Accordingly, the *Catechism of the Catholic Church* acknowledges sin as a "dark reality in human history" that cannot be ignored. The Catholic Church teaches that sin can properly be understood in the context of the relationship between man and God.[11] The true nature of sin is humanity's rejection of God and opposition to his laws. Thus, only the light of divine revelation clarifies the reality of sin and particularly of the sin committed at mankind's origins. Without this revelation, we will be tempted to explain sin as merely "a developmental flaw, a psychological weakness, a mistake, or a necessary consequence of an inadequate social structure." Only in the knowledge of God's plan for man can we grasp that sin is an abuse of the freedom that God gives to created persons so that they are capable of loving him and loving one another.

9. Genesis 3:16–19.

10. Yarnold, *Theology of Original Sin*, 24.

11. *Catechism of the Catholic Church.*

Salvation in Christ through the Church

Christians adopted the doctrine of original sin for soteriological reasons. There is a critical link between the impact of original sin and the redemption in Christ. At the core of the Christian message is that Christ Jesus overcame the estrangement of humanity from God caused by original sin inherited from our first parents. Through his death and resurrection, Christ reconciled humanity with God and the human race regained the lost original privileges. Though a lot was said about sin in the theological discourses, the focus of the church fathers of the Patristic Era was not primarily with the problem of sin, but rather with God's remedy to the problem, which is Christ.[12] The idea of an inherited or original sin served as an explanation for why sin is universal, and thus there is a universal need for redemption in Christ.[13]

Medieval theologians generally accepted the doctrine of original sin without question and the doctrine continued to be assumed as a core component of the divine truths revealed to the church. However, in relation to original sin, medieval theologians preoccupied themselves with issues about human nature itself. The intense speculations of St. Anselm of Canterbury (d. 1109) and Thomas Aquinas (d. 1275), in particular, solidified two important states of human nature: before and after Adam's sin. Human nature before Adam's sin was depicted as the "essence of original innocence," and after Adam's sin as the "essence of original sin."[14] There are two spiritual impacts of Adam's sin on the human person: first, the loss of original justice, which is a state of sin or guilt, and the absence of sanctifying grace; second, concupiscence and weakening of the will.[15] The medieval theologians further developed stratagems to explain and justify the original sin doctrine and the necessity of salvation in Christ.

Later church councils, particularly that of Trent, adopted a perspective that linked the concerns of salvation with the ecclesial establishment, and declared the church the only instrument of salvation. The council, which was held between 1545 and 1563 in Trento (Trent) and Bologna in northern Italy, turned out to be one of the Roman Catholic Church's most important councils. Apart from solidifying the relation between original sin and Christ's redemption, the council significantly declared that human

12. Wiley, *Original Sin*, 54–55.

13. Wiley, *Original Sin*, 57.

14. John Paul II, *Theology of the Body*, 51, 52

15. Yarnold, *Theology of Original Sin*, 66.

beings need the church for the forgiveness of both their original and actual sins. Thus, Christians believe that Christ is the source of the remission of sins through his passion on the cross, but the Catholic Church is the mediator of the forgiveness of sins for the salvation of humanity.

Personal and Actual Sin

A personal sin is to be distinguished from original sin, which is essentially a general sinful human condition. A personal sin is a voluntary act of an individual who transgresses against the law of God. It could be a discrete or a habitual sin committed by the individual. A personal, actual sin is a sin of commission if it violates a negative precept such as the divine precept against theft. It is a sin of omission if it violates a positive precept such as the ecclesiastical precept to fast at an appointed time. One of the champions of a relational understanding of sin and original sin is Tatha Wiley. In her book *Original Sin: Origins, Developments, Contemporary Meanings*, Wiley acknowledges that the doctrine of original sin is relevant in so far as it describes a general human disordered condition or reality, which she refers to as the "sustained inauthentic" human nature, which plays a significant role in the personal and actual sins human beings commit.[16]

Joseph Ratzinger (Pope Benedict XVI) acknowledges that Christian theology adopted the misleading term "original sin" to explain the disordered state of human affairs. He contends that many today fail to recognize original sin as a disordered human condition because they conceive of sin and guilt solely in personal terms.[17] Ratzinger contends further that human beings are relational, and they possess their lives solely by way of relationship. To be a human being, Ratzinger contends, "means to be related in love." But sin means the damaging or the destruction of relationality, which gives authentic meaning to human existence. Sin is a rejection of human relationality, a "loss of relationship, a disturbance of relationship, and therefore it cannot be restricted to the individual."[18]

16. Wiley, *Original Sin*, 207.
17. Ratzinger, *"In the Beginning . . .,"* 72.
18. Ratzinger, *"In the Beginning . . .,"* 72.

SALVATION EXCLUSIVELY FOR MUSLIMS

The general understanding of salvation in Islam is that the Muslim, because he has believed in God, will be saved in heaven. However, whoever dies as an unbeliever will suffer a fate of eternal damnation. This view is mostly expressed in Muslim theological and legal manuals as a unanimous decision by consensus (*ijmāʿ*) of the scholars.[19] Western academics also consider this view of an eternal hell for unbelievers and eternal bliss in heaven for believers as the standard Muslim position on salvation. John Esposito in his book *Islam: The Straight Path* describes the Qur'anic view of what happens to the human being after death as ". . . the Last Judgment, with its eternal reward and punishment, remains a constant reminder of the ultimate consequences of each life. . .the damned will be banished to hell, forever separated from God."[20] However, the believer (the Muslim) is sure of receiving the reward of heaven because he has accepted the message of God through Muḥammad. Another scholar who has written on judgment, heaven, and hell in Islamic thought is Fazlur Rahman (d. 1988). In his book *Major Themes of the Qur'an*, he affirms that "unbelievers and evil persons will earn displeasure and alienation *(sakht)* from God as their greatest punishment."[21] Rahman concludes that the Qur'an urges humanity to endeavor to achieve perfection through the guidance of the Qur'an.

The final judgment will not give humanity any opportunity for personal advancement. "There will be no chance for repentance and reconciliation with God. The human being will be left to accept their fate in heaven or hell."[22] In his *Approaching the Qur'an: The Early Revelations*, Michael Sells describes the Muslim understanding of the Day of Judgment as one in which "[w]hat seems secure and solid turns out to be ephemeral, and what seems small or insignificant is revealed as one's eternal reality and destiny."[23] Elsewhere, he translates surah 98:6 in such a way that the deniers of faith are described as having an "eternal" stay in hellfire.[24]

19. Esposito, *Islam*, 30–31.
20. Esposito, *Islam*, 30–31.
21. Rahman, *Major Themes of the Qur'an*, 113.
22. Rahman, *Major Themes of the Qur'an*, 120.
23. Sells, *Approaching the Qur'an*.
24. Sells, *Approaching the Qur'an*, 106.

It is clear that this view of the Qur'an and of its interpreters and scholars (both Muslim and Western) depicts a significant leaning to exclusivity both explicitly and implicitly in relation to salvation. It is important to note that the Qur'an is stern and explicitly condemns polytheism, calling it *shirk*, meaning "associationism." Polytheists (*mushrikūn*) are associationists who commit a grave error of associating other deities with Allah, which is the worst sin, and renders them incapable of a blissful life in heaven. Polytheists are condemned to eternal damnation because they have refused to accept that Allah is one and has no partners (surah 4:48, 116). Polytheism is a false religion that cannot offer salvation to adherents. Thus, Qur'anic verses consistently call polytheists to repentance and to embrace the right path (Islam) for salvation (surah 9:33; 41:34). Explaining the exclusivist tendencies of these Qur'anic verses, Jacques Waardenburg contends that the Qur'an accuses polytheists on two main grounds: first, of attributing a child to God (surah 17:111); second, of worshiping man-made gods (surah 25:3).[25] In each of these two cases, idols are the objects of worship. Allah is the true and only God who deserves worship, not idols.

Arguing in the same line of Waardenburg, W. Montgomery Watt observes that the Qur'an, in some cases, seems implicitly to make no distinction between polytheism, Christianity, and Judaism, accusing these traditions of committing a grave error. All these traditions, according to Waardenburg and Montgomery Watt, have committed the same error of assigning partners with God. In line with this thought, Christians commit the sin of "associationism" just like the polytheists by believing in the doctrines of the Trinity and the incarnation.[26] This line of thought seems to suggest that Christianity and Judaism are incapable of offering their membership salvation. The Qur'an condemns the Trinity: "And when Allah saith: O Jesus, son of Mary! Didst thou say unto mankind: Take me and my mother for two gods beside Allah?" (surah 5:116). Here, Mary the mother of Jesus is considered to be the third person of the Trinity. The incarnation is also seen in the same light: "It befitteh not (the Majesty of) Allah that He should take unto Himself a son" (surah 19:35). Allah has no son, and therefore Jesus is not the Son of God; he is a mere human being (surah 3:52) and a servant or prophet of God (surah 43:59). The Jews are also accused at times of associationism: "And the Jews say:

25. Waardenburg. *Muslim Perspective of Other Religions*, 56.

26. Watt, "Christianity Criticized in the Qur'an," 197–201.

Ezra is the son of Allah, and the Christians say: The Messiah is the son of Allah. That is their saying with their mouth. They imitate the saying of those who disbelieved of old. Allah (himself) fighteth against them. How perverse are they!" (surah 9:30). Agreeing with Waardenburg and Montgomery Watt, Iqbal S. Hussain regards the Christian doctrines of the Trinity and incarnation as being incompatible with divine unity and an error.[27] By adopting these doctrines, the religious communities are associating partners with God and so could be placed at the same level with or are comparable with the polytheists.

SALVATION EXCLUSIVELY FOR CHRISTIANS

The general notion that Christianity is an exclusivist religion that claims salvation only for its membership cannot be discounted. This is because some verses of the Bible have clear exclusivist tendencies and present Christianity as the only means to salvation. In the Bible, especially the New Testament, there are fundamental verses whose interpretations claim this assertion of salvation. For instance, John 3:16–18 reads: "God so loved the world that He gave his only begotten son, so that everyone who believes in him might not perish but might have eternal life . . . For God did not send his son into the world to condemn the world, but that the world might be saved through him. Whoever believes in him will not be condemned, but whoever does not believe has already been condemned, because he has not believed in the name of the only son of God." The belief in Jesus as the only son of God is depicted, in the above verses, as necessary for salvation. This passage is reinforced by Jesus in his declaration to apostle Thomas in John 14:6: "I am the way and the truth and the life. No one comes to the Father except through me. If you know me, then you will also know my Father." As Jesus is the only way, truth, and life, salvation then can be obtained through no one else. And there is no other name under heaven is given to the human race by which they are to be saved (Acts 4:12). These verses and their theological interpretations claim fundamentally that Jesus—and therefore Christianity—is the only path to the ultimate goal of salvation. Based on these verses, theologians and biblical scholars, Catholic and Protestant alike (Karl Barth,[28] Ernst

27. Hussain, *Beyond Science and Philosophy*, 124.

28. Barth, *Church Dogmatics*, vol. 1/2, 1886/1303–1968/1388.

Troeltsch,[29] and Paul Tillich[30]) have argued extensively to the effect that salvation (or being accepted by God) is realized only through belief in Christ Jesus and membership in the Christian community.

The fathers of Vatican II also made two statements that together reinforce Christian exclusivist claims of salvation and that Jesus, as well as the Christian church, is necessary for salvation.[31] First, the council fathers reaffirmed the centrality of the church in God's plan of salvation: "The Church . . . is necessary for salvation. For Christ, made present to us in His Body, which is the Church, is the one Mediator and unique Way of salvation."[32] Second, the council clearly established the possibility of salvation outside the Catholic Church. Thus, it recognizes other Christian denominations such as the Orthodox and the Protestant churches as members of the people of God: "The Church . . . is linked with those who, being baptized, are honored with the name of Christian, though they do not profess the faith in its entirety or do not preserve unity of communion with the successor of Peter."[33] The two statements reiterate Christianity's unique position both in matters of authenticity of its object of faith and in salvation.

SALVATION FOR NON-MUSLIMS THROUGH MERCY

The exclusivist verses of the Qur'an discussed above and their theological interpretations—which describe Islam wholly in terms that completely exclude members of other religions in terms of salvation—are restrictive. This is because there are certainly other important verses that provide historical and theological points of views that depict other traditions, in particular Christianity and Judaism, in inclusivist terms and therefore as capable of offering salvation to their members. Notable Islamic philosophers and religious scholars have argued for this inclusivist understanding of salvation.

Two of these scholars who are noted for their championing of non-Muslims in God's plan of salvation are al-Ghazālī and ibn al-ʿArabī.

29. Troeltsch, *Christian Faith*, 1901.

30. Tillich, *Systematic Theology*, vol. 1, 150. See also Knitter, *No Other Name?* and *Towards a Protestant Theology of Religions*.

31. The Second Vatican Council was one of the most important mission conferences of the twentieth century for the Roman Catholic Church.

32. Second Vatical Council, *Lumen Gentium* (hereafter *LG*), 14.

33. *LG*, 15.

Al-Ghazālī, in his quest for knowledge, felt the need to free himself from the bonds of conformity and his inherited beliefs. This is because he observed in his social context as a child that each child grew in the religious tradition he was born into.[34] The popular Ḥadith attributed to Muḥammad also reinforced his observation: "Every child is born in the natural state; his parents make him a Jew, Christian, or Magian."[35] By this statement, al-Ghazālī observed that there will always be people who will be outside the *ummah* or Islamic religion for no fault of their own.[36]

Muslims have two main notions of the term "religion" whose critical comprehension could help to espouse the religion's inclusivist claim that other religions are also right paths to salvation. First, the original religion, the *dīn al-fiṭrah* (*religio naturalis*), is religion understood in the generic sense, which everyone (both Muslims and non-Muslims) possesses at birth. It is this original religion that surah 42:13 refers to: "God hath ordained for you that religion which he commanded unto Noah, and that which he inspire in thee (Muḥammad), and that which We commanded unto Abraham, Moses and Jesus, saying: Establish the religion and be not divided therein."[37]

In the light of the original religion, Muslims believe that each human being is born a Muslim.[38] Second, the historical religion, however, refers to the religious traditions of history, which are products of the original religion and containing within them varying degrees of *dīn al-fiṭrah* (surah 2:135; surah 4:123). According to Ismāʿīl al-Farūqī, the Muslim assertion that every human being is born a member of the original religion is based on the belief that what Allah has implanted in human nature, namely, the recognition of his transcendence, unity, holiness, and ultimate goodness, is prior to any religious tradition and significantly remains with the person for life.[39] This means that the non-Muslim could be still rightly guided and be admitted into heaven since their God-given qualities remain with them. In the end, however, al-Ghazālī maintains that though Islam is, in principle, the only path to salvation, yet God's mercy will nevertheless be granted to the many who are not properly exposed to the message.

34. Khalidi, *Medieval Islamic Philosophical Writings*, 60.
35. Khalidi, *Medieval Islamic Philosophical Writings*, 61.
36. Khalil, "Muslim Scholarly Discussions on Salvation."
37. This and all Qur'anic verses are from the Pickthall translation.
38. It is the parents and the environment that make the person a non-Muslim.
39. Al-Faruqi, *Islam and Other Faiths*, 139.

Ibn al-ʿArabī argues that everything is intimately interrelated through their common roots in divine reality. The universe, in its indefinite multiplicity, is nothing but the outward manifestation of God's names, which are the faces that God turns toward creation."[40] In view of this, every religious tradition is rooted in God and the original religion, and so cannot be said to be completely false.

Muslim tradition considers its prophet, Muḥammad, as one of a line of biblical prophets that dates back to Adam and reaches forward through Abraham and Moses, David and Solomon, until it reaches Jesus (surah 19:30). Some of these prophets received messages: Prophet Mūsā (Moses) received *al-Tawrāt* (the Pentateuch), Dāwūd (David) received *al-Zabūr* (the Psalms), 'Īsá (Jesus) *al-Injīl* (the gospel), and finally Muḥammad received al-Qur'an.[41] In line with this, some Qur'anic verses laud the messengers of the Christian and Jewish communities and their message.[42] The previous religious communities are "People of the Book" (*ahl al-kitāb*), which consists, specifically, of the Jews and Christians, who, according to the Qur'anic verses, received revealed Scriptures just as Muslims received the Qur'an. Their error was in their inability to keep the revelations they received intact. They partly corrupted the revelations and fabricated new doctrines that denied the complete truth of the right path to the Supreme Deity.[43] Thus, the Qur'an came as the final and perfect expression of God's will: "And this Qur'an is not such as could ever be invented in spite of Allah; but it is a confirmation of that which are before it and an exposition of that which is decreed for mankind-Therein is no doubt-from the Lord of the Worlds" (surah 10:37). Accordingly, the Muslim concept of prophethood demonstrates that all previous revelations are not completely wrong; some contents of them are right or straight paths that have what it takes to lead people to God and so offer salvation. Thus, any verse in the revelations conveyed by previous prophets that is incompatible with Qur'anic prescription is untrue and so is abrogated.

In relation to abrogation of earlier revelations and their authenticity, ibn al-ʿArabī writes:

40. Chittick, *Imaginal Worlds*, 123.

41. Galwash, *Religion of Islam I*, 179–81.

42. However, Prophet Muḥammad had predecessors but will have no successor. He is the seal of the prophets: "Muhammad is not the rather of any man among you, but he is the messenger of Allah and the seal of the prophets; and Allah is ever aware of all things" (surah 33:40) Muḥammad is not just a messenger of God but also the last of the prophets.

43. Galwash, *Religion of Islam I*, 179–81

> All the revealed religions (sharāᵓī) are lights. Among these religions, the revealed religion of Muḥammad is like the light of the sun among the lights of the stars. When the sun appears, the lights of the stars are hidden, and their lights are included in the light of the sun. Their being hidden is like the abrogation of the other revealed religions that takes place through Muḥammad's revealed religion. Nevertheless, they do in fact exist, just as the existence of the light of the stars is actualized. This explains why we have been required in our all-inclusive religion to have faith in the truth of all the messengers and all the revealed religions. They are not rendered null (baatil) by abrogation—that is the opinion of the ignorant. (III 153. 12)[44]

In these words, ibn al-ʿArabī explains that the previous revelations reflect the true light of God, which cannot be completely wrong. Thus, all the portions of the Word of God that were distorted, deliberately or not, are believed to have been safeguarded in the Qur'an and Islamic religion.[45]

Similar to al-Ghazālī, ibn al-ʿArabī does not conceive of the supremacy of the Prophet Muḥammad's message as being a justification for the eternal damnation of sincere non-Muslims, including the People of the Book. Many of these are non-Muslims through no fault of their own. It is, therefore, difficult to believe that God will punish them in the afterlife. Thus, invoking a theme that is oft-repeated in his discussion on salvation, namely mercy, he states: "God says, 'We do not chastise until We send a Messenger'" (surah 17:15). Note that he did not say, "until We send forth a person." Hence the message of the one who is sent must be established for the one to whom it is directed. There must be clear and manifest proofs established for each person to whom the Messenger is sent, for many a sign (*āyah*) has within it obscurity or equivocality such that some people do not perceive what it proves. The clarity of the proof must be such that it establishes the person's Messengerhood for each person to whom he is sent. Only then, if the person refuses it, will he be taken to account. Hence, this verse has within it a tremendous mercy, because of the diversity of human dispositions that leads to a diversity of views. He who knows the all-inclusiveness of the divine mercy, which God reports, "encompasses all things" (surah 7:156), knows that God did this only because of "mercy toward His servants."[46]

44. Chittick, *Imaginal Worlds*, 125.

45. McAuliffe, *Qur'anic Christians*, 68.

46. Chittick, *Imaginal Worlds*, 156–57; cf. Ibn al-ʿArabī, *al-Futūhāt*, 3:469.

In these statements, ibn al-ʿArabī argues that those who recognize Muḥammad as the Messenger of God and yet choose to reject his message will be punished. He identifies two groups of people who, though they may not be Muslims, could be saved by the mercy of God: first, those who hear the message of God conveyed by Muḥammad but sincerely do not find it convincing; second, those who may not be reached by the message may still be considered among those who submit to God. This perhaps helps to explain why in referring to the Qur'anic statement "The [true] religion (*al-dīn*) with God is 'Islam' (*al-islām*)" (3:19), ibn al-ʿArabī argues that what is meant by Islam in this verse is a generic sense that means "submission" (*inqiyād*).[47]

As Chittick notes, ibn al-ʿArabī's frequently cited "proof-text for [God's] all-pervasive mercy" is the statement found in surah 7:156, "My mercy encompasses all things."[48] In ibn al-ʿArabī's words, "How could there be everlasting wretchedness? Far be it from God that His wrath should take precedence over His mercy . . . or that He should make the embrace of His mercy specific after He had called it general!"[49] As such, if God is as the Qur'an states, "the Most Merciful of merciful beings" (*Arḥam al-rāḥimīn*)" (7:151; 12:64, 92; and 21:83), then we should expect him to be more compassionate and caring than any created being.[50] Accordingly, ibn al-ʿArabī states, "the (final) outcome will be mercy."[51]

SALVATION FOR NON-CHRISTIANS BY GRACE

Thus, in spite of the social and cultural impediments of other traditions, Vatican II recognized that other religions cannot be entirely or wholly wrong. They certainly have some value that has made positive contributions to human development in general. In view of these positive values, *Ad Gentes* acknowledges the presence of "seeds of the word" and points to "the riches which a generous God has distributed among the *other* nations."[52] Again, *Lumen Gentium* makes reference to the good that is "found sown" not only "in minds and hearts" but also "in the riches and

47. Ibn al-ʿArabī, *Fusūs al-hikam*, 95.
48. Chittick, *Imaginal Worlds*, 130.
49. Chittick, *Imaginal Worlds*, 137; cf. Ibn al-ʿArabī, *al-Futūhāt*, 3:466.
50. Ibn al-ʿArabī, *al-Futūhāt*, 3:25.
51. Ibn al-ʿArabī, *al-Futūhāt*, 4:405.
52. Second Vatican Council, *Ad Gentes* (hereafter *AG*), 11.

customs of *other* people."[53] Making its own the vision and terminology of some early church fathers, *Nostra Aetate*, apart from recognizing the presence in these traditions of ". . . a ray of that Truth which enlightens all," goes further to enumerate some of the positive elements of Islamic tradition.[54]

The council toned down the Catholic Church's earlier exclusivist position and spelled out an inclusivist stance on the Church and its relations with other religious traditions in some of its documents, such as *Lumen Gentium* and *Nostra Aetate*. In these documents, the council fathers also took a great step toward acknowledgement in general of non-Christians as capable of salvation and affirmed their high respect, in particular, for Muslims. In the first place, the council asserted that non-Christians, and in particular Muslims, are connected in various ways to the Church:

> But the plan of salvation also includes those who acknowledge the Creator, in the first place among whom are the Muslims: these profess to hold the faith of Abraham, and together with us they adore the one, merciful God, mankind's judge on the last day . . . Those also can attain to everlasting who through no fault of their own do not know the gospel of Christ or His Church, yet sincerely seek God and, moved by grace, strive by their deeds to do His will as it is known to them through the dictates of conscience.[55]

Underlining these two statements of Vatican II is the Church's belief that Christ Jesus calls all people to catholic (universal) union as a family with one creator God. Two implications could be drawn from this position of a catholic union. First, the catholic union of all people stems from the notion of God as the source, creator, and ruler of all. Second, this catholic union of family is not available to only the faithful Catholic or even only to Christians. The union is also available to non-Christians, in particular, Muslims.

The catholic union of all people under one creator and ruler notwithstanding, John Paul II, in his encyclical *Redemptoris Missio*, keenly observes the human obstacles that have prevented certain people from direct embrace of the Paschal Mystery of Christ Jesus: "But it is clear that today, as in the past, many people do not have an opportunity to come to

53. *LG*, 17.

54. Second Vatican Council, *Nostra Aetate* (hereafter *NA*), 2.

55. *LG*, 16.

know or accept the gospel revelation or to enter the Church. The social and cultural conditions in which they live do not permit this, and frequently they have been brought up in other religious traditions."[56]

However, these human obstacles in other religious traditions cannot be a lasting blockage for such people, for salvation reaches non-Christians by virtue of grace. This grace, which emanates from Christ Jesus through the instrumentality of the Holy Spirit, engages the non-Christian in a non-formal, "mysterious relationship to the Church."[57] Grace enlightens the non-Christian in accordance with their spiritual and material circumstances while offering them the possibility of sharing in the Paschal Mystery of Jesus in a manner known to God alone.[58] The World Council of Churches in its landmark document "Christian Witness in a Multi-Religious World: Recommendations for Conduct" affirms to Christians that while it is their responsibility to witness to Christ, conversion is ultimately the work of grace through the Holy Spirit (see John 16:7–9; Acts 10:44–47). The document recognises that the Holy Spirit blows and operates where the Spirit wills in ways over which no human being has control (see John 3:8).

CONCLUSION

Both Christian and Muslim traditions agree on one fact about salvation: salvation is offered to all, it must be made concretely available to all. To ensure that salvation is available to all, Christians and Muslims must acknowledge that in today's world, as in the past, many people do not have the opportunity to come to know or accept revelations of particular religious traditions due to their special circumstances. The social and cultural conditions in which they live do not always permit conversation about particular religions, and many have been brought up in other religious traditions.

For such people outside Christianity, salvation is accessible by virtue of a grace in Christ, which is communicated by the Holy Spirit. For this reason, the Vatican II fathers, after strongly affirming the centrality of the Paschal Mystery of Christ, went on to declare that salvation "applies not

56. John Paul II, *Redemptoris Missio*, 10.

57. John Paul II, *Redemptoris Missio*.

58. John Paul II, *Redemptoris Missio*; and Second Vatican Council, *Gaudium et Spes* (hereafter i), 22.

only to Christians but to all people of good will in whose hearts grace is secretly at work. Since Christ died for everyone, and since the ultimate calling of each of us comes from God and is therefore a universal one, we are obliged to hold that the Holy Spirit offers everyone the possibility of sharing in this salvific deed offered by God and known to Him alone."[59]

Further, the Catholic Church sees no conflict between proclaiming Christ and engaging in interreligious dialogue. Instead, she feels the need to link the two in the context of her mission *ad gentes*. These two elements must maintain both their intimate connection and their distinctiveness; therefore, they should not be confused, manipulated, or regarded as identical, as if they were interchangeable.

BIBLIOGRAPHY

Al-Faruqi, Isma'il. *Islam and Other Faiths*. Edited by Ataullah Siddiqui. Leicester: Islamic Foundation, 1998.

Ali Khalidi, Muhammad. *Medieval Islamic Philosophical Writings*. Cambridge: Cambridge University Press, 2005.

Barth, Karl. *Church Dogmatics*. Vol. 1/2. Edited by G. W. Bromiley, translated by T. F. Torrance and G. W. Bromiley. Edinburgh: T. & T. Clark, 1956.

The Catechism of the Catholic Church. Nairobi: Paulines Publications Africa, 1992.

Chittick, William. *Imaginal Worlds: Ibn al-'Arabi and the Problem of Religious Diversity*. New York: SUNY Press, 1994.

Esposito, John. *Islam: The Straight Path*. 5th ed. Oxford: Oxford University Press 2016.

Galwash, Ahmad. *The Religion of Islam I*. Doha: Modern Printing, 1973.

Hick, John. *Philosophy of Religion*. New Jersey: Prentice-Hall, 1973.

———. *The Second Christianity*. London: SMC, 1983.

Hussain, Iqbal. *Beyond Science and Philosophy: The Qur'ān and Modernism*. Lahore: Adabistan, 2000.

John Paul II, Pope. *Redemptoris Missio: Encyclical Letter on the Permanent Validity of the Church's Missionary Mandate*. United States Catholic Conference, 1990.

———. *The Theology of the Body: Human Love in the Divine Plan*. Boston: Pauline, 1997.

Khalil, M. Hassan. "Muslim Scholarly Discussions on Salvation and the Fate of 'Others.'" PhD diss., University of Michigan, 2007.

Knitter, Paul. *No Other Name? A Critical Survey of Christian Attitudes towards the World Religions*. Maryknoll, NY: Orbis, 1985.

———. *Towards a Protestant Theology of Religions: A Case Study of Paul Althaus and Contemporary Attitudes*. Marburg: Elwert, 1974.

McAuliffe, Jane Dammen. *Qur'ānic Christians: An Analysis of Classical and Modern Exegesis*. Cambridge: Cambridge University Press, 1991.

Paul VI, Pope. *Pastoral Constitution on the Church in the Modern World* (*Gaudium et Spes*). Vatican City, 1965. http://www.vatican.va/archive/hist_councils/ii_vatican_council/documents/vat-ii_const_19651207_gaudium-et-spes_en.html.

59. *GS*, 22.

Rahman, Fazlur. *Major Themes of the Qur'an*. 2nd ed. Minneapolis: Bibliotheca Islamica, 1994.

Ratzinger, Joseph. *'In the Beginning . . .': A Catholic Understanding of the Story of Creation and the Fall.* Grand Rapids: Eerdmans, 1995.

Rhodes, Ron. *The 10 Things You Need to Know about Islam*. Eugene: Harvest House, 2007.

Second Vatican Council. *Gaudium et Spes: Pastoral Constitution on the Church in the Modern World.* 1965. http://www.vatican.va/archive/hist_councils/ii_vatican_council/documents/vat-ii_const_19651207_gaudium-et-spes_en.html.

———. *Lumen Gentium: Dogmatic Constitution on the Church*. November 21, 1964. In *Vatican Council II: The Conciliar and Post Conciliar Documents*, edited by Austin Flannery, 350–426. Collegeville, MN: Liturgical, 1975.

Sells, Michael. *Approaching the Qur'an: The Early Revelations*. Ashland, OR: White Cloud, 1999.

Siddiqi, Muzammil. "Salvation in Islamic Perspective." *Islamic Studies* 32:1 (Spring 1993) 41–48.

Thackston, W. M., trans. *The Tales of the Prophets of al-Kisa'i*. Boston: Twayne, 1978.

Tillich, Paul. *Systematic Theology: Reason and Revelation, Being and God*. Vol. 1. Chicago: University of Chicago Press, 1973.

Troeltsch, Ernst. *The Christian Fait: Based on Lectures Delivered at the University of Heidelberg in 1912 and 1913*. Minneapolis: Fortress, 1991.

Waardenburg, Jacques. *Muslim Perspective of Other Religions*. Oxford: Oxford University Press, 1999.

Watt, W. Montgomery. "The Christianity Criticized in the Qur'ān." *Muslim World* 57 (1967) 197–201.

Wiley, Tatha. *Original Sin: Origins, Developments, Contemporary Meanings*. NewYork: Paulist, 2002.

Yarnold, Edward. *The Theology of Original Sin*. Notre Dame, IN: Fides, 1971.

10

Islamic Philosophy

An Introduction

ALEXANDER E. MASSAD

"What indeed has Athens to do with Jerusalem?" This frequently quoted remark by the church father Tertullian is representative of a strain of Christian thought that believes human reasoning (Athens) has little to offer considering God's revelation (Jerusalem). Such a perspective believes human philosophy is, at best, redundant of the knowledge given in revelation or, at worst, misleading. Indeed, some claim the apostle Paul reflects this disposition in his claim that the gospel is "foolishness to the Gentiles." Yet throughout history, Christians have utilized human reasoning to plumb the depths of Scripture, wrestle with contemporary theological problems, and even develop the foundational doctrines of the Christian faith such as the Trinity.[1] Early church fathers s utilized Greek philosophy to present the rationality of the gospel, such as Justin Martyr in his *First Apology* and *Second Apology*, letters written to the Roman senate a time of Christian persecution.[2] Perhaps the most important use

1. The Greek work *ousia* can be translated as "essence" or "substance." While in Stoicism the term *ousia* seems more appropriately translated as "essence" in Latin the term ousia had been translated into *substantia* from which we get the English word "substance." Therefore, when the Nicene Creed claimed Jesus Christ is of one *ousia* with the Father, although one says "substance" in the English translation, there is an intention of "essence" in the term as well.

2. For a thorough discussion of Justin Martyr and his context, see Justin Martyr,

of Greek philosophy by early Christians is the development of the Nicene Creed's statement that Jesus Christ is *homoousia*, "of one substance," with the Father.[3] At the conclusion of this early church period, Augustine proposed that Christians are free to employ Greek philosophy unless these ideas clearly contradict the gospel. Interestingly, by the Middle Ages (ca. 700–ca. 1550) we find Thomas Aquinas (1225–1274) utilizing not only Greek philosophy, but also the Muslim philosopher Ibn Rushd (d. 1198) to understand philosophical concepts that he finds helpful in illuminating Christian teachings. We even find twentieth-century Christian philosophers like William Lane Craig resourcing classical Islamic philosophical arguments to prove the existence of God.[4]

When considering philosophy's impact on Christian thought, Christians are quick to think of Plato, Aristotle, and even Neoplatonism. However, Islamic philosophy has played an important role as a dialogue partner with Christian theologians for over one thousand years. This chapter is not intended to engage a theological discussion about the merits of using philosophy in understanding the gospel. Rather, the purpose of this chapter is to examine Islamic philosophical thinking about questions that have plagued Christian theologians. There are several benefits from this approach rather than examining the history of Christian philosophical thought. First, the reader will gain a greater knowledge of the history of philosophy. Often the narrative of philosophy begins with the Greeks, taken up by the Romans, and rekindled during the Christian Renaissance and medieval period. The lacunae here is the role Christians and Muslims living in the Islamic world played in the development of philosophical thought from the eighth century onward. Second, examining Islamic philosophy is disarming. Sometimes it is better to examine a question from within one tradition through the lens of another tradition because it is initially less threatening to one's identity. It might be an easier stepping stone to understand how philosophy works within the Christian tradition by examining it through the Islamic tradition and then reflecting on the Christian tradition. Third, Christian engagement with Islamic philosophy is particularly important because of the history of Christian-Muslim engagement. Christian philosophers were seminal in the early years of Islamic philosophy (eighth through eleventh century) and this, I will argue, is an entry point for contemporary

Justin: Philosopher and Martyr.

3. Rusch, *Trinitarian Controversy.*

4. Craig, *Kalām Cosmological Argument.*

Christian-Muslim engagement. Finally, understanding Islamic philosophy opens new avenues for Christian-Muslim dialogue through recognizing the shared philosophical foundation from which Christians and Muslim have constructed theologies about God and the world.

BRIEF INTRODUCTION: HELLENISTIC PHILOSOPHY—PLATO, ARISTOTLE, AND PLOTINUS

It would be difficult to discuss Islamic philosophy without first providing a survey of the Greek philosophical tradition that influenced Islamic philosophy. Any survey, however, will not do justice to the range of Greek philosophical thought that influenced Islamic philosophers. Instead, this section is intended to provide the reader with enough familiarity with Greek philosophers and their concepts to understand how Muslims adopted and transformed these concepts into their own Islamic pietistic frameworks. We will begin with a discussion of Plato's discussion of the soul and epistemology, then move to Aristotelian logic and metaphysics, and conclude with a discussion of Plotinus's emanationist philosophical system.

Plato (d. ca. 348 BCE) wrote much of his philosophical work as a series of dialogues that feature Socrates engaging in philosophical discussions. In Plato's dialogue *Phaedo*, he engages the question of the human soul through a dramatization of Socrates' death.[5] The main idea in the *Phaedo* is that the soul is immortal and separate from the body, which is temporal and will deteriorate. In fact, Plato argues that the soul's immortality entails that the soul pre-existed the body in a metaphysical realm (a place beyond the physical world). In this realm also resides the eternal Forms, the ideal existence of things that exist on earth. For example, when we look at a beautiful sunset, we are looking at the manifestation of the Form of beauty here on earth by means of the sunset. Plato believed things are beautiful or ugly depending on the degree to which they share in the eternal and metaphysical Form of beauty.

Regarding human knowledge, or epistemology, Plato argued in the *Phaedo* that we know something when our soul recollects the Form of that thing. Because the human soul is immortal and pre-existed the human body alongside the universal Forms, the pre-existing human soul knew the universal Forms. However, once the human soul became entrapped

5. Plato, *Complete Works.*

in the human body, the soul lost direct access to these Forms and therefore forgot the Forms. When a person gains knowledge of something, what is occurring is that the soul is recollecting the universal Form of that object that it knew prior to the body but had forgotten. For example, when a person learns that 2+2=4, the soul knows this information by recollecting the Form of mathematics.

Plato's theory of the soul has important consequences for his political philosophy as outlined in *The Republic*. In this dialogue he argued that a city is like the human body, both of which need virtue to flourish. If a city is like a body and the virtue resides in acquisition and maintenance of knowing the universal Forms, then so too should the head of a city be virtuous in knowledge of the universal Forms. This means that the most virtuous ruler of a city must be a philosopher because it is only the philosopher that knows the universal Forms of goodness, beauty, architecture, economics, and all other facets of a flourishing city. Thus, Plato's political philosophy argues that the most virtuous city is one that is ruled by the philosopher-king who knows perfectly how to organize and run the city. To sum up, Plato argued that the soul is immortal, that in its immortal pre-embodied existence the soul knew the universal Forms, that the embodied soul must be reminded of the universal Forms, and that the most realized soul is the one who is the most virtuous, i.e., the philosopher.[6]

In contrast to Plato, who argued that true knowledge comes from understanding how material objects participate in universal Forms, Aristotle (d. 322 BCE) argued that knowledge comes from the soul organizing the world through what it perceives through its senses, or sense perception. Aristotle argued that the essence of a thing resides in itself and not in universal Forms. The essence of an apple is not found in the Form of apple. Rather, the soul understands the essence of an apple by examining and organizing physical apples in the world.

Fundamental to Aristotle's philosophy of the soul and knowledge is his notion of change. In *The Categories*, Aristotle posits there are two types of predicates, things that can be said of an object.[7] On the one hand, there are predicates that are essential and do not change. For example, it is essential for a bicycle to have wheels. On the other hand, there are predicates that are accidental, that change without affecting the object.

6. For more on Plato's influence on Christian thought, see Markos, *From Plato to Christ*.

7. Aristotle, *Philosophy of Aristotle*.

For example, a bicycle may or may not have pedals, yet it can remain a bicycle if it has wheels. For humans to learn what is essential and what is accidental, Aristotle establishes the syllogistic argument:

> Premise 1: All A is B.
> Premise 2: All B is C.
> Premise 3: Therefore, all A is C.

According to Aristotle, in his *Posterior Analytics*, a syllogistic argument can give universal knowledge. For example:

> Premise 1: Cows are animals that chew their cud.
> Premise 2: All animals that chew their cud are ruminants.
> Premise 3: Therefore, all cows are ruminants.

Like Raphael's painting *The School of Athens*, which has Plato pointing upward and Aristotle pointing downward, Plato's understanding of knowledge is that the pre-existent soul recollects the universal forms, whereas Aristotle's understanding of knowledge is that the soul learns through syllogisms derived from the surrounding world.

Finally, Plotinus (d. 270 CE) attempted to bring together aspects of Plato's thought and aspects of Aristotle's thought into a philosophical movement we term Neoplatonism.[8] Plotinus argued there is one pre-existent, immaterial, and universal soul, which he called the "One." The One is pure intellect, which means all it does is think about itself. According to Plotinus, that act of thinking, or "intellecting," creates a derivative being from the One. This derivative being, or *Nous*, desires to return to the One, but cannot because the One's constant act of intellecting prevents union. This constant act of procession and reversion, detailed in diagram 1, repeats itself with the *Nous* intellecting and creating another derivative being until this cycle ends with our sensory world. According to Plotinus, humans contemplate the material world in order to understand the immaterial world and ascend the immaterial intellectual ladder until this person reaches the One. This system is predicated on the notion of unity. The more unified a person is in his or her soul, the more transcendent the person becomes. For example, the more ethical a person acts, the higher this person ascends the immaterial ladder of intellect. How does a person realize what is ethical or what is more unified? Through syllogistic logic. Through discursive reasoning, or logic, the soul learns the higher intellectual forms and ascends the intellectual ladder. Thus, Plotinus attempts

8. Plotinus, *Plotinus Reader*.

to synthesize Aristotle's use of syllogistic knowledge with Plato's notion of Forms to present a metaphysical intellectual cascade of knowledge that people can ascend through philosophy. The movement he inaugurated is called Neoplatonism.

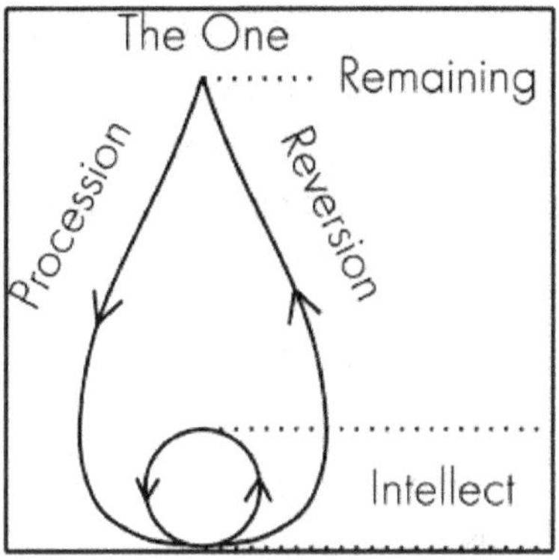

Diagram 1

THE FORMATIVE PERIOD

When discussing Islamic philosophy, there are two general periods. The first period is the formative period and consists of philosophical investigations prior to Ibn Sina (d. 1037). The second period consists of philosophy after Ibn Sina. Most of our discussion of focus on this latter period; however, we must understand the formative period in order to understand Ibn Sina's importance and the critical role Christians and Jews played in the development of Islamic philosophy.

The formative period brings together two strands of logical argumentation occurring under Islamic rule. On the one hand, there were the Mu'tazila. Perhaps the earliest Muslim apologists, the Mu'tazila worked in a style of argumentation called *Kalām*. Known as the *ahl al-tawḥīd wa al-'adl* ("the people of [divine] unicity and justice"), the Mu'tazila intellectually defended their belief that God's unicity disallows distinct attributes (good, wrath, mercy) and the moral responsibility for human actions lies with the individual, not God. After a failed attempt to politically enforce these beliefs through the *mihna* (833–848) under the Abbasid caliphate, the Mu'tazila were eventually eclipsed a century later by a former disciple of theirs—Abu al-Hasan al-Ashʿarī. Al-Ashʿarī and his followers, Ashʿarītes, would become the dominate intellectual position in the Muslim world regarding the relationship between God and God's attributes and the relationship between human moral responsibility and God's sovereignty, omnipotence, and omniscience. Regarding God and God's attributes, al-Ashʿarī argued that Muslims should take a plain reading of the Qur'anic text without anthropomorphizing God and without asking how these two approaches harmonize. Regarding the moral responsibility of human actions as it relates to God's providence, al-Ashʿarī argued that although God creates every act, humans "acquire" (*kasb*) the act and, thus, are culpable for the morality of the act. Al-Ashʿarī maintained that humans could not understand how this operates and must settle for accepting this reality *bi lā-kayf* ("without asking how"). In sum, initial Muslim philosophical inquiry revolved around theological questions regarding the nature of God and the moral responsibility of human actions. Despite the initial Muʿtazila attempts to use philosophical argumentation to rationalize answers to these two problems, it was al-Ashʿarī's approach that recognized the utility and limits of human reason in theological inquiry.[9]

It was in this dialogue between the utility and limits of human reason to scrutinize revelation that Islamic philosophy began to blossom in the ninth century CE. The Abbasid Empire, desiring to become a center of cultural and intellectual progress, promoted the translation of philosophical texts into Arabic because these texts contained not only argumentation useful for theology, but also medical, mathematical, and architectural knowledge. Although Muslims funded the translation movement, it was Christians who were foundational. Christians had been utilizing philosophical concepts for hundreds of years prior to the arrival of Muslim rule, Christians were well versed in Greek, and Christian scholars were already translating texts from Greek into Syriac, which is a linguistic cousin to Arabic. Among the translation circles, it was the Christian scholar Hunayn ibn Ishaq (d. 873) whose translations of Plato and medicinal texts were considered the most reliable.[10]

Within this formative period there are two Muslim philosophers that stand out. The first is Abu Yūsuf Yaʿqūb ibn ʾIsḥāq al-Kindī (d. 873), whom scholars consider the first Arab Muslim philosopher. He argued

9. For a good summary of this period, see Frank, *Early Islamic Theology*.

10. Sidney Harrison Griffith gives an accessible survey into the importance of Christian translators to the early Muslim philosophical movement in Griffith, *Church in the Shadow of the Mosque*.

that the knowing part of a person is the soul, which is rational intellect. Referring to Plato's notion of forms and reflecting Plotinus, al-Kindī argued that humans know something when three separate actions happen simultaneously. First one's soul uses the senses to recognize the potential form in what is known. Second, an external and metaphysical "First Intellect" shines a light, if you will, into the soul of the person to actualize the potential form that the soul sensed. Al-Kindī uses the concept of the First Intellect to address the question of how a soul can actualize a potential form if the soul itself is potential. His response is that it is the First Intellect, which is always actualized and never potential, that shines a light on the soul to actualize the soul's sense perception.[11]

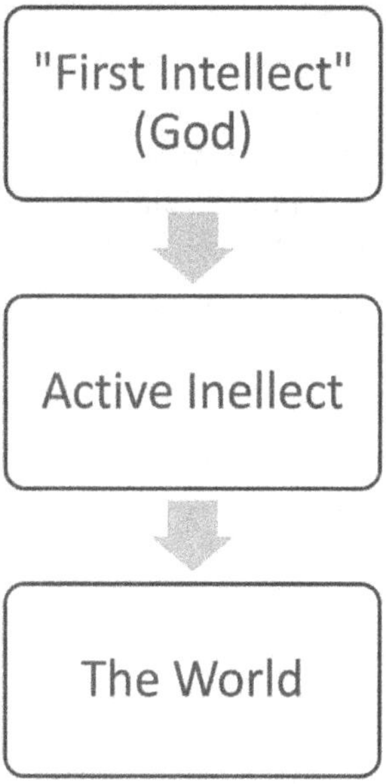

The second, and more influential, is the Baghdadi philosopher Abū Naṣr al-Farabī (d. 950). Building upon the work of al-Kindī, al-Farabī achieved three important philosophical tasks. First, he took the Neoplatonist system of al-Kindī and combined it explicitly with Qur'anic teachings about God creating the universe.[12] Al-Fārābī suggested that

11. For a survey of al-Kindi's life and works, see Adamson, *Al-Kindī*.

12. Instead of "Allah," I am choosing to use the word "God" to denote the concept of a supreme divine being who reveals himself through prophets and scripture and continues to operate in the world. *Allah* is an Arabic word for "God," which is an English word. Since this chapter is in English, it is unnecessary to switch words.

God is pure intellect and the First Intellect who causes all others in the Neoplatonic scheme. God, then, necessarily emanates himself and creates a series of metaphysical entities that culminate penultimately with the "Active Intellect" and finally our world, which is the lowest station of existence. By naming the First Intellect as God, al-Fārābī permanently intertwined the Muslim tradition with Hellenistic philosophy, making philosophy more palatable to subsequent generations. Like al-Kindī's First Intellect, al-Fārābī argued that the Active Intellect stands one level removed from our existence and is integral to the process of human knowledge by actualizing the potential forms the soul senses. However, al-Kindī did not explain how his First Intellect can actualize the potential forms in material object. Al-Fārābī resolved this problem by claiming it is the Active Intellect that gave the potential form in the first place. Therefore, according to al-Fārābī, the Active Intellect gives forms to objects and is the catalyst for the human mind to actualize these forms, which makes the Active Intellect indispensable to human learning.[13]

Let us pause here for a moment and ask why this has importance to the Muslim tradition. After all, much of this philosophy is derived from Greco-Roman, Hellenistic, and Christian sources, and the Muslim tradition existed for a few hundred years prior to these philosophers. It is because of these facts and not despite them that we can better appreciate why these philosophical traditions were important for Muslims in the tenth century CE. Just like Christians were trying to understand God's transcendence in tension with the immanence of the divine in Jesus Christ, so too were Muslims trying to understand how God can transcend creation and send revelation into creation without violating his immutability. Al-Fārābī's use of the Active Intellect seeks to resolve this tension. For al-Fārābī, as well as al-Kindi and others, God remains transcendent as the First Intellect and sends knowledge to humanity through the Active Intellect. The Active Intellect acts as an intermediary, if you will, protecting divine immutability from the flaws of creation.

Indeed, al-Fārābī's epistemology and cosmology provide the foundation of his second important contribution to Islamic philosophy—political philosophy. If the Active Intellect bestows knowledge, then, al-Fārābī believed, the two classes of people whose knowledge is most actualized are the philosopher and the prophet. Although both have fully actualized knowledge, the prophet stands out because he or she can share

13. Fārābī, *Alfarabi*.

this knowledge with ordinary people. Drawing on Plato's *Republic*, which argues that a healthy city needs a philosopher-king, al-Fārābī argues in *On the Principles of the Opinions of the Inhabitants of the Virtuous City* that it is the prophet who is the most virtuous of rulers because he can translate universal knowledge into symbols and metaphors to promote right opinions and right action among citizens. The problem, however, is that prophets die. Without another prophet to take his place, the next best option is to form a group of rulers to embody the various traits of the prophet and encourage the people to adhere to the prophet's laws. This group of leaders ought to be jurists, according to al-Fārābī, because even though they do not have the same knowledge as philosophers, they have the skill of interpreting prophetic laws considering changing circumstances.[14]

Reflection

Before moving onto Ibn Sina's revolutionary philosophy, it would be good to pause and reflect on the formative period of Islamic philosophy from a Christian historical and theological perspective. Historically, we find Christians playing a central role in the translation of Hellenistic philosophy into the Islamic world. In fact, it was the Christian Ḥunayn Ibn Isḥāq whose translations were considered the most reliable among his peers. This is an encouragement for Christians to engage with Muslims in a manner that is mutually enriching toward seeking knowledge.

Theologically, Christians can affirm al-Kindi and al-Fārābī's desire to understand the tension between God's transcendence and God's immanence in revelation. Although many Christians and Muslims today would not subscribe to an emanationist cosmology, both groups affirm God is truth and the totality of all that is real. Indeed, all creation has its being because of God. Pneumatologically, Christians can resonate with al-Fārābī's argument that the Active Intellect illuminates the mind toward knowledge. Many Christians believe that knowledge, especially knowledge of God, is inseparable from the Holy Spirit illuminating the mind. We might also go so far as to say that prophets are those whose minds were particularly illuminated by the Holy Spirit in a manner different from one's day-to-day experiences such that they communicated divine truths to humanity through signs. Thus, from the formative period of

14. Butterworth, trans. *Alfarabi: The Political Writings.*

Islamic thought there are resonances with the formation of the Christian tradition that ought to encourage deeper and more meaningful engagement between the two traditions.

THE TURNING POINT: IBN SINA

Abū ʿAlī al-Ḥusayn ibn ʿAbd Allāh ibn al-Ḥasan ibn ʿAlī ibn Sīnā (d. 1037), known to Latin scholars as Avicenna, instituted a philosophical revolution that upended Aristotle's prominence in Islamic philosophy and philosophy undertaken in the Near East in general.[15] Born in what is today northern Afghanistan, he claimed to have taught himself mathematics and surpassed his teachers to teach himself medicine by the age of sixteen. Although we are focusing on his philosophical work in this chapter, Ibn Sina's medical works were seminal to medical practices in Europe and the Middle East through the Middle Ages. As a philosopher, his most profound work relates to three questions. Ibn Sina's first question regards epistemology and the human soul. Ibn Sina sought to derive a philosophical first principle, a principle that one can be certain without doubts and upon which one could construct a philosophical system. He begins with his "flying man" thought experiment. Imagine, Ibn Sina asks, that you were created in a vacuum with no senses. You cannot see, hear, smell, taste, etc. What would you know? Ibn Sina proposes that you would know that you exist. Knowledge of one's existence, therefore, is the foundation of Ibn Sina's philosophical system. This overturns Aristotle, for whom sense perception and syllogisms were the building blocks of philosophy. For Ibn Sina it is immediate knowledge of one's existence without sense perception that is the foundation of his philosophical system. If self-awareness if the most fundamental form of thinking, then the essence of the self is not the body, which needs sense perceptions, but the soul, which is immaterial and rational.

Ibn Sina's belief that one could have immediate knowledge without sense perceptions is part of his second question: how does one find the middle term of a syllogism? As explained above, Aristotle presented syllogisms as logical tools by which humans discover knowledge. Ibn Sina was interested in the middle term (BC) because this is the explanatory term in a syllogism that gives new knowledge. Ibn Sina proposed there

15. For a summary of Ibn Sina as he relates to Aristotelian and Greek Philosophy, see Gutas, *Avicenna and the Aristotelian Tradition.*

are two types of people when it comes to discovering the middle term of a syllogism. On the one hand, there are normal people, who derive middle terms from other syllogisms or from empirical methods. On the other hand, there are people like the prophets and the philosophers, who have *hads* or "special intuition" whereby one simply knows the middle term of a syllogism without any aids. Therefore, religions like Islam who follow a prophet can rest assured that the prophet has certain knowledge because he is a person who attains the middle term with immediate intuition and does not rely on other factors.

Ibn Sina's third argument, and perhaps his most widely received argument, is his response to the question, how do we know that God exists? Ibn Sina's argument was that God is a "necessary existent." According to Ibn Sina, essences can have three types of existence: impossible, contingent, or necessary. Something that has impossible existence is something whose essence is self-contradictory and, therefore, cannot exist. For example, a round triangle cannot exist because the essence of a triangle, a geometric shape whose internal angles equal 180 degrees, does not allow for the essence of a circle, a geometric shape on a plane whose points are equidistant from the center. Something whose essence is contingent needs something outside of itself to make it exist, or as Ibn Sina puts it, "to preponderate it." For example, people exist because their parents preponderated them. Alternatively, the sun exists because something, either God or the Big Bang, preponderated it. But if all contingent things need something to preponderate them, would not that end up in an infinitely regressive series of contingencies? Ibn Sina responds with a thought experiment. What if we took all contingent things and put them in a bag such that the bag would be the aggregate of all contingencies? Would this aggregate of all contingencies need to be preponderated? Ibn Sina would say yes. Well, then, it cannot be preponderated by something impossible because such a thing does not exist. The aggregate of contingent existences cannot be preponderated by something contingent because it too would be part of the aggregate of all contingent exitances. Therefore, Ibn Sina concludes, only a being whose existence is necessary can preponderate all contingent existences. For Ibn Sina, God is the necessary existent who resolves the problem of infinite contingent regress.

Ibn Sina's philosophy produced certain conclusions that later generations found problematic. For example, his argument that God is a necessary existent entails that God's essence is necessary existence. If God's actions are necessary and God is eternal, then the act of creation is an eternal and necessary. In other words, God did not will the universe at a point in time, but the universe is eternal and necessarily created. Another problem that arises from Ibn Sina's understanding of God regards God's knowledge of particular things. Particular things change from potentiality to actuality. For example, a child grows up to become an adult. Logs can catch fire and then dwindle into charcoal. Knowledge of these particulars entails knowing both the potential (child or log) and the actuality (adult or burning charcoal). Because Ibn Sina affirms God as complete necessity, i.e., having no change, then God cannot have any connection to potentiality because that would involve a change into actuality. Therefore, God cannot know potential things, only actual things. This means God cannot know a particular child that turns into an adult, but God can know the laws of biology that operate in the process of becoming an adult. God cannot know that I started a fire in my fireplace, but God does know the universal laws of combustion that operate when I start my fire.

In sum, Ibn Sina's revolution was to overturn the foundation of philosophical investigation. Prior to Ibn Sina, philosophers like al-Fārābī and al-Kindi employed Aristotelian methods of syllogism, sense perception, and logical argumentation to derive philosophical claims. Ibn Sina argued that philosophical knowledge can be immediately intuitive (*ḥads*) because claims are constructed upon absolute certainty—I know I exist. From this knowledge, Ibn Sina constructs a philosophical system that gives existence a central role. His proof of God as the necessary existence was received not only by Muslims, but also by Christians like Thomas Aquinas and Jews like Maimonides. Still, his legacy is not without controversy.[16]

Al-Ghazālī's Rebuttal

Although there were several Muslim intellectuals who would take on Ibn Sina, perhaps the most seminal was Abū Ḥāmid Muḥammad al-Ghazālī (d. 1111). A jurist, theologian, and Sufi, al-Ghazālī's main texts engaging with "the philosophers"—by which he really means Ibn Sina and those who agree with him—are *The Deliverance from Error* and *The Incoherence of the Philosophers*. In *The Deliverance from Error*, al-Ghazālī argues that one should pursue demonstrative proofs whenever possible. He gives

16. For a reception of Ibn Sina's ideas, see Reisman and Al-Rahim, *Before and After Avicenna*.

mathematics and logic as an example of philosophical pursuits that can provide demonstrative proofs. However, he cautions that philosophy cannot provide demonstrative proofs for all truth. For example, al-Ghazālī believes divine revelation cannot have demonstrative proof because we cannot externally verify its claims. Yet, simply because we have not personally experienced divine revelation does not mean *a priori* it cannot be true. He gives as an example a spark that leads to a conflagration. If one had not seen a fire arise from a tiny spark, would it not seem impossible? Therefore, although al-Ghazālī believes philosophical methods can be useful for certain truth claims, he believes philosophy falls apart when it comes to certain religious truth claims.

It is in *The Incoherence of the Philosophers* that al-Ghazālī takes on three errors he claims "the philosophers" make that rise to the level of heresy—the eternality of the world, God not knowing particulars, and the denial of a bodily resurrection. As discussed above, Ibn Sina argued that God is a necessary existent and consequently the world is eternally necessary. If the world is eternal, then there was no creation moment and God could not be said to be the creator of the universe. Instead, God seems a transcendent monad without a will. For al-Ghazālī, such claims directly contradict Qur'anic claims that God created the universe, God wills events to happen in the universe, and God has an intention for the end of the universe. Secondly, al-Ghazālī sees Ibn Sina's presentation of God as complete actuality unknowing of particulars as contradicting Qur'anic claims that God knows individuals, ordains individual events, and individually judges the righteous and unrighteous. Finally, Ibn Sina's argument that self-aware existence precedes corporeal reality, thus making human essence the soul, has the consequence that a soul could inhabit a second body. To inhabit a second body would entail two different sets of imprints on a single soul, which Ibn Sina thought was impossible. According to al-Ghazālī, such a conclusion entails a rejection of a bodily resurrection and contradicts Qur'anic claims that there is a bodily resurrection with a joyous afterlife for the righteous and a punitive condemnation for the wicked. Thus, according to al-Ghazālī, those who follow Ibn Sina along these three philosophical ideas are in such contradiction to the Qur'an's teachings that they are no longer Muslims (*kufār*).[17]

It is important to note here that al-Ghazālī is not rejecting philosophy altogether. Rather, he is rejecting certain philosophical claims as

17. For more on the juridical consequences of al-Ghazālī's philosophy, see Griffel, *Al-Ghazālī's Philosophical Theology*.

counter to Muslim faith and practice. Indeed, al-Ghazali's work serves to save philosophical inquiry. Al-Ghazālī's argument that philosophical methods such as logic are useful for demonstrative proofs became part of Islamic jurisprudence. Ironically, by placing Ibn Sina at the center of his philosophical critique, al-Ghazālī elevated Ibn Sina's status even further by making him the philosopher *par excellence*. Thus, we might say that al-Ghazālī's legacy regarding the history of Islamic philosophy is that he simultaneously purged the discipline from certain beliefs he found incongruent with the Muslim faith while preserving Islamic philosophy as indispensable to Islamic jurisprudence.

Reflection

What are some takeaways from Ibn Sina's philosophical revolution and al-Ghazālī's response? First, Christians ought to appreciate the historical impact of Ibn Sina's argument that God is a necessary existent. This argument was integral to Thomas Aquinas's philosophy of God and remains an important philosophical apologetic for Christians. The historical reality that Christians drew philosophical inspiration to deepen the Christian tradition and defend it from detractors provides a rationale by which Christians today can act similarly with Muslim truth claims.

From al-Ghazālī, it is important to recognize that he did not undermine philosophical pursuits. His achievement was to purge philosophy from what he saw as diametrically opposed to the Muslim faith. Aspects of philosophical debate over which there was not a consensus was acceptable for al-Ghazālī. Christians can look at this as a model to remain open to philosophical debates and even open-ended conclusions as long as they do not arrive at conclusions that are diametrically opposed to the fundamental tenants of Christian teachings. For example, philosophical debates over human knowledge of God can be open-ended and deepen one's Christian faith. However, concluding that God is fundamentally unknowable would be problematic as that would deny the knowability of Jesus Christ. Thus, Christians can affirm an important role philosophy can serve in deepening and protecting Christian teachings and remaining vigilant against those ideas that would undermine the Christian faith.[18]

18. For a Christian exploration of putting al-Ghazālī and the Jewish philosopher Maimonides in conversation with Christian theology, see Burrell, *Towards a Jewish-Christian-Muslim Theology*.

ISLAMIC PHILOSOPHY AFTER IBN SINA

Islamic philosophy after Ibn Sina branches into two forms. On the one hand, Islamic philosophy in the Iberian Peninsula, Al-Andalus, reasserted Aristotelian philosophy against Ibn Sina. However, this tradition was short-lived as Catholic Europeans expelled Muslims from Spain in 1492. On the other hand, in the Eastern Islamic lands Islamic philosophy developed by further developing Ibn Sina's philosophy into Illuminationism, which maintains a prominent role in Iranian Shiʿa philosophy today.

Al-Andalus

Islamic philosophy in Al-Andalus developed in a religiously diverse milieu, with Jewish philosophers playing a large role in the development and translation of Islamic philosophy into Christian Europe.[19] After the Umayyads were overthrown in Damascus during the Abbasid revolution in 750, they fled through North Africa and into the Iberian Peninsula. It is here that they established the foundation for Islamic rule in Spain, which would last until 1492 with the Catholic conquest of King Ferdinand of Aragon and Queen Isabella of Castile. The intellectual high point of Islamic philosophy in Al-Andalus was the twenfth century, with figures such as Ibn Bajja (d. 1138), Ibn Tufayl (d. 1185), Abū al-Walīd ibn Rushd (Averroes) (d. 1198), and the Sufi saint and philosopher Muḥyī al-Dīn Ibn ʿArabī (d. 1240). There were also major philosophical Jewish figures such as Judah Halevi (d. 1141), Abraham ben Meir ibn Ezra (d. 1167), and Rabbi Moses ben Maimon "Maimonides" (d. 1204). However, here we are focusing on Muslim philosophers.[20]

Generally, Islamic philosophy in Al-Andalus pursued harmonizing Aristotelian, or peripatetic, philosophy with Muslim theology. For example, Ibn Tufayls's book *Hayy ibn Yaqzan* argued that scientific inquiry of nature leads one to the same truths as revelation.[21] In short, Ibn Tufayl tells of a young boy stranded on an island who is raised by animals and through his investigation of nature discovers not only the empirical sciences, but also concludes that souls exist and that God is singular and created the universe, and he even retreats to a cave to pray and contemplate

19. For a thorough history of al-Andalus, see Kennedy, *Muslim Spain and Portugal.*

20. For a good summary, see Adamson, *Philosophy in the Islamic World.*

21. For an English translation, see Ibn Ṭufayl, *Ibn Ṭufayl's Ḥayy Ibn Yaqẓān.*

oneness with God. This young boy eventually meets a Muslim from a city and they discover that they share similar beliefs. Thus, Ibn Tufayl argues the truths of revelation and the truths of empirical sciences (Aristotelian philosophy) are harmonious and mutually affirming.

Ibn Rushd elaborates on the position that the sciences and revelation are harmonious in *The Decisive Treatise*, the *Incoherence of the Incoherence of the Philosophers*,[22] and his major commentaries on Aristotle. Ibn Rushd was a judge for the courts of the Muslim capital of Córdoba and in *The Decisive Treatise* he puts philosophy on trial and concludes, citing Q 88:17–22, that Islamic jurisprudence considers philosophical pursuits obligatory for those who can pursue them. This conclusion leads him to critique al-Ghazālī's *Incoherence of the Philosophers*, which condemns Ibn Sina's philosophy, in his aptly named text *The Incoherence of the Incoherence of the Philosophers*. Ibn Rushd concludes al-Ghazālī's arguments undermine the pursuit of knowledge and, even worse, may lead the uneducated to false beliefs by doubting the teachings of intellectual elites. Yet, Ibn Rushd does not endorse Ibn Sina. Instead, he reaffirms the importance of Aristotelian philosophy. This is the reason why Ibn Rushd wrote extensive commentaries on Aristotle's philosophy.[23] Although Ibn Rushd did not leave a lasting impact on the Islamic philosophical tradition, his Aristotelian commentaries were translated into Latin and were seminal to the development of Christian philosophy into the thirteenth century, such as with Parisian "Averroist" philosophers and Thomas Aquinas's heavy use of Ibn Rushd in his *Summa Theologica*, whom he called "the Commentator."

Perhaps the most influential philosopher to come out of Al-Andalus, at least with regard to the history of Islamic philosophy, was Muḥyī al-Dīn Ibn ʿArabī. Like al-Ghazālī, he believed philosophical pursuits to understanding God were limited. Instead, he sought truth through seemingly contradictory philosophical claims to emphasize God's mysterious nature. Central to Ibn 'Arabi's philosophy was the notion that God is the One Truth (*al-Haqq*) who created the universe, which veils God from human understanding. Humans are responsible for searching out theophanies, moments when God reveals himself in the created universe, and ascending these revelations like rungs in a ladder to ascend the spiritual ladder to God. Humans can ascend the spiritual ladder and become one

22. Van den Bergh, *Averroes' Tahafut Al-Tahafut*.

23. Endress et al., *Averroes and the Aristotelian Tradition*.

with God because, Ibn 'Arabi argues, all reality consists of various degrees of God's existence (*wahdat al-wujud*). Although we perceive a differentiated reality in that the created order does not seem to be a singular unit—trees are not cats and camels are not fish—Ibn 'Arabi argues that the essential existence of all things is singular. Just like white fades to black with degrees of grey in between, so too do all things exist as differentiated degrees from God's divine existence. Although Ibn 'Arabi was not received primarily as a philosopher among Muslim philosophers, his idea of *wahdat al-wujud*, that existence consists of degrees of the divine, had a heavy influence on the development of Illuminationism, a philosophical system that has come to dominate Eastern Muslim philosophy.[24]

Near Eastern Philosophy

In the Eastern Muslim world, what is today Iraq, Iran, and Afghanistan, there arose a new movement that wove together Ibn Sina's philosophy, Ibn 'Arabi's mysticism, and Neoplatonic themes into what is called Illuminationism.[25] The driving question for the Illuminationist was: what is real and how do we know what is real? Yahya ibn Habash al-Suhrawardi (d. 1191) led the movement with his work *Philosophy of Illuminationism*, published around 1154. Against Ibn Sina's argument that existence is the foundation of reality, Suhrawardi argued that essence is more important than existence. For Suhrawardi, terms like "existence" or "essence" are simply mental judgements about the reality that exists external to the philosopher. Reality, Suhrawardi contested, consists of degrees of light, with God being the Light of lights. All things that are real have their reality because they share in God's light. The difference between God, who is pure light, and creation is that the latter consists of light mixed with darkness. Darkness consists of a lack of light, which for Suhrawardi was the material world. Materiality is darkness and material things only have life because God's light inheres to the material darkness. The result is a created being like humans or angels or cows, who are a mixture of light and a darkness.

24. For a substantive survey of Ibn 'Arabi's philosophy, see Chittick, *Sufi Path of Knowledge*.

25. For a survey of the development of Islamic philosophy in the Eastern lands of the Islamic world from the twelfth through fourteenth centuries, see Abdelkader, ed., *Islamic Philosophy*.

Because our reality consists of God's reality—namely, we share in God's light—Suhrawardi contests Ibn Sina's use of Aristotelian syllogisms as the foundation for knowledge. Instead, Suhrawardi argues that direct sense perception gives true knowledge. Ibn Sina, following Aristotle, argued that knowledge comes from two known premises of a syllogism that yield a conclusion. Suhrawardi argues that if one already knows the two premises of a syllogism, then that person already knows the conclusion. Indeed, syllogisms for Suhrawardi are simply fancy wording about knowledge we already have. For Suhrwardi, knowledge comes from the direct apprehension of an object or a concept. If Ibn Sina's "flying man" argument is true, then, Suhrawardi argues, could we not also arrive at other certain knowledge through direct apprehension?[26]

Taking up this argument is a Muslim philosopher that Shiʿa scholars in Iran still engage with today—Ṣadr ad-Dīn Muḥammad al-Shīrāzī (d. 1641), also known as "Mulla Sadra."[27] His genius was not in his carving a path distinct from other philosophers like Ibn Sina. Rather, his genius was in synthesizing previous philosophical movements—Illuminationism, Sufism, and logicians. His two major doctrines are the *gradation of being* and *substantial change*. The concept of the gradation of being builds upon Suhrawardi's Illuminationism. He begins by affirming God as pure light and material things as manifest by limiting light. Material being suffers from darkness, the absence of light. Taking a line from Ibn Sina, Mulla Sadra adds that God's light is necessary, while the light of material beings is contingent upon God. Whereas Suhrawardi had trouble explaining the distinction between God, who is pure light, and the light that makes up material things, Mulla Sadra's addition of the concept of contingency created metaphysical space between God and creation.

Sadra's concept of substantial change is a refutation of Aristotle's position that substances cannot change. Rather, Aristotle argued that the changes we perceive upon a substance are accidental, or "accidents" to the substance. For example, if you see a person walking, you are seeing the "accident" of walking, which may begin or end at any time, imputed upon the person, the substance that does not change due to the walking. Sadra argues that substances can change as well because it is not the substance that defines a thing, it is the degree of light within the object. For example, Sadra argues that a human baby that grows int an adult and

26. For a full discussion of Suhrawardi's *Ḥikmat Al-Ishrāq*, see the critical edition, Suhrawardī, *Philosophy of Illumination*.

27. For a biography and survey of his works, see Rizvi, *Mullā Ṣadrā Shīrāzī*.

then dies proceeds through many substantial changes, yet the essence of being a human whose light is mixed with material obscurity remains the same. Even colors are always in motion. Sadra argues that when we see blue, we are seeing that color in a moment in time. However, in the long run blue is either becoming darker blue or lighter blue. Blue is always in process, in motion toward becoming something else.[28]

These two doctrines, the gradation of being and substantial change, culminate in Sadra's theological anthropology. Humans, according to Sadra, are always in motion toward God or away from God. What determines the direction of motion is one's knowledge of God. For Sadra, this knowledge is found in Islam. The more a person knows, the more knowledge becomes imbued in the soul. The more knowledge the soul obtains, the lighter it obtains and the further it recedes from material obscurity. The final goal of humanity is to escape the confines of material darkness and unite with the oneness of God's pure light. It is here that Sadra is pulling from philosophical Sufis like Ibn 'Arabi. The soul is light, which Sadra takes from Suhrawardi, and the soul is contingent upon God who is pure light, which Sadra takes from Ibn Sina. The soul collects knowledge that brings the soul to a higher state of being, which is in Ibn Sina, and the goal of this higher state is unity with God, which Sadra takes from Ibn Arabi. Thus, Sadra has provided us with a synthesis of the major philosophical streams in the Islamic tradition up to the seventeenth century.

Reflection

A Christian might wonder, what has this previous discussion to do with the Christian life? Indeed, there are a lot of concepts that might not at the outset appeal to the Christian. Why would a Christian be interested in discerning the degree of light in a soul or whether Ibn Rushd was correct in his rebuke of al-Ghazālī's refutation of Ibn Sina? However, there are two important themes that arise from understanding the Islamic philosophical tradition after Ibn Sina. First, there is the importance of historical context. Muslim thought from Al-Andalus has played a significant role in the development of Christianity in the European context. For example, Ibn Tufayl's story *Hayy Ibn Yaqzan* influenced subsequent Christian and European authors who were inspired by the story's harmony between empirical reasoning and religious faith. The famous polymath Pico Della

28. Haq, "Mullā Ṣadrā's Concept of Substantial Motion."

Mirandola helped translate *Hayy ibn Yaqzan* into Latin in the fifteenth century, the book inspired Daniel Defoe's story *Robinson Crusoe*, and it was even translated into English by the American Puritan preacher Cotton Mather in 1721. When we look to Ibn Rushd, we find his commentaries on Aristotle moving into Europe during the thirteenth century and promoting a flowering of Aristotelian philosophy at universities. Even Thomas Aquinas saw Ibn Rushd, whom he called "the Commentator," as indispensable for learning Aristotle. Although Aquinas did not always agree with Ibn Rushd, Aquinas still relied upon him to interpret Aristotle.

The second major takeaway comes from the theological understanding of the human soul we find in Illuminationism and Mulla Sadra. Although one does not have to agree that human souls exist as a degree of light from God intermixed with material darkness, a Christian can find insight into Sadra's idea that we are moving either away from God or toward God. Sadra's belief that substances are always moving, either becoming more of themselves or less of themselves, has strong resonance with Christian the belief about humans being created in the image of God. If a person is created in the image of God, then throughout a person's life this image is either tarnished further with sin or polished through a righteous life in Christ. The question is: what actions will a person do in her or his life? Sadra poses a similar question. If a person acts sinfully, they are denying the essence of their being and losing their light to the material world. A Christian might see sinful life as a rejection of God and a pursuit of the darkness of sin. The inverse would be true as well. In fact, a Christian might go so far as to say that those who live in Christ and pursue a righteous life are more human, in the sense that their image of God is more fully polished and thus shines more brightly, than one who has intentionally tarnished the image of God.

This brief chapter is a brief summary on the breadth and depth of philosophy in the Islamic world. There is much more that can be said about Muslim philosophers, not to mention Jewish and Christian philosophers writing in an Islamic context. However, the purpose of this chapter is to introduce you to some of the major themes, questions, and answers that have surrounded Islamic philosophy. The goal of such a survey is to see how these questions prevail today among Muslims and how Christians can see resonances within the Christian tradition to the questions and answers Muslims have had throughout the centuries. The hope is that when we see more common ground in the philosophical ideas that underpin each tradition, it will become easier to talk about the gospel in a Muslim context in such a way that fits an Islamic framework. Additionally, and perhaps more importantly, realizing our shared historical foundation in philosophy ought to break down walls of division and stereotyping that often lead to fear and violence. As peacemakers, we are to build bridges and promote understanding. The goal of this chapter is to promote this endeavor through a survey of Islamic philosophy.

BIBLIOGRAPHY

Abdelkader, Al Ghouz ed. *Islamic Philosophy from the 12th to the 14th Century*. Göttingen, Germany: Bonn University Press, 2018.

'Abdul Haq, Muhammad. "Mullā Ṣadrā's Concept of Substantial Motion." *Islamic Studies* 11 (1972) 79–91.

Adamson, Peter. *Al-Kindī*. New York: Oxford University Press, 2007.

———. *Philosophy in the Islamic World*. Oxford: Oxford University Press, 2016.

Aristotle. *The Philosophy of Aristotle: A Selection with an Introduction and Commentary*. Translated by J. L. Creed and A. E. Wardman, edited by Renford Bambrough. New York: Signet Classics, 2011.

Burrell, David B. *Towards a Jewish-Christian-Muslim Theology*. Chichester: Wiley-Blackwell. 2011.

Butterworth, Charles E. *Alfarabi: The Political Writings*. Ithaca, NY: Cornell University Press, 2001.

Chittick, William C. *The Sufi Path of Knowledge: Ibn Al-'arabi's Metaphysics of Imagination*. Albany, NY: SUNY Press, 1989.

Craig, William Lane. *The Kalām Cosmological Argument*. New York: Barnes & Noble, 1979.

Endress, Gerhard, Jan A. Aertsen, and Klaus Braun. *Averroes and the Aristotelian Tradition: Sources Constitution and Reception of the Philosophy of Ibn Rushd (1126–1198): Proceedings of the Fourth Symposium Averroicum Cologne 1996*. Leiden: Brill, 1999.

Fārābī. *Alfarabi: Philosophy of Plato and Aristotle*. Edited by Muhsin Mahdi. Ithaca, NY: Cornell University Press, 2001.

Frank, R. M. *Early Islamic Theology: The Mu' tazilites and al-Ash' arī*. Aldershot, UK: Ashgate, 2007.

Gutas, Dimitri. *Avicenna and the Aristotelian Tradition: Introduction to Reading Avicenna's Philosophical Works*. Boston: Brill, 2014.

Griffel, Frank. *Al-Ghazālī's Philosophical Theology*. Oxford: Oxford University Press, 2009.

Griffith, Sidney Harrison. *The Church in the Shadow of the Mosque: Christians and Muslims in the World of Islam*. Princeton, NJ: Princeton University Press, 2008.

Ibn Ṭufayl, Muḥammad ibn 'Abd al-Malik. *Ibn Ṭufayl's Ḥayy Ibn Yaqẓān: A Philosophical Tale*. Edited and translated by Lenn Evan Goodman. Chicago: University of Chicago Press, 2009.

Justin Martyr. *Justin: Philosopher and Martyr: Apologies*. Edited by Denis Minns and P. M. Parvis. Oxford: Oxford University Press, 2009.

Kennedy, Hugh. *Muslim Spain and Portugal: A Political History of Al-Andalus*. London: Longman, 1996.

Markos, Louis. *From Plato to Christ: How Platonic Thought Shaped the Christian Faith.* Downers Grove, IL: InterVarsity, 2011.

Plato. *Complete Works.* Edited by John M. Cooper and D. S Hutchinson. Indianapolis: Hackett, 2002.

Plotinus. *The Plotinus Reader.* Edited by Lloyd P. Gerson. Indianapolis: Hackett, 2020.

Reisman, David C., and Ahmed H Al-Rahim. *Before and After Avicenna: Proceedings of the First Conference of the Avicenna Study Group.* Leiden: Brill, 2003.

Rizvi ,Sajjad H. *Mullā Ṣadrā Shīrāzī: His Life and Works and the Sources for Safavid Philosophy.* Oxford: Oxford University Press, 2007.

Rusch, William G. *The Trinitarian Controversy.* Philadelphia: Fortress, 1980.

Suhrawardī, Yaḥyá ibn Ḥabash. *The Philosophy of Illumination: Ḥikmat Al-Ishrāq: A New Critical Edition of the Text of Ḥikmat Al-Ishrāq.* Edited by John Walbridge and Hossein Ziai. Provo, UT: Brigham Young University Press, 1999.

Van den Bergh, Simon. *Averroes' Tahafut Al-Tahafut: The Incoherence of the Incoherence.* Oxford: Oxford University Press, 1954.

III.

Meeting One Another

11

Contemporary Christian-Muslim Relations

ANWAR BERHE

INTRODUCTION

Islam and Christianity have coexisted for over fourteen hundred years. The adherents of both faiths have interacted with one another in diverse ways, in different regions around the world, and in different time periods. Their relationships have been characterized by periods of tension and competition, peaceful coexistence, cooperation, and in some contexts a developed sense of fraternity and assimilation. Within each encounter, the theological, social, and political context, as well as demographics, ethnic identities, and other factors, have exerted either positive or negative influences on these relationships. In the contemporary period, these interactions have become more diversified and complicated as new thinking toward adherents of a different religion has emerged, and as both Muslims and Christians have undertaken new initiatives and sought to foster interreligious dialogue. This article aims to explore the changes happening in the thinking of the two religious communities and the nature of contemporary Christian-Muslim relations in various regions, particularly in Muslim-majority areas.

NEW DEVELOPMENT IN CHRISTIAN-MUSLIM RELATIONS

The long history of Christian-Muslim relations has witnessed complex and mixed encounters characterized by both cooperation and confrontation. As Shihab noted, "the negative and positive aspects of this [quintessential] encounter stemmed for the most part from the deliberate accentuation of certain biblical and Quranic texts on the part of adherents of both religions."[1] In the Bible, we find an exclusive view of others in passages such as Matthew 12:30 and other verses that state that anyone who doesn't identify with Jesus is not with him. On the other hand, the Bible witnesses to a spirit of inclusivism in the story of Peter and Cornelius in Acts 10, suggesting that God saves people from both Jews and Gentiles who fear him. We also find that the Qur'an denounces key Christian doctrines including the Trinity and the divinity of Jesus (Sura 5:116), and calls Muslims to fight against the People of the Book who rejected Islam (Sura 9:29). Still, the Qur'an also calls Muslims to invite the People of the Book for meaningful dialogue (Sura 16:125) and to consider Christians to be the nearest in affection to Muslims (Sura 5:82).[2] Although there are positive affirmations from both sides, their relationships have been marred by the position of both religious groups as they each opt for an exclusivist view of others, treating them with suspicion and confrontation over the centuries.

In recent years, there have been shifts in the theological perspectives amongst Christians and Muslims. New thinking about religious others and interfaith relations has developed due to the changing environments in the West and the rest of the world after World War II. Muslims and Christians began to realize the need for understanding and engaging with each other in a meaningful way. Christian theologians such as Karl Rahner and John Hicks took up this imperative explicitly and intentionally in the second half of the twentieth century. Karl Rahner advocated for an inclusive view of other religions, claiming that grace is available in all world religions and that those who received grace in their religions are "anonymous Christians." John Hicks, on his part, propounded the

1. Shihab, "Christian-Muslim Relations," 65.
2. Shihab, "Christian-Muslim Relations," 66.

necessity of believing in one divine being as a common ground for interreligious relations.[3] In Islam, some Muslim leaders such as Seyyed Hossein Nursi supported Christian-Muslim cooperation and urged Christian and Muslim communities to come together for unity and collaboration.[4] In his view, interfaith dialogue needs to be "institutionalized," and cooperation should take place between Muslims and Christians in order to carry out joint projects of an interreligious nature. A South African Muslim thinker, Farid Esack, also adopted a new approach of religious inclusivism, promoted an inclusive and friendly attitude toward Christians, and urged all Muslims to collaborate with those of other faith communities, particularly in the "political arena."[5]

In some churches, the doctrine of no salvation outside the church was challenged and they moved from the exclusivist position that salvation is confined to the church to an inclusive position of considering the availability of aspects of truth in other religious traditions. Some churches, however, reaffirmed their exclusivist position toward other religions. The Second Ecumenical Vatican Council, informally known as Vatican II (1962–1964), set a milestone in the relations between the Catholic Church and people of other religions, particularly Muslims. The Catholic Church declared *Nostra Aetate* in Vatican II in 1965 and recognized the availability of "rays of truth" and "seeds of the word" being present in world religions, viewing them as preparations for the gospel.[6] In other words, God's grace is part of human nature and is always embedded in it, so all grace is Christ's grace, and persons of other faiths may live a righteous life because of the presence of Christ and the Holy Spirit in other religious traditions, even without knowing why.[7] The council specifically recognized and applauded the "authentic elements of Muslim spirituality," and identified some aspects of similarities of beliefs between Islam and the Catholic Church.[8]

It was a significant change from the theology of other denominations and a turning point for Catholic-Muslim relations. After this declaration, the *Nostra Aetate* foundation was established and several interreligious dialogue conferences were held between the Catholic Church and various

3. Knitter, *Introducing Theologies of Religions*, 117.
4. Yucel, "Muslim-Christian Dialogue," 198.
5. Goddard, "Christian-Muslim Relations," 201.
6. Knitter, *Introducing Theologies of Religions*, 75–78.
7. Knitter, *Introducing Theologies of Religions*, 72.
8. Riddell, "Christian-Muslim Dialogue," 178–79.

Muslim organizations. Moreover, a significant number of teaching and research centers were established, and materials published.[9] However, due to the shift of the Catholic Church's position from exclusivism to inclusivism, the mission work of the Church has been obscured and the traditional missiological approaches have been repressed.[10]

The World Council of Churches (WCC), which comprises most of the principal Christian denominations, churches, and fellowships, likewise decided to take a new initiative in meeting with Muslims in a consultation that took place in Lebanon in 1966.[11] After this meeting, the council issued significant statements regarding interfaith dialogue in the meetings held at Kandy, Sri Lanka in 1967, and at Cartigny, Switzerland in 1969. The council then "established a new unit, called Dialogue with people of the Living Faiths and ideologies, simply known as the Dialogue Unit" at a conference in Addis Ababa, Ethiopia in 1971. Guidelines for this dialogue were drawn up in the meeting in Chiang Mai, Thailand in 1977.[12] Since then, the WCC has departed from traditional Christian mission and has focused more on Christian-Muslim dialogue.

The World Evangelical Alliance (WEA), however, has tended to adhere more to the traditional practices of Christian mission, and established a unit called the Religious Liberty Commission (RLC), which directly deals with Christian-Muslim relations. This commission works toward ensuring the freedom of "religious education, public and private worship, sharing of one's faith, and freedom to change one's faith"[13] within the framework of Christian-Muslim relations. It emphasizes promoting freedom of religion for all people "in accordance with Scripture" as an essential approach for Christian relations with other faith communities.

Following the changing approaches of Christian relations with other religions, particularly with Islam, Muslims immediately responded to the Christians' call for dialogue. In 2007, 138 Muslim scholars, clerics, and intellectuals issued "A Common Word between Us and You," a document addressed to Pope Benedict XVI and to the leaders of other Christian denominations that aimed at promoting an interfaith dialogue.[14] This document was based primarily on Sura 3:64, which reads, "O people of

9. Berhe, "Muslim Theological Perspectives on Christianity," 69.

10. Riddell, "Christian-Muslim Dialogue," 179.

11. Riddell, "Christian-Muslim Dialogue," 173.

12. Riddell, "Christian-Muslim Dialogue," 175.

13. Riddell, "Christian-Muslim Dialogue," 177–78.

14. Marcinkowski, "Religion, Reason, Regensburg," 162.

the Scripture (Jews and Christians): Come to a word that is just between you and us, that we worship none but Allah, and that none of us shall take others as lords besides Allah. Then, if they turn away, say: Bear witness that we are Muslims." In the "Common Word" document, the absolute unity of God and the necessity of loving God and one's neighbors serve as the common ground for Christian-Muslim relations.[15]

The document received different responses from various Christian institutions and groups. Pope Benedict XVI welcomed the Muslim initiative by stressing the necessity of respect for the dignity of human beings, a commitment to be made by both communities in order to promote mutual respect and acceptance, as well as the need for objective knowledge of other religions to engage in effective interreligious dialogue.[16] Another Christian response to the "Common Word" document came from the Christian scholars at the Divinity School at Yale University Centre for Faith and Culture and was endorsed by three hundred Christian scholars, church leaders, and various denominations. They issued a letter entitled "Loving God and Neighbor Together: A Christian Response to 'A Common Word between Us and You.'" This response from Yale endorsed the title of "Prophet" for Muhammad and explicitly apologized for the Crusades. Yale scholars referred to the document as historic in that it identified some core similarities between Christianity and Islam.[17] Sam Solomon and E. al-Maqdisi, however, expressed their disagreement with the theological standing of the "Common Word" document and the Yale response to the Muslim initiative. In their booklet published in 2009, *The Common Word: The Undermining of the Church*, they contested that "Common Word" undermines the mission of the church and aims to coerce Christians into accepting Islam.[18]

In recent decades, although attempts were made both at the global and local levels to address the problem of tension, mistrust, misunderstanding, and misrepresentation that have existed between Muslims and Christians over the centuries, the development of Islamic extremism has tainted contemporary Christian-Muslim relations. The attacks carried out by Islamic extremist groups against Christians have had severe negative impacts on the peaceful coexistence and mutual understanding between Christians and Muslims. Multiple instances of attacks on churches

15. Marcinkowski, "Religion, Reason, Regensburg,"
16. Marcinkowski, "Religion, Reason, Regensburg,"
17. Solomon and Al-Maqdisi, *Common Word*, xi–xii.
18. Solomon and Al-Maqdisi, *Common Word*, 4.

in northern Nigeria, Indonesia, Egypt, and many other Muslim-majority areas have left the two communities in a state of tension, suspicion, and confrontation.

THE NATURE OF CONTEMPORARY CHRISTIAN-MUSLIM RELATIONS

The changes that have been seen at the global and local levels have had both positive and negative effects on Christian-Muslim engagements. Different regions of the world have witnessed a wide range of Christian-Muslim relations depending on their sociopolitical, historical, and demographic contexts. There are many cases across the globe of conflicts that have a religious dimension, such as Muslims and Christians involved in the recent conflicts in Indonesia, Bosnia, and Kosovo. On the other hand, in countries like Sudan and Nigeria, Christian-Muslim relations "have sometimes been peaceful and sometimes conflictual."[19] In some instances, the religious majority group has enjoyed all the privileges from the state while the minority religious group has suffered discrimination, persecution, and repression due to their religious identity. For example, Christians have suffered persecution and repression in areas where Muslims are the majority. However, in some places where Muslims are the minority, Muslims and Christians have enjoyed cordial relationships and peaceful coexistence, such as in Ghana.

THE MIDDLE EAST

Christians of Middle Eastern countries have a glorious Christian heritage that goes back to the early history of the Christian church. After the region came under the direct rule of Islam, Muslims gained political hegemony and Christians found themselves powerless, persecuted, and treated as second-class citizens (*Dhimmi*). Since the arrival of Islam to the present day, there is an "indissoluble link" between Islam and politics. As Chapman stated, "Muslims, for their part, have lived for around 13 centuries with the assumption that 'Islam must rule' (*al-islām lā budda an yaḥkum*) and have felt it utterly natural that Muslims should rule over Christians."[20] Therefore, they have found it difficult to accept the recent

19. Goddard, "Christian-Muslim Dialogue," 202.

20. Chapman, "Christians in the Middle East," 98.

realities of the political supremacy of Western powers ("Christians") and the notion that Christians living in the Middle East should have equal political rights with their Muslim compatriots. This assumption has played a significant role in the creation of an unequal relationship between Muslims and Christians—superiors vs. inferiors.

Moreover, Muslims see Western policies such as the "war on terror" and Western military intervention in Afghanistan and Iraq "as a repetition of the pattern of the Crusades in which the Christian West waged war on the Muslim East."[21] In this case, Muslims associated Christianity with Western powers and the Christian minorities in Middle Eastern countries have continued to face persecution not only on the basis of their religion but also due to political factors. As Jenkins stated, "Christian communities within the Turkish Empire looked like a clear and present danger to the survival of Ottoman and Muslim power."[22] Due to the fear of any collaboration between domestic and foreign enemies against the Turkish state, Christian minorities in the country have suffered discrimination and persecution. On the other hand, the increasing pressure from Islamist groups in the region continued to create a situation that has resulted in economic hardship for Christians as they faced difficulty in finding any work.[23] This situation led to thousands of Christians emigrating to the Americas, Australia, and Europe. The emigration of the Christians and the decline of the population in the Middle East are not only the phenomena of today. This began in the early twentieth century and accelerated in the mid-1970s.[24]

Christians, for their part, developed various responses to Islam beginning from the early Muslim-Christian contact in the seventh century into the present day. An article published in 2006 by a Lebanese Protestant scholar, George Sabra, describes two fundamental Christian responses to Islam—the "Arab Christian" approach and the the "Eastern Christian" approach.[25] The first approach highlights the avoidance of hostilities with Muslims at all costs. Chapman stated that "Christians of this kind today feel more positively inclined towards Islam, and their basic instinct is 'Don't antagonize Muslims!' They emphasize their Arab identity and history and feel themselves to be part of Islamic civilization. They have

21. Chapman, "Christians in the Middle East," 100.
22. Jenkins, *Lost History of Christianity*, 156–60.
23. Chapman, "Christians in the Middle East," 102.
24. Melcangi and Maggiolini, "Christians Navigating," 176.
25. Sabra, "Two Ways of Being a Christian."

always been strong supporters of Arab nationalism and have often been anti-Western."[26] The second approach, on the other hand, can be summarized as "Save Middle Eastern Christianity at all costs!" Christians of this kind disassociate themselves from anything Islamic and are instead oriented toward the West as they emphasize their "distinctiveness from Arab and Islamic identity."[27] They also consider Islam to be their main threat and are more concerned about their religious freedom. However, it seems that there is no clear boundary between the two approaches—both tendencies are evident within individual Christians in different situations and at different times. In some situations they adopt the first approach, but in other situations they find themselves adopting the other.[28]

Thus, we can see that while Christians in Middle Eastern countries have common issues and have faced similar challenges, every country has a unique history, demography, and set of patterns of Christian-Muslim relations.[29] Egypt contains the biggest Christian community in the region, but it is difficult to find accurate data about the Christian population in the country.

The contemporary history of Christian-Muslim relations in Egypt is characterized by interreligious tensions, attacks on churches by extremist groups, and inequality in public life. In January and February of 2011, Christians protested against the old regime alongside Muslims in the hope that the interim government would ensure more religious freedom and equality amongst religious groups in the country.

Lebanon is another Middle Eastern country that has a significant Christian presence. At the time of its establishment in 1920, the proportion of Christian to Muslims was six to five. The proportional representation of religious groups in the Lebanese government (with a Maronite president, a Sunni prime minister, and a Shiʿite speaker) was able to maintain the power balance between Muslims and Christians for decades.[30] However, the Lebanese Civil War, which last from 1975 to 1990, severely affected the balance of power and "diminished and fragmented Christian leverage, in particular that of the Maronites."[31] The progressive Islamization of politics and the growing influence of Islamist

26. Chapman, "Christians in the Middle East," 101.
27. Chapman, "Christians in the Middle East," 101.
28. Chapman, "Christians in the Middle East," 101.
29. Chapman, "Christians in the Middle East," 102.
30. Chapman, "Christians in the Middle East," 103–4.
31. Melcangi and Maggiolini, "Christians Navigating," 185.

groups also pushed Christian communities to reconstruct their role in the sociopolitical sphere and their presence in the country. Although Lebanese Christians have felt secure for several decades, in recent years, "the decreasing numbers of Christians, and the increase in the power and influence of Hezbollah, have made Christians feel very much less secure, and they have the feeling that their country has been turned into the battleground of the Middle East."[32]

Christianity also came to Iraq in the first century and later spread to the major center of Edessa. Recent statistics show that Christian communities in the country consist of Catholic, Oriental Orthodox, Protestant, and Anglican, representing 3–5 percent of the Iraqi population.[33] The majority of Christians live in urban areas (such as Baghdad, Mosul, and Basra), but their presence in the southern zone has significantly declined due to militant Shia pressure. The 1970 constitution granted the right to the legal existence of the five Christian groups, freedom of worship, the repairing or building of churches, performing religious ceremonies, and conducting theological training in Christian seminaries.[34] This legal provision is not common in many other countries of this region. While Christians felt secure under the rule of Saddam Hussein, they faced enormous pressure from sectarian violence and several thousands of Christians immigrated to Western nations due to the changes that happened after the war in Iraq in 2003. Christians also experienced political marginalization and could not express any opposition to the Iraqi government because the constitution recognizes Islam as the state religion. Despite the fact that Iraq was a secular republic, Islamic (Sharia) law has a strong influence on the daily lives of citizens, which creates a situation of discrimination. O'Mahony asserts that "the Iraqi government widely protected religious freedom in its constitution (all sources to be taken seriously agree with these opinions), one could not hide the fact that in recent years Islam has been more strongly asserted in society. This economic and social pressure on Christians came to confrontations between Muslims and Christians . . ."[35]

Similarly, the arrival of Christianity to Syria dates back to the first century. Christianity has been part and parcel to Syrian history. Syrian Christians live in various cities and villages, comprising about 10 percent

32. Chapman, "Christians in the Middle East," 104.

33. O'Mahony, "Christianity in Modern Iraq," 121.

34. O'Mahony, "Christianity in Modern Iraq," 128.

35. O'Mahony, "Christianity in Modern Iraq," 133.

of the population. For the last couple of decades, the Syrian regime has had special sympathy to Christian minorities, and they practice religious rituals and rites freely both in private and in public. However, since the Arab Spring, "Christians have faced a cruel dilemma: do they support the government or do they side with the opposition?"[36] Consequently, the Syrian civil war brought division among Christians on political lines—some sided with the government, while others joined the opposition in the fight against the regime. Nevertheless, it is evident that the challenge to the Assad regime has had adverse consequences on the lives of Syrian Christians.

SUB-SAHARAN AFRICA

Christian-Muslim encounters in Sub-Saharan Africa can be traced back to the early period of Islam when Muslim refugees from Mecca migrated to Abyssinia (modern-day Ethiopia), seeking protection from the attack of pagan Arabs. From that time, and to this day, Muslims and Christians in Sub-Saharan Africa relate to one another in various ways. It is too simplistic to treat Christians and Muslims as "monolithic communities that interact as blocs" or categorize Christian-Muslim encounters as simply binary—that is, characterized either by confrontation or cooperation. Rather, their relationships should be "understood in their full complexity."[37] The dynamics of their relationships are also determined by different sociopolitical, cultural, religious, ideological, and other factors that emerge locally or are imported from outside. Soares describes Christian-Muslim relations in Africa thus:

> Muslims and Christians in Africa have often lived side by side, have sometimes converted to each other's religions, have shared much in the way of culture in its anthropological sense, and have learned, appropriated and borrowed from each other. This is of course not to deny or downplay the fact that they have also competed and been in conflict with one another. But to focus exclusively on either conflict or peaceful coexistence would be equally erroneous. Moreover, it is worth emphasizing that the analyst should not focus only on religion, since religion is just one of the many possible constituent elements of social identities.[38]

36. Chapman, "Christians in the Middle East," 103.
37. Soares, "Muslim-Christian Encounters in Africa," 1–2.
38. Soares, "Muslim-Christian Encounters in Africa," 2–3.

Ethiopia is one of the ancient nations in Sub-Saharan Africa, and the first country in the world that came into contact with Islam outside of Arabia, when Muhammad sent his followers to Abyssinia. Since then, the hospitality of the Abyssinian king to Muslim migrants laid a solid foundation for Christian-Muslim relations in the country. Over the past thirteen centuries, Ethiopia has experienced a "checkered" relationship between Christians and Muslims: at times characterized by discord, or a sense of competition and interreligious conflict, while at other times there has been peaceful coexistence, cooperation, and harmony. Ahmed argued that the "Christian-Muslim encounter in Ethiopia has gone through a complex and tortuous process characterized by official tolerance and subtle restrictions, outward benevolence and camouflaged antipathy, and liberal declarations of religious equality and popular prejudices and stereo-typical representation."[39]

Over the past three decades, both Islam and Christianity in Ethiopia have undergone internal revival and witnessed freedom of the press, freedom of worship, and freedom of assembly after the restrictions imposed by the communist regime were lifted in 1991. The new political reform and economic liberalization provided ample opportunities for both communities for practicing and propagating their faiths. However, competition for public visibility, theological differences, polemical expressions, as well as the desire for winning souls from the other religion and competition for physical space often incite conflict. Thus, both communities continue interacting with one another in diverse ways.

Anwar Berhe, in his doctoral study, identified five different patterns of contemporary Christian-Muslim relations in Ethiopia.[40] The first pattern is the disengagement pattern, which is characterized by Muslims being polemical, antagonistic, and militaristic. In this approach, demography and theology play an important role "for the antagonistic Muslim approach to other faith communities."[41] The relationship between the two communities is often strained due to the fact that the adherents of each religious group consider themselves to be the exclusive possessors of the truth while other religious groups are perceived as threats. The second pattern of Christian-Muslim relations in Ethiopia is termed as the "resentment approach." "A narrative of Christian hegemony in Ethiopia shows that some Muslims were prompted to develop a sense of resentment

39. Ahmed, "Coexistence and/or Confrontation?"

40. Berhe, *Muslim Theological Perspectives on Christianity*, 260–64.

41. Berhe, *Muslim Theological Perspectives on Christianity*, 262.

and hostility against Christians because they perceived Christians to be the historical oppressors, and because of Muslims suffered all sorts of suppression and persecution under Christian domination."[42] In this relationship pattern, polemics and apologetics become the main means of interreligious interactions.

The third pattern of relationship is competition. Those who uphold this approach focus mainly on winning souls from other religious groups, and Muslims use Islamic daʿwa while Christians use missionary efforts as the primary approach to engage with one another.[43] The fourth pattern of relationship is the tolerance and partnership approach. Those who follow this approach hold the idea of unity and the belief in one God as the basis for interfaith engagement.[44] In many places in Ethiopia, both in urban and rural settings, many Christians and Muslims live together in harmony with the understanding that interreligious solidarity, tolerance, and unity are important aspects of their daily lives. "Thus, there exists a strong sense of community among them without religious and ethnic discriminations."[45]

The last pattern of relationship is the harmony and assimilation pattern. This pattern of relationship mostly exists between Ethiopian Orthodox Tewahido Christians and traditional Sufi Muslims. As Berhe noted, "The assimilation of the two communities is not limited to social engagement, but also covers participation in the popular religious practices of the other group, such as interreligious marriage, participation in religious festivals, conducting prayer (duʿāʾ) together, and contributing money for church or mosque building."[46] In this case, the interreligious dialogue is carried out in daily interactions between Muslims and Christians with the aim of promoting mutual fecundation and fraternity. Religious distinctions are ignored or compromised in these instances.

These patterns of relationships are often influenced by geography (urban vs. rural), demography (Muslims living in Muslim-majority areas are more intolerant towards Christians than those living in Muslim-minority areas), and social dynamics (the history of the first *Hijra* and indigenous solidarity associations).[47] Moreover, ethnic identity, compe-

42. Berhe, *Muslim Theological Perspectives on Christianity*, 262.
43. Berhe, *Muslim Theological Perspectives on Christianity*, 262.
44. Berhe, *Muslim Theological Perspectives on Christianity*, 63.
45. Berhe, *Muslim Theological Perspectives on Christianity*, 63.
46. Berhe, *Muslim Theological Perspectives on Christianity*, 263–64.
47. The First *Hijra* is the migration of the early Muslims to Abyssinia in 615.

tition for physical space, disordered religious expression in public space, and theological orientations (Muslims/Christians who hold exclusive views of other religions are more violent toward others than those who hold more inclusive or pluralistic views of other religions) are other factors that influence community relationships in Ethiopia.[48]

In Muslim-majority Sudan, there is a completely different history of Christian-Muslim relations. Although there has been a long history of Christian presence in the country, its postcolonial history has witnessed the divide of Sudanese communities along regional, ethnic, and religious lines. The government's initiative for the Islamization of society through the introduction of Sharia law and Islamic resurgent programs led to the fight between Arab Muslims in the north and the Christian community in the South. Kukah observes that "the politics of Sudan manifests itself as a conflict between the Arab Muslim North and what is vaguely called an animist/Christian South. Since the forced imposition of Sharia law by the Numeri government in the 1970s, Sudan has plunged further into disaster and chaos, leading to the deaths of millions of its citizens, primarily in the South."[49] Thus, the adoption of Islamic religious and political ideologies in state government played a prominent role in the deterioration of community relationships in the country. In particular, "Islam was a factor of disunity rather than unity."[50]

Nigeria, on the other hand, is one of the largest Muslim-populated countries in West Africa, and its inhabitants follow Islam, Christianity, and indigenous African religions. In modern Nigeria, Islam and Christianity have existed as the predominant religions—49 percent Muslims and 49 percent Christians.[51] The colonial period's pitting of the Muslim north against the Christian south has lasted to the present, and this northern-southern divide has led to an attitude of segregation and limited interaction between Muslims and Christians in the country. Additionally, these two religions compete with one another as rivals rather than being friends. This situation has often caused tensions and conflict.

Indigenous solidarity associations are social associations in Ethiopia, which were established with the aim of supporting the members of a community during the time of a death and in other situations when any member needs social or physical support. No one is discriminated against based on religious or ethnic identity.

48. Berhe, *Muslim Theological Perspectives on Christianity*, 264–68.

49. Kukah, "Christian-Muslim Relations in Sub-Saharan Africa," 157.

50. Voll, "Eastern Sudan," 215.

51. Obeng-Mireku, "Christian-Muslim Relations in Sub-Saharan Africa," 88.

Ottuh asserts that "the problems which have often resulted in frictions and tensions in Nigeria include the evils of fanaticism and bigotism, intolerance, exclusivism, ignorance, etc."[52]

Boko Haram's Islamic political ideology and its assaults against Christians as well as civic law enforcement bodies have also exacerbated the problems of interreligious tensions. In recent years, due to the desire for fulfilling its religious-political cause, the sect has carried out terror activities mainly in northern Nigeria, including bloody insurgence, the killing of dozens of civilians as they primarily target Christian communities, and the destruction of churches and other properties. "The sect regenerates clogs of fundamental division, intolerance and fanaticism. Consequently, the Nigerian religious space is engulfed in a precarious and apprehensive aura."[53] Thus, the relations between the two faith communities have been severely affected due to these extremist activities that have obstructed the development of a genuine dialogue or any potential for harmony and cordial relationships between Christians and Muslims in the country. As Iheanacho stated, "The sect fans the flame of misunderstanding, ill feelings and intolerance between Christians and Muslims."[54]

Emmanuel Obeng-Mireku, in his comparative analysis of the nature of Christian-Muslim relations in Ghana and Nigeria, has identified social, economic, political, and media factors that have contributed to interreligious tensions in Nigeria.[55] First, his analysis shows that there are limited social contacts or inclinations toward interreligious marriage between Muslims in the north and Christians in the south. They live in isolation from one another, which facilitates mistrust, "stereotypes and apprehension," and causes the continuous eruption of conflicts.[56] The development of a negative "social domain," and a lack of sufficient venues to encourage "familiarity and [to] build awareness and trust" between the two faith communities has negatively affected any peaceful coexistence in Nigeria.[57] Second, the environmental degradation in northern Nigeria forced the pastoralist communities (Hausa-Fulani herdsmen) to move southward to search for pasture. This movement led the pastoralists

52. Ottuh, "Christian–Muslim Relations in Nigeria," 51.

53. Iheanacho, "Boko Haram and Renascent Clogs," 47.

54. Iheanacho, "Boko Haram and Renascent Clogs," 50.

55. Obeng-Mireku, "Christian-Muslim Relations in Sub-Saharan Africa," 87–99.

56. Obeng-Mireku, "Christian-Muslim Relations in Sub-Saharan Africa," 87–90.

57. Obeng-Mireku, "Christian-Muslim Relations in Sub-Saharan Africa," 89–90.

(mostly Muslims) into conflict with the Christian farmers.[58] Third, in Nigeria, politicians frequently use politics in relation to religion. Therefore, it serves as an instrument of division rather than unity. "On both sides of the political divide, accusations of Islamization and Christianization of the country have been leveled, all in an effort to mobilize the support of one faith group over the other."[59] Last, media is also used by both communities to spread their ideas of intolerance and polemical expressions, and thus it frequently enhances interreligious division and conflict.[60]

Ghana, in contrast to Nigeria, is characterized by peaceful coexistence between Muslim and Christian communities. It is a Christian-majority country whose population consists of 75 percent Christians and 16 percent Muslims.[61] In the social sphere, Ghanaian Muslims and Christians know much about each other's faith and relate to each other on a personal level due to the fact that many of them are partly influenced by the interactions they had in missionary schools. Both communities also offered opportunities for interreligious interactions and participation in religious ceremonies and festivals. Consequently, there are positive engagements and harmony in social domains.[62] Moreover, in Ghana, there is relatively equal economic opportunity for both Muslims and Christians, which has discouraged anger and resentment among religious minorities.[63] The democratic political system and the demographic realities in Ghana have also contributed to peaceful a coexistence of the two communities; consequently, many Ghanaians—both Muslims and Christians—have no inclination to undermine interreligious harmony.[64]

The East African Christian-majority nation of Kenya hosts different communities from various religious, cultural, and ethnic/racial backgrounds. After the arrival of the British colonizers and Christian missionaries in the nineteenth century, Christianity quickly spread to interior areas. Since then, Muslims continued to dominate mainly the northeast and eastern coast, while Christianity became the dominant religion in the rest of the country.[65] The history of Kenya witnessed a long

58. Obeng-Mireku, "Christian-Muslim Relations in Sub-Saharan Africa," 92–93.
59. Obeng-Mireku, "Christian-Muslim Relations in Sub-Saharan Africa," 93.
60. Obeng-Mireku, "Christian-Muslim Relations in Sub-Saharan Africa," 97–99.
61. Obeng-Mireku, "Christian-Muslim Relations in Sub-Saharan Africa," 88.
62. Obeng-Mireku, "Christian-Muslim Relations in Sub-Saharan Africa," 90–91.
63. Obeng-Mireku, "Christian-Muslim Relations in Sub-Saharan Africa," 93.
64. Obeng-Mireku, "Christian-Muslim Relations in Sub-Saharan Africa," 94.
65. Alio, "Kenyan Christian-Muslim Relations," 125–26.

period of stable and peaceful Christian-Muslim interaction in the social, political, and economic spheres both before and after the country gained independence. However, since 1998 Kenya has experienced a series of terrorist attacks—attacks on the US embassy in Nairobi in 1998, the Kikambala bombing in 2002, the Westgate Mall shooting in 2013, the Lamu attacks in 2014, and the Mandera and Garissa attacks in 2015.[66] Following the terror attacks, the Kenyan government passed an anti-terrorism bill (2013) to control the activities of the Islamic extremist groups. However, Chembea stated that many Kenyan Muslims condemned the attacks and distanced themselves from cooperating with extremist groups; the government used the anti-terrorism bill "to perpetuate the perceived political profiling, marginalization and economic exploitation of Muslims by predominantly Christian regimes."[67]

Despite such developments in recent years having the potential to hurt the peaceful coexistence of the two communities, there are bridging factors that may help to foster healthy relationships. According to Alio, there are five bridging factors for Christian-Muslim relations in Kenya today:[68] first, the historical relationship between Muslims and Christians over the centuries in the coastal areas in which they consistently showed mutual respect and cooperation; second, "the intermarriage process which produced the emergence of Swahili people; whom their cultural and social identities embodied both Bantu and Islamic culture;"[69] third, the democratic political system of Kenya guarantees the fair political representation of the minority Muslim communities despite the Christian majority; fourth, there is freedom of worship, of preaching, and of participation in the political process without religious or ethnic discrimination; fifth, the educational system allows both Islamic religious education and Christian religious education in primary and secondary schools, encouraging positive interfaith relationships.[70]

Tanzania is another East African nation that enjoys peaceful coexistence between Muslims and Christians despite having some cases of interreligious conflicts after September 11, 2001. It is a democratic secular state that guarantees freedom of worship, expression, and assembly to all its citizens. Although some Muslims see themselves as excluded

66. Alio, "Kenyan Christian-Muslim Relations," 125.

67. Chembea, "Negotiating Muslim–Christian Relations in Kenya," 16.

68. Alio, "Kenyan Christian-Muslim Relations," 113–17.

69. Alio, "Kenyan Christian-Muslim Relations," 113.

70. Alio, "Kenyan Christian-Muslim Relations," 117.

and marginalized, "democracy does provide a cross-cutting cleavage that can help to neutralize these tensions."[71] The introduction of the Ujama philosophy by President Julius Nyerere also led the Tanzanian Christian and Muslim communities to capitalize on their African values rather than dividing along religious lines. Japhace Poncian explained Christian-Muslim relations in Tanzania by saying, "although there is some conflict especially in and around Dar es-Salaam (such as in 1993, 1998, 2012) and a little in Morogoro and Mwanza, there is general agreement that at the level of a common person, there are generally good relations between Christians and Muslims."[72]

In Tanzania, Christians and Muslims relate to each other on different levels, particularly at the household, village, and national levels.[73] At the household level, there exist different religious traditions within the same household. The family members of such households "learnt to live together for the common good of the social unit. They began to think first in terms of family or household units rather than as members of different religious traditions."[74] At the village level, the adherents of different religions cooperate together as a social and political unit rather than a religious unit. Although they belong to various religious groups, they recognize and respect each other, and both churches and mosques exist side by side, transcending religious differences. Omari asserts that "in respect of the relation at household and village level, people of different faiths and religious backgrounds participate in various socio-political activities as Tanzanians first and not as members of certain religious groups."[75] At the national level, on the other hand, members of the two communities participate and cooperate in different joint projects and activities. At this level, the members do represent their respective religious groups, including their participation in national festivals and public holidays, as a Muslim sheikh and a Christian priest offer prayers to God standing together side by side.[76]

71. Kukah, "Christian-Muslim Relations in Sub-Saharan Africa," 159.
72. Poncian, "Christian-Muslim Relations in Tanzania," 57.
73. Omari, "Christian-Muslim Relation in Tanzania."
74. Omari, "Christian-Muslim Relation in Tanzania." 379.
75. Omari, "Christian-Muslim Relation in Tanzania."385.
76. Omari, "Christian-Muslim Relation in Tanzania."387.

CENTRAL ASIA

Central Asia is a culturally diverse region in which many different religions, including as Islam, Christianity, Judaism, Buddhism, Zoroastrianism, and Shamanistic beliefs, interact on a regular basis.[77] There are large numbers of Christians in the northern part of the region, with Muslims and Christians more integrated in the south despite Islam playing a larger role. Christian-Muslim interaction in Central Asia can be characterized as at times having been intense and conflictual. According to Gorder, "Some of these tensions, however, have been fanned from faint embers into roaring flames by external influences such as abrasive Islamist missionaries from outside the region and insensitive North American and European Protestant missionaries."[78] Moreover, one of the problems that exists in Christian-Muslim relations in the region is mutual ignorance—both Muslims and Christians do not have enough knowledge about the other religious group.

Each country in the region has unique features and the Christian-Muslim relations are often determined by cultural and legal factors. "While it is generally true that Kazakhstan and Kyrgyzstan are more multireligious, Muslim and Christian interactions are also more tolerant there than in Uzbekistan, Turkmenistan, and Tajikistan, where both legal and cultural challenges are significant."[79] In Uzbekistan, most of the Christians (Orthodox, Catholic, and Protestant Christians) live in the cities, and Christian-Muslim interactions take place primarily in urban settings. The rural Muslim community has limited interactions with Christians and their knowledge about Christianity is limited. Consequently, Christians from an Uzbek Muslim background suffer isolation and persecution from their communities and many of them are forced to leave their country and move to Western countries where they can have protection. On the other hand, "the Uzbekistan government enacted a series of legal ordinances in 1991 and 1992, which sought to limit external religious proselytization. Laws were also put in place to protect those who were vulnerable to outside pressures to become socially displaced from their native Islamic community."[80] Kyrgyzstan's law on religion, however, provides freedom of religion for all religious groups. Christians

77. Gorder, *Muslim-Christian Relations in Central Asia*, 134.

78. Gorder, *Muslim-Christian Relations in Central Asia*, 135.

79. Gorder, *Muslim-Christian Relations in Central Asia*, 134.

80. Gorder, *Muslim-Christian Relations in Central Asia*, 17.

in the country are not required to register their churches and don't face significant restrictions from the government except in the case of the Pentecostal Church of Jesus Christ, which was threatened with closure. There is also a certain level of openness for foreign Christian missionaries to come to Kyrgyzstan to assist the local Christians in "their church growth and pastoral care efforts."[81]

SOUTHEAST ASIA

Southeast Asia contains the majority of the world's Muslim population. Christianity, Islam, Buddhism, and Hinduism have had cultural interactions throughout the centuries in the region, but in recent years interreligious tensions and conflicts have undermined the peaceful coexistence of different religious communities. The changing local realities, the global jihadi narrative, and jihadist propaganda have contributed to a co-radicalization and the threatening of communal relations. It is evident in different countries and regions that both local and global factors "interact in complex ways for good and for ill."[82]

Indonesia is one of the most populous Muslim-majority (87 percent Muslim and 9 percent Christian) nations in Southeast Asia, consisting of 202 million citizens in 1998.[83] In general, Christian-Muslim relations in Indonesia have been "peaceful but fragile," characterized by suspicion and accusation from both sides in their references to "Christianization" and "Islamization."[84] In 1978, the Indonesian government introduced restrictive measures regarding the propagation of religion and foreign support to religious groups. Steenbr argues that the regulations state that "no expatriate missionaries could receive work permits if they came to spread their religion, and foreign workers in other fields were no longer allowed to be active in religious fields save in a few exceptional cases."[85] These regulations affected the missionary activities of churches. On the other hand, the government initiated a new program of interreligious dialogue on three levels to mitigate tensions: first, within each religious group to

81. Gorder, *Muslim-Christian Relations in Central Asia*, 33–34.
82. Bartona and Andre, "Islam and Muslim-Buddhist, 285.
83. Steenbr, "Muslim-Christian Relations," 321.
84. Hutagalung, "Muslim-Christian Relations in Kupang," 442.
85. Steenbr, "Muslim-Christian Relations," 331.

foster internal harmony; second, dialogue among religious groups; and third, dialogue between religious groups and the government.[86]

For the period of 1990–1995 and after the resignation of President Suharto in 1998, Indonesia witnessed several cases of bloody conflict between Christians and Muslims.[87] The interreligious conflict that erupted on Ambon Island was the largest in terms of the scale of destruction and number of casualties. Al-Qurtuby stated that "the Ambon upheavals resulted in thousands of deaths and tens of thousands of injuries. An estimated one-third to one-half of the population was displaced, and countless properties were razed."[88] The conflict expanded into large-scale war because both local and foreign jihadist groups became involved, consequently enhancing the military power of Muslims. People from both sides attempted to engage and refer to their respective religious texts as a theological foundation to justify their actions. However, after all these upheavals, peace and reconciliation was realized after Christians and Muslims engaged in a series of interreligious negotiations and dialogue.[89]

Malaysia is also a Muslim-majority country in Southeast Asia in which the 2000 census shows that the Muslim population is 60.4 percent and the Christian population is 9.1 percent.[90] During the colonial era, the ethnic composition drastically changed and it became normative to equate being Malay with being a Muslim. Although the post-independence constitution has provisions for religious freedom, they consist of articles that ensure the dominance of the Malays in administration and government, while also establishing Islam as the state religion.[91] In recent years, the government has adopted an aggressive Islamization policy, imposing restrictions on non-Muslim communities. The government banned the Malay Bible in 1984, imposed restrictions on Christian literature, banned non-Islamic religious education in all schools, and introduced courses "on Islamic civilization and religion for all students," and established restrictions on non-Muslims in order to hinder their access to land for cemeteries and church building.[92] Northcott explained the current interreligious situation of Malaysia as:

86. Steenbr, "Muslim-Christian Relations," 331.
87. Steenbr, "Muslim-Christian Relations," 336.
88. Al Qurtuby, "Peacebuilding in Indonesia," 351.
89. Al Qurtuby, "Peacebuilding in Indonesia," 354.
90. Walters, "Issues in Christian-Muslim Relations," 68.
91. Northcott, "Christian-Muslim Relations in Western Malaysia," 53.
92. Northcott, "Christian-Muslim Relations in Western Malaysia," 55.

> The genuine pluralism which had characterized government policy towards religion and education since Independence in the multi-religious and multiethnic society of Malaysia has been gradually eroded. Government attempts to restrict the growth and influence of resurgent versions of Islam and non-Muslim religions have produced a real deterioration in inter-religious relationships, both between Muslims of different viewpoints and between Muslims and Christians.[93]

CONCLUSION

This chapter has explored contemporary Christian-Muslim relations by focusing on the recent changes in the various perspectives of different Christian and Muslim communities, as well as the initiatives taken by Muslims and Christians to enhance an interfaith dialogue. It also gave due attention to examining the nature of contemporary Christian-Muslim relations in different regions of the world.

Several important conclusions emerge from this analysis. First, the contemporary Christian-Muslim interaction is diverse and complicated. A limited binary categorization may lead to erroneous conclusions. We can easily notice from the analysis that in different regions and nations Muslims and Christians can relate to each other in various ways, both at the local and national levels. Second, there is a strong tendency for the Islamization of politics in some Muslim-majority areas. The Islamic political narrative and Islamist groups play an essential role in the Islamization process, as well as the deterioration of interfaith harmony and peaceful coexistence. The attacks on churches and the discrimination against Christians have intensified in areas where hardliner Muslims have the political power. Third, the cultural, social, historical, theological, demographic, and political contexts of each country have an impact on both interreligious conflict and peaceful coexistence. Fourth, local and global factors interact with one another in shaping the interreligious contexts. For example, the Indonesian interreligious conflict was aggravated when foreign jihadist groups began to fight against Christians alongside local jihadist groups. Finally, the contemporary global and local realities call each one of us to engage in an interfaith dialogue with Muslims without

93. Northcott, "Christian-Muslim Relations in Western Malaysia," 55.

undermining the mission of the church: to share the good news about Jesus to all nations, including Muslims.

BIBLIOGRAPHY

Ahmed, Hussein. "Coexistence and/or Confrontation? Towards a Reappraisal of Christian-Muslim Encounter in Contemporary Ethiopia." *Journal of Religion in Africa* 36:1 (2006) 19–20.

Alio, Mohamed Sheikh. "Kenyan Christian-Muslim relations: Bridging Factors and Persisting Challenges." *International Journal of Education and Research* 3:12 (December 2015) 125–26.

Al Qurtuby, Sumanto. "Peacebuilding in Indonesia: Christian-Muslim Alliances in Ambon Island." *Islam and Christian-Muslim Relations* 24:3 (2013) 351. http://dx.doi.org/10.1080/09596410.2013.785091.

Bartona, Greg, and Virginie Andre. "Islam and Muslim-Buddhist and Muslim-Christian Relations in Southeast Asia." *Islam and Christian-Muslim Relations* 25:3 (2014) 285. http://dx.doi.org/10.1080/09596410.2014.915097.

Berhe, Anwar M. *Muslim Theological Perspectives on Christianity in Ethiopia between 1974 and 2016: Implications for Interreligious Harmony.* Melbourne: School of Theology, 2019.

Chapman, Colin. "Christians in the Middle East: Past, Present and Future." *Transformation* 29:2 (2012) 98.

Chembea, S. Athuman. "Negotiating Muslim-Christian Relations in Kenya through Waqfs, 1900–2010." *Islam and Christian-Muslim Relations* 1:21 (2017) 16.

Goddard, Hugh. "Christian-Muslim Relations: A Look Backwards and a Look Forwards." *Islam and Christian-Muslim Relations* 11:2 (July 2000) 201.

Gorder, A. Christian van. *Muslim-Christian Relations in Central Asia.* London: Routledge, 2008.

Hutagalung, Stella Aleida. "Muslim-Christian Relations in Kupang: Negotiating Space and Maintaining Peace." *The Asia Pacific Journal of Anthropology* 17:5 (2016) 442. http://dx.doi.org/10.1080/14442213.2016.1226943.

Iheanacho, Ngozi N. "Boko Haram and Renascent Clogs in Muslim-Christian Relations in Nigeria." *Afrrev* 10:2 (April 2016) 47.

Jenkins, Philip. *The Lost History of Christianity: The Thousand-year Golden Age of the Church in the Middle East, Africa and Asia.* Oxford: Lion, 2008.

Knitter, Paul F. *Introducing Theologies of Religions.* New York: Orbis, 2002.

Kukah, Mathew Hassan. "Christian-Muslim Relations in Sub-Saharan Africa: Problems and Prospects." *Islam and Christian-Muslim Relations* 18:2 (April 2007) 157.

Marcinkowski, Christoph. "Religion, Reason, Regensburg: Perspectives for Catholic-Muslim Dialogue." *A Journal of Islam and Civilizational Renewal* 1:1 (October 2009) 162.

Melcangi, Alessia, and Paolo Maggiolini. "Christians Navigating through Middle East Turbulences: The Case of the Copts in Egypt." In *Migrants and Religion: Paths, Issues, and Lenses*, edited by Laura Zanfrini, 176. Leiden: Brill, 2020.

Northcott, Michael. "Christian-Muslim Relations in Western Malaysia: Islam and Christianity in the Colonial Era." *The Muslim World* 81:1 (1991) 53.

Obeng-Mireku, Emmanuel. *Christian-Muslim Relations in Sub-Saharan Africa: A Comparative Analysis of Ghana and Nigeria*. Lethbridge: University of Canada, 2017.

O'Mahony, Anthony. "Christianity in Modern Iraq." *International Journal for the Study of the Christian Church* 4:2 (July 2004) 121.

Omari, C. K. "Christian-Muslim Relation in Tanzania: The Socio-Political Dimension." *Institute of Muslim Minority Affairs Journal* 5:2 (1984) 373–90.

Ottuh, John A. "Christian-Muslim Relations in Nigeria: The Problems and Prospects." *Afrrev Ijah* 3:2 (April 2014) 51.

Poncian, Japhace. "Christian-Muslim Relations in Tanzania: A Threat to Future Stability and Peace?" *Research on Humanities and Social Sciences* 5:3 (2015) 57.

Riddell, Peter. "Christian-Muslim Dialogue into the 21st Century." In *Islam and Christianity on the Edge: Talking Points in Christian-Muslim Relations into the 21st Century*, edited by John Azumah and Peter Riddell, 178–79. Melbourne: Acorn, 2013.

Sabra, George. "Two Ways of Being a Christian in the Muslim Context of the Middle East." *Islam and Christian-Muslim Relations* 17:1 (2006) 43–53.

Shihab, Alwi. "Christian-Muslim Relations into the Twenty-First Century." *Islam and Christian-Muslim Relations* 15:1 (January 2004) 65.

Soares, Benjamin F. "Muslim-Christian Encounters in Africa." In *Muslim-Christian Encounters in Africa*, edited by Benjamin F. Soares, 1–2. Boston: Brill, 2006.

Solomon, Sam, and E. Al-Maqdisi. *The Common Word: The Understanding of the Church*. Charlottesville: ANM, 2009.

Steenbr, Karel A. "Muslim-Christian Relations in the Pancasila State of Indonesia." *The Muslim World* 88:3–4. (July–October 1998) 321.

Voll, John O. "The Eastern Sudan, 1822 to the Present." In *The History of Islam in Africa*, edited by Nehemia Levtzion and Randall L. Pouwels, 215. Athens: Ohio University Press, 2000.

Walters, Albert Sundararaj. "Issues in Christian-Muslim Relations: A Malaysian Christian Perspective." *Islam and Christian-Muslim Relations* 18:1 (January 2007) 68.

Yucel, Salih. "Muslim-Christian Dialogue: Nostra Aetate and Fethullah Gülen's Philosophy of Dialogue." *Australian eJournal of Theology* 20:3 (December 2013) 198.

12

Religious Extremism against Christians

A Pakistani Perspective

MAQSOOD KAMIL

The focus of this chapter is on Islamic religious extremism against Christians. We ought to notice at the outset that Islamic religious extremism is a global phenomenon, and there is hardly any Islamic country where Christians have not experienced some form of extremism. From Egypt to Libya, to Burkina Faso to Nigeria, to the Middle East and South Asia, religious extremism is on the rise against Christians. In what follows, an attempt shall be made to define Islamic religious extremism, identify the sources and forms of extremism, and to suggest how Christians living in the face of extremism can practice their faith in a Christ-honoring manner. It is believed that what follows will be applicable in other majority-Muslim countries; however, the main focus will be on Islamic extremism in Pakistan.

AN OVERVIEW OF THE RELIGIOUS EXTREMISM AGAINST CHRISTIANS IN PAKISTAN

Pakistani Christians have suffered a great disappointment or, as Patrick Sookdeo has called it, "a betrayal" from their compatriot Muslims.[1]

1. Patrick Sookhdeo is the international director of the UK-based Barnabas Fund. He is a former Muslim convert to Christianity and author of many books on Islam. He

Muhammad Ali Jinnah, known as the father of the nation, promised equality for all citizens according to the law and freedom of religion.[2] Christian politicians played a crucial role in the state of Punjab to decide in favor of the anticipated country—Pakistan.[3] Jinnah was a Shi'ia (*Asna Ashari*), a minority Muslim denomination in Pakistan.[4] The Ahmadees, another Muslim sect that was declared non-Muslim by an act of parliament under Bhutto's government, have also suffered tremendously from Sunni extremism. While this is an intrareligious or sectarian problem, Christians, Hindus, Sikhs, and Zoroastrians have all suffered from Muslim extremists. As a consequence of religious extremism, Pakistan's population has changed from 60 percent Muslims and 40 percent other religions in 1947 to less than 4 percent religious minorities within a period of forty-seven years.[5] The discussion below is particularly concerned with extremism against Christians but is largely applicable to other religious minorities as well.

TYPES OF EXTREMISM

Because the topic of this chapter is religious extremism against Christians, some may not consider discussing other forms of extremism appropriate. However, it is hoped that Christians living in majority Muslim counties will agree that religion not only influences, but also dominates all aspects of existence in Muslim-majority nations. Life is not compartmentalized into political, religious, social, and cultural domains but is understood as a whole, which is founded, informed, and undergirded by Islam. Therefore, for the sake of clarity and better understanding the process of extremism, the following distinctions may be helpful.

is deeply involved in helping the persecuted churches, especially in Islamic countries. In his PhD thesis, published as *A People Betrayed*, he explores the history of sufferings of Christians in Pakistan.

2. Shahbazi, "Was Jinnah's Promise to the Minorities Honoured?"; Ahmed, "Fractured Image of Muhammad Ali Jinnah."

3. Ul-Anjum, "Role of Christians in the Freedom Movement."

4. Ahmed, "Was Jinnah a Shia or Sunni?"

5. "Pakistan's Minority Population Is Shrinking."

Intellectual Extremism

Intellectual extremism is the least discussed form of extremism. However, intellectual extremism is the most dangerous form of extremism as it provides a foundation for and legitimizes other forms of extremism. Muslim intellectuals—traditionally known as "imams"—on the basis of their understanding of the Qur'ān, Hadith, and practices of the four caliphs, formulated the rules of engagement for Muslims with non-Muslim citizens of an Islamic state. Sunni Muslim states follow one of the four schools of *fiqh* (Islamic jurisprudence), known as Hanifites, Hanbalites, Malikites, and Shaf'ites. Pakistan is a majority-Sunni (80–85 percent) state and largely follows the Hanifi school of law.

One of the most influential Muslim intellectuals of the twentieth century was a Pakistani of Hanifi leanings, Abul A'la Mawdudi (1903–1979). It is widely recognized that Mawdudi influenced both Hasan al-Bana, the founder of *Jamā' at al-Ikhwān al-Muslimīn* (the Muslim Brotherhood), and his disciple Sayyed Qutb of Egypt (a source of extreme suffering for the Egyptians Christians), as well as Ayatollah Khomeini (who triggered the great and continuing suffering of Iranian Christians). Mawdudi's ideology was based on his basic idea that the predicament of Muslims lies in their forsaking of their faith and thus Muslims of his time were no better than non-Muslims. In his book *Let Us Be Muslims*, he noted that Muslims were no better than *kafirs* in their neglect and disobedience of Allah. Thus, he called Muslims to become "true Muslims." He set out to reform Muslims and bring every aspect of their lives to be shaped by Islam. His political ideology included violent jihad, through which any power from the non-Muslims as well as the unreformed Muslims must be destroyed. He argued that Islam wishes to overthrow the kingdoms of the world and to establish the kingdom of God. His ideological Islamic state has no boundaries. Thus, global jihad is necessary to establish the pan-Islamic state because Allah claims the whole earth and not just parts of it. Mawdudi argued that all other religious duties are geared toward preparing Muslims for jihad. He wrote:

> Briefly speaking, it would be enough to state that the real objective of Islam is to remove the lordship of man over man and to establish the kingdom of God on Earth. To stake one's life and everything else to achieve this purpose is called Jihad; while Salah, fasting, Hajj and Zakat are all meant as a preparation for this task.[6]

6. Abu-'l-A'lā al-, "Meaning of Jihad," 285.

Rafi Aamer, reflecting on Mawdudi's contribution to extremism in his book *Al-Jihād fī'l-Islām*, writes:

> Islam wishes to do away with all states and governments which are opposed to the ideology and program of Islam. The purpose of Islam is to set up a state on the basis of this ideology and program, regardless of which nation assumes the role of standard-bearer of Islam, and *regardless of the rule of which nation is undermined in the process of the establishment of an ideological Islamic state*. Islam *requires* the earth—*not just a portion, but the entire planet*—not because the sovereignty over the earth should be wrested from one nation or group of nations and vested in any one particular nation, but because the whole of mankind should benefit from Islam, and its ideology and welfare program. It is to serve this end that Islam seeks to press into service all the forces, which can bring about such a revolution. The term which covers the use of all these forces is 'Jihad.'[7]

As Islam desires to take over the whole world, including religious, philosophical, economic, social, cultural, and political worlds, Mawdudi understood that Islam advances only by the power of the sword. Ami Isseroff notes from Mawdudi's *Al-Jihād fī'l-Islām* how he extolled the virtues of violent jihad:

> The Messenger of Allah invited the Arabs to accept Islam for 13 years. He used every possible means of persuasion, gave them incontrovertible arguments and proofs, showed them miracles and put before them his life as an example of piety and morality. In short, he used every possible means of communication, but his people refused to accept Islam. When every method of persuasion had failed, the Prophet took to the sword. That sword removed evil mischief, the impurities of evil and the filth of the soul. The sword did something more—it removed their blindness so that they could see the light of truth, and also cured them of their arrogance; arrogance which prevents people from accepting the truth, stiff necks and proud heads bowed with humility. As in Arabia and other countries, Islam's expansion was so fast that within a century a quarter of the world accepted it. This conversion took place because the sword of Islam tore away the veils which had covered men's hearts.[8]

7. Aamer, *Cartoon Crises*, 14:53.
8. Isserof, "Abul Ala Maududi."

Mawdudi's "Jamaat-e-Islami" (JI) movement played an extremely important role in providing ideological and organizational structure to Afghan Jihad against the former Soviet Union. Ayman al-Zwahiri, founder of Egyptian Islamic Jihad and deputy of Al-Qaida's chief, Osama Bin Laden, and present head of Al-Qaida, was a follower of Sayyed Qutb.

JI exercised the highest religious and political influence during the regime of dictator General Zia al-Haq (1978–1988), who most vigorously pursued the policy of Islamization of Pakistan. Zia dissolved the national and provincial assemblies and set up the national and provincial Majlis-e-Shooras. Islamic banking, as well as provincial and federal Sharia courts, were set up, and Hadood laws were enforced. The prohibition of blasphemy and related laws were given new vigor and interpretation. These laws have given constant rise to persecution and extremism against Christians. Non-Muslims were excluded from holding key posts in mainstream politics, and thus excluded from national life. Over ten men from JI were appointed to key positions to implement Zia's program of Islamization, which in fact was Mawdudi's ideology for an Islamic state.

The Islamization of education led to the introduction of new curricula that promoted an extreme version of Islam. The study of Islam was made compulsory. Books on Islamics were overtly anti-Christianity. Christian students were required to study Islamics. They suffered humiliation in their classrooms, both from their teachers and from their fellow students. Educational curricula are understood to be one of the biggest sources of extremism in Pakistan. A report on the relationship between education and extremism noted, "Curriculum and textbooks include hate material and 'encourage prejudice, bigotry and discrimination' toward women, religious minorities."[9] Pervez Hoodbhoy, an avid critic of Pakistan's education system, wrote in *Foreign Affairs*: "Pakistani schools—and not just madrassas—are churning out fiery zealots, fueled with a passion for jihad and martyrdom."[10] Not only Mawdudi, but hundreds of other Muslim intellectuals and Imams have contributed to provide an intellectual basis for religious extremism.

9. Bajoria, "Pakistan's Education System."
10. Bajoria, "Pakistan's Education System."

CONSTITUTIONAL AND LEGAL EXTREMISM

With Mr. Jinnah's promise for the equality of all citizens before the law and for freedom of religion, Christian politicians played a crucial role for the state of Punjab to decide in favor of the anticipated country: Pakistan.[11] The 1956 constitution of Pakistan was secular and guaranteed the freedom of profession and propagation of faith to all the citizens of Pakistan.[12] Pakistan was originally called the Democratic Republic of Pakistan.

However, 1962 amendments to the constitution determined that Islam should be the religion of the state and that Pakistan should be called the Islamic Republic of Pakistan.[13] The 1973 constitution was overtly Islamic and determined the scope and freedom of the Legislative Assembly. It requires the Islamization of the existing laws deemed antithetical to Islam and legislation could be made only in accordance with the Qur'an and the Sunnah. No legislation could be passed that might be deemed repugnant to Islam. This constitution also barred non-Muslims from becoming the head of the state or holding a position in government.[14]It has been correctly observed that "Although the constitution includes adequate accommodation for Pakistan's religious minorities, in practice non-Sunni Muslims face religious discrimination in both public and private spheres."[15]

The first serious attack on freedom of religion in relation to minorities was launched through the 1973 amendment to the constitution. Zia's amendments even changed the Objectives Resolution and silently took away the word "freely," which was central to the clause guarding the freedom of religion for minorities. Before this amendment, the constitution read that minorities would be able "freely to profess and practice their religion." Realizing the seriousness of this amendment, Christians protested, but their voice was smothered. The amendment was then challenged in the Supreme Court of Pakistan. The Supreme Court's decision was a judicial blow that killed the hope of minorities to enjoy freedom of faith in Pakistan. Sookhdeo states: "A landmark decision in the Supreme

11. Shahbazi, "Was Jinnah's Promise to the Minorities Honoured?"; Ahmed, "Fractured Image of Muhammad Ali Jinnah"; Ul-Anjum, "Role of Christians in the Freedom Movement."

12. Berkley Center for Religion, Peace and World Affairs, *Religious Freedom in Pakistan*, 10:34

13. Cohen, *Idea of Pakistan*, 58.

14. Cohen, *Idea of Pakistan*, 58.

15. Cohen, *Idea of Pakistan*, 58.

Court in 1993 ruled that the fundamental rights guaranteed in the constitution were limited by whether they conformed to the injunctions of Islam as contained in the Qur'an and the Sunnah."[16] Thus the Supreme Court's decision judicially reduced Christians to second-class citizens and strengthened constitutional extremism.

The adoption of the Objectives Resolution by the Constituent Assembly in 1949 provided the solid basis for the Islamization of Pakistan and severely restricted the freedom of religion for non-Muslims by resolving that "the future constitution of Pakistan should be based on the Islamic principles of freedom, social justice and equity."[17] Zia tried to legitimize his coup by his promise to turn Pakistan into a purer Islamic state as envisioned in the Objectives Resolution. He implemented a number of Islamic Sharia laws and established the Federal Sharia Court parallel to the Supreme Court. He introduced Islamic banking, reserved headship of governmental institutions exclusively for practicing and confessing Muslims, and replaced Sunday with Friday as the weekly holiday, which made it difficult for Christians to attend church on Sunday. Most significantly, he implemented anti-blasphemy laws that contradict all the established and ratified covenants and conventions of international human rights—of which Pakistan itself is a signatory. Zia's policy of Islamization, his unrestricted use of religion for his own political agenda, and his open alliance with Jamaat-e-Islami contributed to the victimization of minorities. Anti-blasphemy laws have been constantly used by members of the majority as well as the state for mistreating and restricting the freedom of faith of non-Muslims.

Pakistan's legal extremism is most vividly demonstrated through its anti-blasphemy laws, which prescribe life imprisonment for desecrating the Qur'an and a mandatory death sentence for insulting the Prophet of Islam. Many Christians have been falsely accused of blasphemy, arrested, imprisoned, or killed. Sawan Masih, accused of committing blasphemy–which then became a pretext for burning and looting of the Joseph Colony, the Christian community in Lahore—was given the death sentence. Sawan pleaded for his innocence throughout his year-long trial.[18]After making an appeal, Masih was acquitted and released in October 2020, at which point he fled Pakistan.[19] In May 1998, Bishop John Joseph com-

16. Sookhdeo, *People Betrayed*, 102.

17. Sookhdeo, *People Betrayed*, 28.

18. "Sawan Masih: Pakistani Christian Gets Death Penalty."

19. "Sawan Masih: Pakistani Christian Gets Death Penalty."

mitted suicide in front of the court in Sahiwal, which had passed a death sentence for young Ayub Masih, who was falsely accused of blasphemy.[20] Earlier in 1993, Rahmat Masih, Manzoor Masih, and Salamat Masih (only fourteen years old) were accused of blasphemy. They were attacked after a court hearing. Manzoor was killed while the others were injured. The lower court handed down the death sentence to both Rahmat and Salamat. But the high court bench, composed of Justice Arif Iqbal Bhatti and Chaudhary Khurshid Ahmad, acquitted the accused since they were illiterate and did not know how to write Arabic. Following the decision, religious parties led by the Milli Yakjihti Council (Council for National Unity of Purpose) called for a nation-wide strike against the acquittal of the accused. Justice Arif Iqbal was later murdered in his chamber. The assassin confessed that "He killed the judge because he was on the bench that acquitted two Christian men, Salamat and Rehmat Masih, in a blasphemy case."[21] In July 2010, two brothers, pastor Rashid Emmanuel and Sajid Emmanuel, were shot dead as they were being brought by the police to appear before the judge.[22] Frank Crimi sums up Muslim mobs' bloodthirst for those accused of blasphemy:

> Perhaps part of Pakistan's enchantment with its blasphemy laws stems from the fact that many Pakistani Muslims believe killing a blasphemous person earns a heavenly reward, a holy perk that may help explain why at least 30 Christians accused of blasphemy since 2009 have been killed by mobs of Islamist vigilantes.[23]

A Christian couple, Shafqat Emmanuel and Shagufta Kausar. were sentenced to death for allegedly committing blasphemy.[24] Another example is the case of Asia Bibi, a mother of five who has been jailed since 2009 and has since been condemned to death, after her appeal against her punishment was postponed five times.[25] Another startling case, which caught the attention of the Pakistani nation as well as that of the international community, was the accusation of blasphemy against fourteen-year-old Rimsha Masih, who has Down's Syndrome.

20. Bennett-Jones, "Despatches: Karachi."
21. "High-Profile Blasphemy Cases."
22. "Pakistan City Tense"; Khan, "On Trial for Blasphemy."
23. Crimi, "To Jail a Down's Syndrome Girl."
24. "Pakistani Couple Get Death Sentences."
25. "Asia Bibi Appeal Postponed."

Some Muslim clerics have even declared that the Bible is a blasphemous book: as immoral acts of certain prophets are recorded in it, they assert, this is deeply offensive to Muslims. They have demanded that the Supreme Court ban the Bible in Pakistan. Anuragh Kumar noted: "A leader of the Jamiat Ulema-e-Islam (Samiul Haq) or JUI-S party on Tuesday demanded that the Supreme Court of Pakistan ban the Bible, saying 'blasphemous' portions had been 'added to the Bible,' Pakistan's newspaper, *The News International* reported."[26] This attempt to ask the apex court to ban the Bible in Pakistan could have extremely serious consequences for freedom of faith in Pakistan. It is well recognized internationally that the situation of minorities in Pakistan is very serious. Jaweed Kaleem describes the struggle of minorities for survival, stating, "A Pew Research Center report named Pakistan, which is 96% Muslim, one of the most hostile nations for religious minorities. Pew placed the country among the top five overall for restrictions on religion, singling out its anti-blasphemy statutes."[27] Considering the serious condition of the minorities in Pakistan, a US panel urged the US government to add Pakistan to a blacklist of violators of religious freedom. In its annual report, this commission stated that Pakistan "represents the worst situation in the world of religious freedom, among the countries that are not already on the US blacklist and that the conditions in the past year hit an all-time low."[28] Mark Kellner also noted: "Pakistan is a world leader in oppressing religious minorities, the US Commission on International Religious Freedom declared in a report."[29]

SOCIAL EXTREMISM

Since the introduction of the anti-blasphemy and other Islamic laws, freedom to express and propagate one's faith has been severely limited. Not only do minorities not have freedom of faith in the true sense of the word, but they have also been actively persecuted for their faith and, wherever possible, forced to convert to Islam. On February 6, 1997, a mob of 30,000–35,000, led by extremist and militant Muslims, attacked

26. Kumar, "Now Bible Faces Blasphemy Charges"; Rahman, "JUI-S Urges SC to Ban Bible."

27. Kaleem, "Religious Minorities in Pakistan Struggle."

28. AFP, "US Panel Urges Action."

29. Kellner, "Pakistan Tops New List."

and looted a Christian village called Shanti Nagar ("Village of Peace"), reducing it to ashes.[30] In October 2001, Muslim extremists armed with AK-47 assault rifles attacked Christian worshipers in St. Dominic Church Bahawalpur. Sixteen Christians and a policeman were killed, and hundreds were injured. In March 2002, the Protestant International Church Islamabad was attacked with grenades. Five people died and nearly fifty were injured.[31] In August 2002, a church in the Christian Hospital Taxila was attacked with grenades; three nurses died, and twenty-three others were injured.[32] In the same month, Murree Christian School came under fire from extremists and six Christians were killed.[33]

False accusations of desecrating the Qur'ān or insulting the Prophet of Islam against the persons belonging to minorities, especially against Christians, have had a devastating impact on them. In 2005, Yusuf Masih, a Christian, had an angry confrontation with a Muslim, Kalu, who threatened him with dire consequences. He later accused Yusuf of desecrating the Qur'ān. Nearly 1,500 Muslim extremists attacked Christians and burned three churches, a school, and dozens of houses.[34] In 2009, nearly one hundred Christian houses were looted and then torched in the village Bahmani Wala, in the district of Kasur; the same thing happened in Korian, a village near Gojra. But the most devastating attack was carried out on the Christian colony of Gojra, where sixty homes were torched and eight Christians were burnt alive.[35] In March 2013, more than one hundred Christian houses and a number of churches were reduced to ashes in Joseph Colony, Lahore. Two suicide bombers carried out a most horrific attack on September 23, 2013, at All Saints Church Peshawar. Ninety-eight persons, including women and children, died and hundreds of others were seriously injured. Christians in Peshawar had been receiving threats from extremist and terrorist Muslims to convert to Islam or face the consequences. Some of the extremist jihadi groups also started demanding *jizya* from minorities.

Another horrific act of violence against Christians that shocked the world took place on November 5, 2014. A poor Christian couple, Shahbaz Masih and his pregnant wife, were brutally killed by a mob and then

30. George and Alexander, "Pakistan: Mob Attacks."

31 Taylor, "Bloody Sunday."

32. "Nurses Killed in an Attack."

33. Rhode, "Gunman Kills 6."

34. Walsh, "Attack Leaves Churches Gutted."

35. Kharal, "Looking Back."

thrown into the brick kiln and reduced to ashes on the false accusation of desecrating the Qur'ān.[36] There has been a marked escalation of violence against Christians by Muslim mobs. On the popular level, a general understanding prevails among the Muslims that Pakistan is for them, and minorities have no place in it. Pakistan and Islam are considered synonymous. Therefore, if religious minorities want to live in Pakistan, they should convert to Islam. Lipton observes, "Parties and groups with religious affiliations target minority groups."[37] Public outrage against minorities, briefly mentioned earlier, has been increasing to an unprecedented level. Lashker-e-Jhangvi ("the Army of Jhangvi"), an extremist militant organization, was reportedly responsible for the destruction of churches, schools, and Christian homes in Sangla Hill and the Christian colony of Gojra. In all these destructive incidents, the government has failed to punish the perpetrators of violence against minorities. Lipton writes, "The government failed to intervene in cases of societal violence directed at minority religious groups. The lack of an adequate government response contributed to an atmosphere of impunity for acts of violence and intimidation committed against minorities."[38]

CHRISTIAN RESPONSES TO ISLAMIC EXTREMISM

Fear

Faced with this appalling situation, how do Pakistani Christians respond? There is no easy answer to this question because there is no unified Christian response. Since the Iranian Revolution and the ensuing unspeakable sufferings of Christians in this neighboring country, it was feared that Christians in Pakistan may face a similar situation. There was a high likelihood of such persecution because the main inspiration for the Iranian Revolution was the Pakistani religiopolitical ideology of Mawdudi. In Mawdudi's political ideology, non-Muslims may be tolerated in an Islamic state but cannot be allowed to play a role in decision-making. In fact, Mawdudi envisioned Pakistan as the second Madina.[39]

Soon after the creation of Pakistan, Christians began to feel insecure. Renowned Christian scholar, lawyer, and politician Joshua Fazl-ud-din

36. Jillani, "Pakistan Christian Community Living in Fear."

37. Lipton, *Religious Freedom in Asia*, 39.

38. Lipton, *Religious Freedom in Asia*, 39.

39. Singh, "Integrative Political Ideology."

noted: "As a matter of fact, right from the beginning, minor officials had been harassing in Pakistan and openly asking [Christians] to leave Pakistan, which they characterized as a homeland exclusively for Muslims."[40] Consequently, "Loyalty of the non-Muslims to the state of Pakistan is doubted even by the moderate Muslims."[41] Thirty years ago, a survey found that 80 percent of Christians felt they were second-class citizens in Pakistan.[42] With the ever-rising tide of persecution, Christians generally do not see any future in Pakistan. They are living in a constant state of fear. This seems to be the only unified response to Muslim religious extremism. Similar to eighth-century Christians in the Middle East, self-preservation, the security of fellow Christians and church institutions, and survival have been the main concerns of Pakistani Christians.

Mass Migration

Theodore Gabriel observes:

> The sporadic violent incidents against Churches and Christians, the Blasphemy Law and even Islamicisation of Pakistan have filled the Christians with a sense of foreboding and despondency. It is especially so in the case of such a socially and economically struggling community as the Christians. They tend to see Islam as a steamroller force and to panic. This might give rise to a ghetto mentality. Justice Cornelius writing in the *Christian Voice* in 1953 warns against 'A general feeling of despair, a widespread lack of confidence and a common readiness to anticipate the worst.'[43]

Theodore was writing in 2007; major incidents of violence against Christians and a marked escalation in blasphemy cases have since taken place. National newspapers have widely reported the mass migration of Pakistani Christians, who are seeking asylum in Thailand, Sri Lanka, and Malaysia, waiting for their turn in the UN camps.[44] Nazir Bhatti, who has long been advocating for Christians through his paper, *Pakistan Christian Post*, wrote a letter to the Secretary General of the UN claiming

40. Fazl-ud-din, *Future of Christians in Pakistan*, 68.
41. Gabriel, *Christian Citizens of An Islamic State*, 37.
42. Roelle, *Christians Under Siege*, 50.
43. Gabriel, *Christian Citizens of an Islamic State*, 14.
44. Ali, "Packing Their Bags"; "Pakistani Christians Moving."

that 90 percent of Pakistani Christians favor refugee status from the UN.[45] This claim might seem like an exaggeration. However, it is true that Christians neither feel safe nor have equal rights as other citizens of Pakistan. Therefore, anyone who can—especially the middle class of Pakistani Christians—is emigrating from Pakistan.

Agitation and Protests

Constant suffering at the hands of extremists and the denial of justice from the courts (for all the atrocities committed against Christians, no one has been convicted or punished by the courts) have driven Christians to take to the streets in the hope that the authorities and the international community may take notice of their plight. It has become a common cultural norm to protest and force the government to take some action. In May 1998, Bishop John Joseph took an extreme step and committed suicide in front of the court in Sahiwal that gave the death sentence to young Ayub Masih, who was falsely accused of committing blasphemy.[46] This sparked further protests, and protestors faced further violence from police and Muslim gangsters. Hundreds of Christians were severely beaten, arrested, and imprisoned. Some government hospitals refused to treat injured protesters. After twin suicide bombers killed twenty worshippers in Youhanabad on March 15, 2015, Christians seized two terrorists and burned them before taking to the streets. Government authorities dubbed this as the worst form of terrorism because they had burned two Muslim terrorists. Hundreds of Christians were arrested, beaten, and harassed. A large number of residents of Youhanabad fled and have not returned even to this day.

Living in Ghettos

An overwhelming majority of Christians are living in a state of fear, insecurity, and mistrust. Social, political, constitutional, and religious hostility, coupled with extreme socioeconomic and political vulnerability, have forced Christians to live in unseemly ghetto communities. Nearly half a century of growing persecution and constant betrayal have seriously

45. Bhatti, "90% Pakistani Christians."

46. Bennett-Jones, "Despatches: Karachi."

affected Christian-Muslim relations. In his recent article, Bishop Michael Nazir-Ali writes:

> These laws [blasphemy laws] have not just muzzled freedom of belief and of speech but they have made Christians and other non-Muslims perpetually fearful about being targets of the next accusation. It has created a ghetto mentality amongst them and further removed them from the ambit of public life. The removal of the moratorium on the death penalty, ostensibly to deal with terrorism, raises the real prospect of someone now being executed for blasphemy. This would be a tragic development indeed.[47]

Messianic Response

One thing that puts Christianity in stark contrast to its persecutors is its message of forgiveness. Islam as a religion and culture justifies taking revenge. Tribal, sectarian, and family feuds have taken thousands of lives as a vicious cycle of taking revenge continues to grow. However, the New Testament of the Bible teaches not to take revenge because judgment belongs to God (Romans 12:19). Christ's unimaginable suffering and his prayer for forgiveness for those who crucified him has always inspired Pakistani Christians to follow their Savior and to forgive the perpetrators of violence against them. The worst carnage of Christian worshippers took place in All Saints Church in Peshawar on September 22, 2013. Two suicide bombers killed ninety-eight and injured approximately two hundred people. The response from the bereaved families was amazing. A veteran South Korean missionary did thorough research after this most heinous attack against innocent Christians. He interviewed 337 persons and asked about their response to the killers. These are their remarks:

> "I believe God will do all the judgment. So, I entrust God for HIS judgment, and I forgive them."
> "They don't know what they are doing. Even the beast doesn't do this. I already forgive them, and I pray to God to show them His mercy so that they would repent and be restored back to good human beings."
> "I forgive them and pray for them that they would know how precious life of a human is."

47. Nazir-Ali, "Persecution of Pakistan's Christians."

> "Jesus Christ shed his blood to forgive such a sinner as I am. . . Human's blood is so sinful and filthy which is nothing compared to the precious blood of Jesus. . . why can't I forgive them?"
> "I forgive. But I wish and pray for them to repent, begin to love other people, and stop killing."[48]

This attitude of forgiveness by the wounded souls sets them apart from the perpetrators of extremism against them.

AN AUDACIOUS TENACITY OF FAITH

One of the most unexpected and stunning responses by ordinary Christians in the face of tremendous suffering has been to remain firmly grounded in their commitment to and faith in Christ. After horrible carnage in many of the churches, church leaders were afraid that churches might become deserted. However, the Christian response has been exactly the opposite. Pakistani churches are filled with people of all ages. Their persecution testifies to the truthfulness of the teachings of Christ: "You will be hated by everyone because of me, but the one who stands firm to the end will be saved" (Matthew 10:22); and "Then you will be handed over to be persecuted and put to death, and you will be hated by all nations because of me" (Matthew 24:9). They take seriously the challenge and promise of Christ to remain faithful until death and receive the crown of life (Revelation 2:10). Thus, Pakistani Christians continue to demonstrate a remarkable tenacity of faith in the face of intense persecution emanating from religious extremism.

INTELLECTUAL RESPONSE

While Pakistani Christians have demonstrated a unique Christian virtue in their forgiveness of their enemies—even when these enemies have not sought forgiveness—this does not necessarily mean that any love for them has been inspired in enemy hearts. Nor does it create peace. Christians need to engage Muslims at sociopolitical and religiocultural levels in order to create mutual understanding and an environment for peaceful, respectful, and accommodative coexistence. This requires a comprehensive

48. Matthew Jeong, "Report to the Diocese of Peshawar and All Donor Friends about Our Visit to Victims of the Bomb Blasts on 22 April 2014" (2014, unpublished, quoted with permission).

dialogue between Christians and Muslims. Unfortunately, Muslims in Pakistan do not feel such a need. Michael Nazir-Ali contends that Muslims and Christians have a "grave responsibility for maintaining peace."[49] This would require dialogue and cooperation. Nazir-Ali argues that committed and genuine dialogue naturally requires critical evaluation of other faiths by Christians and allows others to critically evaluate the Christian faith.[50] Nazir-Ali also asserts that the catholicity of the church demands its dialogue with and mission to the rest of the world. He argues that if the church, in John Knox's words, is an "ever-widening sphere and ever-deepening reconciliation . . . then the Church must always be in dialogue with the community, with the people of other faiths and with all those of goodwill."[51] Nazir-Ali refers to four types of dialogue discussed by Eric Sharpe and another similar four types by the Vatican. These are the dialogue of life, the dialogue of deeds, the dialogue of specialists, and the dialogue of the interior life. Regarding the third kind, he writes, "People, sometimes, do not give enough value to the dialogue of specialists. In some cases, this *has* been sterile: where it has been overly concerned with classical issues and there has been a danger in some respect of a merely antiquarian interest."[52]

While the dialogues of life and deeds are unavoidable (to some extent even preferable) and take place, almost involuntarily, on a daily basis, they lack intentionality and Christian moorings. When it comes to the dialogue of specialists, Christians in Pakistan suffer from a lack of specialists who can engage with Muslim scholars. The training institutions for Christian leadership are largely responsible for such a dearth. None of the major theological institutions teach courses on Islam or Christian-Muslim relations. Sadly, constitutionally, politically, socially, and intellectually, the Christian voice has been smothered and Pakistani Christians are without influence. They constantly look toward the Western world to save them from these appalling and life-threatening situations. However, in many cases it proves counterproductive.

49. Nazir-Ali, *Unique and Universal Christ*, 86.

50. Nazir-Ali, *Unique and Universal Christ*, 87.

51. Nazir-Ali, *Mission and Dialogue*, 72.

52. MNazir-Ali, *Mission and Dialogue*, 82.

FOLLOWING THE EXTREMISTS

Peaceful protest is not only justified but also necessary to challenge unjust authorities and injustices (John 18:22). Muslim extremists, to a certain extent, have influenced some Christians to become extremists themselves. Reacting to the violence committed against Christians, Christian demonstrators have also turned to violence and damaged public property. The most shocking incident took place after the twin suicide attacks in Youhanabad on March 15, 2015. Reportedly, police arrested two Muslim suspects from the scene. Angry Christians snatched them from the police, killed them, and set their bodies on fire. As the fire engulfed them, Christians shouted: "*Halailuya and Khudawand Yasu Masih ki Jai*" ("Praise God and victory to the Lord Jesus Christ"). This has no small similarity with the Muslim chanting of "Allahu Akbar."[53] Chaudhary Nisar Khan, the Minister of the Interior, quickly condemned this Christian reaction as the worst act of terrorism.[54] From time to time, certain Christian leaders have threatened to set up militant organizations modelled after Islamic extremist organizations to defend Christians. This is of course an incredibly sad and completely un-Christian response.

FOLLOWING THE EXTREMIST

Contrary to being influenced by Muslim religious extremism, however, Christians ought to respond with a different kind of extremism—to wholeheartedly follow the one who is most extreme: Jesus Christ. Christ could be considered extremist in two ways: (i) what he taught and what he did and, (ii) what people thought about him. To consider the second item first, Jesus' opponents, as they considered his teachings and his claims about himself, took him to be an extremist who was so dangerous that they had to eliminate him. At his first sermon in Nazareth, his audience tried to kill him by throwing him from the top of the mountain (Luke 4:28–30). When Christ claimed that he and God—whom he called his "Father"—were one, Jews called him a blasphemer and tried to stone him (John 10:30–33). On another occasion, even his disciples thought his teachings were too extreme, to the point that many of his disciples left him and never came back (John 6:60–66). His cleansing of the temple

53. ARY News (live TV), March 15, 2015, https://www.youtube.com/watch?v=9OlpIdrBhWo.

54. Haider, "Mob Lynching."

was certainly understood by the temple authorities as the act of an extremist, inciting them to kill him (Mark 11:15–18). The understanding of the Jewish opponents of Christ might have been clouded by many different factors; however, Christ was not only an extremist, but rather *the* Extremist. His choice to become human, to be born as a vulnerable baby, and to offer himself as the sacrifice to save humanity and honor his Father were extreme acts. His teaching to "love your enemies and pray for those who persecute you" (Matthew 5:44) goes beyond our mental and ethical extremes. Christ's call and demand to his disciples to deny their very *self* and carry their cross daily is an extreme demand.

Thus, in my view, the most appropriate Christian response to religious extremism is Christian extremism, or perhaps messianic extremism. Christian moderation ultimately leads to the betrayal of Christ. It is somewhat similar to Peter's walking at a distance behind Christ after his betrayal. Soon after, Peter denied that he even knew Jesus, let alone that he was one of his closest disciples. In other words, the Christian response to religious extremism should be not only our extreme commitment to Christ, but also living out our call to radical discipleship. Only messianic extremism can counter religious extremism. Only extreme love can overcome extreme hatred. Only carrying the cross can deliver us from the fear of death and assure us of the victory that Christ has already won over the powers of extreme destruction, including the destructive power of religious extremism. Only by losing one's life for Christ and the gospel may one find life (Matthew 10:39; Mark 9:34–35; Luke 9:23–25). This is the way of the cross, the way of the crucified and resurrected Lord and all his true disciples and apostles. Only following the Extreme One with extreme commitment could be called an appropriate Christian response to religious extremism.

BIBLIOGRAPHY

Aamer, Rafi. *Cartoon Crises*. http://familyofheart.com/DOC/FOS/Comments_AR02.htm.

AFP. "US Panel Urges Action on Pakistan Religious Freedom." *Dawn*, April 30, 2014. https://www.dawn.com/news/1103293.

Ahmed, Khaled. "The Fractured Image of Muhammad Ali Jinnah." *Himal Southasian*. February 1, 1998. https://www.himalmag.com/the-fractured-image-of-muhammad-ali-jinnah/.

Ahmed, Khalid. "Was Jinna a Shia or Sunni?" *Friday Times* 22:45 (December 2010). http://www.thefridaytimes.com/24122010/page27.shtml.

Ali, Rabis. "Packing Their Bags: Christians Moving to Thailand to Escape Violence, Insecurity." *The Express Tribune*, July 15, 2014. http://tribune.com.pk/story/735724/packing-their-bags-christians-moving-to-thailand-to-escape-violence-insecurity/.

ARY (TV live) News, March 15, 2015. https://www.youtube.com/watch?v=9OlpIdrBhWo.

"Asia Bibi Appeal Postponed for a Fifth Time." *Christian Today*, May 27, 2014. http://www.christiantoday.com/article/asia.bibi.appeal.postponed.for.a.fifth.time/3701.htm.

Bajoria, Jayshree. "Pakistan's Education System and Links to Extremism." *Council on Foreign Relations*, October 7, 2009. http://www.cfr.org/pakistan/pakistans-education-system-links-extremism/p20364.

Bennett-Jones, Owen. "Despatches: Karachi." *BBC News*, May 7, 1998. http://news.bbc.co.uk/1/hi/world/south_asia/88890.stm.

Berkley Center for Religion, Peace and World Affairs. *Religious Freedom in Pakistan*. https://berkleycenter.goergetown.edu/essays/religious-freedom-in-pakistan. 2014.

Bhatti, Nazir S. "90% Pakistani Christian Favour Refugee Status from UN after Rising Violence." *Pakistan Christian Post*, June 15, 2011. https://www.pakistanchristianpost.com/editorial-details/112.

Chaudhary, Wilson. "Lahore Christians Face Further Attack after Man Accused of Blasphemy." *British Asian Christian Association*, May 25, 2015. http://www.britishpakistanichristians.co.uk/blog/tag/Gulshan_Ravi/.

Cohen, Stephen P. *The Idea of Pakistan*. Washington, DC: Brookings Institution, 2004.

Crimi, Frank. "To Jail a Down's Syndrome Girl." *Front Page Magazine*, August 23, 2012. http://www.frontpagemag.com/2012/frank-crimi/to-jail-a-downs-syndrome-girl/.

CTS Admin. "Crucial Time for Christians in Pakistan after the Churches Attacked in Youhanabad Lahore." *Christians' True Spirit*, March 31, 2015. http://christiantruespirit.com/?p=89.

Dictionary.com. "Extremism." http://dictionary.reference.com/browse/extremism.

Fazl-ud-din, Joshua. *The Future of Christians in Pakistan*. Lahore: Punjabi Darbar, 1949.

Gabriel, Theodore. *Christian Citizens of an Islamic State: The Pakistan Experience*. Aldershot, UK: Ashgate, 2007.

George, Naseem, and Aftab Alexander. "Pakistan: Mob attacks on Shanti Nagar." *Human Rights Solidarity* 7:1 (1997). http://www.hrsolidarity.net/mainfile.php/1997vol07no01/237/.

Gledhill, Ruth. "Michael Nazir-Ali: Christians in Pakistan Are 'Sitting Ducks' for Terrorist Attack." *Christian Today*, March 18, 2015. http://www.christiantoday.com/article/michael.nazir.ali.christians.in.pakistan.are.sitting.ducks.for.terrorist.attacks/50239.htm.

Haider, Mateen. "Mob Lynching Is 'Worst Kind of Terrorism,' Says Nisar." *Dawn*, March 18, 2015. http://www.dawn.com/news/1170157.

"High-Profile Blasphemy Cases in the Last 63 Years." *Dawn*, December 8, 2010. http://www.dawn.com/news/589587/high-profile-blasphemy-cases-in-the-last-63-years.

Isserof, Ami. "Abul Ala Maududi." *Encyclopedia of the Middle East*. December 20, 2008. http://mideastweb.org/Middle-East-Encyclopedia/abul-ala-maududi.htm.

Jillani, Shahzeb. "Pakistan Christian Community Living in Fear after Mob Killing." *BBC News*, November 8, 2014. http://www.bbc.co.uk/news/world-asia-29956115.

Kaleem, Jaweed. "Religious Minorities in Pakistan Struggle but Survive amid Increasing Persecution." *Huffington Post*,. June 20, 2014. www.huffingtonpost.com/2014/02/10/religious-minorities-pakistan_n_4734016.html.

Kellner, Mark A. "Pakistan Tops New List of Religious Freedom Abusers, Panel Says." *Desert News*, May 1, 2014. http://national.deseretnews.com/article/1395/pakistan-tops-new-list-of-religious-freedom-abusers-pane l-says.html.

Khan, Fareed. "On Trial for Blasphemy, Two Christian Brothers Murdered in Pakistan." *AsiaNews*, July 19, 2010. http://www.asianews.it/news-en/On-trial-for-blasphemy,-two-Christian-brothers-murdered-in-Faisalabad-18977.html.

Kharal, Asad. "Looking Back: Not a Single Person Convicted for Gojra Riots." *The Express Tribune*, March 10, 2013. http://tribune.com.pk/story/518585/looking-back-not-a-single-person-convicted-for-gojra-riots/.

Kumar, Anuragh. "Now Bible Faces Blasphemy Charges in Pakistan." *Christian Post*, June 3, 2011. http://www.christianpost.com/news/now-bible-faces-blasphemy-charges-in-pakistan-50789/.

Liebman, Charles S. "Extremism as a Religious Norm." *Journal for the Scientific Study of Religion* 22:1 (1983) 75–86. http://users.clas.ufl.edu/kenwald/pos6292/liebman.pdf.

Lipton, Edward P., ed. *Religious Freedom in Asia*. New York: Nova Science, 2002. http://www.thereligionofpeace.com/Quran/009-friends-with-christians-jews.htm.

Maudūdī, Sayyid Abul A'la. "Meaning of Jihad." In *Let Us Be Muslims*, edited by Khurram Murad, 285–92. Leicester: Islamic Foundation, 1985.

Nazir-Ali, Michael. *Mission and Dialogue: Proclaiming the Gospel Afresh in Every Age*. London: SPCK, 1995.

———. "Persecution of Pakistan's Christians by Fanatical Islam is a Betrayal of Jinnah and Founding Fathers." *International Business Times*. June 12, 2015. http://www.ibtimes.co.uk/persecution-pakistans-christians-by-fanatical-islam-betrayal-jinnah-founding-fathers-1505766.

———. *The Unique and Universal Christ: Jesus in a Plural World*. Milton Keynes, UK: Paternoster, 2012.

"Nurses Killed in an Attack on Christian Hospital." *The Telegraph*, August 9, 2004. http://www.telegraph.co.uk/news/1403992/Nurses-killed-in-attack-on-Christian-hospital.html.

"Pakistan: 13 Year Old Boy Set on Fire for Being Christian." *Independent Catholic News*, April 13, 2015. http://www.indcatholicnews.com/news.php?viewStory=27193.

"Pakistan City Tense after 'Blaspheming' Christians Shot Dead." *BBC News*, July 20, 2010. http://www.bbc.co.uk/news/world-south-asia-10696762.

"Pakistani Christians Moving to Foreign Countries Out of Fear." *Deccan Chronicle*, July 15, 2014. http://www.deccanchronicle.com/140715/world-neighbours/article/pakistani-christians-moving-foreign-countries-out-fear.

"Pakistani Couple Get Death Sentences for Blasphemy." *BBC News*, April 5, 2014. http://www.bbc.co.uk/news/world-asia-26901433.

"Pakistan's Minority Population Is Shrinking." *Union of Catholic Asian News*, June 25, 2021. https://www.ucanews.com/news/pakistans-minority-population-is-shrink ing/53801.

Parshall, Janet. "How Do You Define an Extremist?" *Christian Post*, April 15, 2013. http://www.christianpost.com/news/how-do-you-define-an-extremist-93956/.

"Qur'an, Hadith and Scholars: Friendship with Non-Islam." *WikiIslam*. May 21, 2002. http://wikiislam.net/wiki/Qur%27an,_Hadith_and_Scholars:Friendship_with_Non-Muslims#Ibn_Kathir.

Rahman, Atika. "JUI-S Urges SC to Ban Bible within 30 Days." *The Express Tribune*, June 9, 2011. http://tribune.com.pk/story/185452/jui-s-urges-sc-to-ban-bible-threatens-consequences/.

Rhode, David. "Gunman Kills 6 in a Christian School in Pakistan." *New York Times*, August 6, 2002. http://www.nytimes.com/2002/08/06/world/gunmen-kill-6-at-a-christian-school-in-pakistan.html.

Roelle, Patrick J., Sr. *Christians Under Siege*. Bloomington, IN: AuthorHouse, 2009.

"Sawan Masih: Pakistani Christian Gets Death Penalty for Blasphemy." *BBC News*, March 28, 2014. http://www.bbc.co.uk/news/world-asia-26781731.

Shahbazi, Ammar. "Was Jinnah's Promise to the Minorities Honoured?" *The News*, December 25, 2012. http://www.thenews.com.pk/Todays-News-4–150305-Was-Jinnah%C3%A2%C2%80%C2%99s-promise-to-the-minorities-honoured.

Singh, David Emmaneul. "Integrative Political Ideology of Mawlana Mawdudi and Islamisation of the Muslim Masses in the Indian Subcontinent." *South Asia Journal of South Asian Studies* 33:1 (2000): 129–48.

Sookhdeo, Patrick. *A People Betrayed: The Impact of Islamization on the Christian Community in Pakistan*. Fearn, Scotland: Christian Focus/Isaac, 2002.

Taylor, LaTonya. "Bloody Sunday." *Christianity Today*, March 1, 2002. http://www.christianitytoday.com/ct/2002/marchweb-only/3–25–33.0.html.

Ul-Anjum, Munir. "The Role of Christians in the Freedom Movement of Pakistan: An Appraisal." *Pakistan Journal of Social Studies* 32:2 (2012) 437–43.

Walsh, Declan. "Attack Leaves Churches Gutted and Religious Minorities Living in Fear." *The Guardian*. November 28, 2005. http://www.theguardian.com/world/2005/nov/28/pakistan.declanwalsh.

13

Working for the Common Good

PACKIAM T. SAMUEL

The concept of working for the common good has come into common usage in recent years. Rather than defining a situation in terms of *problems*—such as problems of racialism, tribalism, or communalism—an attempt is instead being made to focus on the *opportunities* for building a united and tolerant community. There has also been a shift away from conceiving such a united society in terms of a majority's patronizing acceptance of its neighboring minorities; "integration" is a self-defeating notion if it inhibits the survival and further development of diverse traditions; "tolerance" is an empty boast if it cannot extend, however taxingly, to others' stubborn desire for insulation and even to their intolerance and fanaticism. Community is forged not from uniformity but from potentially enriching, albeit also potentially destroying, diversity.

The dreaming and the hard work involved in building better community relationships have two main thrusts. First, there are those with a smaller vision of community; they work for the betterment of their own tradition's social, cultural, and religious heritage. Second, there are those who have a wider, sometimes nebulous but sometimes prophetic vision of community: they work for cooperation between the various communities toward the realization of a new concept of community. If the former group can degenerate into self-seeking communalism, the second can slip into impatient and impoverishing syncretism. Both groups can lose momentum for unity if they are impatient with each other and refuse to recognize that they have a mutually supportive function. The wider community cannot exist without the contribution of the various particular communities, large and small; and those particular communities will have nothing to contribute unless they can catch a glimpse of how others stand in need of them.

The tensions and hostilities in society need to be analyzed, not so much in terms of the inherently bogus or at least short-sighted criteria of race or nation, but much more in terms of an aspiration to draw on the riches of many mutually respectful traditions and to work toward achieving a microcosm of the racial and cultural diversity that is part of the human condition. It must then often be in the fields of intellectual, technical, and physical partnership in the solution of *practical* questions that growth may occur toward some sense of *spiritual* communication participation and wider contribution.

It may be that the time is ripe for a new initiative of interreligious contribution to the needs in our societies. Such an interreligious initiative would not be intended as a substitute for the work of existing secular or religious agencies; it might, however, help revive some such agencies, especially if the new interreligious group could work inside of or in close cooperation with the earlier agencies.

The integrity of the existing communities must be respected, but a determination to participate in building a new sense of community need not be incompatible with that. An openness to each other as adherents of great and related religious worldviews, and still more urgently, perhaps, an openness to our countless and increasingly numerous fellow humans who deny or do not know any religious outlook, will help to create a new sense of community. Today we wish to move beyond communalist relationships toward the collaboration of communities in the building of one community, working with each other but also, in the case of Christians and Muslims, with a vivid sense of working together with and in obedience to God.

COMPETITION OR COOPERATION

The tensions and hostilities of past and even recent history have often made it difficult to conceive of real *cooperation* between Christians and

Muslims. Muslims in the Philippines or Chinese Christians in Indonesia, Muslims in Cyprus or Christians in Turkey, Muslims in Uganda or Christians in eastern Nigeria: all these communities have fresh memories of real or imagined discrimination; the real reasons for the friction may have been political, economic, or tribal. But the fact that a religious frontier lay along the same line of friction meant that it was easy to interpret the differences between them as religious. It is therefore remarkable and encouraging to hear of new ventures, however small, to restore a sense of brotherhood between estranged Christians and Muslims.

Between active hostility and active cooperation, there is often the insidious stage of *competition*. Whether at the level of building ever grander churches and mosques within spitting distance of each other, duplicating educational and health facilities to ensure that each community can be self-sufficient, or missionary competition for the spiritual scalp of the animist or adherent of traditional religion, energies are being diverted from serving one's fellow man and from serving God toward serving one's own sense of personal or communal pride. Christians and Muslims, working and preaching in competition with each other, sometimes give the impression that they are sharing about God with the world. One may ask whether it would not be truer to recognize that God shares his mercy and love with all people and that the missionary's task is to show that God knows us before we ever knew him. Conversion is not the process of virtuoso indoctrination by a Christian or Muslim preacher, but a man or woman's turning to God because they realize that he has turned toward them.

If we may reject competition as a form of human pride, we must also be critical of the sort of cooperation that is little more than a self-indulgent feeling of *camaraderie*. A cooperation that will endure will not be a mood of wishful thinking, do-gooding, or ecumenical euphoria; it will be a sense of working together with each other and with God, obedient to God's purposes for human brotherhood and sustained by his reconciling power.

The forms of work into which Christians and Muslims may together be led are various. They may be colleagues as doctors or nurses in state hospitals, in Christian hospitals, or in Muslim hospitals. They may teach together, or they may be fellow students in schools and colleges. They may work together in the same docks, on the same building site, or in the same fields. Sometimes, of course, there may be tensions. Yet, while such shared professional or domestic relationships may be difficult, this does not mean that they are automatically to be discouraged or frowned upon. New patterns of mutual respect and partnership learned in such contexts may make a visionary contribution to society at large.

OUR MUTUAL NEED AND OTHERS' NEED OF US

Muslim and Christian participants in wider interreligious conversations have discovered and illuminated the recognition of a possible *mutual need*, not only in terms of past history, but also in the present and future. Yet this is not only a need for each other in building a new community. Adherents of world religions are becoming a dwindling minority against proponents of secular ideologies. Perhaps if we are honest with ourselves, we shall admit that people of deeply held and ongoing faith have always been a minority; perhaps we must accept our minority role as within God's inscrutable purposes, while also recognizing our responsibility to others as all the more urgent.

As we see the way in which it is God who sends and directs people in mission, and the way in which it is he, again, who converts men to himself, we recall our duty in both the Christian and Muslim traditions to preach and to teach but to do so in such a way that the hearer may freely appropriate for himself or herself the implications of the message. As Christians and Muslims, we have much to learn from each other about patterns of obedience to God's call to us to testify of our faith.

It is at a still more elementary level, however, that it seems to me that Christians and Muslims most urgently need to work together, namely in the delicate area of young peoples' religious education; it should, of course, be borne in mind that religious education can be widely defined to include religious interpretations of history, politics, sociology, and science. It should also be borne in mind that for many modern theorists of education and for many theologians, religious education is not to be understood in terms of indoctrination or inculcation but rather in terms of guiding a student to discover what is true for himself. There may be a place for a somewhat more dogmatic approach to religious education within a church or Muslim association, etc. If religious education can be conceived and implemented in this more open way, it becomes possible and enriching to teach young people about the religion of their neighbors without imposing any relativist and syncretistic—or, alternatively, disparaging and triumphalist—innuendoes.

The lessons in patience, sensitivity, communication, and cooperation that Christians and Muslims may learn as they deepen the relationships between their two communities are lessons that they may go on to share with others. It is not only our own communities that stand in such need of such transforming relationships; it is the whole world. If we who have so much in common are content to remain apart and, still worse, to allow our differences to harden, then we will have failed in our duty to our own communities, to each other, to the wider world, and to God.

Our talk of concepts of human brotherhood will seem so hypocritical if we cannot be seen to stand scrupulously for religious freedom, both in the defensive sense of allowing each to do what seems right to him and in the more constructive sense of creating a climate of opinion where men are liberated from social constraints and enabled to appropriate their religious allegiance with integrity of conscience. The Qur'anic dictum that "There is no compulsion in religion" will guide our two communities into a more free and glad sharing of their riches with each other and with the whole world. In working together, in witnessing together to new generations and to all our other neighbors, we may grow closer to that *community* of mankind.

For many of us there is a still more pressing reason why we should intensify deliberate efforts to meet each other. Beyond the sense of a common humanity and the inter-involvement of Christians and Muslims in history, there is a desire—belated for some of us—to honor together our conscious dependence upon God in a world that often seems to deny him. We wish together to obey God in the place of our fellow men and in the pursuit of justice and peace.

Some of us also wish to find a theological and, on occasion, perhaps, a devotional framework for our mutual recognition and awareness. There is rich promise in trying to bind together both the social and the spiritual ties that can unite us on a common basis. We know that we have sometimes widely differing political expectations and motivations and sometimes widely differing theological language and doctrine between our respective traditions. Yet, we have found that as we meet we can be renewed in our commitment to God and our fellow beings.

OUR HOPES IN THE DIALOGUE

It has been established that dialogue is not an attempt to suppress differences but rather to explore them frankly and self-critically together with those who come from another tradition. Rather than being satisfied with the lowest common denominator, we must confront sometimes poignant points of tension. One must hope that we can shed all caricatures of each other's social and theological positions. Our image of each other is often based on outmoded and, by now, reformulated positions. We can endeavor to retrieve more positive evaluations of each other. While we see that the same language or symbols could convey different meanings to our respective communities, we could also hope to clarify how fundamental or how incidental those differences are. Such mutual discovery can lead us to a better awareness of what the authentic issues for our dialogue are.

In approaching these issues in this manner, we accept a clear individual responsibility. We must test for ourselves whatever emerged as a claimant upon us. We do not invite others to undertake something that some of us have not already tried or have not pledged ourselves to try. We dare to hope that such faithful experience may contribute not only to the renewal of our personal commitment to God but also to that of our respective communities.

We see that there is a challenge from the secular world to our religious communities that they should never again prove to be the instruments of mutual hatred and division in society. Only if we heed this may we, as religious men, challenge others to ask ultimate questions of life and death, of truth and goodness, of forgiveness and responsibility, of true community and suffering. For our dialogue is not only for our personal enrichment and for the enrichment of our mutual relationships; it is something that we wish to contribute to the world and to offer to God.

GUIDING PRINCIPLES FOR OUR DIALOGUE

We do not desire to confine our conversation and our collaboration to a group of experts. We feel an obligation to help make possible a wider spirit and practice of dialogue in our communities. We recognize that different situations call for different sensitivities, but that certain irreducible principles should be respected. The implications of these principles will be particular to various contexts and will need to be patiently and practically worked out.

A. *Frank Witness*: We do not ask each other to suppress or conceal our convictions. In dialogue with one another, each should bear witness of his motives to his fellows and to God. This frank witness can help to remove complacency, suspicion, or unspoken fears.

B. *Mutual Respect*: We believe that mutual respect is a necessary principle for our dialogue. This does not involve a stale coexistence of "live and let live," but a sensitive regard to the partner's scruples and convictions, a sympathy for his difficulties, and an admiration for his achievements. We should avoid all invidious comparisons of strength in our tradition with weakness in the other, of the ideal in one with the actuality in the other.

C. *Religious Freedom*: We should be scrupulous about our protection of religious liberty. This involves not only the rights of any religious minority, but also the rights of each individual.

WHAT HAVE WE FOUND IN OUR MEETING TOGETHER?

Talking together with frankness and mutual respect and aspiring to create conditions for full religious liberty and freedom of conscience, we have explored several major theological themes. Written papers and spoken contributions from members of both religious traditions have begun to show us a wider vision of world community, of our understanding of revelation, and of our role as religious men and women in many different nation-states.

We recommend all these issues for further study. Ideally this should be undertaken in partnership between a Christian and a Muslim group or individuals. We believe that theological and spiritual renewal can prepare us for social renewal.

A. *World Community*: Muslims and Christians are called upon to a wider vision of community, including interracial, intercultural, and international. This must often be tested and realized at the local level, where religious pluralism provides a microcosm of the world's diversity. The quality of openness and cooperation in such local situations should make a vital contribution to the extension of interreligious harmony and international justice.

We recognize the fact that it is desirable for a community to dedicate itself to the welfare of a focal situation or nation. There may also be instances where a religious community must exercise its critical faculty against a local political or socioeconomic framework that is narrowly nationalistic and hinders the establishment of world community, justice, and human dignity. Christians and Muslims must actively contribute to redressing the wrongs of society, even at the expense of their own vested interests.

We expressed our very deep concern about many situations that are a threat to world peace and create tensions among religious communities. We noted in particular the human tragedy of the Middle East and the many injustices against the people of Palestine, for which the world at large bears responsibility. We hope that this crisis will be solved in the spirit of compassion and justice.

B. *Revelation*: In our attempt to be obedient to Truth, our respective religious communities are wrestling with their understanding of revelation. We are aware of the suspicions and doubts of many modern men and the rapidly decreasing impact of traditional language and symbolism. Within our religious traditions there is scope for reconsidering many of our theological and legal constructions; in this we should ensure continuity with the past, notably with our authoritative sources.

C. *Religion and Society*: Dialogue does not take place outside a given political and socioeconomic context. We deliberately avoided insisting upon a desideratum of a secular state or a religious state as being the more conducive setting for growth toward world community and obedience to divine revelation. The conviction of our conference members was that social justice, spirituality, and dialogue can and should be pursued in many differing political and cultural contexts.

Our involvement in society is part of our duty toward God. Some Muslims and Christians can speak of being coworkers with God in making history and in transforming society. We are aware of how we are confronted in new ways with the issue of religion in society. How far have our traditions failed our fellow men? How far do they hold new promise? We work together for self-critical reevaluation of our roles and of our mutual relationships.

D. *Our Devotional Practice*: Our theological and socioeconomic concerns need the spiritual basis and eschatological dimension of worship and prayer. Worship and prayer demand of us more than definitions, for they are the experiences of witnessing God and confronting the world. If our belief in the mercy and the justice of God impels us to work in the affairs of the world, how can Christians and Muslims relate their spiritual life to man's demands for justice, brotherhood, and human dignity?

WHAT PRACTICAL STEPS DO WE SUGGEST?

We endorse again a variety of situations in which Muslims and Christians live, talk, think, and work together. The dialogue may well carry political or social implications that must be consciously faced. Yet no local situation is completely immune from the possibility of it providing an inspiring example for men in other situations across the world, nor yet from the possibility of its discouraging and embarrassing those others. Accordingly, we propose a catalog of practical steps, some of which may be opportune in some situations but not in others. Yet in our worldwide concerns and in our sense of worldwide community, we desire to be alert to as many possible ways forward as there may be.

A. *In our national and local communities*: Christians and Muslims can and do cooperate with all their neighbors, as well as with each other, actively and prayerfully in nation-building, in ensuring human and religious rights, in struggling for justice and peace. They may work as colleagues in teams engaged in rural development, in literacy campaigns, or in medical clinics. They may together try to meet the problems of alienated youth through more patient response to their protests and through providing counseling services or recreational facilities. Deliberate and conscious collaboration between Muslims and Christians, and with others, in such contexts may sometimes produce tensions, but it may also contribute to our mutual reconciliation.

B. *Within our own religious communities*: In working for the removal of our prejudices and for the furthering of a deeper mutual appreciation, we reaffirm the urgency of avoiding all polemic and of providing textbooks, teacher training, and seminary programs, which should be worked out in consultation with each other. We welcome the emerging willingness for religious communities' gifts of material and practical aid, not to be channeled through a particular religious community but given to the whole community, wherever the need is greatest.

C. *In further interreligious dialogue*: We determined to keep in touch with the results of local and international dialogues, and to work together, not least on our own home situations, in order to establish theological, missiological, and societal principles for our dialogue and to find more opportunities for dialogue. By dialogue we have in view not only meetings such as this, but also social collaboration and intellectual cross-fertilization.

FURTHER READING

Aminrazavi, Mehdi. "Philosophia Perennis and Scientia Sacra in a Postmodern World." In *The Philosophy of Seyyed Hossein Nasr*, edited by Lewis Edwin Hahn, Randall E. Auxier, and Lucian W. Stone Jr. Library of Living Philosophers 28. Chicago: Open Court, 2001.

Baharudin, M., and Muhammad Aqil Luthfan. "The Transcendent Unity behind the Diversity of Religions and Religiosity in the Perspective of Perennial Philosophy and its Relevance to the Indonesian Context." *Walisongo: Jurnal Penelitian Sosial Keagamaan* 25:2 (2017) 325–60.

Chittick, William C. The *Sufi Path of Knowledge: Ibn al-'Arabi's Metaphysics of Imagination*. Albany: SUNY Press, 1989.

Clarke, J. J. *Oriental Enlightenment: The Encounter between Asian and Western Thought*. London: Routledge, 1997.

Coomaraswamy, A. K. "The Pertinence of Philosophy." In *Contemporary Indian Philosophy*, edited by S. Radhakrishnan and J. H. Muirhead. London: Allen & Unwin, 1952.

D'Souza, Diane. *Evangelism, Dialogue, Reconciliation: The Transformation Journey of the Henry Martyn Institute*. Hyderabad, India: HMI, 1998.

Eliade, Mircea. *The Quest: History and Meaning in Religion*. Chicago: Chicago University Press, 1969.

Gangadean, Ashok K. "The Quest for the Universal Global Science." In *The Philosophy of Seyyed Hossein Nasr*, edited by Lewis Edwin Hahn, Randall E. Auxier, and Lucian W. Stone Jr. Library of Living Philosophers 28. Chicago: Open Court, 2001.

Jawad, Haifaa. "Seyyed Hossein Nasr and the Study of Religion in Contemporary Society." *American Journal of Islamic Social Sciences* 22:2 (2005) 49–68.

King, Sallie B. "The Philosophia Perennis and the Religions of the World." In *The Philosophy of Seyyed Hossein Nasr*, edited by Lewis Edwin Hahn, Randall E. Auxier, and Lucian W. Stone Jr. Library of Living Philosophers 28. Chicago: Open Court, 2001.

Subhan, John A. "Henry Martyn Institute of Islamic Studies, Hyderabad—Its History and Work." *Al-Basheer: The Bulletin of Christian Institute of Islamic Studies* 1:2 (April–June 1972) 11–26.

Taylor, J. B. "Community Relationship between Christians and Muslims." *Al-Basheer: The Bulletin of Christian Institute of Islamic Studies* 2:1 (January–March 1973) 37–42.

Lings, Martin. *What Is Sufism?* Los Angeles: University of California Press, 1975.

Merton, Thomas. *Mystics and Zen Masters*. New York: Farrar, Strauss & Giroux, 1967.

Sharma, Arvind. "Revisioning Classical Hinduism through Philosophia Perennis." In *The Philosophy of Seyyed Hossein Nasr*, edited by Lewis Edwin Hahn, Randall E. Auxier, and Lucian W. Stone Jr. Library of Living Philosophers 28. Chicago: Open Court, 2001.

Sharpe, E. J. "Some Problems of Method in the Study of Religion." *Religion* 1 (1971) 1–14.

14

The Future of Muslim-Christian Dialogue

A Reflection on the Past

WAGEEH MIKHAIL

INTRODUCTION

Islam appeared in the Arab region in the seventh century CE in a context that was distinctly pluralistic, both ethnically and religiously. At the time, Christians formed the majority of the region's residents, in addition to a number of Jewish communities, as well as many who practiced ancient Eastern religions. Muslims found themselves at the heart of numerous religious conversations, especially with Christians and Jews, the so-called *Ahl al-Kitāb*, or "People of the Book." Both the large degree of similarities between Islam and Christianity, as well as the essential, fundamental differences between them, were an important reason for these conversations. These conversations reached their peak in the first era of the Abbasid Empire, at a time when Christians, Muslims, Jews, Sabians, and others mingled. They would gather for theological conversation at meetings in which they discussed matters concerning their beliefs with great freedom and respect.

These Abbasid gatherings played a crucial role in enriching the quality of the conversations taking place. In these meetings, many different people would gather and each one would take to discussing the truthfulness of his denomination and creed. There was no threatening, nor derision. Precedence was given to reason and to logic. We read, for example, in the *Biographical Dictionary of the Spanish Arabs*, which dates back to the eleventh century and was written by Abū ʿAbdallāh ibn Muḥammad al-Humaydī (d. 1095), about a man named ʿUmar Aḥmad ibn Muḥammad ibn Sajdī. It reads: "He visited Baghdad at the end of the tenth century, shortly after the death of the philosopher and Christian apologist Yaḥyá ibn ʿUḍayy"[1] (d. 974). During his stay there, ʿUmar twice attended the gatherings of the city's most famous Muslim scholars, but then vowed never to attend one again. He was shocked by what he found there. He wrote about it, providing this description of his experience:

> At the first session I attended I witnessed a meeting which included every kind of group: Sunni Muslims and heretics, and all kinds of infidels: Majūs, materialists, atheists, Jews and Christians. Each group had a leader who would speak on its doctrine and debate about it. Whenever one of these leaders arrived, from whichever of the groups he came, the assembly rose up for him, standing on their feet until he would sit down, then they would take their seats after he was seated. When the meeting was jammed with its participants, and they saw that no one else was expected, one of the infidels said, "You have all agreed to the debate, so the Muslims should not argue against us on the basis of their scripture, nor on the basis of the sayings of their prophet, since we put no credence in these things, and we do not acknowledge him. Let us dispute with one another only on the basis of arguments from reason, and what observation and deduction will support." Then they would all say, "Agreed." Abū 'Umar said, "When I heard that, I did not return to that meeting. Later someone told me there was to be another meeting for discussion, so I went to it and I found them engaging in the same practices as their colleagues. So, I stopped going to the meetings of the disputants, and I never went back.[2]

When confronted with this very significant text, we cannot miss an important truth about the eastern Arab world during the Middle Ages. As we see here, the Middle East was very diverse, the home to many

1. Quoted from Griffith, *Church in the Shadow of the Mosque*, 63–64.
2. Griffith, *Church in the Shadow of the Mosque*, 64.

denominations and religions. The followers of each sect defended their doctrine and presented arguments and evidence for its soundness. By doing so, they entered into dialogue with those who differed with them. These conversations resulted in the appearance of numerous Islamic theological schools of thought. The *Mu' tazilah* played an important role in formulating Islamic thought during the Abbasid caliphate. At the same time, many Arab Christian authors took it upon themselves to explain Christian doctrine with the common theological vocabulary and imagery they shared with their Muslim and Jewish counterparts—the impact of their context is absolutely clear in these texts. Look, for instance, at how this anonymous author wrote this prayer in the preamble to his book on the oneness of God:

> Praise be to God,
> before whom nothing was,
> and who was before everything,
> after whom there is nothing,
> and He is the heir of all things,
> and to Him all things return;
> who kept the knowledge of all things,
> by His knowledge,
> and nothing but His intellects
> is sufficient for this;
> in whose knowledge is the end of all things,
> and He counts everything by His knowledge. . .
> We ask you, O God, by your mercy and power,
> that you make us to be among those who know your Truth,
> who follow your good pleasure,
> and who avoid your wrath;
> who give praise using your most beautiful names,
> and who speak using your most sublime similitudes.
> You are the merciful one, the merciful Lord of mercy.
> You sat on the throne,
> were exalted above all creatures,
> and filled all things.[3]

This text gives the reader the impression that the writer is without a doubt a Muslim. The prayer itself is full of clear Islamic—even Qur'anic!—expressions. We read, for example, expressions quoted word-for-word from the Qur'an, such as, "Open our hearts . . . your beautiful names." Additionally, there are other Islamic phrases that aren't directly derived from

3. Gibson, ed., *Arabic Version of the Acts of the Apostles*, 2.

the Qur'an. Regardless, the prayer either contains direct quotes from the Qur'anic text or is full of implicit allusions taken from Islamic thought. This prayer has a distinctly Islamic tint; its wording resembles the way Muslims pray, even today! What's exciting about this is that the prayer isn't Muslim at all, but rather the prayer from the preamble of an anonymous Arab Christian author's book from the early ninth century. It was the introduction to his theological treatise entitled *On the Triune Nature of God*. This work is preserved in a manuscript at the Monastery of Saint Catherine and written in approximately the year 800.

Moreover, what is surprising is that the Arab Christian author sees no issue with using these Islamic expressions in a Christian book, for the terms used in the Qur'an—Islamic terms—were a genuine part of his identity. That's why, when he wanted to present a supplication to God before writing his book on Christian doctrine, it was only natural that his language had clear traces of Islamic influence. Interreligious dialogue calls for "each religion to redefine its theological vocabulary so that it conforms to the vocabulary of other religions."[4] In his commentary on this text, S. K. Samir says:

> The author is impregnated with the Qur'anic culture. He does not live in a "Christian ghetto," nor does he use what some might call a "Christian Arabic" vocabulary or style, and much less a "Christian Arabic grammar." He shares with Muslims . . . the common Arabic culture, which carries many Qur'anic words and expressions, and a certain style and even some Muslim thoughts.[5]

The first century of the Abbasid era saw an unrivaled movement of interaction between Christian theological scholars and Muslim intellectuals. It is even said this was one of the richest periods of Middle Eastern history generally, and Islamic history specifically. On the one hand, the Middle East witnessed an academic revolution under Abbasid rule, as the rulers strongly encouraged striving after knowledge. The "House of Wisdom," *Dār al-Ḥikmah*, was the first school that specialized in translation, and all those who worked there attached importance to the translation of Greek and Syriac intellectual and philosophical heritage into Arabic. There is no doubt that *Dār al-Ḥikmah* had a massive impact on this intellectual movement. It's well known historically that Arab Christians were

4. Borrans and al-Nayfar, *Mustaqbal al-ḥiwār al-Islāmī al-Masīḥī*, 136.
5. Samir, "Earliest Arab Apology for Christianity," 109.

leaders in the translation movement in *Dār al-Ḥikmah*—we have only to mention names such as Ḥunayn ibn Isḥaq, Isḥaq ibn Ḥunayn, Ḥubaysh ibn al-Ḥasan al-Aʿsam al-Dimashqī, and others to show their pivotal role.[6] It's only rational that this intellectual openness would cause doctrinal divisions between followers of these different religions, especially Christianity and Islam, given the crucial nature of preaching in Christianity and the Islamic *daʿwah.* The testimony of history shows that it was natural that the Christian-Muslim dialogue was colored by disagreement, as Muslims saw Christianity as deviating from the truth. Some Muslim scholars took to writing books to refute Christian doctrine using reason and tradition. Among the oldest of these works are *In Response to the Naṣārá* (the Christians) by the Zaydī Imām al-Qāsim ibn Ibrāhīm (d. 860),[7] *In Response to the Various Sects of the Naṣārá* by ʿAlī ibn Rabn al-Ṭabarī (d. approx. 870),[8] *In Response to the Naṣārá* by al-Jāḥiẓ (d. 869),[9] the letter by Abū ʿĪsá al-Warrāq (d. approx. 861) entitled "Refutation of the Christian Sects,"[10] and others.[11] At the same time that all of these Islamic rebuttals called "responses" were being penned, Christians, in their turn, responded to these responses, giving the title "The Proof" or "The Book of Proof" to their responses. It is well known that a large number of Christian theologians used the title "Proof" for their writings, such as: Boṭros al-Bayt Ra'sī (mid-ninth century),[12] Yaḥyá ibn ʿUdayy (d. 974),[13] Īliyā al-Nuṣaybīnī,[14] Īshūʿāb ibn Malkūn (d. 1049),[15] and ʿAmmār al-Baṣrī.[16] There is no doubt that *āyah* 111 of *Sūrat al-Baqarah* was at

6. See for example Baum, "Age of the Arabs," 42–83.

7. Ibrāhīm, *Ar-Radd 'alā-n-Naṣārā*, 301–64; cf. Madelung, "Al-Qāsim and Christian Theology," 35–44.

8. Khalifé and Kutsch, eds. "Ar-Radd 'alā-n-Naṣārā de aṭ-Ṭabari.»

9. Muḥammad 'Abd Allah al-Sharqawī, *Al-Mukhtār fī al-Radd 'alā al-Nasārā li-Abī 'Uthmān al-Jāḥiẓ* (Beirut, Lebanon: Dār al-Jīl, 1991); al-Jāḥiẓ, *Rasā'il al-Jāḥiẓ*, ed. 'Abd al-Salām Mahmūd Hārūn (Cairo, Egypt: Maktaba al-Khanijī, 1964).

10. Thomas, ed. and trans., *Anti-Christian Polemic in Early Islam*; cf. Thomas, ed. and trans., *Early Muslim Polemic against Christianity.*

11. For more, see the work of 'Abd al-Majīd al-Sharafī, *Al-Fikr al-Islāmī fī al-Radd 'ala al-Naṣārā ilā Nihāyat al-Qarn al-Rābiʿ/al-'Āshr* (Tunis, Tunisia: al-Dār al-Tunisia lil-Nashr, 1986).

12. Cachia and Watt, eds. *Top of Form Eutychius of Alexandria, Kitāb al-Burhān*, 192, 193, 209, and 210.

13. Platti, "Une Cosmologie Chrétienne."

14. Horst, *Metropoliten Elias von Nisibis Buch.*

15. Sbath, *Vingt traités philosophiques et apologétiques*, 152–58.

16. See Makhlouf, "Burhān," 281–96.

the forefront of these Christian theologians' minds, as though they were saying, "Our books are proof of our truth; that we are right." But unfortunately, it is not within the scope of this study to elaborate on this kind of Christian-Muslim dialogue, because the goal of this paper is to draw out lessons from this rich history that can be applied to future Christian-Muslim relations.

Undoubtedly, the open-mindedness of the Muslim caliphs in the first century of the Abbasid period and their desire to acquire knowledge in science and literature opened the door for new ideas to filter in. Greek philosophical thought, both that which was translated at that time to Arabic and that which was already present in the Syriac Christians' heritage, was the common ground on which Christians and Muslims met. As a result of this fraternization, Christian theologians were faced with new questions they hadn't ever pondered. In the same way, Muslim theologians found themselves confronted with philosophical dilemmas that Christians were familiar with because of their longstanding knowledge of Greek philosophy. To get out of this, Christians came up with authentic Arabic ways of expressing Christian theology that took into account the nature of the issues related to theology and translation that Muslims brought up. Islamic scholars, in turn, referred to Greek philosophy in search of patterns and formulations that agreed with the Qur'anic text. These undertakings were not without challenges, for every Christian and Muslim theologian needed to know the other side's beliefs well. Throughout the process of formulating their ideologies, both sides displayed a high degree of eagerness and openness. Therefore, Christians knew the nature and the reasons behind the Islamic "attack" on their beliefs. Muslims also knew the different sects of Christianity and the doctrinal differences between them. Both sides entered into a logical and theological discussion that left a significant impact on their understanding of themselves and of each other, as well as on the new terms in Arabic theological vocabulary.

WHAT ABOUT THE FUTURE?

Often when people try to predict the future, and especially the future of Christian-Muslim relations, we find that some want to turn their backs on the past with the pretext of moving forward with what is new and innovative. They want to throw off a yoke that was perhaps quite heavy. This side believes that looking solely to the future is sufficient because it causes people to come up with creative ways of interacting with the new realities of the present age. The other side, meanwhile, looks to the past and practically drowns itself in it, crying over the ruins of the "good ole days." But, in my opinion, both sides are wrong. The error of the former lies in disregarding the past and failing to see its value; the error of the latter lies in living in the past. We must see how we can view the past critically and use it constructively. On the one hand, we must appreciate the past as we look toward the future. On the other hand, we cannot trap ourselves in days gone by. A balanced and critical reading of history allows us to derive useful lessons from past that help to build a better future. Based on this conviction, I would like to paint a picture of the past to highlight some important elements for us to consider for the future of Christian-Muslim relations.

A RENAISSANCE PROJECT

It would not have been possible for Christian-Muslim relations to be as we just described them if Muslims and Christians hadn't participated in a renaissance project to build Arab civilization; something that dazzled the world at that time. This renaissance project was *Bayt al-Ḥikmah*, the "House of Wisdom," which was the first school to specialize in translation. Those who worked there took care to translate Greek and Syriac intellectual and philosophical heritage into Arabic. There are different opinions regarding who the true founder of *Bayt al-Ḥikmah* was. Some argue that it was the Abbasid caliph Hārūn al-Rashīd (d. 809), who planted the first seeds of *Bayt al-Ḥikmah* in Baghdad when he established what is known as *Khizānat al-Ḥikmah*, the "Treasury of Wisdom." However, it is well known that *Bayt al-Ḥikmah* reached the height of its glory during the reign of the caliph ʿAbdallāh al-Ma'mūn (786–833), the son of Caliph al-Mahdī. He had leanings toward the *Mu' tazilah* sect, which called for a balance between scriptures and reason. This eventually led them to adopt the doctrine of the creation of the Qur'an, which caused what is known in Islamic history as *al-Miḥnah al-Kubrá*, or the "Great Tribulation."[17]

Tradition tells us that Caliph al-Ma'mūn founded *Bayt al-Ḥikmah* after seeing Aristotle in a dream, as Ibn al-Nadīm recounts for us in *al-Fihrist*. The story goes that:

17. See Rifāʿī, *'Aṣr al-Ma'mūn*, 1:295–99; cf. al-Durūbī, "al-Tarjamah wal-Taʿrīb bayna al- 'Aṣrayn al-ʿAbbāsī wal-Mamlūkī," 14–15; Mez, *al-Ḥaḍārah al-Islāmiyyah*, 80–82.

> The caliph al-Ma'mūn saw in his sleep a white man, a bit red in the face from drinking, with a wide forehead, sitting on his bed. He had the impression that he was standing in awe in front of him.
> He asked, "Who are you?"
> He said, "I am Aristotle."
> He was overjoyed and said, "Oh wiseman! May I ask a question?"
> He replied "Ask."
> Al-Ma'mūn said, "What is good?"
> He replied, "Whatever is good according to reason."
> Al-Ma'mūn asked, "Then what?"
> Aristotle responded, "What is good according to the law."
> Al-Ma'mūn asked, "Then what?"
> Aristotle replied, "What is good according to society."
> Al-Ma'mūn asked, "Then what?"
> Aristotle said, "There is no then what." That is, there is nothing else other than that.[18]

Al-Ma'mūn was convinced that religious law did not contradict reason. Therefore, he saw that strengthening this institution that specialized in translating Greek sciences would undoubtedly contribute to the advancement of knowledge and building a state on the basis of science, open to others and to new ideas. This state of affairs continued until the Mongols razed Baghdad in 1258.

It is well known historically that Arab Christians were the leaders of the translation movement in *Bayt al-Ḥikmah*. To show the critical role they played, we only have to mention figures such as Ḥunayn ibn Isḥāq, Isḥāq ibn Ḥunayn, Ḥubaysh al-Ḥasan ibn al-Aʿsam al-Dimashqī, Isṭifān (Stephen) ibn Bāsil, ibn Baṭrīq, Jāwrjiyūs (George) ibn Jibrā'īl, Yaḥyá ibn Māsawi, Qusṭā ibn Lūqā, Yaḥyá ibn Baṭrīq, Diyonīsiyus Yaʿqūb al-Ṣalībī, Yaḥyá ibn Harūn, Yaḥyá ibn ʿUdayy, and ʿAbd al-Masīḥ ʿAbdallāh ibn Nāʿimah al-Ḥumṣī.[19] It's no exaggeration to say that Arab Christians played such an essential role in *Bayt al-Ḥikmah* that it's impossible to imagine Arab civilization being established without it. However, it is important to remember that Muslims and Christians, as well as Sabians (such as Thābit ibn Qurrah) and Jews, all worked together to build Arab

18. Ibn al-Nadīm, *Al-Fihrist* (Beirut, Lebanon: Dār al-Maʿrifa, 1978), 339.

19. Samīr, *Dawr al-Masīḥīyīn fi al-ḥaḍārah al-ʿArabīyah-al-Islāmīyah*; Samir, "Christian Communities," 77–82; cf. Khalil, *Dawr al-Masīḥīyīn al-Thaqāfi fil-ʿĀlam al-ʿArabī*; Lamoreaux, *Ḥunayn ibn Isḥāq on His Galen Translations*; Treiger, "From al-Biṭrīq to Ḥunayn," 143–81.

civilization. It is therefore clear that Muslims and Christians, especially, made a great effort in building the Arab East. They did not view the doctrinal differences between the two religions, of which they were very much aware, as an impediment to this project. The primary goal of all became advancing their nation and their passion was centered on gaining knowledge and applying it.

Medical Regime for the Pilgrims to Mecca recounts anecdotes on this subject. This book was written by the Christian theologian, translator, and doctor Qusṭā ibn Lūqā after the Abbasid vizier Abū Muḥammad al-Ḥasan ibn Makhlid ibn al-Jarrāḥ (824–882) asked Qusṭā to accompany him on the Ḥajj. For reasons of which we are uncertain historically (likely having to do with his family and needing to care for his children), Qusṭā excused himself from the trip. He wrote this book instead, which is considered the first medical resource dedicated to the healthcare of pilgrims on Ḥajj. This means that what we see here is a Christian theologian being invited to accompany a friend on the Ḥajj, and he writes a work to advise on the healthcare of pilgrims on Ḥajj![20] This book isn't a theological treatise, but a medical book discussing the medical principles one must follow on the Ḥajj.

Today, as we look toward a better future for Christian-Muslim relations in countries that includes all people without discrimination based on religion, race, gender, or color, we must define the framework for a renaissance project. This project must rival *Bayt al-Ḥikmah* in its glory. It must enable our countries to overcome this pitiful state that conjures up images of violence whenever Christian-Muslim relations are brought up. It must enable our countries to arrive at a world in which each citizen enjoys his rights and performs his duties. I am not asking us to repeat history; that we copy *Bayt al-Ḥikmah*. Copies are usually nothing more than a poor imitation of the original. However, I do hope that we can come together around a common vision we seek to accomplish, a project we endeavor to accomplish for the good of our countries. How can we take pride in the civilization that Christian and Muslims shared in building in the past—a civilization that enlightened the whole world in the Middle Ages—when many Muslims and Christians in the developing world today are illiterate? How can we take pride in the Muslim and Christian doctors in the Abbasid period, like the Bukhtyashūʿ family and ibn Sīnā, and be resigned to the fact that a high percentage of Muslims and Christians in

20. Bos, ed., *Qusta ibn Luqa's Medical Regime.*

the developing world are suffering from life-threatening diseases? Christians and Muslims must search for a shared renaissance project that will benefit their countries, relieve people of their suffering, and give them the chance for a better life.

If Christians and Muslims were to share in a renaissance project, it might strengthen good relations between the two communities and promote a spirit of nationalism. Or perhaps it might be more realistic for Christians and Muslims in a specific geographical area to work together on a project to raise awareness about an issue (or a set of issues) that matter to people's everyday lives. Working together is an important value, and both sides can and should affirm it. The number of theological similarities between Christianity and Islam will play an important role in accomplishing a renaissance project that is beneficial to people. Both religions share many values, which could be used as a jumping off point or as common ground for building a better future.

These kinds of projects can overcome one of the most important obstacles to Christians and Muslims coming together—the fact that the classical conversation between the two sides was limited to the elite and excluded the general public. Of course, the elite have a very important part to play—there is no doubt about that. However, this issue is apparent by the way meetings for religious dialogue are confined to these groups. This limitation, which isn't grounded in the reality of the lives of the general population, gives a false impression of the nature of the dialogue, making many think that the dialogue is merely an academic luxury, a chance for a group of experts to discuss matters that are mostly impractical. This assumption is dangerous, for it detaches the dialogue from the reality of people's lives. Actually, the general population are the ones who are truly involved on a daily basis in Christian-Muslim dialogue. They are the employees in government offices who discuss (almost daily) matters related to religion. They are the businessmen, the shop owners, and the repairmen who bring up religion in their daily conversations and interactions. And yet the gap between the "elite" who call for this dialogue and the general public continues to widen.

How, then, can we allow Christian-Muslim dialogue to be limited to academic discussions between the elite, far from all of these people?

MUTUAL UNDERSTANDING

We must recognize that agreement on a renaissance project can only come about after we have reached a mutual understanding and erased all *religious illiteracy*, that is, ignorance about the other's religion. Coexistence requires understanding; those who do not get to know each other cannot coexist. If they are coerced into coexisting, there would always be quarrelling and conflict. Conversely, those who understand themselves and recognize their strengths and weaknesses are better suited to live in harmony. Thus should it be for Muslims and Christians. In terms of self-understanding, I do not see any shortcomings from either side, Christian or Muslim; our heritage is full of Christian and Islamic religious writings. Where the shortcoming lies is in understanding the other. It is often said the history of Christian-Muslim understanding is in fact a history of *mis*understanding. ʿAmmār al-Baṣrī, in what could be considered a key section of his book *The Proof*, emphasizes that Christian-Muslim mutual understanding is plagued by misunderstanding.

> We now come to what they find distasteful when we say that Christ is the Son of God. They beleaguered people with this by telling them about us, that we say that God took for Himself a female companion and a son from her. God is far too exalted for that. When we mention that God has manifested His economy in a body like ours, they distort it by making us say that He descended into the womb of Mary and limited Himself in her. When we mention that Christ was crucified, they distort this understanding to say that we impute weakness to God's [character]. And when we mention baptism, and taking the Eucharist as the Body and Blood of Christ, and our belief that our reward in the lasting world is not found in sexual intercourse or food and drink, they oppose us.[21]

Muslims have serious shortcomings in understanding Christianity, and Christians likewise fail to understand Islam. The biggest proof of this is that the vast majority of the information each side has about the other's beliefs is the result of popular folklore; it is usually superficial, incomplete, and selective. Often, we find that this knowledge is used by some Christians and Muslims to stir up controversy when speaking against the doctrines and practices of the other. The bitter truth in which most Christians and Muslims live is the partial, or shall I say selective,

21. Michel Hayek, 56–57.

knowledge of the other. About this King Ḥasan II says: "We [Christians and Muslims] often err in our understanding of one another. Occasionally in the past we opposed one another to the point of exhaustion in a number of disputes and wars. I believe that today God is calling us to change our old ways. We must respect one another and encourage one another to do good works in service of God."[22]

Erasing religious illiteracy will help to create mutual understanding. Once that happens, Muslims and Christians will realize their need to develop their religious vocabulary so that it can express understanding of the self and of the other. The prayer discussed above provides us with a contextual model that bridges between faith and reality, between the stable and the variable. We must make sure that the language used in our religious speech is understood by the other. We must make sure that we use a distinctly Arabic vocabulary in order to emphasize how deep our Arab roots go. If Muslims and Christians realized the importance of using the same terms, especially religious terms, our understanding of one another would be laudable and our dialogue beneficial. Then, many would no longer stop to define terms or to debate their meaning, but instead could dive deeper into the actual work, into a shared, collective renaissance project, far from selective language and partial knowledge.

A large number of Christians know some Qur'anic verses that they believe talk about the eternal nature of Christ, such as when the Qur'an refers to Jesus as the Word of God and a spirit from him (*Sūrat al-Nisā'* 171). They very easily bring up this verse as an indication in the Qur'an of Christ's eternality. But these same people, whose selective knowledge of the Qur'an is for apologetic purposes only, fail to see the full picture that the Qur'an paints of Christ: Qur'anic Christology. Likewise, the majority of Muslim polemicists refer to a number of verses from the Bible in which they see violence against some city of another (like in the Book of Joshua) or teachings that seem to talk of Christ as no more than a prophet (Matthew 19:17) without having a wider understanding of what the Bible says about Christ. These tendencies toward being selective in one's knowledge of the other are very dangerous. Their true danger manifests in giving the false impression of knowledge of the other's holy text. Incomplete knowledge might even be more dangerous than complete ignorance![23]

22. Quoted in Borrans and al-Nayfar, *Mustaqbal al-ḥiwār al-Islāmī al-Masīḥī*, 127.

23. See Ebeid, "Can the Qur'ān Be Read," 37–74; Swanson, "Beyond Proof Texting," 297–318.

Frequently, Christians and Muslims are ignorant of one another even though they believe themselves to be somewhat acquainted. In this case, there must be objective knowledge that calls for mutual exchange of information about human and spiritual experience, so that this work is not limited to researchers specializing in Islam or Christianity. What is needed are encounters for the sake of mutual understanding, so that each might learn about the other, not just about who he is now but also who he wants to be. It is the Christian's duty, therefore, to seek to understand Islamic culture clearly, as well as *ʿ Ilm al-Kalām* (speculative theology), and the testimonies of *Ṣūfī* mystics. The Muslim, for their part, must inquire about a Christian's culture and theology. So, those in conversation will discover the spiritual treasures of the other group and how they endeavor to incorporate them in their personal journey.[24]

INTERACTION AND THE NEED FOR CHANGE

Arab Christians had extensive knowledge of Islamic thought and the intellectual context in which they lived during the Golden Age of Islam. They knew the techniques and arguments of theologians very well, to the point that they parodied them to defend their theological positions and prove the truth of their doctrine. This would not have been possible if they had chosen to be isolated or closed off, in the interest of keeping their doctrine pure and intact. This also would not have been possible if Muslim theologians hadn't been open to Greek philosophy. It was inevitable that this intellectual openness would have a dual impact on both sides of the discussion. Arab Christians were molded as they reshaped their Greek and Syriac heritage in an authentic Arab mold, far from any artificiality or exaggeration.

As for Muslim theologians, they too were molded. They began to realize the deep logic that supports the doctrine of the Trinity, and so they began to look at passages of the Qur'an that talked about God's life and his Word from a new perspective—a perspective whose framework was defined by Christian thought. And far from the traditional accusation that Christians worship three gods, the *Muʿ tazilah* took it upon themselves to evaluate the argument of the divine attributes with which Arab Christians always armed themselves. On refuting this assertion, the *Muʿ tazilah* found themselves in faced with a broader, more

24. Borrans and al-Nayfar, *Mustaqbal al-ḥiwār al-Islāmī al-Masīḥī*, 156–57.

comprehensive question related to the essence of God's attributes. In Abū ʿ Īsá al-Warrāq's refutation of the doctrine of the trinity we have the strongest evidence that ʿ Ammār al-Baṣrī's propositions were reasonable—his assertions about the eternality of the attributes and his claim that God is one being, existing eternally with his Word and Spirit. They were reasonable, even though al-Warrāq himself refused to accept them but wrote instead to refute them.[25]

However, we cannot allow ourselves to forget that the process of shaping one another has conditions: openness is its pillar and flexibility is its soul. How can we begin to imagine a Christian theologian impacting the formulations of a Muslim theologian without both sides having a great deal of openness and flexibility? And how could ʿ Ammār have had such depths of knowledge of the arguments of scholars of Islamic theology if he had not been open to them? And how could they have listened to his opinions if they were also not open to him? Moreover, how can "iron sharpen iron" if both sides are not already "iron" and are not equal? Can wood sharpen iron? Would iron be shaped if it were hammered with the branch of a tree?

Before openness and flexibility can exist, each side must befriend the other—a person cannot sharpen another unless he can first call him friend. Enemies do not sharpen one another; they kill one another. However, those who have befriended one another can sit together as partners and listen to one another—when this happens, that's when the process of sharpening takes place. Both sides stand before the greatness of God, knowing fully that their thoughts are limited and that their words are unable to express the Righteous One, who has no equal. They draw closer to one another, hoping that together they might realize new dimensions of knowledge. Of course, I do not mean that either side will abandon the foundations of his creed or the firm convictions of his faith. On the contrary, is not the acceptance of others the greatest proclamation of one's steadfastness to their beliefs? Let us conclude by reading these words, by which ʿ Ammār al-Baṣrī expressed his conviction of the truth of his position while also acknowledging the inability of the human mind to fathom the essence of God:

> Goodness me, if our description of Him with oneness and Trinity is false and invalid; though some of His creatures are found to be as such, their description of Him as one in meaning, since

25. Thomas, ed. and trans., *Anti-Christian Polemic in Early Islam*, 132.

> needy powers, and vile accidents are found to be as such, is false and invalid. And if both descriptions fall short of [knowing] the truth of His majestic essence, and the splendor of His quiddity; goodness me, [at least] we have attributed to Him the best of the qualities and names, unlike them. However, truth is in our description, given how we described Him; and falsehood is in their description, since they did not know what they said, and did not reason the corruption of their depiction.[26]

To conclude, I would like to say that both Islam and Christianity are comprehensive religions, interacting with all aspects of human life and addressing every person. Hence, they should not be limited to the individual or to personal life. Islam is not practiced only on Fridays, and Christianity not only on Sundays! God did not create us to live as individuals, to live isolated from one another on islands. We are one human community, united by values and principles that were first and foremost formed based on religious precepts. What is needed is not a call to copy repulsive Western political philosophies, but a return to deep Christian-Muslim dialogue like the one that was taking place in the Arab world in the ninth century. This time, the conversation must take a political bent instead of a dialectical one, as was appropriate to the context of the first centuries of interaction between Muslims and Christians. This dialogue will be focused, in part, on allowing Christians and Muslims to go out with shared political principles that serve their countries and their worship.

"As iron sharpens iron, so one person sharpens his friend" (Proverbs 27:17). Our destiny (and here I mean the positive meaning of the word) is for Muslims and Christians in the Middle East to live as brothers, reflecting our belief that the God we worship is the Most Merciful, the God of Love. Our destiny is to befriend one another and to sharpen one another. Our destiny is to build a free society in which man lives to experience the presence of God and bless his fellow man. Our destiny is to revive our countries. Whatever our destiny might be, it is inevitable that we influence one another and be influenced in turn, that we form one another and be formed. "As iron sharpens iron, so one person sharpens his friends." So, have we become friends?

26. Michel Hayek, 164.

BIBLIOGRAPHY

Ibn al-Nadīm. *Al-Fihrist*. Beirut, Lebanon: Dār al-Maᵉrifa, 1978.

G. Sordell, *Muᵉjam al-Islām al-Tārīkhī*, trans. al-Ḥākim. Beirut, Lebanon: al-Dār al-Lubnanīya lil-Nashr al-Jāmaᵉā, 1995.

Abū 'Uthmān al-Jāḥiẓ. *Rasā'il al-Jāḥiẓ*, ed. 'Abd al-Salām Mahmūd Hārūn. Cairo, Egypt: Maktaba al-Khanijī, 1964.

Baum, Wilhelm. "The Age of the Arabs: 560–1258,." In *The Church of the East: A Concise History*, edited by Wilhelm Baum and Winkler Dietmar, 42–83. London: Routledge Curzon, 2003.

Borrans, Maurice, and Aḥmīdah al-Nayfar. *Mustaqbal al-ḥiwār al-Islāmī al-Masīḥī*. Bayrūt: Dār al-Fikr al-Mu'āṣir, 2005.

Bos, Gerrit, ed. *Qusta ibn Luqa's Medical Regime for the Pilgrims to Mecca*. Leiden: Brill, 1992.

Cachia, Pierre, and W. Montgomery Watt, eds. *Eutychius of Alexandria, Kitāb al-Burhān*. Louvain: Secrétariat du CorpusSCO, 1960.

Cooper, Glen M. "Ḥunayn Ibn Isḥāq on His Galen Translations." Edited and translated by John C. Lamoreaux." *Journal of the AOS* 140:3 (September 19, 2021) 750–51.

Cragg, Kenneth. *Sandals at the Mosque: Christian Presence Amid Islam*. Edited by Pierre Cachia and W. Montgomery Watt. New York: Oxford University Press, 1959.

Di Matteo, Ignazio. "Confutazione contro i Cristiani dello Zaydita al-Qāsim b. Ibrāhīm." *RSO* 9 (1921–123) 301–64.

Ebeid, Bishara. "Can the Qur'ān Be Read in the Light of Christ? Reflections on Some Melkite Authors and Their Use of the Holy Book of Islam." *Collectanea Christiana Orientalia* 18 (2021) 37–74.

Eutychius of Alexandria. *Kitāb al-Burhān*. 4 vols. Corpus scriptorum Christianorum Orientalium, t. 192–93, 209–10, v. 192–93, 209–10. Louvain: Secrétariat du CorpusSCO, 1960.

Gerrit Bos, ed. *Qusta ibn Luqa's Medical Regime for the Pilgrims to Mecca*. Leiden: Brill, 1992.

Gibson, Margaret Dunlop, ed. *An Arabic Version of the Acts of the Apostles and the Seven Catholic Epistles: From an Eighth or Ninth Century MS. in the Convent of St. Catherine on Mount Sinai*. London: Clay, 1899.

Griffith, Sidney. *The Church in the Shadow of the Mosque: Christians and Muslims in the World of Islam*. Princeton, NJ: Princeton University Press, 2009.

Horst, Ludwig. *Des Metropoliten Elias von Nisibis Buch vom Beweis der Wahrheit des Glaubens*. Colmar, 1886.

Ibn Ibrāhīm, Al-Qāsīm. Edited by Ar-Radd 'alā-n-Naṣārā. Ignazio de Matteo, "Confutazione contro i Cristiani dello Zaydita Al-Qāsīm ibn Ibrāhīm." *Rivista degli Studi Orientali* 9 (1922) 301–64.

Khalifé, I. A., and W. Kutsch, eds. "Ar-Radd 'alā-n-Naṣārā de aṭ-Ṭabari.» *Mélanges de l'Université Saint Joseph* 36 (1959) 115–48.

Khalil, Samīr. *Dawr al-Masīḥīyīn al-Thaqāfī fil-'Ālam al-'Arabī*. 2 vols. Mawsū'at al-Ma'rifah al- Masīḥiyyah 5: al-Fikr al-'Arabī al-Masīḥī. Bayrūt: Dār al-Mashriq, 2004.

———. "The Earliest Arab Apology for Christianity (c. 750)." In *Christian Arabic Apologetics during the Abbasid Period (750–1258)*, edited by Samir Khalil and Jørgen Nielsen. Leiden: Brill, 1994.

Kraemer, Hendrik. *World Cultures and World Religions: The Coming Dialogue.* London: Lutterworth, 1960.

Lamoreaux, John. *Ḥunayn ibn Isḥāq on His Galen Translations.* Provo, UT: Brigham Young University Press, 2016.

Madelung, Wilferd. "Al-Qāsim Ibn Ibrāhīm and Christian Theology." In *Studies in Medieval Shi'ism*, by Wilferd Madelung, edited by Sabine Schmidtke, 35–44. Farnham: Ashgate Variorum, 2012.

Makhlouf, Avril. "Burhān—A Word on a Journey from the Heart to the Mind and Back." *Parole de l'Orient* 30 (2005) 281–96.

Mez, Adam. *Al-Ḥaḍārah Al-Islāmīyah fī al-Qarn al-Rābiʿ al-Hijri.* Translated by Muḥammad ʿAbd al-Hādī Abū Rīdah. Al-Qāhirah: Maṭbaʿat Lajnat al-Taʾlīf wa-al-Tarjamah wa-al-Nashr, 1940.

Platti, Emilio. "Une Cosmologie Chrétienne." Introduction and édition of the Livre de la démonstration, attributed to Yaḥyā ibn ʿAdī. *Mélanges de l'Institut Dominicain d'Études Orientales du Caire* 15 (1982) 75–118.

Rifāʿī, Aḥmad Farīd. *ʿAṣr al-Maʾmūn.* Vol. 1. al-Qāhirah: al-Hayʾah al-Miṣriyyah al-ʿĀmmah lil-Kitāb, 1997.

Samīr, ʿAbduh Samīr. *Dawr al-Masīḥīyīn fī al-ḥaḍārah al-ʿArabīyah-al-Islāmīyah.* Damascus: Dār Ḥasan Malaṣ, 2005.

Samir, K. Samir. "The Christian Communities, Active Members of Arab Society throughout History." In *Christian Communities in the Arab Middle East: The Challenge of the Future*, edited by Andrea Pacini, 77–82. Oxford: Clarendon, 1998.

———. "The Earliest Arab Apology for Christianity (c. 750)." In *Christian Arabic Apologetics during the Abbasid Period (750–1258)*, edited by S. K. Samir and J. S. Nielsen, 57–114. Studies in the History of Religions 63. Leiden: Brill, 1994.

Sbath, Paul. *Vingt traités philosophiques et apologétiques d'auteurs arabes chrétiens du IXe au XIXe siècles.* Cairo: H. Friedrich, 1929.

Swanson, Mark. "Beyond Proof Texting: Approaches to the Qur'an in Some Early Arabic Christian Apologies." *The Muslim World* 88:3–4 (July–October 1998) 297–318.

Thomas, David, ed. and trans. *Anti-Christian Polemic in Early Islam: Abū ʿĪsā al-Warrāq's "Against the Trinity."* University of Cambridge Oriental Publications 45. Cambridge: Cambridge University Press, 1992.

———. *Early Muslim Polemic against Christianity: Abū ʿĪsā al-Warrāq's "Against the Incarnation."* University of Cambridge Oriental Publications 59. Cambridge: Cambridge University Press, 2002.

Treiger, Alexander. "From Al-Biṭrīq to Ḥunayn: Melkite and Nestorian Translators in Early ʿAbbāsid Baghdad." *Mediterranea: International Journal on the Transfer of Knowledge* 7 (2022) 143–81.

www.ingramcontent.com/pod-product-compliance
Lightning Source LLC
Chambersburg PA
CBHW050618300426
44112CB00012B/1560
* 9 7 9 8 3 8 5 2 0 5 2 4 0 *